T0326247

The Humanist Controversy

The Humanist Controversy
and Other Writings
(1966–67)

LOUIS ALTHUSSER

Edited by
François Matheron

Translated and with an Introduction by
G.M. Goshgarian

VERSO
London • New York

This book is supported by the French Ministry for Foreign Affairs
as part of the Burgess Programme, headed for the French Embassy
in London by the Institut Français du Royaume Uni

Liberté · Égalité · Fraternité
RÉPUBLIQUE FRANÇAISE

First published by Verso 2003
This edition © Verso 2003
Translation © G.M. Goshgarian
First published in *Écrits philosophiques et politiques. Tome II* and
Écrits sur la psychanalyse © Éditions Stock/IMEC 1993 and 1995

All rights reserved

The moral rights of the author and translator have been asserted

1 3 5 7 9 10 8 6 4 2

Verso
UK: 6 Meard Street, London W1F 0EG
USA: 180 Varick Street, New York, NY 10014–4606
www.versobooks.com

Verso is the imprint of New Left Books

ISBN 978-1-85984-408-3

British Library Cataloguing in Publication Data
Althusser, Louis
    The humanist controversy and other writings (1966–67)
    1. Philosophy, French – 20th century 2. Philosophy, Marxist
    3. Psychoanalysis and philosophy
    I. Title II. Matheron, Francios III. Goshgarian, G. M.
    194

Library of Congress Cataloging-in-Publication Data
A catalog record for this book is available from the Library of Congress

Typeset in 10/12 Palatino by SetSystems Ltd, Saffron Walden, Essex
Printed and bound in Great Britain by the Bath Press Ltd, Avon

Contents

List of Abbreviations

Books or book-length manuscripts by Althusser

EI = *Essays in Ideology*, trans. Ben Brewster *et al.*, London, Verso, 1984.

EPP = *Écrits philosophiques et politiques*, 2 vols, Paris, Stock/Imec, 1994–95.

ESC = *Essays in Self-Criticism*, trans. Grahame Lock, London, Verso, 1976.

FM = *For Marx*, trans. Ben Brewster, London, Verso, 1996.

LF = *Lettres à Franca*, Paris, Stock/Imec, 1998.

LP = *Lenin and Philosophy and Other Essays*, trans. Ben Brewster, New York, Monthly Review Press, 1971.

MRM = *Montesquieu, Rousseau, Marx: Politics and History*, trans. Ben Brewster, London, Verso, 1972.

PSH = *Psychanalyse et sciences humaines: Deux conférences*, ed. Oliver Corpet and François Matheron, Paris, Librarie Générale Française/Imec, 1996.

PSPS = *Philosophy and the Spontaneous Philosophy of the Scientists and Other Essays*, ed. Gregory Elliott, trans. Ben Brewster *et al.*, London, Verso, 1990.

RC = *Reading Capital*, trans. Ben Brewster, London, Verso, 1979.

SH = *The Spectre of Hegel: Early Writings*, trans. G.M. Goshgarian, London, Verso, 1997.

SISS = *Socialisme idéologique et socialisme scientifique*, Alt2.A8-02.01 to Alt2.A8-02.04 (part of *TP*).

SM = *Solitude de Machiavel*, ed. Yves Sintomer, Paris, PUF/Actuel Marx Confrontations, 1998.

TP = Mss. on the union of theory and practice, Alt2.A7-01 to Alt2.A7-02.

WP = *Writings on Psychoanalysis: Freud and Lacan*, trans. Jeffrey Mehlman, New York, Columbia University Press, 1996.

Note: The manuscript of 'The Historical Task' and other Althusser manuscripts referred to in the text are housed at the Institut Mémoires de l'édition contemporaine, Paris.

All the texts consulted in Althusser's archives are designated with a string that begins 'Alt2.A', omitted in the notes.

Shorter texts by Althusser

'ACP' = *Aliénation et culte de la personnalité*, Alt2.A3-04.

'ESC' = 'Elements of Self-Criticism', *ESC* 101–50.

'ISMP' = 'Is it Simple to be a Marxist in Philosophy?', *PSPS* 203–40.

'LP' = 'Lenin and Philosophy', *PSPS* 167–202.

'MHMD' = 'Matérialisme historique et matérialisme dialectique', *Cahiers marxistes–léninistes*, no. 11, April 1966, pp. 88–122.

'MPH' = 'Montesquieu: Politics and History', *MRM* 10–109.

'MRH' = 'Marx's Relation to Hegel', *MRM* 161–86.

'NCA' = 'Note critique et autocritique pour le lecteur de *Pour Marx* et *Lire le Capital*, 16 oct. 1967', Alt.2.A9-05.07 and Alt.2.A10-03.05.

'NSP' = 'Notes sur la Philosophie', *EPP* II, 299–348.

'OEYM' = 'On the Evolution of the Young Marx', *ESC* 151–62.

'OTW' = 'On Theoretical Work: Difficulties and Resources', *PSPS* 43–67.

'PRW' = 'Philosophy as a Revoutionary Weapon', *LP* 11–22.

'PSH' = 'Philosophie et sciences humaines', *SM* 43–58.

'PSPS' = 'Philosophy and the Spontaneous Philosophy of the Scientists', *PSPS* 69–166.

'R' = 'Rectification', Alt2.A9-05.01 to Alt2.A9-05.05 and Alt2.A20-03.02.

'RSC' = 'Rousseau: *The Social Contract*', *MRM* 111–60.

'RTJL' = 'Reply to John Lewis', *EI* 61–140.

'SRC' = 'Sur la révolution culturelle', *Cahiers marxistes–léninistes*, no. 14, November–December 1966, pp. 5–16.

'TPh' = 'The Transformation of Philosophy', *PSPS* 241–65.

'TTPTF' = 'Theory, Theoretical Practice and Theoretical Formation: Ideology and Ideological Struggle', *PSPS* 1–42.

Where the author of a text is not named in the notes, it is always Althusser.

Other texts

AFC = Archives of Francis Cohen, Bibliothèque marxiste, Paris.

AWR = Archives of Waldeck Rochet in the Archives of the French Communist Party, Paris.

Annales = *Annales de la Société des amis de Louis Aragon et Elsa Triolet*, no. 2 (2000): Aragon et le Comité central d'Argenteuil.

Choisy = Transcript of an assembly of Communist philosophers held at Choisy-le-Roi on 22–23 January 1966.

CW = Marx/Engels, *Collected Works*, London, Lawrence & Wishart, 1970–2002.

EC = Ludwig Feuerbach, *The Essence of Christianity*, trans. George Eliot [Great Books in Philosophy], Amherst, NY, 1989.

FB = Ludwig Feuerbach, *The Fiery Brook: Selected Writings of Ludwig Feuerbach*, ed. and trans. Zawar Hanfi, Garden City, NY, 1972.

GI = Marx and Engels, *The German Ideology*, in *The German Ideology, Theses on Feurbach, and The Introduction to the Critique of Political Economy*, trans. anon. [Great Books in Philosophy], Amherst, NY, 1998.

Secretariat = Archives of the PCF Secretariat, Archives of the PCF, Paris.

Introduction

G.M. Goshgarian

Louis Althusser wrote the studies collected in the present volume between June 1966 and July 1967. Except for the ten pages of 'The Humanist Controversy' incorporated into 'Marx's Relation to Hegel' in 1968, and a version of 'The Historical Task of Marxist Philosophy' published in Hungarian the same year, all were stranded in his archives until after his death in 1990.[1] Of the completed texts of any importance that their author did release in this fourteen-month span, only an anonymous paean to the Chinese Cultural Revolution dates from it; the others are light revisions of earlier work.[2] As for Althusser's most substantial manuscript of the day, a 'vast, shapeless mass' of writing on the union of theory and practice (here called *Theory and Practice*) that had swelled into 'matter for two or three books' by mid-1966, all but two chapters were abandoned to the gnawing criticism of the mice, together with some dozen shorter pieces and the materials assembled below.[3] While many of the unpublished writings did enjoy, in the form of lectures or circulating papers, what has aptly been termed 'semi-public status',[4] this hardly alters the general picture, dominated by the contrast between the rich production of 1966–67 and the smattering that made its way into print.

Yet Althusser was persuaded, after the autumn 1965 publication of *For Marx* and *Reading Capital* had catapulted him from respectable academic obscurity at Paris's École normale supérieure to the centre of French intellectual life, and from nearly twenty years on the fringes of the Communist Party to his moment of glory as one of its 'three great men',[5] that the 'theoretico-political' situation urgently required a statement from his camp. 'Between now and ... February-March-April', he wrote to his lover Franca Madonia in August 1966, '*it is impossible that nothing appear*, given what we've already written, the way some people are reading it ... and the ambiguities and omissions in our publications.' The 'ambiguities' had bred an alarming perception of his work as 'a counter-signature of the structuralist claim', although he had been decrying structuralism, 'idealism's last hope', as a philosophical fraud since his 1962–63 seminar on the subject.[6] In the spring, the Party's General Secretary had joined the chorus of those bewailing his 'omission' of the problem of the union of theory and practice, although Althusser had 'anticipated the possibility ... even necessity of a materialist definition' of it, doing no more only because one could not do everything at once. *Marxist Theory and the Communists* would fill in the blanks that autumn, he assured other Party intellectuals at a 'Homeric' dinner-debate on May Day.[7] The ambiguities would be laid to rest in a long-planned Althusserian review (later baptized *Théorie*, but never born); the first issue, it was decided over the summer, would focus on the difference between structuralist and Marxist conceptions of structure.[8]

These concessions aside, Althusser initially stood by the positions staked out in *For Marx* and *Reading Capital*. They were commanded by the thesis, adapted from Gaston Bachelard, that the major sciences had emerged from revolutionary 'epistemological breaks' with the practically motivated systems of thought that their emergence retrospectively identified as ideologies. Marxism had originated in one such 'theoretical revolution', which transformed the raw material of its three sources – German idealism, French utopian socialism, English political economy – into a pair of new sciences, historical and dialectical materialism. The object of the first was the history of social formations, a realm opened up to scientific analysis by 'Marx's fundamental discovery', 'the topography' of distinct practices combined in distinct ways in distinct modes of production. Dialectical materialism, or Marxist philosophy, was the Theory of theoretical practice; it studied 'the relation between theoretical practice and *the other practices*, and therefore, simultaneously, the specific nature of *the other practices* ... and the types of determination linking them'.[9] Like the science of history, then, philosophy, too, took all the practices and their relations as its object, but 'only in so far as they participated in the production of knowledge as knowledge'. Its main task was to construct, using means of analysis analogous to those that historical materialism brought to bear on social modes of production, the science of the modes of production of theory.

It followed that dialectical materialism was engendered by historical materialism, which *practised* a break with ideology whose history and results philosophy had to theorize. This exemplified the law that a nascent philosophy necessarily lags behind the science that calls it into being, the Althusserian variation on the theme that the owl of Minerva takes wing at dusk. Yet a science depended for its continued existence on the philosophical 'guide' that depended on it. Unless it was armed by philosophy with the theory of its own theoretical practice, any science, although its discoveries were irreversible, had to fear the 'constantly recurring ideological temptations' that could always reverse it, drawing it back within the embrace of the ideology from which it had torn itself. The danger was acute in the case of historical materialism, given its novelty and the obvious reasons for the hostility to it. Dialectical materialism's lag behind its sister science therefore implied a politics: philosophy's task was to save Marx's theoretical revolution by finishing it. But to save the theoretical revolution was to save the revolution *tout court*: without revolutionary theory, as Althusser never tired of repeating after Lenin, there could be no revolutionary practice.[10]

By summer 1966, Althusser had admitted that his critics were right in one crucial respect: the logic of the break isolated the theory required to make the revolution from the realm of the non-theoretical practices in which the revolution had (also) to be made. Theory became theory by virtue of a distantiation that ruled out both its internal determination *by* ideology and its direct intervention *in* ideology: a theory, by

definition, had no *practical* relation to the ideological practices
with which it broke. This put philosophy, 'the highest form of
the theorization of ideology',[11] at a double remove from all
other practices. It had no practical relation to ideology, one of
its objects; nor did it have, as the science of the 'relation
between [theoretical] practice and the other practices', any
practical relation to that relation – which, since philosophy,
too, was a theoretical practice, included its own relation to
itself. Althusser's philosophy thus found itself at odds with
two basic contentions of the science on which it claimed to be
based: that theory was co-determined – indeed, primarily
determined – by its non-theoretical outside, specifically by the
ideologies, where 'the class struggle figures in person';[12] and
that the vocation of revolutionary theory was to intervene in
the ideological class struggle. What Althusser had called
'omissions' thus turned out to be symptoms of the fact that
he could think the 'union of theory and practice', of theoretical and non-theoretical practice, only as the impossible
encounter of two heterogeneous orders ('our union of the
body and soul', he quipped in a letter)[13] or the tautological
consequence of their prior identification.

He concluded, in retrospect, that he had proceeded by
identifying them, 'posing the theoretical question in place of
the political' and thus, if not quite calling theory politics,
demoting politics to the rank of an 'extension of theory'.[14]
This 'theoreticism', a term he began applying to his work in
mid-1966, sprang from an overreaction to the historicism that
defined Marxism as an immediate expression of history,
rather than an autonomous theory irreducible to it. Historicism led, as in Gramsci, to an identification of history and the
Marxist 'philosophy of history'; it collapsed dialectical materialism into historical materialism and treated the result as the
world-view of a class possessed of the Marxist science of
itself. Thus, at least tendentially, it made Marxism a form of
absolute knowledge, one which differed from Hegel's only in
that it situated the union of history and the theory of history
in the historical process rather than at its term. The crux of
Althusser's self-criticism of 1966 was that he had finally only
inverted this schema, absorbing history in theory rather than
the reverse, to produce what was, tendentially, another Marx-

ist theory of absolute knowledge. Witness his treatment of the relation between philosophy and politics: the attempt to avoid the Gramscian conclusion (which, if for different reasons, was also Stalin's) that 'the real philosopher is simply the politi-cian'[15] had ended up standing it on its head. 'It is the bearers of theory', ran his ironic summary of the theoreticist tendency in his early work, 'who make history.'[16]

Althusser would, in 1966–67, mobilize Spinoza against his theoreticism, which, however, his appeal to Spinoza also reinforced. Against the conception of knowledge as a shad-owy reflection of a real lying outside it, For Marx and Reading Capital silently invoke the Spinozist principle that 'substance thinking and substance extended are one and the same sub-stance', insisting that ideas, no less than their real objects, are also the real, albeit in the form of thought.[17] But this material-ist defence of the materiality of both ideological and theo-retical practice came at a price, set by the quest for an equivalent of substance that runs through Althusser's work of the 1960s. In For Marx and Reading Capital, this equivalent is production, supposed to have a general structure common to all its forms, theoretical and non-theoretical alike; it exorcizes the spectre of the parallelism that might otherwise haunt attempts to contest, via the thesis that ideas are quite as real as their objects, the historicist empiricism for which theory is simply a reflection or an expression of its times. Philosophy is accordingly conceived as the 'science' that provides knowl-edge of this general structure, and, with it, of the unity-in-diversity of the whole of the real. Even after Althusser begins to criticize his own theoreticism, he explicitly reaffirms this theory of philosophy on the basis of a (mis)reading of Spi-noza's Ethics summed up in the affirmation that 'the parallel-ism of the attributes is tempered and corrected in Spinoza by the concept of substance ... it is the concept of substance which plays the role of the concept of the articulation of the attributes'. 'Our attributes', he adds, are the general scientific theories whose articulation it is philosophy's business to think; only by doing so can it avoid the dilemma of the par-allelism of the attributes.[18] A year later, in mid-1967, Althus-ser was still contending that philosophy must concern itself with the unity-in-diversity of all the theoretical and also the non-theoretical practices.[19] It was above all by way of this contention that his theoreticism continued to resist his ongoing break with it.

The idea that the general structure of production is common to 'substance thinking and substance extended' provides the point of departure for Althusser's first, theoreticist approach to the relation between Theory and politics. Thus *For Marx*, borrowing its concept of the conjuncture ('current situation') from Lenin's political writings, affirms that 'the essence of the object (the raw material) of *political* and *theoretical* practice [is] the structure of the "current situation" (in theory or politics) to which these practices apply'.[20] Althusser doubtless considered this one of the places in which he had 'anticipated the necessity of a materialist definition' of the problem of the union of theory and practice. Here it is clearly posed in terms of the 'parallelism of the conjunctures'; for we are dealing with two, political and theoretical. Or, rather, with three, since the 'raw material' of politics proper must be distinguished from political theory, as a letter of Althusser's spells out: 'the science of the political is a different practice [than politics]; it is a theoretical practice by nature independent of its application in politics, i.e., of political practice'.[21] On closer inspection, it turns out that there is yet another pole in this dual mirror structure: the theory of the political conjuncture is in its turn an element in the structure of the *theoretical* conjuncture, which has its own Theory. Yet the passage draws these distinctions only to efface them. For we have two conjunctures and two theories, but only one Theory.

The reason is not that the essence of both conjunctures is a *structure*, but that the structure of both conjunctures is an *essence*, and that only Theory *knows* it. Theory is the science of this essence or general structure, to which political science, however inventive – and Althusser's aim here is precisely to stress the potential contribution of Lenin's political thought to philosophy – has access, like any other science, via Theory alone. The Theory of theoretical practice (dialectical materialism) meets no corresponding limitation in the practice it theorizes: it is independent of its application in theory (historical materialism), which is in turn independent of its application in politics. Theory alone, to cite Althusser's 1976 self-criticism, can unify the whole under its aegis and 'speak the Truth about all human practices'.[22] Thus the same essay that assigns the philosophical and political 'attributes' their distinct conjunctures and theories but a common substance/essence solves, in advance, the problem it might seem to pose, serenely affirming that dialectical materialism is 'the general Theory in which is theoretically expressed the essence of theoretical practice in general, through it the essence of practice in general, and through it the essence of the transformations, of the "development" of things in general'.[23]

Althusser's critique of the epistemological essentialism that bred this species of speculative 'Spinozism' unfolds in the texts collected below, as well as *Theory and Practice* and a handful of others. It is carried out in the name of a defence of the singularity of Marxism that is only the most conspicuous figure of a Marxism of the singular whose presiding spirit, in this period, is *also* Spinoza, read through a prism provided by Machiavelli, Marx, Lenin and Mao. It issues in a philosophy that proposes to account for itself as the always singular effect of a singular political 'conjuncture' on a singular philosophical 'conjunction': a philosophy that takes its place within the field of what Althusser christens, in notes dating from summer 1966, the 'theory of the encounter'.[24] What disappears from this new conception of philosophy is the notion, at the heart of the old, of the general as 'essence'. What takes its place is a theory of the singularity of generality.

The way to the philosophy of the encounter was paved by the argument, developed in *Theory and Practice*, that casting Theory as both philosophy and science inevitably made it a form of absolute knowledge. On the one hand, Althusser said, in sum, that the sciences and ideologies were the objects of the Theory of theory, which was therefore distinct from both. On the other, because it was itself a science, it took its place among the objects it studied. It established the scientificity of the *other* sciences, and thus their difference from ideology, on the basis of criteria laid down by their own historical practice, not with reference to the kind of (ideological) a priori guarantees provided by classical epistemology. But by what criteria did it then distinguish *itself*, the scientific theory of scientificity, from the ideological theories of science – for instance, classical epistemology – that it set out to combat? These criteria could be provided only by its own theoretical practice, for no other science studied scientificity as such. What counted as scientificity, however, could be determined only by these criteria. Theory accordingly intervened in a field encompassing Theory in order to define Theory by its intervention. It was thus the self-creating science of itself: the theoreticist equivalent of Gramsci's historicist absolute knowledge.[25]

The condition for elaborating an alternative to both consisted in situating philosophy in the conjuncture without benefit of the transcendental guarantee provided by its extra-conjunctural double, scientific Theory. Althusser takes this step in the earliest of the texts below, the June 1966 lecture 'The Philosophical Conjuncture and Marxist Theoretical Research', when, in passing, he faults his earlier work for failing to distinguish the 'theoretical status' of historical materialism, which is a science, from that of philosophy, which is not. Attending to this distinction, he predicts, will generate 'a long string of related developments'. The most important is encapsulated in a jotting that probably dates from the same summer – 'in the broad sense, every philosophy is practical or political: an *Ethics*'.[26] The beginning of the break that separates the two halves of Althusser's philosophical career might well be dated to that note.

What justified calling philosophy political? Althusser's, as he saw in retrospect, was political by its own involuntary confession, and in this it was typical. Its pretension to being the science of itself was the very symptom of what denied it scientific status: like any other philosophy, it forged its identity in a struggle with its adversaries, participating in a war of ideas precisely by virtue of its claim to judge it from a position above the fray. Thus it was, as Althusser had said of *ideology* in a May revision of *Theory and Practice*, 'both judge and party to the action'.[27] This implied more than that materialist philosophy was immersed in the *philosophical* conjuncture; for, in that conjuncture, it contended with the philosophical 'detachments' of the *ideologies*, in which the 'class struggle – and, with it, politics – 'figure in person'. In a word, a very short road led from the demise of Theory to the birth of the thesis that philosophy had an 'intimate, organic relationship with politics'.[28] It is short enough to awaken the suspicion that, having first demoted politics to the rank of an extension of philosophy in reaction to the distortions of historicism, Althusser contritely restored philosophy to its subaltern place as an extension of politics. His new definition of philosophy could be, and has been, held up as evidence that he did: 'philosophy', he wrote early in 1968, 'represents the people's class struggle in theory'.[29] But philosophy was saved from this 'politicism' by the fact that, even after it had ceased to be the scientific Theory of theory, it maintained a privileged relationship with the sciences: it represented the sciences in politics, Althusser said, while simultaneously representing politics in the sciences. Thus it was itself an element in the 'union', or, at least, articulation, of (scientific) theory with (political-ideological) practice. With this, Althusser had negotiated the turn initiated, not quite two years earlier, in 'The Philosophical Conjuncture'.

Few of his previous positions survived it intact. By February 1968, philosophy was said to operate not with concepts, but with categories; to produce not verifiable truths, but theses; and, in the sense that it generated no cumulative body of knowledge, to have no real history. Its 'object' disappeared along with the idea that it had one: the unity of the 'two great systems' comprising the theoretical and non-theoretical practices – finally only another name for 'what is improperly called the totality of the real'[30] – was no longer, under any name, a possible object of knowledge. Indeed, the sciences themselves no longer formed a totalizable whole: they could perfectly well subsist as isolated 'continents', islands in the void of the ideologies from which they emerged. Their history, previously assigned to dialectical materialism as if the Theory of theory transcended the study of concrete theoretical practices, was now put under the jurisdiction of the science of history. Even the 'law' according to which philosophies are precipitated by the appearance of new sciences was called into question: in November 1967, Althusser privately endorsed the idea – although he retreated from it soon after, and was not to defend it publicly until 1973[31] – that the birth of the science of history had been induced by the change in

Marx's philosophical position which came about when he threw in his lot with the Parisian communists. This attested both the key role still attributed to philosophy, and the logical priority of what Althusser now thought under that name to the break between science and ideology, redefined as the beginning of an endless process, a 'continuing break'. 'Politics in the broad sense' or 'in the last instance' had come to signify something akin to the idea of the primacy of opposition, and thus to Derridean *différance*: no longer conceived as a product of the break, philosophy was, rather, the activity of the continuing break itself, a purely differential operation that consisted in drawing and redrawing a line within itself between the idealist/ideological tendencies that blocked the advance of science and the materialist tendencies that opposed them. It was, said Althusser, the 'repetition of a "nothing"'.

Some of these theses are to be found in 'The Historical Task' and the nearly contemporaneous 'Humanist Controversy', alongside others incompatible with them. The rest crystallized with implausible rapidity in a 'theoretical aggiornamento' undertaken shortly after Althusser abandoned 'The Humanist Controversy' in July. The first fruits of the 'theoretically rigorous summer'[32] of 1967 were harvested in his introduction to an autumn lecture course on the spontaneous philosophy of scientists as well as a celebrated February 1968 lecture, 'Lenin and Philosophy'.[33] The same period yielded a long reassessment of his work which contained much of the matter, and even something of the manner, of the well-known self-critical texts that he released only in 1973–74; the guarded reconsiderations that began appearing in print in 1968 do not begin to capture the flavour and force of this still unpublished 'rectification' (probably destined to appear in the journal *Théorie*).[34] The kernel of it was the charge that Althusser's neglect of the union of theory and practice had been, not a sin of omission, but a 'stupendous mistake'. It was attested, added a related text, by the assumption that Theory could simply be 'applied' to the class struggle from outside it.[35]

Yet if the 'omissions' of May 1966 had become stupendous mistakes, the 'ambiguities' remained ambiguities: the sheer mass of structuralist terminology purged from the 1968 second edition of *Reading Capital* notwithstanding,[36] Althusser pleaded from first to last, and always in the same terms, a resounding not guilty to the charge of structuralism. The vehement polemics against Claude Lévi-Strauss included in the present volume show that he protested his innocence in all good faith – the more so as his earlier judgements of 'the most dangerous fellow around' are quite as one-sidedly hostile.[37] Whether he was a structuralist none the less is a question that need not detain us. The relevance of his critique of structural anthropology to his own development lies elsewhere: in his 1966 discovery that the commitment to 'the primacy of unity'[38] which he took to be the chief manifestation of Lévi-Strauss's idealism also haunted his own. The mark of this complicity was, however, less his concept of structure than his Theory of theory, a bastion of the primacy of unity in a philosophy whose basic tendency was to affirm the primacy of opposition. Thus it is no accident that Althusser's settling of accounts with Lévi-Strauss, a central concern of three of the texts below, should have ushered in his turn of 1966–67: it was a critique of his own theoreticism *avant la lettre*.

There was another: Althusser's 1959 discussion of Montesquieu's 'mythical notion of the nature of the State', which was based on the premiss 'that a political power [could] be established and exercised outside classes and over them'. Theoreticism was the philosophical equivalent, the mythical notion that Theory could establish and exercise its power outside (class) ideologies and over them; it was the native doctrine of what Althusser would later describe as the party of the state in philosophy. 'Every ideology is also a practice': Althusser's, practised on the terrain of the party of the state *tout court*, aimed to establish the power of Theory over politics by fusing the 'party of the theoretical' with the Party of Maurice Thorez. The ultimate objective was to bring 'the masses on to the historical stage, not only to make the revolution, but to remain there afterwards ... so that the dictatorship of the proletariat would be the power of the masses'. But Althusser's attempt to realize this objective ignored the masses; it took the form of a campaign to convince the leadership of the French Communist Party to let him create the conditions required to make its activists into (Althusserian) theoreticians.[39] The resulting organizational battle intensified from 1963 on. It peaked, in mid-1966, in a resounding defeat for the partisans of Theory. It was in the conjuncture shaped by this defeat of Althusser's theoreticist *practice* that his anti-structuralism helped to precipitate the anti-theoreticist *theory* capable of accounting, among other things, for the encounter between philosophy and politics that spawned his 1966–67 turn.

This would seem to warrant a departure from the practice of the now immortal, if otherwise unknown titular figure of 'Reply to John Lewis', whose unconcern for 'such concrete things as politics' has been diligently emulated by most of Althusser's other critics, and unabashedly endorsed by the last to date.[40] It is, at any rate, more in keeping with the spirit of Althusser's enterprise to consider his 'theoretical qualities' as they appear, not when 'detached from the political debates of his day',[41] but, rather, when firmly reattached to them. We shall therefore say a word about Theory's long march through the French Communist Party before sketching the beginnings of Althusser's break with the party of the state in philosophy.

II

Stalinism with a humanist face

'In real history,' *For Marx* affirms, 'determination in the last instance by the economy is exercised precisely in the permutations of the principal role between the economy, politics, theory, etc.' The last example is not on the list by accident. For Althusser, who – like his Machiavelli, thought in extremes – the 'noteworthy interest shown in ... Marx's Early Works by young Soviet scholars', as he diplomatically stated the matter in *For Marx* – that is, the 'pitiful ideological rumination of the works of Marx's youth' – was 'an important sign of the present direction of cultural development in the USSR' – that is, the symptom of a 'catastrophic' revision of Marxism that implied nothing less than the imminent collapse of socialism.[42] Such revisionism represented, at the level of theory, the alarming progress of the offensive against the socialist camp. But it was more than just an *index* of the inauspicious course of the global class struggle; the battle to overturn the revolution in society was proceeding *by way of* a reversal of the Marxist theoretical revolution being carried out on the authority of the early Marx. Under these conditions, interpreting the world was the fastest way to changing it. Indeed, interpreting *Marx* was: in the post-Stalin era, the 'struggle for a correct conception of Marxist theory' would decide 'the fate of the socialist revolution itself'.

The seeds of the disaster that theory had to avert had been sown by Lenin's direct heirs. Their failure to finish the revolution by carrying it into the ideological realm had 'ensur[ed] the survival, that is, the reactivation, of older elements' in the superstructures of Soviet society, while blocking the development of Marxist thought needed to transform them. Stalin's 'crimes and repression' were one consequence of the marriage between the revolution and the barbarism that had survived it; the dogmatic sleep he had imposed on Marxism was another. Thus Stalin had 'snuffed out not only thousands upon thousands of lives, but also, for a long time if not for ever, the theoretical existence of a whole series of major problems', eliminating 'from the field of Marxist research and discovery questions that fell by rights to the province of Marxism'. After 1956, bourgeois ideologies rushed to fill the resulting theoretical vacuum; reactivating 'old petty-bourgeois reflexes', they sowed the illusion that protest couched in terms of 'alienation, freedom, or man' could produce social change. This was the 'ultimate posthumous effect of the dogmatism' of the Stalin period: the moral-liberal 'diversions' that took the place vacated by Marxist analysis, beginning with Khrushchev's denunciations of 'violations of socialist legality' and 'the personality cult', reinforced a depoliticization that shored up the foundations of the social system they were supposed to help reform. Truly to put Stalin's legacy behind it, the post-Stalin CPSU would have to resume active leadership of the class struggle, at home and abroad. But its Twenty-Second Congress preferred to declare the USSR a 'state of the whole people', while espousing the ostensibly Marxist humanist ideology ('everything in the name of man') that stifled class-based political initiative in the USSR itself, and, at the international level, justified class collaboration. In both respects, the Stalinist regime that had never seriously come forward in humanist garb, according to the

Althusser of the 1960s, was perpetuated by the Khrushchevite regime that did.[43] What was emerging after Stalin was less an alternative to Stalinism than Stalinism with a humanist face.

Theory's historical task was therefore to overcome the poverty to which Stalin had condemned it, while combating the ideology with which Khrushchev was replacing it. Instead, what passed for Marxist theory, East and West, was colluding with what it should have been countering. Its celebration of a Feuerbachian–Hegelian Marx revived the twin ideological problematics with which Marx's revolution in thought had broken: the economism ('the poor man's' Hegelianism) which assumed that the 'autodevelopment' of the economy would by itself bring indefinite progress in every other social sphere, and thus implied, tendentially, the outright suppression of political practice; and economism's 'theoretical complement', the humanism which, putting a ghost in the economic machine, cast it as the motor of the continuous self-realization of a universal 'human spirit', thus tending to the same end, 'negation or attenuation' of class struggle. But these were *bourgeois* ideologies. What loomed on the post-Stalinist horizon was, accordingly, capitalism: 'the revolution in society, like the revolution in thought, runs a very great risk: that of being smothered by the old world, and, directly or indirectly, falling back under its sway'.[44]

This was why it was crucial to develop dialectical materialism, which alone could draw the line between theory and the humanist/evolutionist ideology threatening to engulf both Marxism and socialism. But only the Party could lead the fight to translate theory into revolutionary practice; that was why it was crucial to win it over to revolutionary positions by importing Marxist science into it, at the price of an organizational battle against the foes of theory squatting in its ranks. At mid-decade, Althusser found himself in the thick of this battle.

The profound noxiousness of Althusser's ideas

Since the late 1950s, the PCF had been lumbering towards a de-Stalinization that lent some semblance of plausibility to efforts to hoist it back on to the rails of a class-based revolutionary socialism. There were two main reasons for its new-found desire for change. One was that its deep-seated loyalty to Moscow had finally got the better of its faith in Stalin: by late 1961, the Party leadership had endorsed the Khrushchev reforms and begun selectively adopting them. The second was a revival of its electoralist traditions: in 1962, still smarting from a 1958 setback that had sharply reduced its usual quarter of the postwar vote, the PCF set off in pursuit of an alliance and a common programme with the socialists, confident that it could dominate a left coalition government after a victory at the polls. The need to win over socialist and Catholic voters, especially from the then burgeoning white-collar strata, was thought to mandate both doctrinal and organizational change. It would be necessary, in particular, to stress the commonalities between Marxist and progressive non-Marxist thought, advocate a peaceful, gradual, parliamentary transition to socialism, and lift, wherever possible, the bureaucratic constraints still imposed on Communist thinkers and artists.

The policy of the outstretched hand, as the bid for socialist and Catholic support was called, found its spontaneous translation in the language of humanism and evolutionism. 'Unity of action with Catholic workers,' said one of its leading Communist partisans, Gilbert Mury, 'is a necessary moment in our march towards, first, democracy, and then socialism; it naturally means that Christian humanism is not wholly alien to us ... the unity of history ... is that of a [humanist] project that runs through it, and if Marxism is not the application of this project in the age of the rise of the working class, what is it?'[45] The PCF's advances in the mid-1960s plugged the gaps in this logic. The Party registered solid gains in legislative and local elections in 1962–64, saw its membership figures swell, and, most importantly, negotiated its support, albeit without a common programme, for François Mitterrand's bid to unseat de Gaulle in the 1965 presidential elections, in which the socialist candidate polled a promising third of the votes in the first round. These successes came in a climate warmed by Vatican II, a papal call to ban the bomb, and intensifying dialogue between the PCF and a Church that had, in the not-too-distant past, excommunicated Party members and put Communist publications on the index. French Communism's 'official philosopher', the Marxist-humanist Roger Garaudy (who would later confess that he had wanted to widen 'the spiritual opening that Christ could bring to Marxism' in order to 'hasten the advent of man'), eagerly exploited the new philosophical opportunities jointly afforded him by Khrushchev and the Pope. His Feuerbacho–Marxian 'creed of the whole man', whose first article of faith was that the aim of proletarian revolution was to overcome alienation so that man, Marxism's alpha and omega, could return to himself and live a universal life as the true subject of his history,[46] seemed, to many Communists, admirably suited to ensuring both that the Christian–Marxist dialogue would deepen and that the Communist–Socialist alliance would eventually reach the end of the parliamentary road to socialism.

In the face of these massively practical arguments for Marxist humanism, Althusser's hair-splitting 'gobbledygook' (to cite the Party's literary eminence Louis Aragon) about the early Marx's relation to Feuerbach and Hegel carried little weight indeed. As for his 'revolutioneering' (Aragon again) to the effect that, say, 'the fight for peace implied anti-imperialist struggle', not 'peaceful coexistence and ecumenism', it could be dismissed out of hand for making it 'virtually impossible' to apply a Party line calculated to garner the magic 51 per cent of the vote.[47] Moreover, the revolutioneering had, off the record, acquired a conspicuous 'Chinese' tinge that was highly suspect in a Party which had, from early on in the Sino–Soviet split, outdone Moscow in excoriating Beijing's 'sectarianism'. If not in 1963, when he had gone on 'theoretical trial' for, in sum, hiding his true (Maoist) aspirations from the Party, then certainly by mid-decade, Althusser richly deserved the '"Chinese" albatross' that his judges had hung around his neck,[48] and the PCF's leaders could no doubt prove it. Thus they had solid reasons to turn a deaf ear to his 'theoretical anti-humanism'; and, despite his claims to the contrary, there is scant evidence that it cost them a struggle to do it. 'There is no question but that', the Party's Secretary General Waldeck Rochet noted in his voluminous philosophical papers under the rubric 'Althusser's theories', 'we mean to fight for the most consistent humanism possible.' All indications are that he spoke for the vast majority of his peers.[49] Yet, in 1965, the Party's real decision-making body, the Political Bureau, chose to fan the flames of the humanist controversy, promoting a major inner-Party debate around Althusser's claim that Marxist humanism was a contradiction in terms.

If everything militated against giving this claim a fair hearing in the Party, everything militated in favour of pretending to. To begin with, the excitement generated by Althusser's work had given Marxism new respectability in the University, where it had long been a poor cousin; by launching its own discussion of theoretical anti-humanism, the Party could improve its position in academia, while raising its standing in the eyes of 'the many Communist teachers and college professors, along with a fringe of intellectuals around them', over whom he had 'real authority' (as an inner-Party affidavit in his defence put it).[50] Second, the quarrel about humanism flared up at a time when the Political Bureau had resolved to discipline its unruly student union, the Union des étudiants communistes, which included an influential proto-Maoist grouping (the 'Chinese') whose leaders were politically, and in some cases personally, close to Althusser. Moving his anti-humanism stage centre might – and eventually did – disarm the UEC's young Althusserians, making it more likely that they would countenance manoeuvres designed to neutralize their rivals in the organization, the Trotskyists and 'Italians' (so called because they sought their political models among the reformist currents of the Italian CP). Third, and most important, Althusser and his humanist antagonists in the Party could be played off against one another; in the prevailing political conjuncture, this proved an opportune means of both implementing and limiting the de-Stalinization on the PCF's agenda.

Key to this strategy was the fact that Stalinism wore a humanist face in Paris as well as in Moscow. The point is almost too conveniently demonstrated by the political career of Mury, who, in November 1966, nine months after making the ringing profession of humanist faith quoted a moment ago, left the PCF for a Maoist group out of the sort of 'deep, tragic attachment to the work of Stalin'[51] that had, by the early 1960s, disappeared from the Party's discourse, but still flourished in its methods of quelling dissent. These methods were also Garaudy's, Althusser had hinted in a 1963 review of the Marxist–humanist Bible, the *1844 Manuscripts*: it was not surprising that the humanists who confused the young Marx's un-Marxist philosophy with his communist politics should regard theory as a pliant tool for realizing the political tasks of the hour, given that their attachment to a 'whole historical past' encouraged them in their ways. As if to substantiate the charge, Garaudy promptly shot back, in an organ of the Political Bureau directed by none other than Garaudy (who was himself a member of the Political Bureau), that 'the consequences [of Althusser's work] seem to me grave from both a theoretical *and* a practical standpoint'. Three years later, he was substantiating the same charge with a vengeance: 'all the comrades have recognized', he wrote to the head of the Party, 'the profound noxiousness of Althusser's ideas, and even the fact that they have the character of an organized platform'[52] – that is, constituted grounds for expulsion.

Althusser's defence of the autonomy of theory was thus not a purely theoretical affair; it was also a call to break the Stalinist-humanist stranglehold on the Party's intellectual life. On a widely shared view, the garrotte was in the hands of the PCF's 'official philosopher', who used it to establish an 'intolerable, dangerous monopoly' redounding to the benefit of the Feuerbacho–Marxian religion of man.[53] By mid-decade, prevailing opinion in the PCF's upper echelons was – de-Stalinization *oblige* – that Garaudy's power had to be curbed; granting his anti-humanist adversaries a forum was the shortest way to curbing it. They had, however, to be curbed in their turn: if one of the objectives was to bridle Garaudy's increasingly religiose enthusiasms, this must not be done in such a way as to give free rein to his adversaries' anti-humanism. Nor should the advocates of the autonomy of theory be encouraged to make a habit of contesting the Party line, as Althusser all but openly had; the Political Bureau's monopoly on political discussion had to be restored with all deliberate speed. A relatively free debate between Garaudy's and Althusser's partisans, which the leadership could easily close off whenever it threatened to get out of hand, was the likeliest means of checking Garaudy at small risk to Marxist–humanist orthodoxy, while establishing freedom of expression with all the requisite reservations. The humanist controversy was, from the Political Bureau's standpoint, intended to serve these limited ends. As it turned out, it did.

The debate proper began early in 1965. The year before, Althusser had had difficulty publishing in the French Communist press.[54] It was a Party monthly for politics and culture, the *Nouvelle critique* (*NC*), which stepped in to redress the situation after the July 1964 death of long-time Party leader Maurice Thorez. Its editor, Jacques Arnault, accepted one of the texts

Althusser had been unable to place, 'Freud and Lacan'. He followed up in December, before the ink was dry on Jorge Semprun's spirited attack on another, 'Marxism and Humanism', by inviting his editorial board to conduct a written debate on theoretical anti-humanism. In March, the *NC* reprinted Semprun's and Althusser's essays, together with a rejoinder by Althusser[55] and a more neutral piece. The humanist controversy was on; it would fill the pages of the *NC* for the next year.

There is no space here to review the contributions to this debate, which brought together diverse and diversely informed evaluations, more of them pro-Althusserian than not, of the idea that Marx's philosophical development had been marked by a break with humanism and Hegel. More important for present purposes is the fact that the debate took place at all, and Althusser's reactions to it.

Allowing the controversy about humanism to go forward in the *NC*, the Party leadership was, as all involved understood, striking a blow for Althusser. For the *NC* was not neutral. It had taken up the cudgels for the autonomy of theory in a December 1963 issue on the 'personality cult' that had earned it a rebuke from the Political Bureau instigated, in the opinion of its editorial board, by Roger Garaudy; and it continued to trespass on grounds 'reserved for those in positions of political responsibility', some of its editors going so far as to endorse the heresy, as one wrote in a memorandum sent to Rochet, that 'democratic centralism does not apply in the realm of theory'.[56] Moreover, if the review was hardly 'animated by a sectarian current that defended Althusser',[57] it was no secret that there were close ties between him and many of those associated with it. Some were former students of his from the early 1950s. One, a member of the Central Committee, had declared himself to be in basic political agreement with his former teacher in a theoretical correspondence begun in 1964; another, a confidant since 1948, published the first major popularization of his work, submitting it to his scrutiny in August 1966.[58] Aragon's condemnation, after the fact, of 'the perfectly unwarranted, scandalous scope' of the discussion in the *NC*, like Garaudy's charge that it was 'a muted version' of the 'systematic attack on the politics of the Party led by the group of philosophers influenced by Althusser', suggest how bitter resistance to the debate must have been when there was still hope of repairing 'the very bad mistake' the Political Bureau had made in *'letting* the *NC's* campaign against humanism *go on* (even encouraging it)'.[59]

Garaudy was not wrong: at stake in this campaign was, in the view of Althusser and many of his allies, the post-Stalinist reformism for which humanism and a vulgar Hegelianism provided ideological cover. But if it was at stake, it was never in question. The proof was that a Political Bureau whose unconcern for inner-Party democracy was matched only by its devotion to the gradualist, electoralist strategy that 'the most consistent humanism possible' underpinned did not hesitate to widen the scope of the humanist controversy, moving it beyond the venue of the *NC* to the far more prestigious arena of the Party's Central Committee. It did so in two stages, convening, in Choisy-le-Roi, a January 1966 assembly of Communist philosophers conceived as a dress rehearsal for a Central Committee meeting on 'problems of ideology and culture' held in Argenteuil two months later. Althusser seized the chance to rally the PCF to the 'left-wing anti-Stalinist positions'[60] he had been defending for years. Everything suggests that he thought he could succeed, if only because his predictable failure to make the slightest dent in the Party's politics worked a revolution in his own. In the direct aftermath of Argenteuil, he began moving towards a rupture with French Communism which, in the event, begot a politically paralysing compromise with it – while prompting, in philosophy, his resignation from the party of theory.

Although he was absent from Choisy-le-Roi because of illness, and from Argenteuil because he was not a member of the Central Committee, Althusser had the starring role at both. The January assembly, held in the presence of the assembled Political Bureau, showed that he enjoyed far greater support among the Party's philosophers than he had thought: the Stalinist–humanist tirade that Garaudy delivered against him provoked unusually sharp replies in his defence, and even sharper critiques of his rival's methods of muzzling dissent. The hostilities engaged at Choisy were pursued in long volleys of mostly invidious letters for and against Althusser addressed to Party authorities; inside a committee appointed to draft the resolution of the forthcoming Central Committee meeting; and in a series of Byzantine manoeuvres and counter-manoeuvres which signalled, on balance, that a relaxation of constraints on free expression was in the offing, and Garaudy's personal power on the wane. The climax, Argenteuil, consisted in three days of oral jousting that was at once erudite and so bitter that the order was later given to purge the version released for public consumption of 'polemical passages of a personal nature'. 'Much of the debate', as Aragon maliciously remarked, 'revolved around a proper name . . . comrade Althusser's.' Yet the defence of his positions was restrained, in conformity with what he later understood to be the meeting's general purpose: to strike 'a blow to the left, a blow to the right'. The upshot was a resolution which roundly declared that 'there is a Marxist humanism', while self-contradictorily promising an end to bureaucratic interference in intellectual debate.[61] Thus Argenteuil both closed the door to left-wing anti-Stalinism and limited the freedom needed to prise it back open: the resolution itself, intervening in the debate on humanism in violation of its own promise, was proof that the unrestricted liberties it granted in most spheres did not include that of questioning the Party line.

The same message had been broadcast even more loudly well before Argenteuil, when the Party leadership seized on the NC's chronic insolvency to push through a restrictive 'modernization' of it. If it were carried out as planned, its editor-in-chief warned, 'there would no longer be room' in the review for the equivalent of the debate about humanism. In the event, there no longer was. On the day Althusser delivered 'The Philosophical Conjuncture', Arnault's staff were giving him a farewell banquet. A note in his successor's archives sums up the limits on the de-Stalinization approved at Argenteuil: the new NC was to contain 'nothing opposed to the Party's political line (nor even anything different)'.[62] Althusser's reaction was to make it known that he would not be contributing anything to the 'new Nouvelle critique'.[63]

Theoreticist practice

In an unposted November 1963 letter, Althusser imagines the key witness at the investigation that preceded his 'theoretical trial' penitently reciting an Althusserian lesson before his former teacher. The 'theoretical dead-end' in which Marxist thought finds itself after thirty years of Stalinist repression and dogmatism, his interlocutor admits, can become, under defined 'circumstances', in the sense in which you use this word in . . . 'On the Materialist Dialectic', Louis . . . more important politically than the political contradiction itself (and ultimately, Louis, that is what you were thinking, deep down, when you told me that, in your view, 'today everything depends on Theory', which simply means that, in your view, Theory is today the 'decisive link' in the Leninist sense).

A statement Althusser probably read at his trial leaves no doubt as to which branch of Theory he had in mind: 'everything ultimately depends on . . . Marxist Philosophy'. Yet Althusser's 'everything depends on philosophy' did not spring from a faith in the 'critical omnipotence' of a theory that could 'become *practical* by dissipating the aberrations of History in the name of its truth'; he by no means believed that 'a general reform could be obtained by what might be called the Improvement of the Understanding'. That had been the error of the Enlightenment or the neo-Hegelians, labouring under the crippling illusion, as *For Marx* notes, that 'everything depends on philosophy'. Emerging, like them, 'from the world of reflection to transform the political world', but aware, as they had not been, that Theory's objective was not to convert 'History to History's truth', or even the Party to the Party's, Althusser set himself a properly *political* task: converting the Party to Theory's.[64]

This theoretical distinction made no practical difference. Althusserian philosophy's historical task was the transformation of ideology; to transform ideology, it had to reform the Party's understanding, translating philosophy into politics by tutoring the modern Prince. Concretely, this called for the development of two parallel programmes. The curriculum for one was set by Althusser's writings and seminars. His and his co-authors' 'difficult, austere' work, he confessed in 1967, was read mainly by intellectuals without 'organic (in the Gramscian sense) links to the workers' movement'. Yet, as he saw it in 1963, this by no means precluded their sallying forth from the world of reflection to revolutionize the political world. Was he not training up 'a mass of theoreticians' in whom Theory would one day take flesh, acquiring the '*historical* existence' that neither Party nor class had yet succeeded in giving it?[65] What was more, matters were proceeding apace. In 1964, students of his had created a heavily attended School for Theoretical Formation in which the classics of Althusserian Marxism stood high on the syllabus, and founded a review, the *Cahiers Marxistes–léninistes*, that bore their mentor's mark on every page. As for the faction of the UEC piloted by the Althusserians, it had, by March 1965, climbed its way into the leadership of the organization on the backs of the revisionist 'Italians', whose exit it had helped to engineer a few months after their idol Khrushchev's fall from grace. The 'young lions' of the École normale would now proceed, their professor exulted, to make a 'practical application' of his principles. This 'direct transition from theory to politics' was 'wholly within the norms': no arms were as powerful as those provided by 'a correct conception of things'.[66]

The Party proper was a less receptive pupil. Not until the changing of the guard after Thorez's death did Althusser even risk broaching – in February 1965 – a plan for 'obtaining certain key modifications required for the indispensable work of theoretico-political formation' in the PCF. Heartened by the response, he turned out, in three days, a forty-page memorandum combining a simplified review of key points of Althusserian doctrine, a vigorous plea for freedom of research and expression, and instructions how to 'build theoretical activity into the practice of the Party itself'.[67] He followed up with a primer that he submitted to French Communism's official theoretical journal. Entitled 'Theory, Theoretical Practice and Theoretical Formation', it argued that 'it is theoretical formation that governs ideological struggle'.[68]

'Genuinely optimistic' when he initiated this bid to become the guide of the future French Revolution, Althusser was jubilant by April, convinced by recent developments that the union of Althusserian Theory and Communist practice was now squarely on the historical agenda. 'Things were only just getting under way' in the UEC; the debate on humanism had commenced in the pages of the *Nouvelle critique*, whose editors were living 'proof ... that people older' than his *normaliens* could hold their own on 'the front lines of the battle for theory'; lecturing once-mistrustful Communist colleagues on the teaching of philosophy, he had observed that his 'ideas were making their way' 'in the Party itself'. 'Very soon' the Althusserian 'ranks would be swelled' by an inrush of new recruits; 'the union of generations' would give them 'great force'. His work had 'triggered ... an irreversible

movement much bigger than he was'; 'events continued to confirm all his certainties and predictions'.[69]

A year later, his enthusiasm was unabated. Was the international response to *For Marx* and *Reading Capital* not proof that
theory was indeed the decisive link in the present conjuncture,
as he had proclaimed four years earlier? Even the fact that his
essay on theoretical formation was still 'sleeping in a drawer'
months after he had expected it to appear in the PCF's theoretical
review could not dampen his optimism. He had arranged to have
part of it read out at the January assembly of Communist philosophers at Choisy, hopeful of convincing the members of the Party
leadership in attendance of 'the importance of philosophy', and
was now rewriting it into a book (*Theory and Practice*) destined,
for reasons of 'theoretical politics', for the Party's publishing
house. Although one had 'to keep in mind what the Party was',
the reports on the proceedings at Choisy furnished by several of
the editors of the *NC* were grounds for 'deep satisfaction'.
'Nothing would be as it had been before in the French Party,'
Arnault had told him, after this 'historic event'. All Althusser's
correspondence of the day suggests that he believed it.[70]

In the immediate aftermath of Argenteuil, he quite unambig-
uously changed his mind. Calculated public statements notwithstanding, he was conscious, from the first, that he had been dealt
a major defeat. His reaction was one of 'indignation' over what
'he and his team-mates unmistakably regarded as the triumph'
of their philosophical antagonists.[71] The first public expression of
his disenchantment came by way of his Maoist students, whose
uneasy alliance with the UEC's Party orthodox had already
foundered early in 1966. After a secret conclave with their tutor
on the eve of the UEC's 2–3 April Congress, they roared out their
disapproval of the PCF's 'revisionism' in a ferocious broadside
strikingly similar, in content if not in its 'Chinese' style, to his
own (probably unsent) letter to the Central Committee blasting
the Argenteuil resolution in no uncertain terms. Althusser, too,
vowed to 'go on the offensive', for there was 'no question of
accepting the revisionist theoretical compromise contained in the
resolution'; it would be necessary to 'co-ordinate the initiatives'
of those opposed to it, and 'fight the battle to the bitter end'.[72]
This was more than a reaction of the first hour. As surely as the
course Althusser steered down to Argenteuil was that of someone

who expected to redeem the Party, the course he struck after the fiasco of March was that of someone who had consigned it to perdition.

Objective anti-Stalinism

As the conjuncture would have it, while the Althusserians in the UEC were grouping for their final battle with the PCF, Chinese students, defying the (Soviet) party of the state and shaking off the tutelage of even the Chinese Party and state, set about 'realizing a Marxist thesis' advanced in 'Contradiction and Over-determination'. In a revolution 'of and by the masses', they carried the class struggle into the relatively autonomous instance in which the CPSU had failed to 'liberate mass initiative', 'the ideological superstructure'. Althusser promptly concluded that the Chinese masses were practising the left-wing anti-Stalinism of which his Marxism offered the theory. But if they confirmed that theory in one sense, they exposed, in another, the ideology sapping it from within: China provided living refutation of the notion that it was the bearers of theory who made history. It was, plainly, the masses, making what was plainly an 'ideological revolution'; what was more, indications were that they were making it without benefit of any vanguard, that of the working class not excepted.[73] So, at all events, ran the Althusserian myth of the Chinese Cultural Revolution, anti-Stalinist 'not in words but in deeds'.[74]

Althusser elaborated this version of events under the dual impact of Argenteuil and the news arriving from Beijing, system-atizing it in the autumn 1966 essay on China which, had its author's identity been revealed, would have been sufficient pre-text for expelling him from the PCF. Was he, like the UEC's 'Chinese', courting expulsion? A tête-à-tête with Rochet that took place a week after his lecture on 'The Philosophical Conjuncture' left no doubt that the Political Bureau had opted for a form of Garaudyism without Garaudy. In Althusser's view, the Party that emerged from the battle of Argenteuil must have offered a sorry contrast with his young lions, 'the embryo of a revolutionary future'.[75] There could be no question of helping the PCF to quash the revolution, in Paris or Beijing. In July, Althusser and his closest associates agreed among themselves that they would not actively seek a break with the PCF, but would not 'publicly criticize the Chinese' either.[76] Around the same time, the UEC's rebels (already stigmatized as 'oppositional elements' by the Party) held a cloak-and-dagger conclave to lay the groundwork for an independent organization. On one account, Althusser originally planned to attend; on another, Étienne Balibar, who did, read a message to the assembly on his behalf, to the effect that he disagreed with their tactics but approved their general political line.[77] By autumn, as the Party manoeuvred to torpedo the core Althusserian section of its student union while giving a wide berth to its prestigious helmsman, it seemed to Balibar, writing from Alger after a summer in France, that the motives for 'abandoning ship' had become 'powerful'; they indicated that Althusser should bail out of the Party 'at the head of a crew' including 'the people in the UEC'.[78] If Althusser was not of the same mind, it is hard to see why he hailed the Cultural Revolution in the *Cahiers Marxistes–léninistes*, which had become the ensign of the 'Marxist–Leninist' vanguard organization launched by the Maoist rebels in December.

His essay on China was more, in any case, than the fruit of a momentary enthusiasm; it crowned a shift in his assessment of the political situation amply attested by the metamorphosis that comes over his private correspondence in the wake of Argenteuil. The same friends and allies he had cheered, a few months earlier, with sanguine accounts of the swift gains Marxist Theory was making on impending disaster were now, and for a long time to come, assailed with prognostications as dark as those featured in the Chinese Communist Party's *Pékin Information*. 'Ninety-nine per cent of the economic bases of Soviet ideology', warns an August letter, lie 'outside the USSR', in which 'bourgeois ideology is spreading into so many areas that there is no counting them all.' 'It may well be that ours is a day in which the union of Marxist theory and the workers' movement is breaking up,' a left Catholic group heard Althusser say in May 1967; 'it is a highly precarious historical achievement that can literally be lost.' Even the occasional burst of optimism of the will came out sounding rather like a dirge: 'yes, socialism too can perish, as Marx knew; we have to theorize the possibility of its death precisely so as to prevent it – nothing less'. An August gloss on 'The Philosophical Conjuncture' points to the source of the threat without mincing words: 'Following the Soviet CP, the French and Italian CPs are objectively pursuing reformist, revisionist policies; they are becoming Social-Democratic parties: they have ceased to be revolutionary . . . in their present state, our parties are all but lost.' That is, 'despite its often very dogmatic form', the Chinese criticism of them was '*basically* . . . correct'. And Beijing was right about more than what was wrong with the Moscow-loyal Communist movement. The 'encounter' between the Althusserians' writings and the pronouncements of the Chinese revolutionaries spoke volumes. Indeed, a good part of Althusser's future task would consist in providing a 'theoretical foundation' for 'what certain Chinese theses affirm[ed]'.[79]

The stage was thus set for a collective exit from the PCF/UEC. It would have to be, Balibar argued in November, 'unambiguous, well-explained, and public'. In the event, it was, in Althusser's case, private, unexplained, and ambiguous in the extreme. It was, moreover, not an exit properly so called, but an inner emigration; and, far from being co-ordinated by Althusser and his collaborators on the one hand and Paris's junior Red Guards on the other, it materialized amid a series of manipulations designed by the rebels to push him into their camp by forcing his and his associates' hand. These machinations backfired. Hospitalized for a depression in November, Althusser concluded in January, while still ill, that he and his collaborators 'had to stay in the Party *for as long as possible* in order to fulfil, *for as long as possible* . . . the long-term theoretical function that the conjuncture had assigned' them – for they were 'currently irreplaceable'. He had, he added, 'been truly reckless' the year before; he had nearly 'squandered the theoretical credit' patiently amassed over the years. Letters sent to friends at the NC gently but firmly disowned the Althussero–Maoists and their new 'Marxist–Leninist' vanguard organization. His 'whelps' had, for lack of anything better, 'thrown themselves on his writings', bending them and everything else they could find to their own uses; unfortunately, they 'were completely out of his control'.[80]

If the last act was not an open break with French Communism, neither was it quite a return to the fold. In spring 1967, pursuing plans discussed the previous June, Althusser welded a handful of his co-thinkers into a vaguely 'clandestine' philosophical-political organization (the 'Groupe Spinoza') in which it would at last be possible to speak freely – behind closed doors. Thus one of the group's founding documents, drawn up by Althusser, uncompromisingly condemns the PCF's slide towards a 'petty-bourgeois, Social-Democratic socialism' associated with the CPSU's 'right-opportunist, petty-bourgeois revisionism' and contrasted with Beijing's 'Marxist–Leninist positions'. Yet the Groupe Spinoza's political colour did not, in its founder's view, imply that members who also belonged to the Communist Party should turn in their cards; they could occupy the 'empty place' of Marxist-Leninist philosophy 'from outside the Party without necessarily quitting'. its ranks.[81] It was a good retrospective definition of what Althusser had, as Argenteuil must have taught him, been doing all along.

How did the change in Althusser's politics affect his philosophy? In sum, it yielded the argument that politics shapes philosophy and, more generally, that, by way of philosophy, the ideological must continue to affect the theoretical even after the birth of Marxist science. For the Althusser of 1966–67, 'the ideological' had come to mean, not primarily discourse, but the non-discursive practices – 'behaviours and practical attitudes', or *moeurs* – that are sometimes embodied, as well, in the 'systems of ideas' he called theoretical ideologies. To say that politics/ideology shapes philosophy was therefore also to acknowledge the formative influence of non-theoretical on theoretical practice. But this was by no means to abandon the thesis that Marxist philosophy's task is to transform politics/ideology; Althusser's new argument was, rather, that philosophy's implication in the transformation of ideological practice transformed philosophy itself. His own philosophical evolution was a case in point. Coming on the heels of his failure to advance the cause of left-wing Stalinism with the sole weapon of theory, had the Chinese struggle to do so by transforming 'ideological social relations' not also sparked the transformation of Marxist philosophy inaugurated with Althusserian Marxism's 1966–67 turn? Marx's 'philosophical evolution', Althusser would soon conclude, 'was based on his political evolution'.[82] The political evolution that yielded this insight was Althusser's.

Yet if, in Marx's case as well, nothing would have happened without the politics, without the philosophy, the politics would not have found its theoretical expression. Finding it was a matter of making the external logic that led from Choisy-le-Roi to the Groupe Spinoza over into the internal logic that saw scientific philosophy become class struggle in theory.[83] It is to that inner logic that we now turn.

III

Althusser takes his distance from the party of the state in philosophy in 'The Philosophical Conjuncture and Marxist Theoretical Research' with the remark, noted above, that he had been mistaken in calling dialectical materialism a science. It is not elaborated. But 'there is a way of not talking about B when discussing only A', to cite a 1967 fragment, 'that takes account of B in one's discussion of A'.[84] Like everything Althusser wrote in 1966–67, 'The Philosophical Conjuncture' provides an illustration: it takes account of Althusser's incipient break with the idealist tendencies in Althusserian Marxism in a critical discussion of the idealist philosophies dominating the philosophical conjuncture in France. Better: it *effects* that break, drawing a dividing line *in* Althusser's own work in the act of drawing up battle lines *between* it and that of his adversaries. Moreover, by way of its sketch of the philosophical conjuncture, it *figures* the results of the break it only begins to theorize: the idea that Lenin's conception of the 'current situation' in politics applies to philosophy as well finds, at the descriptive level, an astonishingly complete realization here.

The germ of Althusser's lecture is contained in a 1963 letter detailing plans for a theoretical review. Letter and lecture envision a broad philosophical alliance along lines cutting conspicuously across the frontiers of what counted as Marxism: both range materialism and its prospective non-Marxist allies – notably Canguilhem, Lacan, Foucault and, 'somewhat later', Derrida – against 'the dominant French philosophy' (phenomenology and hermeneutics, Marxist or not) and the '"philosophical" ideologies' bringing up its rear (both structuralism and, more generally, the technocratic thought with which Althusser associated it). Between 1963 and 1966, however, the terms of the alliance change. In 1963, Althusser envisages rallying all the partisans of rational philosophy, materialists and idealists alike, to a broad 'party of the theoretical'. After all, they have a common foe in ideology; there is no pressing need 'to shoot down all idealist philosophers in flames'.[85] That, however, is a fair statement of the aim of the lecture. Yet if Althusser now issues a polite declaration of war on his allies within the party of the theoretical, he has no intention of dissolving the alliance: his objective is, rather, to open an 'anti-critical-idealist Front' in a complex war of position pitting materialists and close confederates (for example, Derrida) against others fighting alongside them in a subordinate struggle against a reactionary French spiritualism. It is in this context that he allusively traces the corresponding lines of demarcation between theoreticism and materialism in his own work, and predicts the long string of developments to which it must lead.

In a sense, the prophecy is fulfilled as soon as it is made, as even a cursory comparison of 'The Philosophical Conjuncture' with the 1972 'Elements of Self-Criticism' suffices to show. From the idea that the history of philosophy is that of an endlessly renewed battle between its materialist and idealist tendencies, through the claim that, in this struggle, neither is realized in a pure form in any philosophy, to the affirmation that philosophy's divisions and subdivisions are 'fixed in a series of *meeting*-points', or a main 'front' and secondary 'fronts', the view that the task of Marxist philosophy is to wage a war of position on the idealist adversary it (in both senses) contains emerges in the practical state as soon as Althusser begins to question his theoreticism.[86] To produce it, he had only to theorize his own theoretical practice.

More exactly, he had to extend the theorization of it begun elsewhere. To *For Marx*'s assertion that the diverse practices have in common the 'general essence of practice', *Reading Capital* adds – or objects – that 'there is no production in general, there is no history in general'. History, like production, can be thought only as singularity: as the 'always exceptional' situation of 'Contradiction and Overdetermination', whose necessity is that of its contingency, the structure of its conjuncture, a 'cause immanent in its effects' – all expressions of 'the principle', attributed to Mao, that 'the universal only exists in the particular'.[87] Situating philosophy in the conjuncture, 'The Philosophical Conjuncture' effectively affirms that this principle holds for philosophy too: there is, its author might have said, no philosophy in general. The task before Althusserian theory was thus that of thinking its own singularity: it would have to bring itself under the sway of its own law, aligning its theory of a now fully historicized philosophy with its theory of history, politics, or the social formation. That is, Althusser would have to 'rectify' the early Althusser as he had the early Marx: via 'the *application* of his works *to themselves* ... of their more elaborated forms to their less elaborated forms ... their theoretical system to certain terms of their discourse'. In practice, this 'folding back'[88] was carried out incognito: in 1966–67 and beyond, Althusser took account of Althusser by discussing Lévi-Strauss, Feuerbach, Lacan and Marx.

Initially, he did so unawares. Although he devoted much of 1966 to criticizing structuralism, it was hardly with the intention of settling accounts with his own theoreticism by proxy but, rather, in order to show, in an unambiguous attack on Lévi-Strauss, that the structuralist 'ambiguities' in his previous work were that and no more. The new onslaught on structuralism was to have been the opening battle in a campaign to concretize the anti-critical-idealist, anti-structuralist alliance proposed in 'The Philosophical Conjuncture' by creating a national network of 'theoretical study groups'. Althusser drew up fliers promoting these study groups in the autumn, but the project, overtaken by events, foundered soon after; it is unlikely even that the fliers were ever sent out.

One of the motives for the renewal of Althusser's quarrel with structuralism, and the broader campaign it was meant to spearhead, was his long-standing desire to seal an alliance with Jacques Lacan. If only by offering 'the science of history' lessons on the non-teleological nature of historical process that Althusser had been shouting from the rooftops, Lacan's 1965–66 course on the object of psychoanalysis, the opening lecture in which had appeared in a review founded in January 1966 by students of his and Althusser's, had fuelled visions of joint initiatives with the Lacanian school. But the materialist strands in Lacan were, Althusser thought, interwoven with others of Lévi-Straussian origin that tied him to a subjectivist, intentionalist notion of the unconscious. After seeing Lacan in July, he said as much in a note covering a copy of 'The Philosophical Conjuncture'; Lacan's 'theoretical relations with Lévi-Strauss' could be, '*to a certain extent*, a problem' for him and his associates, who, unlike 'everyone else', had no interest in 'confusing [him], under the term of structuralism, with Lévi-Strauss'.[89] Thus when, over the summer, Althusser revived plans to launch the review *Théorie*, he opted to give questions related to structuralism and psychoanalysis a large place in it; the first issue was to include work on the relations between structuralism and Lévi-Strauss, Lacan, linguistics, and ' "structure" in Marx'.[90]

The task of leading the anti-structuralist charge – or counter-attack, since structuralism was 'invading everything' – was initially entrusted to one of the co-authors of *Reading Capital*, Roger Establet. Establet, however, demonstrated the urgency of his task by example: he defected, persuaded of the 'genuinely materialist character of structure in Lévi-Strauss'. For Althusser, this apostasy was merely further confirmation that the French Party and left in general were becoming 'increasingly Lévi-Straussian'. It was in this climate that, after setting *Theory and Practice* aside in July, he dashed off 'On Lévi-Strauss', originally part of a 20 August letter that even its author considered 'extreme' – though not extreme enough to prevent him from distributing it widely in the autumn to anthropologists and others likely to rally the anti-structuralist offensive.[91]

The gravamen of Althusser's charge against structural anthropology is anticipated in his book on Montesquieu: Lévi-Strauss explains the 'prodigious and daunting diversity of manners and morals' that constitutes the anthropologist's basic problem by reducing them (as Montesquieu does not) to 'an ideal and abstract model'.[92] Everything that resists such reduction he consigns to the realm of contingency. Thus he annuls the historical 'diversity' (whether that of distinct cultures or the distinct levels of a particular culture) from which he sets out: the characteristic structuralist operation consists in producing 'explanations of real history' through an appeal to the 'varied combination . . . of "elements" ' in a combinatory, deemed capable of 'explaining historical effects *by itself*'. This latter-day Platonism is animated by a 'spiritualist conception' that makes structure a principle of coherence 'latent' in what it structures, typically identifying it with the unconsciously operating 'laws of the human mind'. Althusser's other criticisms of Lévi-Strauss are all predicated on these two.

The first, however, is quoted here from Étienne Balibar's 1973 assessment of his own contribution to *Reading Capital* – faulted for, among other things, its reliance on something suspiciously akin to a combinatory. The second occurs in a 1966 letter in which Pierre Macherey questions Althusser's conception of the 'structured whole' on the grounds that it is tied to a notion of 'latent structure' reminiscent of the structuralists'. Balibar goes on to reject the 'temptation' of constructing what Althusser holds up, in 1966, as an example of the *legitimate* formalism that contrasts with its structuralist parody: 'a formalized theory of modes of production in general'. Such a formalization, Balibar says in 1973, 'can only be a theory of *the* mode of production *in general* and its *possible* "variations"';[93] in other words (Althusser's, protesting his *innocence* of structuralism), it can only lead to 'the crazy formalist idealism of the idea of producing the real by a combinatory of elements'.[94] As for the notion of 'the structural whole', Althusser himself acknowledged that it was 'ambiguous': it could be construed as an 'interiority' and 'the correlate . . . of a unity'.[95]

Why does Althusser approve a 'formalized theory of modes of production in general' while condemning structuralism for 'explaining' social phenomena as 'mere *variations* of a purely formal *mode of combination*' – and affirming that 'to understand a real phenomenon is not . . . a matter of producing the *concept of its possibility*, [but] the concept of its *necessity*'? The reason, in brief, is that he had from the beginnings of his enterprise 'set out to think *singularity*', while acknowledging that 'it is possible to think the singular and concrete only in *concepts* (which are thus "abstract" and "general")'. The general concept he mobilized to think this way of thinking the singular was the Spinozist 'singular essence',[96] which might be defined as a complex unity itself made up of internally complex unities that nothing beyond the 'contingent necessity' of their encounter predestines to coalesce in an organized whole. From the overdetermined social formation to the conjunction of Marxism's three sources, from the political/philosophical conjuncture to its complement, the structure present only in its effects, a great many of the basic building-blocks of *For Marx* and *Reading Capital* had been conceived with reference to this idea. The formalism that 'On Lévi-Strauss' both condemns and exemplifies stems, paradoxically, from the attempt to conceptualize the 'question of empirical knowledge'[97] (and thus the union of theory and practice) in its terms.

This yielded a new insistence that there could be no knowledge of anything 'other than the singular and particular', since 'a general principle yields knowledge only if specified in the forms required by its singular object'. Singular objects were now named 'empirical concepts', an equivalent for 'singular essences' that brought out the dependence of the knowledge of 'facts' on the system of concepts that produced it. This clarification gave rise to another, worked out in notes dating from summer 1966; it bore on the relation between 'theoretical objects' and the singular objects of which they produced knowledge. The crux of it was that a particular theory produced, not knowledge of 'its' object, but new relations among 'theoretical objects' situated within a field whose limits it defined; the field contained both real and virtual objects, and could thus produce knowledge of (real) singular essences only if it was combined with '(empirical) knowledge of the determinate forms of existence that make for the singularity of these essences'. As each particular or 'regional' theory transformed relations between the theoretical objects in its field, so it was itself one of the objects of another, more comprehensive 'general theory' which, in its turn, transformed the relations among a number of regional theories.

The task of philosophy, at this point in Althusser's thinking, was to combine existing general theories, identified as the Althusserian 'attributes', by theorizing the conjunctural relations between them. Since philosophy was now also conceived as contained in the conjuncture it theorized, 'to say that it is the Theory of the conjuncture of all existing Theories does not mean that it is their General Theory = there is no general theory of General Theories, for, if there were, it would be absolute knowledge; it is merely the Theory of the combination of existing Theories in their present conjuncture'.[98] In the philosophical conjuncture, philosophy thus had its singular object, apparently analogous with those of all other forms of knowledge. This particular 'singularity', however, was a manifestation of the unity of the totality of the real, testifying to the still transcendent nature of a philosophy which, albeit 'conjunctural', provided knowledge of the 'combination of [all] existing Theories' or 'attributes'. The singularity of the object of Theory was thus deceptive; philosophy concerned itself with the present moment of a totality whose universality could *not* be said to 'exist only in the particular'.

The structuralist potential of this scheme is plain: if General Theories are conceived as subsuming regional theories which in turn subsume the fields containing their (real and virtual) objects, one can perfectly well conclude that in this version of the Althusserian dialectic, as in its theoreticist predecessor, 'the moment of the "pure" theory of historically representable sets ... precedes the theory of historical structures'.[99] As for the proviso that theoretical objects must be combined with 'empirical knowledge' to produce the concept of 'the necessity of a real phenomenon', it begs the question: how is this combination to be thought, if not, in Lévi-Straussian fashion, as knowledge of a necessary form supplemented by knowledge of its contingent content? Althusser's response was to eliminate the question (his own) by replacing it with another: how could the 'conjunctural' combination of theories be conceived without recourse to notions of generality that cast it in terms of genus and species? The new question begins to materialize in 'Three Notes on the Theory of Discourses', in which his thinking about general and regional theories moves centre stage.

Dated September–October 1966, 'Three Notes' opened a formal exchange between Althusser and his associates that he initiated in the course of writing it, in the unrealized hope of turning out a book by several hands, *Elements of Dialectical Materialism*. The text is a taxonomy of the types of discourse specific to theory, ideology, art and the unconscious. It focuses on the production of the singular essence Althusser calls the subject of ideology, which is one way of defining the theory of interpellation it introduces. Developing ideas indebted less to Lacan's essay on the mirror stage than to a symptomatic reading of Feuerbach, it describes the ideological mirror structure that transforms the conflictual encounter at the origins of what Althusser initially terms the 'subject of the unconscious' by recasting it as the ideological subject's 'subsumption' under a Subject. It also pursues an attempt, begun in 1963, to assign psychoanalysis its general theory;[100] and, in the process, it presses the attack on Lévi-Strauss-in-Lacan. Attributing to Lacan the misconception that the 'regional theory' of psychoanalysis has its general theory in linguistics, which, says Althusser, he intermittently conceives, after Lévi-Strauss, as the 'mother-discipline of the human sciences', 'Three Notes' objects that the theory of the unconscious must, rather, be assigned to historical materialism, but also to a nascent general theory of 'the signifier'. It moves towards the fundamentally anti-Lacanian conclusion, which the third note opposes to what the first affirms, that only one type of discourse, the ideological, has a subject properly so called.

If so, ideology is one thing and the unconscious is something else entirely – a premiss that makes it possible to think the effects of each on the other: that is, their articulated combination. This might be regarded as Althusser's posthumous contribution to the ongoing debate about the thesis for which he is best known in the Anglophone world: 'ideology interpellates individuals as subjects'. Broached in a 1963 discussion of the 'imputation of forms of behaviour' to the subject, the mechanism of interpellation is here named and sketched in the context of a critique of Lacan that is absent from the canonical text on the topic, although that critique remained central to Althusser's project.[101] 'Three Notes' thus points to the need for a reinterpretation of his thinking on the relations between the unconscious and ideology, attested by the fact that a knowledgeable critic could write, shortly before the text was published, that the Althusserian school never made any 'real attempt . . . to "articulate" historical materialism and psychoanalysis' – precisely what 'Three Notes' tries to do. Thus Althusser anticipates the objection that he lacks a theory of the subject, or misses the dimension of desire underpinning interpellation, with the argument that ideological discourse is overdetermined by those effects of the unconscious to which it offers a 'hold', even as certain effects of the unconscious are in turn overdetermined by the ideological subject-effect. As if to refute the charge that he nurtures 'hegemonic ambitions' at the expense of psychoanalysis,[102] 'Three Notes' leaves it to a psychoanalytic theory that has ceded the category of the subject to ideology to explain how the process of interpellation is conditioned by the unconscious, present in the subject-centred mirror structure of ideology only in the form of its absence – an absence masked, precisely, by the presence of the ideological subject-effect. To the end of his life, Althusser continued to plead for the division of labour outlined here.[103]

About the idea that psychoanalysis has *two* general theories, 'Three Notes' remarks, in passing:

> Naturally, this case will seem 'special' to us if we cling to an idea of the G[eneral] T[heory] mired in the Aristotelian categories of inclusion and subsumption. On this conception of 'generality', which it seems to us absolutely necessary to reject, the GT maintains relations of extension with its RTs (since every RT is *included* in *its* GT, one GT is enough to account for an RT). On this conception, an RT cannot depend on *two* GTs; it can depend on just one.

The relationship between the two general theories on which certain regional theories depend is, Althusser adds, comparable to the 'overlap' between two machines; one of the French terms he uses (*empiétement*) suggests, more clearly than the English, that what is involved is interference or encroachment rather than mere redundancy. In an aside reminiscent of *For Marx*'s affirmation that the 'exceptional' social formation is not an exception but the rule, he suggests that the case of a regional theory ascribable to two general theories is not an 'isolated instance'. Further discussion of the subject is postponed.

Althusser returned to it in spring 1967, which saw him working on a spate of projects after the depression that afflicted him from November to March: the creation of the Groupe Spinoza; plans to launch the review *Théorie* under its auspices; a revision of *Theory and Practice*, which he hoped to publish as two separate books that autumn; and the last three of our texts, 'On Feuerbach', 'The Historical Task of Marxist Philosophy', and 'The Humanist Controversy'. 'On Feuerbach' is part of a spring 1967 lecture course based on his translations of Feuerbach's early work and eight-year-old draft chapters of a monograph on it; a version of the course was earmarked for a (never completed) book on *The German Ideology*, on the drawing board since early 1966.[104] As the course was beginning, a 'summary of Althusser's research' was unexpectedly commissioned (only to be later refused) by the leading Soviet philosophical journal; Althusser seized the occasion to turn out 'The Historical Task', intended, as the pedagogical style shows, for readers unfamiliar with the complexities of Western Marxist debate. In May, he rounded off the first draft of this essay with an innovative chapter on philosophy and politics, born of the reflections he had been pursuing in *Theory and Practice*, and decided to issue the expanded text in France; the result was a projected monograph which reached proof stage before it was abandoned. In June, after dispatching 'The Historical Task' to Moscow, he began planning a French version of a collection proposed by a Mexican publisher the previous autumn; it was to include his 1963 'Marxism and Humanism' and selections from the debate that the essay had touched off in the *NC*. What exists of 'The Humanist Controversy' was produced at a furious pace early in the summer to introduce the (abortive) French book.[105] It is not surprising, then, that the last three texts in the present volume should share many of the same themes. Among them – although this is rarely explicit – is the search for a new 'conception of generality' capable of accommodating the new conception of a 'conjunctural' philosophy.

'Thought', we read in 'On Feuerbach', 'that "*seeks to encroach upon its other*" – and the "other of thought" is being – *is thought that oversteps its natural boundaries*. This encroaching upon its other on the part of thought means that it *claims for itself that which does not properly belong to thought but to being*. That which belongs to *being* is *particularity* and *individuality*, whereas that which belongs to *thought* is *generality*.' Taken from Feuerbach's critique of Hegel, this Althusserian passage, says Althusser, raises the spectre of nominalism: if Feuerbach admits that only individuals exist, he risks making his version of essence, the human genus, nothing but a name, 'bound up with history and the politico-ideological conjuncture'. But 'Feuerbach is not a nominalist'. He has a theory of 'the unity', under reason, of the 'attributes of the human essence' (reason, will, and the heart), such that 'everything that is an object of reason simultaneously is, or can be, an object of [non-theoretical] practice'. Feuerbach's philosophy is thus 'simultaneously a theory of knowledge and of practice'. 'This, of course, has implications', remarks his critic, 'not only for the nature of ideologies, philosophy, and the sciences, but also for politics, which is reduced to a critique of the illusions of consciousness about itself, with the whole resting on the thesis of the practical and theoretical primacy of consciousness.' Feuerbach is not a nominalist, but a theoreticist.[106]

Yet it is not his theoreticism which founds his realism, but the reverse. Feuerbach's basic claim, according to Althusser, is that the general/the essential exists as the human genus, which constitutes the essence of each individual. Man has an existential experience of this in sexuality and an alienated consciousness of it in religion, which, objectifying his essence, constitutes his essential object. The founding principle of Feuerbach's philosophy is accordingly that man's relationship to his fellow (wo)man, like his relationship to the objects of his consciousness, is a relationship to his own attributes, that is to say, to his generic essence.

In making this demonstration, Althusser says, Feuerbach produces an account of ideology which, albeit ideological, nevertheless lays bare the speculary structure informing all ideology. Feuerbachian man finds the reflection of Man everywhere; Feuerbach 'puts all humanity through the mirror stage'.[107] So, Althusser adds, does Lévi-Strauss. The characteristic operation of structural anthropology is to show that apparently diverse or even contradictory practices of a society (or of several) are structurally equivalent – that is, result from determinate, if unconscious, transformations of a set of unvarying rules. 'On Feuerbach' identifies this isomorphism, the *'homology* of *structure* that makes it possible to think *unity through convertibility'*, with the Feuerbachian mirror structure that makes all man's objects reflections of his essence. Since Lévi-Strauss is said to trace the isomorphism of only apparently diverse practices to the operations of the immutable, unconscious 'laws of the human mind', it is a short step to the argument that the dean of the structuralists, who had declared in a polemic with Sartre that 'the ultimate goal of the human sciences [is] not to constitute, but to dissolve man',[108] is a secret sharer in the (Feuerbachian) humanism he contests. 'On Feuerbach' extends the argument to phenomenology and hermeneutics, emphasizing the fact that all three are 'Feuerbachian' philosophies of consciousness conceived as a mirror structure. But the text also shows that the question of consciousness is not essential to its argument; the more fundamental point is that the mirror structure as such ensures the primacy of unity over diversity, the 'imposition of difference under non-difference'.

Stated in those terms, the criticism of Feuerbach and his unwitting heirs applies to its author as well. In the Althusser of *For Marx*, it was theoreticist theory which ensured the primacy of unity over diversity by assigning all the social practices their subordinate place within the totality of which theory alone provided the knowledge. But the resulting mirror structure, which invested Theory with the unity of the totality and the other way around, did not disappear as soon as Althusser rejected his theoreticist definition of philosophy; rather, it survived in a form which sought to compensate for the fact that there was now no 'general theory of General Theories'. Witness the attempt, in 'Three Notes', to find a functional equivalent for the supposedly unifying role of Spinozist substance: 'if we do not think the possibility of an articulation between GTs, we will remain at the level of the *parallelism of the attributes* and of the temptation that constantly accompanies it, the *conflation* of the attributes'. That is, the only way not to fall back into theoreticism of the kind that made theory 'simultaneously a theory of knowledge and of practice' – or, according to Feuerbach-in-Althusser, an expression of 'the essence of theoretical practice in general' and thus of 'the essence of practice in general' – was to produce a substitute for it: philosophy had, at all events, to be charged with preserving the unity of the whole of which it was supposed to be a reflection. Moreover, the persistence of philosophy's unifying function at the 'horizontal' level, that occupied by the major sciences (or General Theories) and philosophy itself, had its counterpart in the 'vertical' unity between the various 'theoretical objects' and their real and virtual "variations": that is, in the persistence of something not unlike an originary essence down through the long line of transformations that ultimately culminate in something rather like their phenomena. The previous sentence paraphrases the criticism of the ideology of genesis sketched in 'On Feuerbach' – which thus marks out a place for its author in the Feuerbacho-phenomenologico-hermeneutic family portrait it paints.

The contradiction this points to is not resolved but exacerbated in 'The Historical Task of Marxist Philosophy'. It is here that Althusser first elaborates the twin insights that to make dialectical materialism a science is to make it a species of absolute knowledge, whereas to recognize that it is not a science because ideology is a 'squatter' inside it is to recognize that it has an 'intimate, organic relation' to politics.[109] But these new ideas remain tied to others commanded by both the variant of geneticism that sets out from a 'theoretical object' only to find it again in 'its' variations, and the affirmation that philosophy, although no longer a science, provides knowledge of 'what is improperly called the "totality" of the real'. Indeed, geneticism and 'post-theoreticism' are increasingly intertwined: the totality which, whatever its alias, is still both philosophy's 'theoretical object' and 'the real', has its variations in the conjunctures which can only be 'determinate forms of existence' of this totality. The conjuncture is thus a singular essence which is a form of existence of a higher unity. Philosophy in Althusser, like structure in Lévi-Strauss, continues to impose 'difference under non-difference': the non-difference it imposes is indifferently the totality's and its own.

How is this squared with the thesis that materialist philosophy is caught up in constant combat with the ideology it contains – that, as 'The Humanist Controversy' affirms, a science's break with ideology is 'an event of very long duration that, in a sense, never ends'? The answer is that the 'continuing break' is here conceived as secondary; it has its origins in another, inaugural break, which institutes a science that must be further developed on the one hand and protected, on the other, from the ideologies that 'besiege' it. The theory of the encounter, then, applies only up to the moment of the emergence of a science. Thereafter, philosophy's defence of the sciences against the ideologies it contains – that is, fends off – is the purely external confrontation required by a defence of the scientific *fortress* against the incursions of its foes. The metaphor is on prominent display in 'The Historical Task'.[110]

The conception of philosophy that sustained it was, however, already under attack from within Althusser's own work. The critique of the ideology of genesis, or of 'genus' in Feuerbach, was implicitly a rejection of it. An alternative had begun to emerge in the thesis that the regional theory of psychoanalysis was rooted in the conflictual conjunction of two general theories. Althusser's work on Lévi-Strauss contained the structurally similar idea that even 'primitive' societies, invested by 'the ethnographic attitude' with an 'originary simplicity', had to be conceived, like all others, as resulting from the combination of at least two modes of production;[111] thus they represented, as it were, an originary duplicity or multiplicity. These concrete instances of 'the unevenness of origins' (the subtitle of the 1963 'On the Materialist Dialectic')[112] prefigure the affirmation, in 'The Humanist Controversy', of the 'non-originary nature of the origin', an idea whose paternity Althusser here rather inconsistently attributes to a single father, Jacques Derrida, even while arguing that concepts, like modes of production and most other things of consequence, tend to have several. Althusser's second definition of philosophy – a statement of its non-originary origin in science and ideology – would crystallize when this concept got the better of the geneticism informing his theory of theory.

Once it had, Althusser possessed the means for thinking his politically determined insight into the political nature of philosophy. The alternative to the theoreticism for which Marxist philosophy had been fathered by the theoretical revolution that spawned the twin sciences of historical and dialectical materialism was not regression to the historicism for which philosophy was a mere extension of politics. Philosophy could, rather, be conceived as originating in an origin that is not one, *in* and *as* the conflictual encounter between science and politics/ideology. The concept of generality adumbrated in 'Three Notes', in other words, was the condition for extending the theory of the encounter beyond the moment of the break: philosophy could then be thought as a continuing break with the ideological that ceaselessly constitutes and reconstitutes itself through the *process* of the break, rather than as its result. The principle underlying this conception of its activity as a division or dividing neither preceded nor followed by a unity is spelled out in a well-known passage of Althusser's self-criticism:

> It is impossible to separate the classes from class struggle. The class struggle and the existence of classes are one and the same thing. In order for there to be classes in a 'society', the society has to be *divided* into classes; this division does not come *later in the story* . . . it is the class struggle which constitutes the division into classes.

The passage dates, it is true, from 1972. But here is another, written early in 1966:

> The opposition of particular interests [in Rousseau's *Social Contract*] means that particular interest is constituted by the universal opposition which is the essence of the state of war. There are not first

individuals each with his own particular interest, opposition intervening subsequently as an accident. The opposition is primary.[113]

In the realm of theory as well, opposition is primary. This is
perhaps the shortest way of summarizing Althusser's turn of
1966–67, whose concrete implications can be restated in the
terms of his 1972 remark on the primacy of class struggle:
philosophy and the existence of the division between the sciences
and the ideologies are one and the same thing. Fundamentally,
there is not, contrary to what he had maintained down to the
turn, and even a little beyond it, first ideology, and then science,
and then the opposition between them. Rather, the opposition
between the scientific and the ideological stems from a process
of division that does not come later in the story, but is constituted by philosophy, the class struggle in theory; it takes the
form of an internal division between philosophy and the ideology it contains, carried out in the name of a defence of the
scientific that is, in the last instance, political. In philosophy, the
'second' Althusser might have said, opposition is all.

Before he could say anything of the sort, however, he had to
establish the primacy of opposition within his own theory of
theory. He would do so explicitly only with the first formulation,
in autumn 1967, of his new definition of philosophy. The new
and deeper self-criticism that cleared the way for it was fully
stated only afterwards. But, although Althusser might not have
realized it at the time, it was presented indirectly in the July
1967 'Humanist Controversy', by way of a discussion of the
tribute that the Marx of the *1844 Manuscripts* paid to an ideological conception of unity even as he struggled to formulate, on the
terrain of the emergent science of historical materialism, the
principle that opposition is primary.

Conceived as a rejoinder to Althusser's critics at Argenteuil,
'The Humanist Controversy' claims to be nothing more than a
'labour of critical repetition' of Marx's break with Feuerbach,
and thus of Althusser's own polemic against the Marxist humanism of his own day. But, as in 'The Historical Task', repetition
paves the way for a major innovation. *For Marx* and *Reading
Capital* had treated the Hegelian dialectic as an epistemological
obstacle that Marx had to clear away to become Marx; 'The
Humanist Controversy' says, rather, that Marx owes Hegel the

key concept of the 'process without a subject'. More generally, Althusser suggests that, purged of the teleology that is nevertheless built into its very structures, the Hegelian dialectic can be rewritten in materialist terms. As a process whose only subject is 'the process itself', it offers an alternative to the humanism that was the lynchpin of bourgeois ideology; the Hegelian conception of the non-originary nature of the origin is incompatible with the geneticism, and thus with the evolutionism, which Hegel is more commonly taken to underwrite. To combat the resurgence of humanism and carry out the concomitant 'radical critique of the ideology of genesis' called for in 'On Feuerbach', the implicit thesis would seem to run, Marxism could do worse than to make, following Marx, a critical return to Hegel.

Any such return must, however, set out from a criticism of Marx's. The early Marx contracted his debt to Hegel, Althusser says, while trying to historicize Feuerbachian humanism by grafting the Hegelian dialectic onto it. The result was an impasse, because it proved impossible to marry Hegelian process to the inherently ahistorical categories of Feuerbach's philosophy, above all the one that epitomized its 'radical negation of history', Man. Hegelianized, humanism could only yield an essentially religious ideology of genesis, a version of process that always began with a subject always discovered again at the end, because everything that lay in between was a reflection or emanation of it. Man, in other words, ensured the primacy of unity over a historical dialectic which, in a certain Hegel, a Hegel read against the grain, proceeded from the idea that opposition is primary.

It was this genuinely materialist notion of process that Marx put beyond his reach by imprisoning Hegel in Feuerbach in the *1844 Manuscripts*. He continued to suffer the consequences in *The German Ideology*, in which an incipiently Marxist conception of dialectic is lamed by a geneticism that subordinates historical difference to a principle of unity represented, not now by Man, but by 'concrete individuals', historicized representatives of the transhistorical Feuerbachian Subject. Such historicization of the inherently transhistorical involved a contradiction in terms; it was the form in which, in Marx, the (Feuerbachian) attack on history survived Marx's critique of it, although that critique had already initiated the revolutionary break that would issue in the Marxist dialectic.

If this is an accurate account of Marx's theoretical crisis of 1844–45, was Althusser's turn of 1966–67 not a 'critical repetition' of it in a sense that he could scarcely have intended? Like the Marx of the *1844 Manuscripts*, Althusser too had put a massive 'epistemological obstacle' in the path he had himself begun to open up.[114] Moreover, it was, broadly speaking, the same obstacle, a transhistorical category implying a radical negation of history; and, in Althusser as in Marx, it checked the development of the key category of process. The difference was that, in Althusser, this transhistorical category was not Man, but Theory, and that it thwarted the progress not of historical, but of dialectical materialism, standing in the way of a conception of *philosophy* as process initiated by his recognition of its basically political nature. In Althusser too, the epistemological obstacle briefly survived the critique that would lead to its disappearance, and for much the same reason: Althusser's 'conjuncturalization' of philosophy, like Marx's historicization of Feuerbachian Man, was predicated on a contradictory union of transcendence and immanence that situated philosophy in the historical singularity of a conjuncture while also making it the guardian of an always already given totality of which the conjuncture was the ephemeral manifestation. So conceived, the philosophical conjuncture was, like the 'concrete individual' of *The German Ideology*, the idealist 'premiss' squatting within a tendentially materialist theory of theory – even while it pointed the way to its own suppression, as do many of the ideological obstacles which, Althusser notes in 'The Humanist Controversy', have a curious kinship with the theoretical concepts whose emergence they block.

If it is legitimate to associate this relation of a still-transhistorical theory to 'its' conjuncture with the conception of generality and the ideology of genesis that, in one way or another, all the texts collected below contest, then 'The Humanist Controversy' offers a clue as to why its author abandoned this unfinished attempt at founding what 'On Feuerbach' calls a 'non-genetic theory of historical irruption' in order to attend to more urgent matters. Althusser no doubt realized, in the course of the witty attack on the Marxist variant of geneticism that comes near the end of 'The Humanist Controversy' as we have it, that he was still in league with the adversaries he was trying to drive from the field: in a consistently non-genetic theory – a theory of the encounter – materialist philosophy had to be conceived as derivative of nothing but the encounter that engendered it, while its 'historical irruption' had to be approached less as a datable event than as an endlessly ongoing process. It followed that the notion of the continuing break put forward in 'The Humanist Controversy' had to be invested with a meaning very different from the one that it had there, another way of saying that Althusser's continuing break with himself had only been initiated in his writings and political struggles of 1966–67. We have barely begun to come to terms with the transformation of philosophy that it augured.

Notes

1. For the French text of 'Three Notes on the Theory of Discourses', as well as François Matheron's and Olivier Corpet's introduction and notes, see *Écrits sur la psychanalyse*, ed. Matheron and Corpet, Paris, 1993, pp. 111–70. 'The Historical Task of Marxist Philosophy' is translated from the proofs of a monograph (9-02.05) that Althusser did not pass for press; the authorized Hungarian edition of an earlier, somewhat shorter version appeared in his *Marx – az elmélet forradalma*, trans. Ernö Gerö, Budapest, 1968, pp. 272–306. The originals of the other writings translated below may be found in EPP II: 169–251, 393–532.

2. 'RSC', a major study of the *Social Contract*, is culled from a course Althusser gave early in 1966; 'SRC', the essay on the Cultural Revolution, was written nine months later. Eric Marty offers an unintentionally hilarious analysis of these two texts (*Louis Althusser*, Paris, 1999, pp. 143–62), pillorying the article on China as an 'apology for totalitarianism' before torturing the inevitable 'inevitable retraction' for it out of its ancestor. The proleptic recantation was, be it noted, *reprinted* in 1972 – about the same time its author dropped some rather spectacularly unrepentant remarks on the Cultural Revolution ('RTJL' 131–2) that Marty magnanimously overlooks.

3. Guy Besse, Letter of 14 May 1966 to Henri Krasucki, AWR 8, 5, e; Letter of 12 July 1966 to Besse. Althusser released the two chapters of *Theory and Practice* as 'MHMD' and 'OTW' (April 1966 and 1967, respectively).

4. François Matheron, Introduction, SH 2. Key passages are sharply condensed in Althusser's later work, notably parts of 'The Philosophical Conjuncture' in 'LP' 172–3 and 'PSPS' 122; 'The Humanist Controversy' in 'ESC' 113–14; 'On Feuerbach' in 'ISMP' 231 ff. 'On

Lévi-Strauss' is liberally quoted in Emmanuel Terray, *Marxism and 'Primitive' Societies*, trans. Mary Klopper, London, 1972, pp. 178–9 and *passim*.

5. Interview with Gérard Bellouin, 6 November 1992, cited in Frédérique Matonti, 'La double illusion: *La Nouvelle critique*, une revue du PCF (1967–1980)', Doctoral thesis, University of Paris I, 1996, p. 159. Bellouin was a member of the Party's Section for Intellectuals and Culture. The PCF's other two great men of the hour were Louis Aragon and Roger Garaudy.

6. *LF* 699, 4 August 1966; Perry Anderson, *In the Tracks of Historical Materialism*, London, 1983, p. 37; 'Teoria e metodo', *Rinascita*, 25 January 1964, p. 28.

7. Waldeck Rochet, *Le Marxisme et les chemins de l'avenir*, Paris, 1966, pp. 288–9; 'A propos des ouvrages publiés', 9–05.06, pp. 2–3; *LF* 671, 12 May 1966; unposted letter of 7 June 1966 to Lucien Sève.

8. On the phantom career of the long-planned review, see François Matheron, 'L'impossible revue *Théorie* de Louis Althusser', *La Revue des revues*, no. 32 (2003), pp. 33–51.

9. *SISS* 84; 'MHMD' 105, 117.

10. 'MHMD' 105, 117, 121–2; 'TTPTF' 8, 13; 'Projet de réponse à Jorge Semprun', 3–05.02, p. 2.

11. 'TTPTF' 27.

12. 'The Historical Task', p. 215.

13. Letter of 12 May 1966 to Étienne Balibar.

14. Letter of 2 September 1966 to Michel Verret; 'NCA', 4.

15. *RC* 128.

16. 'R', 9–05.01, pp. 43–4.

17. As is spelled out, in what Althusser considered a 'prodigiously illuminating' essay (letter of 14 May 1965 to Pierre Macherey), in Macherey, 'On the Rupture', trans. Ted Stolze, *The Minnesota Review*, 26, 1986, pp. 122–3.

18. 'Three Notes on the Theory of Discourses', p. 65. See also Peter Thomas, 'Philosophical Strategies: Althusser and Spinoza', *Historical Materialism*, 10, no. 3, 2002, p. 78.

19. 'The Historical Task', p. 213.

20. *FM* 210.

21. Letter of 22 January 1964 to Michel Verret.

22. 'TPh' 246.

23. *FM* 169.

24. 'Sur la genèse', 11–02.01. The theory of the encounter is associated with a 'theory of the clinamen' in contemporaneous notes on Pierre Macherey's *Towards a Theory of Literary Production* (11–02.06).

25. *TP*, 8–01.04, p. 3 and *passim*; 'The Historical Task', p. 214.

26. 'The Philosophical Conjuncture', p. 12; Diverses notes 1966, 11–02.02. For the view that it was Jacques Lacan who taught Althusser, late in his career, that 'the union of theory and practice must be thought at the level of ethics', see Joon-kee Hong, *Der Subjektbegriff bei Lacan und Althusser*, Frankfurt, 2000, p. 215.

27. *TP*, 7-01.10, pp. 93–4; see also 'TTPTF' 23. A Spanish version of this passage is available in Althusser *et al.*, *Polémica sobre marxismo y humanismo*, trans. Marta Harnecker, Mexico City, 1968, pp. 183–6.

28. 'The Historical Task', pp. 215, 209.

29. 'PRW' 21 (an 'interview' that Althusser in fact conducted with himself). The canonical formulation of 1972 reads: 'philosophy is, in the last instance, class struggle in the field of theory' ('RTJL' 67).

30. 'The Historical Task', p. 212.

31. 'NSP' 318; 'OEYM'. Compare 'LP' 181, 183.

32. Letter of 21 July 1967 to Michel Simon; *LF* 751, 754, August 1967 and 6 December 1967.

33. Four of the five lectures Althusser gave to lead off this course taught with half a dozen associates are available in *PSPS* 69-165. The fifth, published posthumously as 'Du côté de la philosophie', *EPP* II: 253-98, has yet to be translated.

34. For the earliest published self-criticism, see *RC* 7–8. Most anglophone readers discovered a somewhat bolder version of it when they discovered Althusser; see *FM* 14–15, 256.

35. 'R', 9-05.01, pp. 43–4; 'NCA' 3.

36. See *Lire le Capital*, ed. Étienne Balibar, Paris, 1996, pp. 635–61.

37. Letter of 10 October 1963 to Michel Verret. See also 'PSH' 55–7.

38. 'Notes sur Lévi-Strauss, *La Pensée sauvage*', 60–04, pp. 18–19.

39. 'MPH' 102; 'TPh' 263–4; unposted letter of 24 November 1963 to Lucien Sève; letter of 21 December 196[3] to Pierre Macherey; 'NCA' 4-5; 'La conjoncture, 4 mai 1967', 11-03.01, p. 2.

40. 'RTJL' 66. The exception that proves the rule is Gregory Elliott, *Althusser*, London, 1987, still the best book available on the relation between Althusser's politics and his philosophy.

41. Isolde Charim, *Der Althusser-Effekt*, Vienna, 2002, p. 15.

42. *FM* 213, 51n.; 'ISMP' 209; 'La coupure', 8-03.06, p. 2; letter of 14 August 1966 to Michel Verret.

43. *FM* 116, 237; 'ACP', passim; 'R', 9-05.01, pp. 5–6, 10, 12, 15; 'The Humanist Controversy', p. 224n.

44. *FM* 214; 'OTW' 56; 'The Historical Task', p. 192; 'R', 9-05.01, p. 19; 'Lettre aux camarades du CC du PCF', 42–04.01, p. 18; *SISS* 17.

45. Gilbert Mury, Choisy 47, 49.

46. Roger Garaudy, *Mon tour du siècle en solitaire*, Paris, 1989, p. 210; Garaudy, *Perspectives de l'homme*, Paris, 1959, p. 1 ff.

47. Aragon, Letter of 19 January 1966 to Waldeck Rochet, pp. 132–4; letter of 14 May 1965 to Michel Simon (part of this letter was published in *Polémica sobre marxismo y humanismo*, pp. 192–8).

48. *The Future Lasts a Long Time*, ed. Olivier Corpet and Yann Moulier Boutang, trans. Richard Veasey, London, 1993, p. 183, translation modified; Jacques Arnault, 'Note en vue de la rencontre du mercredi 15 November 1965', AFC, 4, B.

49. AWR, 8, 4, a (1966?); see also 'Entretien avec Waldeck Rochet', ed. François Matheron, *Annales* 185, where Althusser first makes the claim that Rochet confessed to pretending to be a humanist for political reasons.

50. Jacques Arnault, Letter of 4 March 1966 to the Section for Intellectuals and Culture, AFC, Box 11.
51. Suzanne Mury, Letter to all the friends and comrades of Gilbert Mury, cited in Christophe Bourseiller, *Les maoïstes*, Paris, 1996, p. 269.
52. *FM* 159–60; Roger Garaudy, 'Les "Manuscrits de 1844" de Karl Marx', *Cahiers du communisme*, no. 39, March 1963, p. 118; Garaudy, letter of 28 January 1966 to Waldeck Rochet.
53. Michel Simon, Letter of 15 January 1966 to Louis Althusser.
54. See 'The Humanist Controversy', p. 224.
55. *FM* 242–7.
56. Michel Verret, personal communication, 23 July 2000; François Hincker, 'Michel Verret et *La Nouvelle critique*', in *Philographies*, Saint-Sébastien, 1987, p. 223; Verret, 'Note soumise à la réunion des philosophes du PCF des 22 et 23 January 1966', AWR, 7, 1, c, p. 8.
57. Roger Garaudy, Interview with Robert Geerlandt, in Geerlandt, *Garaudy et Althusser*, Paris, 1978, p. 29.
58. Michel Verret, 'Sur Théorie et pratique', in *Théorie et politique*, Paris, 1967, pp. 127–85.
59. Louis Aragon, Letter of 19 January 1966 to Waldeck Rochet, *Annales* 132; Roger Garaudy, Letters of 16 June 1966 (AWR 8, 2, g) and 14 February 1966 (AWR 9, 2, b) to Waldeck Rochet.
60. 'La conjoncture, 4 mai 1967', 11-03.01, p. 2.
61. Secretariat, 15 March 1966; *Cahiers du communisme*, May–June 1966, no. 5–6; 'Intervention de Louis Aragon au titre de rapporteur du projet de Résolution', *Annales* 139; 'Analyse de la Résolution du Comité Central', 42–04.02, p. 2; 'Le Parti communiste, les intellectuels et la culture: Résolution sur les problèmes idéologiques et culturels', *Annales* 294.
62. Jacques Arnault, Letter of 7 December 1965 to the Section for Intellectuals and Culture; Arnault, 'Écrit de mémoire', unpublished Ms., 1994, p. 6; [Francis Cohen], unsigned handwritten note, AFC 4, B.
63. Letter of 30 September 1966 to Étienne Balibar.
64. 'Réponse à une critique', *EPP* II: 365; *FM* 65, 80n; 'L'homme Helvétius' (radio programme), *France Culture*, 15 January 1962.
65. 'R', 9–05.02, p. 34; unposted letter of 24 November 1963 to Lucien Sève.
66. *LF* 608, 611, 18 March and 18 April 1965.
67. Letter to Michel Verret of 23 February 1965; 'Note pour H. Krasucki sur la politique du Parti à l'égard des travailleurs intellectuels (25/2/1965)', 42-03.01, pp. 12–13, 18–20, 22.
68. Letter of 6 January 1966 to Michel Verret; 'TTPTF' 38.
69. *LF* 608, 611, 18 March and 18 April 1965; Letters of 23 February 1965 to Michel Verret and 5 April 1965 to Michel Simon.
70. *LF* 663, 10 March 1966; letters of 6 and 26 January 1966 to Michel Verret; letters of 17 and 28 January 1966 to Pierre Macherey.
71. Letter of 28 April 1966 to Étienne Balibar; Guy Besse, Letter of 14 May 1966 to Henri Krasucki (responsible for the Party's relations with intellectuals), AWR 8, 5, a. See also 'RTJL' 111.
72. Letter of 4 April 1966 to Pierre Macherey; 'Lettre au Comité central

d'Argenteuil', 42-04.01 f.; [Benny Lévy *et al.*], 'Faut-il réviser la théorie Marxiste-léniniste?', in Patrick Kessel, *Le mouvement 'maoïste' en France*, vol. 1, Paris, 1972, pp. 149–61; letter of 17 or 24 March 1966 to Pierre Macherey.

73. 'SRC' 5, 9; 'R', 9-05.02, p. 22. An unpublished draft of 'SRC' confines the role of the 'vanguard party' to accomplishing the 'political revolution', leaving the ideological revolution to the masses themselves, in an echo of the Chinese Communist Party's August 1966 'Sixteen-Point Declaration' ('Sur la révolution culturelle', 7-01.03, p. 2). The published version of 'SRC' is more orthodox; see SRC 10.

74. Letter of 9 March 1967 to Michel Verret. See also 'RTJL' 131–2.

75. 'Entretien avec Waldeck Rochet', *Annales* 183–5; *LF* 667, 29 March 1966.

76. Pierre Macherey, Letter of 28 November 1966 to Étienne Balibar; Balibar, Letter of 2 January 1967 to Macherey.

77. Secretariat, 24 May 1966, p. 2; Bourseiller, *Les maoïstes*, p. 60; Hervé Hamon and Patrick Rotman, *Génération*, Paris, 1987, vol. 1, p. 318. Balibar recalls being driven blindfolded to the meeting, but has no memory of delivering a formal message (Interview of 13 March 2000).

78. Étienne Balibar, Letter of 24 November 1966 to Pierre Macherey.

79. 'Exposé devant le groupe "Esprit"' (5 May 1967), 8-03.07, p. 44; Letter of 14 August 1966 to Michel Verret; *LF* 693–4, 729, 26 July and 26 September 1966.

80. Étienne Balibar, letter of 24 November 1966 to Pierre Macherey; letters of 28 January and 7 February 1967 to Balibar; letter of 24 February 1967 to Michel Verret.

81. 'La conjoncture, 4 mai 1967', 11-03.01, pp. 2, 4, 7.

82. 'SCR' 10; 'RTJL' 105; 'NSP' 318.

83. 'OEYM' 160; 'ESC' 102–3.

84. 'R', 9-05.05, folder 2.

85. Letter of 21 December 196[3] to Pierre Macherey.

86. 'ESC' 143–5.

87. *FM* 188n, 208–10, 183; *RC* 108, 188–9.

88. 'OTW' 61. 'Folding back' is an equivalent for *repliement* ('Sur le travail théorique', *La Pensée* 132 [March–April 1967], p. 17). The word is not translated in 'OTW'.

89. Jacques Lacan, 'La Science et la vérité', *Cahiers pour l'analyse*, no. 1, January 1966; letter of 11 [13?] July 1966 to Lacan, *WP* 171–2. If Althusser's letter reached its destination, its message did not: Lacan pointedly called his would-be ally a 'structuralist' in a November 1968 lecture (Lacan, *D'un Autre à l'autre*, vol. 1 [Paris, 1969], pp. 11–12). No Lacano-Althusserian alliance ever came about.

90. *LF* 699–700, 4 August 1966; letter of 4 August 1966 to Michel Tort.

91. Roger Establet, personal communication, 24 April 2000; Letters of 4 August 1966 to Michel Tort and 6 September 1966 to Alain Badiou; *LF* 724, 15 September 1966.

92. 'MPH' 20.

93. Étienne Balibar, 'Self-Criticism', trans. anon., *Theoretical Practice* 7–8

(1973), pp. 60–61; Pierre Macherey, Letter of 10 May 1965 to Louis Althusser; 'On Lévi-Strauss', p. 21.

94. 'ESC' 129.

95. Letter of 19 February 1966 to Pierre Macherey, cited (and misdated) in Warren Montag, Introduction to Pierre Macherey, *In a Materialist Way*, London, 1998, p. 7; Macherey, *A Theory of Literary Production*, trans. Geoffrey Wall, London, 1978 [1966], pp. 136–56.

96. 'On Lévi-Strauss', pp. 26–7, 30. The term 'singular essence' makes a fleeting appearance in the first edition of *Lire le Capital*, pp. 654–5 as well as in 'On Lévi-Strauss', p. 30 and *LF* 712, 13 September 1966. Althusser deems it 'too dangerous' for public consumption in a 23 October 1966 letter to Yves Duroux.

97. 'The Philosophical Conjuncture', p. 13.

98. Diverses notes 1966, 11.02–01, p. 1; and, for a diagram of the relations very summarily sketched here, 11.02–02; 'The Historical Task', p. 214; *LF* 712, 13 September 1966.

99. Alain Badiou, 'Le (re)commencement du matérialisme dialectique', *Critique*, 23, May 1967, p. 464.

100. *PSH* 27, 76.

101. *PSH* 107; *Sur la reproduction*, ed. Jacques Bidet, Paris, 1995, pp. 223–42 ('Ideology and Ideological State Apparatuses', *EI* 1–60, was extracted from this text, not yet translated into English); Letter of 21 February 1969 to Ben Brewster, *WP* 32.

102. David Macey, 'Thinking with Borrowed Concepts: Althusser and Lacan', in *Althusser: A Critical Reader*, ed. Gregory Elliott, Oxford, 1994, pp. 144, 147.

103. Letters of summer 1977 (*WP* 4–5) and 11 May 1984 to Gudrun Werner-Hervieu, in Werner-Hervieu, *Begegnungen mit Louis Althusser*, Berlin, 1998, pp. 27–30.

104. Most of the translations were published in Ludwig Feuerbach, *Manifestes philosophiques: Textes choisis, 1839–1845*, ed. and trans. Louis Althusser, Paris, 1960. Althusser's letters of 28 April 1966 and 17 April 1967 to Étienne Balibar show that the book on *The German Ideology* was to be co-authored with Balibar and, perhaps, Roger Establet.

105. Letters of 18 February 1967 to Étienne Balibar and 21 June 1967 to Michel Verret; *LF* 749, 12 July 1967; Arnoldo Orfila Reynal, Letter of 19 November 1966 to Louis Althusser; Althusser *et al.*, *Polémica sobre marxismo y humanismo*; correspondence Althusser/Mark Mitin, 1967–68.

106. 'On Feuerbach', pp. 140–1.

107. 'Projet de livre sur Feuerbach', 35-01.01, p. 7. Althusser's work on the Feuerbachian 'mirror stage' is anterior to 'Three Notes', which is obviously based on it.

108. 'Notes sur Lévi-Strauss, *La Pensée sauvage*', 60–04, p. 17a; Claude Lévi-Strauss, *The Savage Mind*, Chicago, 1966 (1962), p. 247.

109. *TP*, 8-01.02, p. 2; 'The Historical Task', p. 209.

110. 'The Historical Task', p. 192 and note.

111. 'On Lévi-Strauss', p. 22. The critique of the 'nostalgic' 'modern myth'

of primitive society is developed in 'Une question posée au cours du séminaire du 10.1.1964 par Louis Althusser', 40–03. 04, p. 3.

112. *FM* 161.
113. 'RTJL' 82; 'RSC' 120.
114. 'The Humanist Controversy', p. 252.

The Philosophical Conjuncture and Marxist Theoretical Research

(26 June 1966)

Althusser's archives contain two very different versions of the lecture 'The Philosophical Conjuncture and Marxist Theoretical Research'. The one published here is taken from a mimeographed text that bears the notation 'lecture delivered at the École normale supérieure on 26 June 1966'. There are no handwritten modifications on this copy, which closely matches the lecture that Althusser actually gave, as is indicated by a tape-recording he kept in his files. (Also recorded was part of the often spirited discussion that followed Althusser's talk, notably an exchange with Jean-Pierre Vernant.) Several copies of the text of the lecture were found in Althusser's archives after his death. All indications are that it circulated widely, that is, enjoyed semi-public status.

The other extant version of 'The Philosophical Conjuncture' (eight typed pages, preceded by the handwritten words 'not delivered' and covered with handwritten emendations) is older, and shorter only because it was left unfinished. The substance of it has been incorporated into the first two pages of the final version, the style of which is much more concise. We saw no compelling reason to publish the whole of the first version.

François Matheron

I take the floor for two reasons: a bogus reason, and a real one. The bogus reason is that someone has to start, after all. But that question has been settled, because I've already started. The real reason is that I owe you certain explanations.

I owe you certain explanations, quite simply, by way of

response to a question we are all asking ourselves; it is the question of this meeting. Why this meeting? What have we French philosophers come here to do, in June 1966? What can and what will come of this meeting?

If I'm to give you the explanations I owe you, I shall have to say things without beating about the bush, bluntly, perhaps even harshly – both to save time and also to eliminate all possible confusions, ambiguities and lingering doubts. We all have an interest in calling a spade a spade.[1]

So: why this meeting? Let me tell you how it came about. I personally invited some of you. I invited certain philosophers of my acquaintance because I know that they are working in the field of Marxist theory. I also invited certain non-Marxist philosophers because I know that they take an interest in the work of Marxist scholars. Lastly, I put up a notice in the École [normale supérieure] announcing this meeting and indicating that it was open to the public. In the invitations and the notice, I said that the purpose of the meeting was to allow Marxist scholars to come together and bring each other up to date on their work, and also to take stock of the major theoretical questions that Marxist research has by all means to address.

In deciding to call this meeting, in signing the invitations and the agenda, I was not acting on my own behalf, but neither did I make this decision on the suggestion of any authority. The decision was made for us by the effects of the theoretical conjuncture itself: it had become necessary. I drew the appropriate conclusions. And I would also suggest that we draw the appropriate conclusions as to the *object* of our meeting: to define this, it is enough analyse the structure of the theoretical conjuncture.[2]

I am going to be extremely schematic. The most we can do here is to set out, very roughly, the elements that make up the basic structure of the theoretical conjuncture prevailing in the field that interests us, French philosophy and Marxist theory today.

It seems to me that we can set out, very roughly, a few *elements,* and, at the same time, indicate the *relations* between them. Basically, my analysis will bear on two areas: (a) *French philosophy* and (b) *Marxist theory.* I shall be using the term 'French philosophy' broadly, to include both philosophy in the strict sense and also disciplines still associated with it for historical reasons, such as the sciences known as the 'human' sciences – sociology, psychology, and so on. I shall be using the term Marxist theory in the twofold sense of Marxist philosophy or dialectical materialism, and the Marxist science of history or historical materialism. Hence the two areas that I shall analyse in schematic terms will be distinguished, but will also overlap. These distinctions and these intersections can serve us as pertinent indices.

A.   French philosophy

It seems to me that we can describe the theoretical structure of French philosophy in 1966 by setting out the following elements. We shall see that, in order to define them, we have to turn back to the past, going a very long way back indeed. We shall therefore define these different elements and the relationship between them both as elements and, at the same time, as sedimented historical layers. What will be of the greatest interest to us is the relationship among these different elements today.

1. At the very deepest level of the theoretical conjuncture of present-day French philosophy, we still find a persistent, sedimented layer whose origins can be traced back to the philosophy of the Middle Ages. Certain forms of medieval philosophy subsist in explicit and sometimes rigorous form in the contemporary Thomist and Augustinian schools. In general, however, the philosophy of the Middle Ages does not survive in person today: rather, it serves as the support for what can be called a *religious* and *spiritualist* tradition that we will encounter again in a moment, for this tradition was revived by another historical period of French philosophy.

2. Alongside the *religious-spiritualist* element, with a heritage going back, in part, to the Middle Ages, there is a *rationalist-idealist* element deriving from Descartes which also features in the theoretical conjuncture of French philosophy. As is well known, Cartesian philosophy has served as the basis for two different interpretations, the interpretation of *mechanistic materialism* on the one hand and that of *critical idealism* on the other.

As in the previous case, we are dealing here not with Descartes in person but with philosophies that have taken up and developed his thought, interpreting it in a particular direction and thus giving it a particular bent.

The Cartesian machinery is still flourishing today in one whole sector of the human sciences, first and foremost experimental psychology, and also empirical sociology. Critical idealism of narrowly Cartesian – that is, dualistic – inspiration was incarnated in Alain's philosophy; today it is dying a natural death. However, a form of critical idealism of broadly Cartesian inspiration was taken up and developed by Kant and Husserl. It is very much alive today, and currently constitutes what is doubtless *the dominant element* in the theoretical conjuncture of French philosophy.

3. Alongside these two elements – *religious-spiritualist* and *rationalist-idealist* – there subsists another element, another theoretical layer, whose origins may be traced back to the eighteenth century: *rationalist empiricism* in its two forms, idealist and materialist. Materialist rationalist empiricism lives on in the ideology of certain scientific practices (psycho-physiology, etc.). Idealist-rationalist empiricism does too, and has produced the more interesting results. It was this current which, setting out from other, materialist aspects of Descartes's work, spawned the great work of the *Encyclopédie*, d'Alembert, Diderot, and so on. This tradition was taken up by the only great French philosopher of the nineteenth century, Auguste Comte. It saved the honour of French philosophy, if one may use a term from the sports world here, during the terrible spiritualist reaction of the nineteenth century. It has given us the only philosophical tradition that we can trace, almost uninterruptedly, from the seventeenth century down to our own day: the tradition of the philosophy of the sciences to which we owe such great names as Comte, Cournot, Couturat, Duhem, and, closer to our own time, Cavaillès, Bachelard, Koyré, and Canguilhem.

4. After setting out these elements, in the perspective arising from their very historical distance from us, we can now begin to approach our own period. Let us, then, say something about the nineteenth and early twentieth centuries. Philosophically speaking, this period is massively dominated by a profound philo-

sophical reaction, that is, a profoundly reactionary philosophy. From Maine de Biran to Bergson, we can compile, to our dismay, a long list of names: Victor Cousin, Ravaisson, Boutroux, Lachelier, and all their epigones. This tradition is defined by its virulent, vicious theoretical crusade against all forms of rationalism, idealist or materialist. It is this tradition that takes up – in a form which, moreover, shows only contempt for the authentically theoretical aspects of medieval thought – the *religious spiritualism* preserved for us by the Church, its theologians and its ideologues. This nineteenth-century philosophical spiritualism was so narrow-minded that it twisted the idealist Cartesian tradition in a frankly spiritualist direction, and quite simply ignored a philosopher like Kant; the only one of Kant's works it familiarized itself with – and belatedly, at that – was the *Critique of Practical Reason*. Suffice it to say that Bergson, for example, never really took the trouble to read Kant, and in any event, did not understand anything of what he read. This spiritualism compromised the tradition of the philosophy of the sciences in apologetic works such as Boutroux's and Lachelier's. It fought, unremittingly, a battle to the death with the one great philosopher of the nineteenth century, Auguste Comte, and, as can be seen in the work of Péguy and Bergson, also relentlessly attacked a very great mind, Émile Durkheim, who was, moreover, a disciple of Comte. There is no need to add that these pseudo-philosophers, who did not even take the trouble to read Descartes seriously, scorned the philosophy of the eighteenth century, and knew neither Kant nor Hegel (remember Cousin's *bon mot!*), while regaling themselves on the scraps of Schelling and Schopenhauer that served them in place of thoughts – there is no need to add that the ignorance, scorn and hatred of these pseudo-philosophers, veritable watchdogs of religious ideology and reactionary political ideology, was extended to the work of Marx once it had acquired objective existence. Our existence is still shaped by the effects of these sweeping condemnations and this ignorance, which – albeit explicable for class reasons – are of an unbearable stupidity. Many were those who were thus condemned to philosophical death, covered with insults and blows or covered over with the earth of forgetfulness: the whole current of utopian philosophy, notably Fourier and Saint-Simon; Cournot, Auguste Comte, Nietzsche, Freud and Durkheim; and, of course, Marx. We should also be aware that these philosophical *auto-da-fés* were celebrated to religious and moralistic chanting, or, once religion had become a little too embarrassing, to the chants of the secular religion of modern times, the religion of art.

We should be aware of all of this, because this reactionary spiritualist philosophy still weighs heavy on us today, and also because our task is to struggle against it and *rehabilitate its victims*. It is the conjuncture that sets even our philosophical tasks for us, and identifies them as necessary. Thus I include among these tasks, along with the struggle against spiritualism in all its forms – particularly religious ideology and the ideology of art, and all the aesthetic treatises it has spawned in our country – the task of philosophically rehabilitating Saint-Simon, Fourier, Auguste Comte, Cournot, Durkheim, and others.

5. The fact that philosophical spiritualism massively dominates our recent heritage accounts for the present philosophical conjuncture. For certain things have happened, after all, since Maine de Biran and Victor Cousin, and even Lachelier and Bergson. A number of minor historical events have occurred, known as the Revolution of 1848, the Commune, World War I, the 1917 Revolution, the rise of Fascism, the Popular Fronts, the Spanish Civil War, World War II, the Resistance, the defeat of Hitler, the Chinese Revolution, the liberation of the Third World, and so on. A few events that have somewhat unsettled the world of religious, moral, aesthetic, chauvinistic and, quite simply, ignorant and inane spiritualism bequeathed us by the nineteenth century. Starting thirty years ago, after Alain's timid Cartesian-Radical-Socialist reaction and the half-baked beginning made by Brunschvicg, who sought to bend the tradition of the history of the sciences to the service of a supposedly rationalist religious ideology, something has begun to happen in French philosophy, and the balance of power has begun, hesitantly, to swing the other way.

It is still in the process of swinging the other way; the work of history is still in gestation, before our very eyes. I would like to try to sketch the features and also the moments of the present conjuncture.

I will distinguish *two essential moments*.

We may say that *in a first moment*, whose effects are there for all to see, spiritualism had to give ground under the pressure of a renewal of French philosophy: to be very precise, under the pressure of a movement inspired by *critical, rationalist idealism*. Return to Descartes, return to Kant, discovery of Hegel and Husserl, serious readings of these authors, and studies and commentaries on them. We can draw a fairly complete map of this Philosophical Front, which I shall call *Front number 1*, and name the spiritualists who are still carrying on the good fight, disguised as old Descartes or Husserl, Heidegger and Freud, interpreted in their fashion (unfortunately, this is the direction in which Merleau-Ponty was increasingly tending, and in which Ricœur has frankly struck out). But we can also mention the critical rationalist idealists on this Front who have forced the enemy to retreat: besides the Marxist philosophers who, like Politzer, Mougin[3] and others, played their part in this battle, we can name Sartre, our Rousseau, a man of the eighteenth century, more of a moralist and political thinker than a philosopher, and yet a rationalist idealist; we can name Jean Hyppolite, thanks to whom French philosophy has recognized the importance of Hegel and Husserl; Guéroult, a master at teaching the basics of how truly to *read* texts; and others as well. And we can single out a few great names among them: Cavaillès, Bachelard, Koyré, Canguilhem, and others, epistemologists and historians of the sciences, with the small yet very important reservation that they often *consciously* associated themselves with the tradition of critical idealism, even if much of their work actually tends in a totally different direction. Such, then, is the first moment of the transformation of the conjuncture, a transformation that has basically been accomplished: the retreat of spiritualism under the joint pressure and combined blows of rationalist idealism or critical idealism and Marxism, on *Front number 1*.

Today, no doubt, we are living through a *second moment*. To some extent, this moment exists only in a latent state: the element I shall go on to discuss is still defining itself, and there can obviously be no question of suggesting that it is at all *dominant*. The idealist element, rationalist or critical, is still dominant. Yet there is, at least, something new in the making that has to be taken into account – something which is of great interest to us, because we, too, are playing a certain role in it.

What is in the making is the discovery that the problematic of critical, rationalist idealism no longer answers to the profound needs of the theoretical conjuncture: *the crisis of critical, rationalist idealism has now begun*. It has begun, but it has not yet been resolved. Whence a profusion of attempts to seek out new paths; whence the presence of philosophy everywhere, and a recognition of philosophy's leading role in the attempts at renewal springing up left and right, in literary criticism, the novel, cinema, painting, ethnology, the history of knowledge, the history of cultural formations, and so on, generally under Lévi-Strauss's aegis but also under Bachelard's. Philosophies of this and that are now shooting up like mushrooms, overnight, in all the private gardens of official culture, and preventing even academic worthies like Picard[4] from cultivating their gardens – that is, their rubbish [*navet*, which literally means turnip] – in peace. What interests us is not the mushrooms – after all, most of them aren't even edible – what interests us is the terrain.

If we leave aside the manifestations of typically Parisian culture and the culture of the 'Parisian Internationale' in order to discuss what is taking place at the *properly* philosophical level, we can plainly perceive a situation of objective crisis. Guéroult taught us how to read, but he too often commits the 'blunder' of taking the disorder of reasons for the 'order of reasons'.[5] Merleau-Ponty went over to spiritualism. Sartre is alive and kicking, combative and generous, but he does not teach us anything about anything, especially not the authors and subjects he discusses: Marx, Freud, sociology, politics, and so on. Sartre will not have any posterity whatsoever: he is already philosophically dead, although he may suddenly be born again, as we hope he will. The truly vital work that is now being done is being done elsewhere – around Marx, Freud, and also Nietzsche; around Russell, Frege and Heidegger; around linguistics, epistemology and the history of the sciences. What is truly vital in what is under way is challenging, profoundly, the *theoretical problematic* not only of spiritualism (Front number 1), but also, on Front number 2, of critical rationalist idealism. By the same token, it is challenging the *ideological problematic* of the 'human' sciences, as they are called.

We can provide a fairly accurate measure of the revolutionary theoretical import of this nascent renewal by gauging the extent to which the critical-idealist problematic has been challenged, and determining the direction the challenge is taking. This criterion authorizes diagnoses that are independent of mere cultural success. Thus we can already say that Lévi-Strauss, his great scientific merits notwithstanding, will not, *philosophically* speaking, play a role commensurate with the highly suspect success he has been accorded; whereas other authors – well known, less well known or unknown – already hold, and in some cases have long held, *keys*, or, at least, *some of the keys* to our future (I have in mind the real Bachelard, Canguilhem, the real Lacan, etc.). But enough of these questions of individuals, or, rather, of the variations of individual structural effects produced by the theoretical conjuncture.

At all events, it is in the context of this second moment that the Marxist philosophical enterprise can take its place – indeed, has already begun to take its place. As we conceive it, Marxist philosophy naturally has a part to play in the *anti-spiritualist* struggle on Front number 1, side by side with the critical rationalist philosophies; but it also struggles on Front number 2, the *anti-critical-idealist Front*, against the problematic of critical, rationalist idealism and for a new materialist problematic. There can be no doubt that this struggles poses strategic and tactical problems, especially the problem of alliances in the theoretical and ideological struggle. We make no bones about this. We know, and our friends do too, that the problems are rather simple on a Front as sharply defined as the anti-spiritualist or anti-irrationalist Front number 1. We do not hide the fact, from ourselves or from others, that these problems are much more difficult on the anti-critical-idealist Front, Front number 2, because it is a Front which is still confused and sometimes ill-defined, so that we have to take into consideration not only the overall development of the philosophical situation, fashionable Parisian ideological by-products included, but also the hesitations and experimentation of all the actors, carefully distinguishing the actions that represent real commitments on their part from those by which they simply continue to search for their identity. Our non-Marxist friends should be aware that these criteria and scruples apply to us as well, and that we are striving to take them into account for our own internal use.

But, in saying all that, I have just defined new objectives for us Marxist philosophers: to have it out not only with Merleau-Ponty and Ricœur (Front number 1), but also with Sartre and Guéroult (Front number 2), and to try to gain as clear a sense as possible of the work of those who, like us, albeit sometimes in very different ways, seek [to] challenge the critical-idealist problematic that we are struggling against on Front number 2. For the stout of heart, then, there is a long list of pressing tasks in view.

In saying all that, I have also just indicated some of the urgent tasks facing Marxist philosophy, which must make a thorough critique of the empiricist, formalist and idealist ideology that holds sway in most of the human sciences; distinguish, in the field of the human sciences, between the real objects and the imaginary ones; and identify our objective allies, the specialists who are in reality fighting alongside us – either because their practice corresponds to a real object, as in sociology and linguistics; or because they derive from their practice concepts that can contribute to the philosophical transformation currently in progress; or, again, because they have already taken their place on the two Fronts of the philosophical struggle.

B. Marxist Theory

But, in saying all that, I have in effect already broached the question as to which elements of the conjuncture are pertinent to Marxist theory. As I have already written quite a few pages explaining my views on the matter, I shall be more concise, but, at the same time, much more explicit and precise.

The basic task of Marxist theory, its strategic task, has Marxist theory itself for its object. I mean, to be quite precise, that Marxist theory has to know *exactly* what it is as a theory, and to know exactly what point it has reached in its development, in order to know what kind of theoretical work it must and can accomplish.

This task is not exactly an easy one, a simple matter of definition. Or, more exactly, defining the specificity of Marxist theory as rigorously as we can today, in 1966, is an undertaking that can be carried out only in struggle and through struggle. There can be no defining Marxist theory in the absence of a struggle against ideological interpretations of Marxist theory –

not only the misinterpretations, distortions, prejudices and ignorance of Marxism that reign *outside* the Marxist context, but also the misinterpretations, ideological distortions, and so on, that reign *within* it, nationally and internationally. We, too, have our spiritualists – to be quite precise, our ideologues of the creation of man by man, who define man in terms of his consciousness of the future, and interpret Marxism as a humanism. We, too, have our critical or rationalist idealists and our vaguely Kantian or Husserlian ideologues of transcendental praxis; it sometimes even happens that the spiritualists and idealists lend one another, as circumstances dictate, the concepts they need. We, too, have our rationalist empiricists (who are often, incidentally, also humanists), especially in the ranks of the psychologists, psychiatrists, and so on. We, too, have our partisans of mechanistic materialism, monism, and economism, in all fields, not just in political economy. It is impossible to define Marxist theory with any precision if we do not wage a rigorous critical struggle, in both senses of the word 'rigorous', against all these ideological distortions of Marxism. The struggle has to be waged on the anti-ideological Front (anti-spiritualist and anti-critical-idealist, anti-mechanistic, anti-economistic, anti–voluntarist, etc.), which means that we have to *study* these ideological distortions at the same time as we undertake to define Marxist theory. We will therefore constantly find ourselves writing texts in two columns; if, in what follows, I say nothing about column 2 (works of anti-ideological criticism) and speak only about the first column (works of definition and positive research), I would ask that the existence of the *second column* be kept constantly in mind. It, too, requires its specialists.

The number one task consists, then, in *defining Marxist theory*. This means, above all, distinguishing the Marxist science of history or historical materialism, which is a science, from Marxist philosophy or dialectical materialism, which is a philosophy. It means defining the specific object of each discipline and the respective status of each of the two disciplines; defining, first and foremost, that which makes Marxist philosophy a philosophy and not a science in the strict sense, albeit a philosophy of a scientific character.[6]

Let me note straight away that this last point – that is, the *difference in theoretical status* which distinguishes Marxist philosophy from Marxist science – was in fact *evaded* in my published works. I distinguished the Marxist science of history from Marxist philosophy solely with regard to the difference in their *objects*, without bringing out, as I should have, the difference in *their theoretical status*. Among the important questions that need to be examined, therefore, I include the question of the specific difference in theoretical status between Marxist science and Marxist philosophy.

Naturally, this question could open the door to a long string of related developments and questions, but I cannot go into them here.

Once we have defined the Marxist science of history and Marxist philosophy, once we have defined the difference in their objects and theoretical status, we can broach two important subjects: the theoretical work to be done in the field of Marxist philosophy on the one hand and the Marxist science of history on the other. I shall use the traditional terms: in the fields of dialectical and historical materialism.

Let me say right away that my aim is not to provide an exhaustive list of possible questions: there are an infinite number of them. I would merely like to note the major questions that in fact occupy a *strategic theoretical position* in the development of Marxist theory today.

1. In the field of dialectical materialism

Strategic questions: I will provide a list of these questions and comment on some of them.

Strategic question number 1: *The difference in theoretical status between Marxist science and Marxist philosophy.*

Strategic question number 2: The theory of *structural causality*. Experience has shown that this question commands everything else – if not at the primary, then at the secondary level [*en seconde instance, sinon en première*]. It commands the theory of *practice* in general, and thus the theory of *theoretical practice itself*. It commands the general theory of *practice* and, at the same time, the theory of the *dialectic* (including the theory of the tradition).[7] On this question, we have more and more elements that stand as so many signs of its decisive importance, but the more of them we find and the more closely we home in on the question, the more difficult it appears. What was said on the subject in *Reading Capital* is quite rudimentary; but we have at least identified the question and called it, I hope, by the right name.

Strategic question number 3: The theory of *theoretical practice*, that is, of the practice productive of knowledge [*connaissances*]. Here, too, I draw attention to a point that was – I am to blame for this – evaded in the published works. There, the question of theoretical practice was posed much more than it was resolved, and it was posed, as is always the case (reflection and research progress in no other way), both to bring out certain features that had been only poorly distinguished in the past, and to combat ideological interpretations. *In the published works, it was a matter of combating, above all, an empiricist and pragmatist conception of Marxist theory.* This explains the fact that the accent fell, as they say, on the specificity of theoretical practice. This ideological opposition, which is, I think, basically correct [*juste*], induced an *effect of elision*: I failed to deal with an extremely important question, which we can provisionally term '*the question of empirical knowledge*'. Lenin, for example, says that the soul of Marxism is '*the concrete analysis of a concrete situation*'. I did not produce the theory of this formulation, or even outline such a theory. I do not say that what I wrote makes it impossible to produce it: but the *absence* of the theory of empirical knowledge generates, like all absences, effects of distortion and displacement even in what is present, that is, in what was said. One can state this differently by saying that putting the accent squarely on the specificity of theory and theoretical practice resulted in a *few* (troubling) *silences*, or even *ambiguities*, in what was written. Let me say right away that this elision was not without consequences. The main consequence was to put us at daggers drawn with the historians and especially the sociologists, who spend their time and their lives – at any rate, a good part of their time – producing empirical knowledge. The upshot was Homeric discussions with our friends among the historians and sociologists – direct discussions or discussions pursued in the absence of our interlocutors, that is to say, via third parties and the associated rumours. While these friends have been charitable enough to say nothing about this in public to date, that hardly means they have no objections to raise.[8] They are right about this elision. I am currently trying to make up for this deficiency in a text that will, I hope, see the light some day.[9]

On the question of the theory of theoretical practice, research is already in progress.[10]

Strategic question number 4: This question is bound up with the preceding one, but I believe that we are well advised to treat them separately. I have in mind *a theory of the knowledge-effect*. Such a theory presupposes a *general theory of discourse* and a distinction between the specific types of discourses that would bring out the characteristic features of scientific discourse. On this problem, too, researchers are already at work; some of them have been working for quite some time.

Strategic question number 5: The theory of *ideology*. On this point as well, what was said in the published works is important, but marked by the struggle against empiricism and pragmatism. Whence possible silences and distortions. It is necessary, first, to undertake to produce a *general theory of ideology*, and, to this end, to note that it is possible to identify something as ideology only retrospectively, from the vantage point of non-ideological knowledge. One must also note that the science–ideology relationship constitutes *a field of variations*, marked off by two limit-positions (that of science on the one hand and ideology on the other), a vector field orientated *by the retrospection I have just mentioned*. Finally, it has to be noted that this field is itself one moment (in constant transformation) of a process, and that it is this process which defines the existence and nature of the field.

One could conjointly pursue other studies bearing on *ideology*, its place or places of implantation in the *social structure*, and also on the different regions of ideology. Work is in progress here too.

Strategic question number 6: The theory of a particular structural effect: what we might call *the subjectivity-effect* or theory of the *subject*. This is a problem of great consequence, but it is extremely difficult; some of us have already done some work on it.[11]

Strategic question number 7: The theory of individuality, which is indispensable for developing, in historical materialism, the theory of the historical forms of individuality (including not only all the problems of what is ordinarily called the individual, but a considerable number of other problems as well, first and foremost the theory of the social formation).

There are many other questions; I have mentioned only those which seemed to me to be the most important.

2. *In historical materialism*

Here again, I shall give a list of questions that seem to me to be of *strategic* importance from a theoretical standpoint.

Strategic question number 1: A systematic definition of the currently available, tried-and-tested concepts of the *general theory*[12] of historical materialism.

Strategic question number 2: The theory of social classes and political parties.

Strategic question number 3: The theory of the legal-political superstructure (theory of law, theory of state power, theory of the state apparatus).

Strategic question number 4: The theory of political practice.

Strategic question number 5: The theory of transitional forms.

Strategic question number 6: The theory of the forms of historical individuality (including the social formation).

Here again, countless questions need to be addressed, but we have to limit ourselves. Be it noted that the questions we have to pose in historical materialism are infinitely better defined than those in dialectical materialism; we have many more elements and theoretical and practical experiences on the basis of which to pose them. This is one effect of the theoretical lead that historical materialism has over dialectical materialism.

C.

In closing, I would like to mention a few questions that are pertinent to *the history of the historians*, whether they are historians of philosophy, ideology, politics or the economy. These questions are questions that have to be treated historically if certain theoretical problems are to be posed and solved; at the same time, they are questions that can be treated historically only if certain theoretical concepts are developed. I believe it would be useful to turn this circle to our advantage, regarding it not as an impasse but as the condition for joint progress in empirical history and in theory.

These questions are:

1. A theoretical and political history of the Second International, in broad outline.
2. A history of the Third International, in broad outline.
3. The personality cult[13] (a typical example of an empirical impasse due to the lack of a theory of politics and transitional forms).
4. Imperialism,[14] and so on.

To conclude, I shall return to my point of departure. I owed you explanations. I was about to say that I have given them to you. In fact, it is the analysis of the structure of the theoretical conjuncture that has given them to us.

I submit this analysis and its conclusions to you for discussion.

Notes

1. In the first draft of the text, the first three paragraphs differ considerably:

   My dear friends, you are as familiar as I am with the profound and, incidentally, apocryphal aphorism in which Machiavelli defines the universal Law that governs men: what goes without saying goes even better unsaid [*ce qui va sans dire va encore mieux en ne le disant pas*; the second part of the saying usually runs '*va encore mieux en le disant*', 'goes even better if it is said'].

   This aphorism states a principle that informs not only official meetings and the thoughts we keep to ourselves in everyday encounters, but also classical philosophy and the classical dialectic. As our encounter has all the marks of an official meeting, as we are all keeping certain thoughts to ourselves, if only because we are wondering what thoughts our neighbours are keeping to *them*selves, and as we are about to talk about philosophy, I propose that we apply Machiavelli's law in order to abolish its effects.

2. This paragraph condenses in a few lines a passage developed at length in the first draft:

> I now move on to another kind of presentation, which will acquaint us with the object of our meeting. For we are to some extent in the position of people who have been invited to a play that nobody has seen or talked about yet; they have a vague notion of its title but no idea of what it is about, and do not even know who the author is.
>
> We will attend to the question of the author first. This play is a play without an author. If we are here, it is as the effects of a theoretical conjuncture. The person who is addressing you is, like all the rest of us, merely a particular structural effect of this conjuncture, an effect that, like each and every one of us, has a proper name. The theoretical conjuncture that dominates us has produced an Althusser-effect, as it has produced a Rancière-effect, a Balibar-effect, a Macherey-effect, an Establet-effect, a Bettelheim-effect, and so on. Of course, this effect exhibits variations: thus the Vernant-effect and the Althusser-effect do not coincide – which means that we have serious philosophical differences of opinion. Without wishing to presume on their personal motivations in any way, I would even hazard the statement that our philosophical friends who are not Marxists but take an interest in Marxism also feature here as effects of the theoretical conjuncture, each in a particular form, though in a form different from that of the Marxist philosophers I have just named. My friend Jacques Derrida will not take it amiss, I hope, when I say that if he is here today, it is not only out of friendship and philosophical indulgence, but also as a structural effect of the philosophical conjuncture. There is therefore also a Derrida-effect.
>
> I am not joking when I say that the play performed here is a play without an author, and that we are all particular structural effects of the conjuncture. It is the philosophical conjuncture which brings us together here, and provides our meeting with its object. No one should be surprised if, in order to provide a precise definition of the object of our meeting, I dwell on the conjuncture. Here, too, I should like to try to say what naturally goes without saying, and lend my voice to an analysis of the philosophical conjuncture that dominates us.

3. Henri Mougin is the author of *La Sainte Famille existentialiste* (Paris, 1947), among other works. Althusser may be thinking of Mougin's article 'L'esprit encyclopédique et la tradition philosophique française', *La Pensée*, nos 5, 6, and 7, October 1945-April 1946.

4. See Raymond Picard, *Nouvelle critique, nouvelle imposture*, Paris, 1965, a polemic directed against the French New Criticism, especially Roland Barthes's *Sur Racine*. In 1966, Barthes riposted with *Critique et vérité* (*Criticism and Truth*, trans. Katrine P. Keuneman, Minneapolis, MN, 1987).

5. An allusion to Martial Guéroult, *Descartes selon l'ordre des raisons*, Paris, 1953. See *FM* 69.

6. 'Philosophy of a scientific character' is a transitional formula that reflects Althusser's conception of philosophy at this stage in his thinking.

7. Probably an error for 'the transition' [*Trans.*].

8. Here Althusser is probably thinking of Jean-Pierre Vernant and Pierre Vilar in particular. Vernant attended Althusser's lecture and took issue with it in the ensuing discussion. Vilar later published an essay on Althusser (to which Althusser began to write a response): 'Histoire marxiste, histoire en construction', *Annales ESC*, 1, January–February 1973, partially translated as 'Marxist History, a History in the Making', trans. anon., in Gregory Elliott, ed., *Althusser: A Critical Reader*, Oxford, 1994, pp. 10–43.

9. Althusser is no doubt thinking of his projected book on the union of theory and practice (1966–67), which he ultimately abandoned.

10. See 'NSP'.

11. See especially 'Three Notes on the Theory of Discourses' below.

12. On the concept of 'general theory', see ibid.

13. In 1964, Althusser began working on a book he planned to call *How to Pose the Problem of the Cult*. The first three chapters are extant. This text is closely related to an untitled book which undertakes a critical analysis of theories of alienation. That book, too, was left unfinished.

14. In 1973, Althusser began working on a book on imperialism; he intended, in particular, to refute the theory of 'monopoly state capitalism' which then held sway in the French Communist Party, and also to criticize the notion of a 'socialist mode of production'.

On Lévi-Strauss

(20 August 1966)

Only one version of the text Althusser entitled 'On Lévi-Strauss' exists. It was typed by a secretary at the École normale supérieure, probably from a letter whose salutation and closing signature were dropped. Althusser's archives contain many mimeographed copies of this text, which seems to have been rather widely distributed. Thus Emmanuel Terray acknowledges receipt of a copy in a 12 January 1967 letter to Althusser in which he comments on the text at length, and announces that he plans to put it on the syllabus of his seminars at the University of Abidjan, where he was then teaching. In a letter dated 13 March 1968, Althusser asks Alain Badiou what he thinks of Terray's proposal to include this text in an appendix to Terray's book Le Marxisme devant les sociétés 'primitives', *which ultimately appeared without it in the series, 'Théorie', that Althusser edited for François Maspero's publishing house. Badiou's response, if there was one, has not been found.*

François Matheron

The question of Lévi-Strauss and structuralism is of the utmost importance today, and will continue to be important for a long time.

Basically, the criticism that I would address (that I do in fact address) to Lévi-Strauss (there's no point in talking about his epigones, because he is *partially* responsible for them – in other words, there are *certain things* in Lévi-Strauss that authorize his epigones to utter and write inanities) is the fact that he *claims to draw his inspiration from Marx, but doesn't know him* (not only doesn't know him, but thinks he does, and so declares that this or that thesis of his is Marxist, and that his ultimate aim is to *produce a theory of ideologies*).[1] Since that is his ambition, we may examine his qualifications for the task; it is, at least on a first approach, legitimate to examine Lévi-Strauss in relation to Marx.

In speaking of Lévi-Strauss's misunderstanding of Marx, I am stating my basic criticism of him here in deliberately *limited* fashion. But you[2] will see that I could (and shall) make the same criticism *without mentioning Marx*. In other words, I criticize him not because his thought fails to conform to that of an individual, however great that individual might be, but, in the final analysis, because it *fails to attain its object* (which can be defined altogether independently of Marx). Thus I merely utilize Marx as a reference point and guidepost in order to situate a criticism that can be formulated altogether independently of Marx. So don't be misled by *the form* my criticism takes.

Very schematically, to adopt the terms Lévi-Strauss uses when he calls himself a Marxist and claims to be producing a *theory of ideology* (he sometimes stretches the term to take in the 'super-structure' or 'superstructures' in general), I would say that Lévi-Strauss's thought is

1. formal; and
2. misses its object;
3. which means that there is a serious defect in the formalism of his thought.

These are necessary distinctions, because I would not for a moment consider criticizing anyone's thinking for being *formal*, or, more precisely, for bearing on forms and seeking to *formalize*, as fully as possible, the concepts in which it thinks those forms. Any body of thought qualifying as knowledge thinks in terms of *forms*, that is, relationships which combine determinate elements. If Marx ranked Aristotle as high as he tells us he does in *Capital*, it is because Aristotle is the thinker of *forms par excellence*, and of form in general. Marx, too, repeatedly called himself a thinker and 'developer' (a barbarism, but I'm taking short cuts) of *forms*. And nothing prevents the thought of forms (which is scientific thought itself) from rising one level higher than that of the forms it brings to light, and thinking the (theoretical) *form* of existence, of combination, of these *forms*: it is then that thought becomes formalizing thought, and rightly so. There are not only partial formalizations in *Capital*, but also all the prerequisites for a formalized theory of modes of production in general, together with all their internal forms of articulation (on this crucial point, see Balibar's text in *Reading [Capital]* II, a text of the greatest importance). Don't be misled on this point either. I'm not criticizing Lévi-Strauss for formalism in general, but for *the wrong kind of* formalism.

That said, let us go into detail.

Lévi-Strauss hasn't the slightest idea what a *mode of production* is. He is unfamiliar with Marx's thought. The first result of this ignorance is that he conceives the 'primitive societies' he deals with (and practically, or in any case *originally*, he deals *only with them* – 'originally' means that when he talks about non-primitive societies, all he does is transfer to non-primitive societies the categories and results of his work on primitive societies, that much is plain) – the first result of this ignorance is that he conceives the phenomena of the 'primitive societies' he deals with in the basic, classical categories of ethnology, without criticizing those categories. The *fundamental* source of ethnological prejudices, and thus of ethnological ideology, consists, *basically*, in the belief that 'primitive' societies are of a very special sort that sets them apart from others and prevents us from applying to them the categories, particularly the Marxist categories, in which we can think the others. *Basically*, in the ethnological ideology of 'primitive societies', we find, besides this notion of the irreducible specificity of the nature of these societies and the phenomena peculiar to them, the notion that they are *primitive* not only in a *relative*, but also in an *absolute* sense: in 'primitive society', the word *primitive* always more or less means – for the ethnological ideologue and for Lévi-Strauss as well (see *Tristes tropiques* and his lecture at the Collège [de France])[3] – *originary*. Not only are primitive societies primitive, they are also originary: they contain the truth in empirical, perceptible form, a truth that is masked and alienated today, in our non-primitive, complex, civilized, etc., societies. This is Rousseau's old myth (Lévi-Strauss often refers to it, taking only this myth from Rousseau, although there are so many *other* things of genius in Rousseau), resuscitated by the bad conscience of the ethnologists, those sons of the colonial conquest who, to assuage their bad consciences, discover that the primitives are 'human beings' at the dawn of human civilization, and then cultivate their friendship (see Lévi-Strauss's evocations of the friendships that sprang up between him and his primitives). I know that all this may seem 'facile', but that's how it is: the difficult thing is to see what the consequences of this 'facileness' are.

The basic consequence of the fact that Lévi-Strauss makes things easy for himself – by omitting to call the *very foundations* of ethnological ideology into question, and so succumbing to it in his turn – is that he is *prevented* from attending to the essence of what Marx says. If we really read and listen to Marx, we have no choice but to draw the following conclusions:

1. there are no 'primitive societies' (this is not a scientific concept); there are, however, *'social formations'* (a scientific concept) which we can *provisionally* call primitive, in a sense wholly uncontaminated by the idea of *origin* (of pure, nascent civilization, of the truth of transparent, pure, native human relations, and so on);

2. like any other *social formation,* a primitive social formation comprises a structure that can be thought only with the help of the concept of *mode of production,* and all the *subordinate concepts* implied by it and contained in it (i.e. a mode of production consists of an economic base, a legal-political superstructure, and an ideological superstructure);

3. like any other social formation, a primitive social formation possesses a structure that results from the combination of *at least two distinct modes* of production, one dominant and the other subordinate (for example, hunting and cattle-raising, hunting and farming of such-and-such a type, hunting and gathering, gathering and fishing, or farming and gathering and hunting or cattle-raising, etc.);[4]

4. as in any other social formation, this combination of two or more modes of production (one of which dominates the other or others) produces specific effects that account for the concrete form taken by the legal-political and ideological superstructures. The effects of the dominance of one mode of production over the other or others often produce paradoxical effects at the level of superstructural forms,

particularly of the ideological superstructure, the only superstructural form Lévi-Strauss ever really considers. By this I mean that every mode of production necessarily *induces* the existence of the (superstructural) instances that specifically [*en propre*] correspond to it, and that the hierarchical *combination* of several modes of production, each inducing its own specific instances, produces as its actually existing *result* a *combination* of different (superstructural) instances induced by the different modes of production which are combined in a given social formation. It follows that the superstructural instances that actually exist in this particular social formation have *forms* that are intelligible only as the specific *combination* of the instances induced by the different modes of production involved (combined in the social formation under consideration) and by the effects of the dominance of one over the others. This effect of dominance can be *paradoxical*: this means, as history shows us time and again, that a mode of production which is dominant (economically speaking) can nevertheless exist in a social formation under the dominance of *superstructural* instances that derive from some other, *subordinate* mode of production. (For example, the *form* of the Prussian state in the mid-nineteenth century was induced by the *feudal* mode of production, which was none the less subordinate to the capitalist mode of production in the Prussian social formation: what *dominated* in the superstructure was a form of state corresponding to the feudal mode of production, which was nevertheless *dominated* in the economy by the capitalist mode of production.) It is these cross-effects which account, even in 'primitive' societies, for *ideological differences* (in the structure of ideologies; differences that Lévi-Strauss quite simply associates with purely *possible* formal variations, that is, with the merely logical categories of opposition, substitution, etc., without once pausing to wonder about the reasons for these substitution[s], variations, etc., precisely because he does not know what a social formation or a mode of a production or the combination of modes of production and their superstructural instances is).

5. If this is so, then we are no longer entitled to use the

concept of *anthropology*, as Lévi-Strauss does in the wake of all other ethnologists. *There can be no such thing as* anthropology. It is a concept which simply sums up ethnological ideology (see my remarks above) in the illusory belief that the object of ethnology is constituted by phenomena different from those studied by the science of history (of social formations, of whatever kind). That Lévi-Strauss calls himself an *anthropologist* gives him his membership card in ethnological ideology, and, at the same time, a theoretical programme: a claim to forging the specific concepts appropriate to the unique (and *exemplary*) reality called a primitive [*primitif*] society, and a claim to forging, with these concepts, concepts that are primordial [*primitif*] (that is, *originary*) with respect to all the others with whose help we think the reality of other 'social formations' – Marxist concepts in particular.

(What I have just laid out for you concerning 'primitive social formations', modes of production, their necessary coexistence and combination in any social formation, the effects induced by each mode of production and, lastly, the combination of the effects induced by each mode of production on their superstructural levels, together with the possibly paradoxical effects of this combination – none of this, if I may be permitted to say so, is *for sale in the shops*. These are ideas that we have drawn, that I have drawn, from our studies of Marx. They are, in and of themselves, a small 'discovery' that I will present in my book.[5] In particular, the conclusions about anthropology that we derive from this are of very great theoretical, and therefore, indirectly, ideological, and of course political consequence. You can see, too, that this gives us, for the first time, *something with which we can think* what transpires at the level of the forms of the superstructure, especially their often paradoxical forms, not just at the level of the state or the political in general – the political does not always take the form of the state! – but also at the level of the forms of the *ideological*. This has certain major political consequences.)

My basic criticism of Lévi-Strauss is that he discusses the ideological and aspires to provide a theory of it *without knowing what it is* or *being able to say what it is*.

The consequences of this are incalculable, if you recall *that not knowing what the ideological is* means, to begin with, not knowing what a social formation is, or what a mode of production is, or what the instances (economic, political, ideological) of a mode of production are, or what their combination (primary, secondary) is, and so on.

These consequences are readily identifiable in Lévi-Strauss's theory. Let me mention the most important, *besides* those I've already pointed out.

1. When Lévi-Strauss analyses the structure or structures of kinship relations, what he fails to say is that if kinship relations play so important a role in primitive societies, this is precisely because they play the role of *relations of production* – relations of production that are intelligible only as a function of the *modes of production* whose relations of production they are (and as a function of the combination of these modes of production). As a result, in Lévi-Strauss, kinship relations are 'left hanging in the air'. They depend, when one reads his texts, on two different *conditions*; he shifts constantly back and forth between them. Either they depend on a formal condition (the effect of a formal combinatory that depends, in the final analysis, on the 'human spirit', the 'structure of the human spirit', and ultimately the . . . 'brain'[6] – this is Lévi-Strauss's 'materialist' side, which combines a binary linguistic approach with a cybernetic conception of the human brain, and so on; you get the picture), which is, ultimately, a logical 'principle' or a brute material reality (Boolean logic as revised by binary linguists, or the physiology of the brain . . .) 'incarnated' in kinship structures. Or, on the contrary, kinship structures depend in Lévi-Strauss on another, purely *functionalist* condition that can be summed up as follows: if certain rules governing marriage, and so forth, exist in primitive societies, it is *so that* these societies can live, survive, and so on. (A functionalist biologist subjectivism: there is a 'social unconscious' which ensures, exactly as an acute intelligence would, that 'primitive society' possesses the *means* it needs to live and survive. Just as one must criticize this functionalism, which, on the theoretical plane, invariably takes the form of a subjectivism that confers upon 'society' the form of existence of a subject endowed with intentions and goals, so one must criticize and

reject the concept of the *unconscious*, its indispensable correlative, of which Lévi-Strauss *is compelled* to make liberal use. I would go so far as to say that the concept of the unconscious is no more scientific a concept in psychoanalysis than in sociology or anthropology or history: you see how far I am prepared to go!). In short, because Lévi-Strauss does not know that kinship structures *play the role of relations of production* in primitive social formations (for he does not know what relations of production are, since he does not know what a social formation or a mode of production is, and so on), he is compelled to think them either in relation to the 'human spirit' or the 'brain' and their common (binary) formal principle, or else in relation to a social unconscious that accomplishes the *functions* necessary to the survival of a society.

One of the most spectacular consequences of his theory is that it leaves him *utterly incapable* of accounting for the fact that kinship structures in primitive societies are not always and everywhere the same, but exhibit significant variations. For him, these variations are merely the *variations* of a purely formal *mode of combination* – which is simply tautological and explains nothing. When you grant yourself a mode of combination that allows for an infinity of *possible* forms in its combinatory matrix, the relevant question is not whether the *possibility* of such-and-such a real phenomenon (such-and-such an observable kinship structure) is from the outset already included among the variations of the combinatory (for that is tautological, and consists in establishing that what is real was *possible*). The pertinent question is, rather, the following: why is it *this possibility* and not another which *has come about, and is therefore* real?

But Lévi-Strauss never answers this question, because he *never asks it*. It is entirely beyond the confines of his theoretical horizon, of the field delimited by his basic concepts. He takes, on the one hand, the real as he observes it and, on the other, the possibilities that he has generated with his type of universal combinatory: when he comes up against a real, the whole problem consists, for him, in *constructing the possibility* of this real, setting out from the play of the combinatory. Yet it is not by producing the possibility of an existing real that you render it intelligible but, rather, by producing the concept of its *necessity* (*this particular* possibility and *not another*). To understand a real phenomenon is not, I would say, a matter of producing the *concept of its possibility* (that is still classical philosophical ideology, the typical juridical operation that I denounce in the preface to *Reading* [*Capital*] I; it is, rather, a matter of producing the concept of its *necessity*. That Lévi-Strauss's formalism is the *wrong sort* of formalism can be seen, now, in connection with this very precise point: Lévi-Strauss takes the formalism of *possibility* for the *formalization* of *necessity*.

2. What I have just said about Lévi-Strauss's analyses of kinship structures also applies, *a fortiori* and in an infinitely more compelling way, to his analyses of the *ideological*. Yet I know that some people who would go along with what I say about kinship structures would be much more reticent when it comes to ideology and Lévi-Strauss's analysis of it. For his formalism seems better adapted to his analyses of myths, since he does not appear to confuse things in the case of myths the way he does in the case of kinship structures. If he doesn't know that kinship structures function as relations of production (that is why they display the observable structures, structures that disappeared in our societies *once relations of production were no longer conflated with kinship structures*) – if, that is, Lévi-Strauss is wrong about the nature and role of kinship structures – he seems, on the other hand, to be right about myths, because he takes them for what they are: myths, *forms of the ideological*. He himself says that they are forms of the ideological! He appears to have going for him, then, the fact that his object is a real one, and that he has found the right name for it. Unfortunately, a name is not *ipso facto* a scientific concept. As Lévi-Strauss *does not know* what the ideological is (although he says he is dealing with the ideological), since he does not know what the ideological level is in the complex articulation of a mode of production and, *a fortiori*, in the combination of several modes of production within one social formation, he falls back – instead of giving us a theory of the ideological, that is, instead of producing the concept of the *necessity* of its *differential* forms – on the *procedure* and ideological temptations that worked (so well!) in the case of kinship structures. That is why we find him going through the same 'theoretical' procedure *again*. He traces the forms of the ideological back to *possibilities* constructed on the basis of a combinatory (with its

classical, ultimately binary procedures); the combinatory itself is in turn traced back either to a 'faculty' of the human spirit, as if this combinatory were one of its effects, or, when hope dies within him (or begins to stir again), to . . . the brain! Rather than retreating, then, he forges ahead under the banner of the wrong sort of formalization (once again, that of the possible, a formalization that is fundamentally ideological). Either the same forms are *identified* as *homologous* with other existing forms (by virtue of the 'virtues' of the procedures of the combinatory), the forms of kinship or economic or linguistic exchange; or they are ultimately identified with certain 'economistic' factors ('mode of life', 'geographical conditions', etc.) which Lévi-Strauss takes for the equivalent of a Marxist theory of the economic level of a mode of production, whose conceptual existence he knows nothing about. Here too, the 'sticking-point' for Lévi-Strauss is that he is absolutely incapable of accounting for the *real* diversity of the *existence* of a given form of the ideological in a given primitive social formation: he only ever accounts for the *possible*, and once he has produced the concept of possibility, he assumes that he need no longer worry about the concept of necessity, to which he is royally indifferent.

I do not say that it is easy to see one's way clearly in all of this. In particular, it does not work very well at all simply to take for good coin the handful of Marxist concepts circulating in the market, and then try to 'apply' them as found to so-called 'primitive' societies. But Marx explains at sufficient length that the laws governing the mechanism of a social formation vary as a function of the structure of this social formation; this implies that one has to *produce* the concepts required to account for the specific social formations known as primitive social formations. When we observe them, we discover that while, in principle, things function in accordance with the same laws of necessity in primitive social formations, they take different forms. We discover, for instance, that the *function* of the relations of production is not accomplished by the same 'elements' in primitive societies as in ours; that the political, the ideological and, in general, the *instances* do not take the same form or, consequently, occupy exactly the same fields as they do in our societies, but, rather, include other elements, relations, and *forms*. These differences, however, are intelligible only on the basis of Marx's fundamental theoretical concepts (social formation, mode of production, etc.), the appropriate differential forms of which have to be produced if the mechanisms of primitive social formations are to be rendered intelligible.

I would say, then, that the whole of Lévi-Strauss's thought, with its merits as well as its defects, becomes intelligible if we set out from his misunderstanding of Marx; not because Marx is Marx, but because Marx thought the very *object* that Lévi-Strauss prevents himself from thinking when he sets out to think it (and affirms that he thinks it).

Lévi-Strauss furnishes very good *descriptions* of certain *mechanisms* (kinship structures, the forms in which one myth is transformed into another, and so forth), but he never knows *what the object* whose mechanism he is describing is, because what makes it possible to define this object in the existing science (Marx's concepts) is a dead letter for him. He is talking about relations of production when he describes kinship structures, but is unaware that he is talking about relations of production. When he talks about myths, he is talking about an *instance* (the result of a complex and often paradoxical combination) that takes its place in a social formation structured by a combination of modes of production, but he is unaware that he is talking about this determinate, real, necessary instance: he thinks he is talking about the human spirit! This profound 'blunder' has very serious consequences. The most serious is that Lévi-Strauss is forced to invent an *object* out of whole cloth (or, rather, to scavenge it from the most vulgar ideology, where it has been lying around for thousands of years of religion) – ostensibly the object of his discourse: the 'human spirit'! The other consequences are no less serious: this 'human spirit' is endowed with the 'faculty' of combining possibilities, in binary fashion (either this human spirit or the 'brain'), with the result that, for Lévi-Strauss, the production of the concept of the necessity of an object is replaced by the production of the concept of its *possibility*. What he *describes* (often very well) is thus associated one hundred per cent with the mystical power of a human spirit combining possibilities and producing them as possibilities. Everything that *distinguishes* the reals from one another, in other words, everything that makes for the differential necessity of existing phenomena, of distinct instances – all this is glossed over, so that all that we encounter in the world is homologies, isomorphisms: words, women, goods, and so on, are all exchanged in the same way, because they have the same 'form' (isomorphic forms by virtue of their *common birth*: isomorphic because they are born of the same combinatory matrix of pure possibilities!). We then find one and the same 'human spirit' everywhere; this is the proof that the 'Savage Mind' thinks,[7] a proof that puts Lévi-Strauss's philosophical ignorance on display. I'll give you just one example for the sake of a laugh; it's worth its weight in gold. Lévi-Strauss has taken it into his head that, in certain respects, the 'savage mind' is far in advance of the 'non-savage' mind – for example, when it comes to conceiving 'secondary qualities', individuals, singularity, and so forth.[8] This is practically Bergson! It is an ideological myth in the true sense. It would be easy to show that modern scientific thought sets out to think *singularity*, not only in history (Marx and Lenin: 'the soul of Marxism is the concrete analysis of a concrete situation') and psychoanalysis, but also in physics, chemistry, biology, and so on. The one little problem (for Bergson and Lévi-Strauss!!) is that it is possible to think the singular and concrete only in *concepts* (which are thus 'abstract' and 'general'); but that is the very condition for *thinking* the singular, since there can be no thinking without concepts (which are, consequently, abstract and 'general'). Philosophers such as Spinoza (the 'singular essences') and Leibniz did not wait until our day to assign the non-savage mind the task of thinking singularity (that is, to register the *reality* of modern science in philosophy)!! Of course, Lévi-Strauss is unaware of this; he prides himself on having revealed to the world that modern science, *too*, is in the process of gradually drawing closer to the savage mind and thinking the singular, when *it has been doing so* from the very beginning of its existence. It as if he were to reveal that we shall, at last, begin inching our way down the path that will lead to the discovery of America – which was, alas, for better or for worse, discovered a very long time ago.

Of course, the critique I have just outlined, like any critique, is to some extent unjust, because it is *one-sided*. I have said that Lévi-Strauss *describes* certain mechanisms *very well indeed*. It often happens that, in describing something, he *goes beyond* description: this is especially true of his studies of kinship structures, which will endure as an important discovery. His analyses of myths also sometimes contain things of great value. And the fact remains that he is a thinker with a concern for rigour who knows what scientific work is. In short, I would have to rectify and temper my criticism with all sorts of qualifications to make it equitable. But I do not think that the points I have just developed can be left out of a *just* [*juste*] evaluation of Lévi-Strauss's work. Even if some of my formulations are too hasty, I believe that they are *on the mark* [*touchent juste*]: they touch on the precise point that distinguishes us from Lévi-Strauss himself and, *a fortiori*, from all the 'structuralists'.

Notes

1. See especially Claude Lévi-Strauss, *Structural Anthropology*, trans. Monique Layton, Chicago, 1983.
2. See the Editor's Introduction above.
3. The 5 January 1960 inaugural lecture that Lévi-Strauss delivered after being appointed to the newly created Chair of Social Anthropology at the Collège de France. See Lévi-Strauss, 'The Scope of Anthropology', *Structural Anthropology II*, trans. Monique Layton, Harmondsworth, 1976, pp. 3–32. [*Trans.*]
4. Althusser asked a secretary at the École normale supérieure to type out an extract from a letter written by Emmanuel Terray in which Terray comments on this paragraph in particular. While indicating his agreement with Althusser's basic argument, Terray insists that the examples Althusser gives leave something to be desired, for they can lead to confusion between a 'mode of production' and a 'sphere of production': hunting and fishing are not, in themselves, modes of production. The original letter has not been preserved.
5. Althusser is probably referring to one of his unfinished works on the union of theory and practice, which originated in a mimeographed text, still unpublished in French, dated 20 April 1965, 'TTPTF'.
6. See, for example, Claude Lévi-Strauss, *The Savage Mind*, Chicago, 1966, p. 248n:

> But mathematical thought at any rate reflects the free functioning of the mind [*l'esprit humain*], that is, the activity of the cells of the cerebral cortex, relatively emancipated from any external constraint and obeying only its own laws. As the mind too is a thing, the functioning of this thing teaches us something about the nature of things.

7. *'La démonstration de La Pensée sauvage'*: *La Pensée sauvage* is the French title of the book that appeared in English under the title *The Savage Mind*. [*Trans.*]

8. See in particular ibid., p. 22:

> Physics and chemistry are already striving to become qualitative again, that is, to account also for secondary qualities which when they have been explained will in their turn become means of explanation. And biology may perhaps be marking time waiting for this before it can itself explain life.

Three Notes on the
Theory of Discourses

(1966)

Althusser delivered his 26 June 1966 lecture 'The Philosophical Conjuncture and Marxist Theoretical Research' with two objectives in mind: to assess, some eight months after the publication of For Marx *and* Reading Capital, *the prevailing theoretical conjuncture, and to lay the groundwork for the organization of a broad national structure in which it would be possible to carry out collective theoretical work. In November, he drew up a text he called 'Circular No. 1', and had it typed. The stated purpose of this circular was 'to organize this collective work': it called for the 'formation of Theoretical Work Groups' throughout France. These were to be based on the following principle: 'We believe that a Theoretical Work Group, at least given the present state of philosophical and epistemological problems, cannot be straightforwardly organized on the basis of the existing "disciplines", that is, on the basis of divisions that in many cases must rather be criticized and rejected. Today most of the decisive theoretical problems, at least in philosophy and the "Human Sciences", are obfuscated by "disciplinary" divisions and their effects. We therefore propose that the Theoretical Work Group be organized around, not a discipline or "interdisciplinary theme", but a* theoretical object, *a fundamental* theoretical problem *which, while it may well touch on the domains of several existing disciplines, will not necessarily appear in person in any of them, whether in its content or the form of its theoretical object.' Although the organization envisaged in this 'circular' never materialized, Althusser did indeed create a collective work group around himself. 'Three Notes on the Theory of Discourses' constitutes the first stage in its history.*

In a letter preserved in his files, dated 7 October 1966 and addressed to Alain Badiou, Étienne Balibar, Yves Duroux and Pierre Macherey, Althusser outlined his conception of the work that he proposed to undertake with them. He began by noting that the object was to prepare a 'work of Philosophy (Elements of Dialectical Materialism) that we will publish collectively, say, a year from now, or, at the latest, in a year and a half' — a work which, he added in a 14 October letter to Balibar, in an explicit reference to Spinoza, was to be 'a true work of philosophy that can stand as our Ethics'. *He went on to define the kind of research that he had in mind. 'At the present stage,' he wrote, 'this collective work should be carried out* in written form, *via an exchange of* research notes *drawn up by each of us and distributed to all five collaborators.' 'So as to avoid provoking reactions from certain oversensitive people,' he added, 'it should be a matter of* strict agreement among us *that we will maintain the* most complete secrecy *about our agreement, that is, our project, our collective work and its organizational forms. I want a* formal commitment *from you on this point. You can easily see why.' He further explained what he meant by 'research notes': 'it should be understood that these are research notes, that is, essays, tentative approaches, reflections that involve theoretical risks of error and invite corrections and criticism. Thus we should not be at all afraid to engage in attempts that may go awry, or put forward hypotheses that may be risky and have to be rejected or put to rights.' Finally, Althusser insisted on what was, in his view, the basic condition for the success of the project: 'everything depends on our awareness of the importance of what is at stake in this undertaking; without that, there is every chance that the circuit will soon be interrupted. Each of us should pledge not to leave a Note he has received* unanswered. *Each of us should put in writing, in a Note, thoughts and remarks (of whatever kind) that stand in direct or indirect relation to the projected* Elements.'

As is well known, the projected book never saw the light. Yet, in a certain sense, it exists. In the space of two years, Althusser and his collaborators exchanged more than four hundred pages of Notes of greatly varying lengths. And, however ambiguous the undertaking, given the institutional rank of the now internationally famous Althusser, the facts are there for all to see: an unprecedented intellectual adventure did indeed take place. One would be hard pressed to name others like it.

Posted on 28 October 1966, 'Three Notes on the Theory of Dis-

courses' was the first Note to be exchanged. It was followed, in November 1966–January 1967, by Étienne Balibar's fifty-seven-page 'Note on the Theory of Discourse'. But, since things are never simple, we cannot be certain that Althusser initially wrote his text with a collective project in mind. As he himself says in the accompanying letter, his first Note was written 'over the month of September'; typed by a secretary,[1] it was one of the three Notes sent in a single batch to his four collaborators, and probably also to Michel Tort, who participated in the organized exchange. We have, however, found an earlier version of the first Note in Althusser's files. Entitled 'On Psychoanalysis', it was typed by Althusser himself and dated 13 September. Althusser sent this text to René Diatkine on 5 October 1966; alluding to his recent 'Letters to D[iatkine]', he says: 'This text, as you will see, if you have the patience (and time) to read it, rectifies a number of the theses that I proposed in my letters this summer. In particular, I now think that what I said earlier about the universality of the "two storeys"[2] does not stand up. The "two storeys" of the economic are not of the same nature as the "two storeys" of discourses.'

Althusser sent the same text to Franca Madonia on 13 September, along with a detailed commentary on its status and stakes:

> Bear in mind that this writing exercise is research in the true sense, not an exposition of things already known. One result is that there are modifications (tending towards increased precision) between the terminology used in the beginning and that used at the end.... The 'thesis' defended here depends to a large extent on a point of theory that I've been working out for a few months now, concerning the difference between a general theory and the regional theories that depend on it. The need for this distinction has made itself felt in connection with Marx's works. Let me tell you, to give you the general idea, that I would today say that historical materialism is the general theory of which the theory of the capitalist mode of production, or the theory of the political and of politics ... or the theory of the ideological, or the theory of the stages of the transition towards the socialist mode of production, or the theory of the economic instance of the capitalist mode of production (which Marx explicitly discusses in Capital), etc., are regional theories. These regional theories are theories of a theoretical object (the capitalist mode of production, etc.), not knowledge of real objects (the capitalist mode of production is not a real object, for it exists only in one or another historical social formation, nineteenth-century England, Russia in 1917, France and Italy in 1966, etc.). That which exists, in the narrow sense of the word 'to exist', is real objects (which I today call, using a concept of Spinoza's, 'singular essences'): the knowledge of real objects

presupposes the intervention of the concepts of the general theory and the regional theories involved, plus the (empirical) knowledge of the determinate forms of existence that make for the singularity of these essences. Thus a record of analytical practice (one or another episode of a cure as described by a psychoanalyst) presupposes – in order to be understood as such, situated and brought into relation with the mechanism that produces it – an appeal to the regional theory of psychoanalysis, which in turn presupposes an appeal to the general theory. In the text I've sent you to read, the emphasis is on the absolutely indispensable nature of an appeal to the general theory, and on the fact that (this is its theoretical tragedy) the regional theory of psychoanalysis still has no general theory at its disposal, for it does not know which general theory it depends on. I try to say which one it depends on, and I show that this general theory is a combination of two general theories, one known (historical materialism) and another whose existence is as yet unsuspected, or very nearly so, and in any case confused, even today, with either linguistics or psychoanalysis (this confusion is to be found even in Lacan): the general theory of the signifier, which studies the mechanisms and possible effects of every discourse (signifier).

If all this is true, it should, despite its aridity, have the effect of a bomb. I'm going to get as many guarantees as I can by consulting a few, but only a very few, knowledgeable young lads before publishing it, in a form I've yet to decide on. For I'm advancing here in a field bristling with people packing pistols of every imaginable calibre; they fire without warning and without mercy, and, if I don't watch out, I risk being shot down in cold blood.[3]

Not long after producing the first text, Althusser came to the conclusion that certain points in it required modification. He proceeded to write the other two Notes, which he dated 12 October 1966, and had a secretary type all three. He did not modify his first Note before the 12th, but the typed version of it bears many critical comments in his hand. If another passage in the letter to Madonia just quoted is to be believed, these emendations were made before he began to compose the last two Notes: 'There are in this text not only terminological variations, but one or two passages that contain quite a few imprecise statements and are sprinkled with question marks – passages that didn't stand up in my own view even as I was writing them. Since then I've refined a few ideas which can help put these passages to rights – but I haven't had a chance to revise my text.'[4]

The very fact that the texts published here were left unfinished helps us to see a dimension of Althusser's enterprise that has been ignored or misunderstood. Althusser is often accused of attempting to establish *the hegemony of a system. But what we find in these texts is quite the opposite: a mode of thought that attends to the singularity of the sciences and carefully eschews, at a time when 'structuralism' was at its apogee, any unification of the 'human sciences' under the hegemony of one of them, 'historical materialism' and 'dialectical materialism' not excepted – even while attempting a differential definition of the status of each one of them (in the present instance, psychoanalysis). We also discover in these texts an original attempt at least to pose the question of the relationship between the unconscious and ideology. If today we know – thanks to the 'late Althusser', among others – that the problems men pose are not always those they are capable of solving, we cannot pretend to believe that they have solved a problem simply because they have ceased to pose it.*

What follows contains the whole of the text of 'Three Notes on the Theory of Discourses' in the form in which it was sent to the members of the group mentioned above. We have supplemented this text with certain passages which were included in the copy that Althusser typed, but which were then omitted, obviously by mistake, when someone else retyped it. As for Althusser's handwritten addenda to the version of the first Note that he himself typed, they are reproduced, without exception, in our Notes to the text.

Olivier Corpet and François Matheron

Cover letter

Paris, 28 October 1966

I attach to this letter, as a personal contribution to our exchange, 'Three Notes' about the theory of discourses. This text grew out of a reflection on the status of unconscious discourse and its articulation with ideological discourse.

I have recopied the first Note, written in September, without changing anything in it.

Obviously, it has been partly superseded, as appears in Notes 2 and 3.

(a) I believe that everything I have said about the place of the 'subject' *in every one of the discourses* must be revised. The more I work on it, the more I think that the category of the subject is absolutely fundamental to *ideological* discourse, that it is one of its central categories: it is bound up with the *truth-guarantee* in the centred, double mirror structure.

Drawing the consequences of this 'pertinence', I do not think it is possible to talk about a 'subject' of the unconscious, although Lacan does, or of a 'subject of science', or of a 'subject of aesthetic discourse' – *even if* certain categories of the discourses in question do bear a relation to the category of the *subject*, inasmuch as all are articulated with ideological discourse, each in a specific way.

All this already provides a basis for refinements and rectifications, but I don't have the time to work them out right now; others can say what they are and develop them at length, under more favourable conditions.

(b) all of the last part of Note 1 has to be revised and *very seriously* modified, both because of the status it implicitly ascribes to the subject of the general theory and also because of the General Theory which it suggests is determinant.

Note 1

[On Psychoanalysis]

1. The current situation of psychoanalytic theory

We can describe psychoanalytic theory in its current state by saying that, apart from *a few* attempts discussed below, it takes the form, in the best of cases, of a *regional theory* which lacks a *general theory*, although it is, *in principle*, the realization of this general theory.

To approach psychoanalytic theory as a *regional* theory is to approach it as a *theory*, a *system* of theoretical concepts that makes it possible to account for the structure and functioning of its object, currently known as the psychoanalytic *unconscious*. The unconscious is the theoretical object (or object of knowledge) of psychoanalytic theory (a regional theory).

This *theory* of the unconscious, as found in Freud (the first topography, the second topography) or Lacan, has, as a theory, to be carefully distinguished from its *application* (precepts, practical rules for the conduct of the cure) as well as from observations of psychoanalytic practice (the cure), which are nevertheless *registered* in the concepts of that theory. The concepts by means of which the experimental data of the cure are thought (and manipulated) are *practised* concepts, not (theoretically) thought concepts.

The concepts that are systematically thought in the regional psychoanalytic theory do not take as their object the real object on which the practice of the cure and its observations bear, but a *theoretical object* that allows us to think, *among other things*, what goes on in the cure. Freud's topographies think the unconscious *in general*, that is, provide the concepts that account *not only* for what goes on *in the cure*, especially in 'pathological' cases – psychoses and neuroses – but also for what goes on *outside the cure*, and elsewhere than in so-called 'pathological' cases. It is no accident that Freud first wrote an *Interpretation of Dreams*, then went on to produce a *Psychopathology of Everyday Life* and a theory of the *Witz*, or that he discussed art, religion, and so on. The theory of the unconscious is, in principle, the theory of *all the possible effects* of the unconscious – in the cure, outside the cure, in 'pathological' as well as 'normal' cases. What characterizes it as a theory is what makes any theory a theory: it takes as its object not this or that real object, but an object of knowledge (and thus a theoretical object); it produces the knowledge of the (determinate) *possibility* of the *effects*, and thus of the *possible effects* of this object in its *real* forms of existence. Every theory, then, goes beyond the *real* object that constitutes the empirical 'point of departure' for the historical constitution of the theory (in Freud, this point of departure is the 'talking cure') and produces its own theoretical object as well as knowledge of it, which is knowledge of the *possibilities* [*les possibles*] of this object, and the forms of existence in which these determinate possibilities are realized, that is, exist as *real* objects.

In this perspective, we may say that a psychoanalytic theory does indeed exist, that this theory has its theoretical object and produces knowledge [*connaissances*], the knowledge of the possibilities (in particular, the possible effects) of this object.

At the same time, however, we must say that this theory is a regional theory which exhibits the peculiar feature of depending in principle on a general theory that is *absent*.

In the history of the sciences, this situation is not unique to psychoanalysis. Every[5] new 'science' irrupts, when it is 'founded', in the form of a regional theory that depends in principle on an *absent* general theory. This *de jure* dependence on a general theory which is absent in fact means that:

- we can observe, within the regional theory itself, the absence of the general theory (the effects of this absence) at the theoretical level: for as long as the general theory is lacking, the regional theory strives to 'achieve closure', but fails to; or, to put it in other terms, it tries to define its own object *differentially* (in contradistinction to other theoretical objects: in the present case, those of biology, psychology, sociology, etc.), but *fails to*. This attempt and failure are the presence of this *de facto absence* of a general theory, the existence of which is nevertheless called for, *de jure*, in order to found these attempts;
- we can also observe the absence of the general theory at the *practical* level. The theoretical problem of the limits, and thus of the differential definition of the object of psychoanalysis – a problem which, in the absence of a general theory, remains unsolved – produces specific effects in the field of technique and the field of practice. For example: if the psychoses can be made accessible to psychoanalytic technique, how should the cure of psychotics be conducted, and so on? For example: what is the relationship, practically and technically speaking, between the psychoanalytic cure and the psychotherapies, between psychoanalysis and psychosomatic medicine, and so on? For example – this is the *most serious consequence*: because of the lack of a general theory, we are witnessing the decline of the regional theory, ignorance of it as a theory, and its retreat into the empiricism of psychoanalytic practice or its unwarranted conflation with other regional theories (biology, psychology, etc.) even at the *technical* level (consider the technical deviations of certain schools, whether Adler and Jung or the English and American schools).

It must, however, be pointed out that the effects of this absence *can* be relatively *limited*, confined within limits that safeguard both Freud's psychoanalytic rules (the technique of the cure) and the regional *theory* on which they depend.

The practice of many practitioners may well be technically correct even if they do not master, at the theoretical level, the regional theory (it is enough for them to master it in its technical forms, the guarantee of effective practice) – (it is enough for them to 'practise' it). By the same token, the regional theory, despite the dangers just evoked, can survive more or less intact in the absence of a general theory, the need for which nevertheless makes itself felt in principle in that theory's very absence.

These are the features which define the situation of psychoanalytic practice and psychoanalytic theory today. We find either practitioners who 'practise' the regional theory (and whose practice is correct, whatever ideas about the regional theory, correct or not, they may have in their heads); or practitioners who do not practise it (but, rather, practise a false theory); or, again, psychoanalysts who master the regional theory *theoretically* (and who, at the same time, can simultaneously – this is not inconceivable – 'practise' it badly). In the immense majority of cases, psychoanalysis does not go beyond the *regional theory*.

The fact that psychoanalysis does not have a general theory at its disposal, only a practice or a regional theory, confers a very peculiar status upon it: *it is not in a position to provide objective proof of its scientificity* – that is to say, it is not in a position differentially to define (or locate) its theoretical object in the field of theoretical objectivity (a field constituted by the differential relations of the different theoretical objects in existence). Indeed, the only possible way to provide proof of the scientificity of a regional theory is point to the differential articulation which assigns that regional theory its place in the articulated field of existing theoretical objects. The general theory alone can fulfil this function, by thinking the object of the [regional][6] theory in its articulated relationship with the other objects whose system constitutes the existing field of scientific objectivity.

2. The question of the general theory

Certain authors have attempted to answer this question, to resolve this problem, with varying degrees of success; some of these attempts have proven aberrant, others interesting.

The aberrant attempts: these are, in their way, manifestations of the *existence* of the problem, in the very form of their aberration.

Let us mention the biologistic attempt, the psychologistic attempt, the ethologistic attempt, the sociologistic attempt, the philosophical attempt. These attempts are distinguished by their *reductive* character: in setting out (or not) to think the difference between the theoretical object of psychoanalysis (the unconscious) and some other theoretical object (that of biology, psychology, philosophy, etc.), they in fact *reduce* the object of psychoanalysis to the object of these other disciplines.

The interesting attempts: Freud's own, and, today, Lacan's.

We find in Freud (in the metapsychological essays, *Three Essays on Sexuality*, and also in *Totem and Taboo* or 'The Future of an Illusion') an attempt to situate the object of psychoanalysis with respect to other objects belonging to existing disciplines. The interest of Freud's attempts lies in the fact that they are not reductive but, rather, *differential* (consider the theory of the drives in its differential relation with the theory of the instincts). One may say that the *existence* of these attempts and their *differential* character are proof that Freud was aware, very keenly aware, of the need to think the theoretical object of psychoanalysis within the limits of the field of scientific objectivity. His constant references to science, scientific objectivity, and the various sciences already in existence, including the myths in which he anticipated the future theoretical 'solution' of the problems of psychoanalytic theory that would result from the development of some other discipline – all this offers direct and indirect evidence (right down to certain myths) of Freud's recognition of the need for a general theory. Once again, what is remarkable here, in the absence of the theoretical conditions that would have made it possible to constitute this general theory (we are quite possibly still at the same stage), is the fact that, even when he had to borrow certain of his concepts from some other discipline (from the sciences, or even from a certain philosophy) in order to outline this general theory, Freud always conceived it as in principle *distinct* from the regional theories from which he borrowed. He never lapsed into a biological general theory, a psychological general theory, or a philosophical general theory. Whence the paradox of his attempt: he had to sketch the broad outline of a general theory that intended to be a general theory in so far as its function was concerned, and did not intend to be one in so far as its content was concerned. Freud *reproduced*, in his general theory (the metapsychology), what might be called the compulsory solitude of the regional theory, which it is the effect of a general theory, precisely, to eliminate. To say that Freud's general theory reproduced his regional theory means that the concepts of the general theory are just as 'isolated' as his regional theory: instead of furnishing the differential link between his regional theory and other regional theories, instead of serving as general concepts that would make possible several different regional theories, *including* the regional theory of psychoanalysis, they express a (hollow) claim to generality rather than the reality of this generality in its true, concrete role. These concepts *reproduce* the concepts of the regional theory; they are nothing but replicas of it cast in the form of generality – when they are not simply concepts *of* the regional theory decked out with a *name* that assigns them a function in the general theory, a function *of which this name is not the concept*. A single example will suffice to illustrate this point: the concept of the *death instinct* (opposed to the Libido) actually belongs to the regional theory; by dint of its *name*, however, it is *charged* with functions in the general theory.[7] Yet its *name* does not transform the regional concept into a general concept: its name is a programme that does nothing more than delimit a function in its very absence.

Lacan's attempt very lucidly takes up what is best in Freud's. The labour of conceptual denomination that Lacan has carried out on the concepts of Freud's regional theory goes beyond the limits of the regional theory. This rectified terminology, rendered systematic and coherent, is one from which Lacan has drawn extremely far-reaching theoretical effects (within the regional theory); it is an elaboration that could not have been conceived of and realized without (i) an awareness of the need to elaborate a general theory; (ii) a correct[8] conception of the nature of a general theory; and (iii) the beginnings of an elaboration of this general theory. The most spectacular sign of this threefold imperative, of which Lacan is cognizant, is his use of linguistics. Lacan not only fiercely defends the principle, found in Freud, according to which the object of psychoanalysis must be differentiated from that of biology, psychology and philosophy (especially phenomenology); over and above this defensive, negative effort, he makes a positive effort to show, with respect to linguistics, both what distinguishes the (theoretical) object of psychoanalysis from that of linguistics and what makes them similar. In short, he thinks a difference not only in its negative, but also in its positive aspect; that is, he thinks a differential *relation*. And it is this differential relation with the object of linguistics that serves him as a fundamental principle for thinking the other differential relations: with the objects of biology, psychology, sociology, ethology and philosophy.

It is certainly no theoretical *accident* if one *specific* differential relation (here, the one that brings the object of linguistics into a relation of pertinent difference with the object of psychoanalysis) – this relation and no other – turns out to be the right principle for bringing out the *other* differential relations. If this differential relation plays this privileged role, it is because it *commands* the others, at least in the present state of thought on the subject. It should be added that we can discern, thanks to one of its effects (which is usually completely ignored), the function 'general theory' which is fulfilled by the recourse to linguistics in the conceptual elaboration of the concepts of the regional theory of psychoanalysis: for Lacan is led to clarify not only the theoretical concepts of the regional theory of psychoanalysis, but also certain theoretical concepts of the regional theory of *linguistics itself*. What we see here is a specific effect of any general theory: whenever it clarifies a given regional theory about itself, helping it to formulate and rectify its concepts, it necessarily has the *same effect of rectification–reclassification* on the concepts of the other regional theory brought into play in this operation of differential definition. The linguists have perhaps not yet realized what they owe, in their own discipline, to an undertaking that *apparently has no bearing* on it. Yet what we see here is a standard effect of any general theory: in setting out to develop one regional theory by confronting it with another, it rectifies–reclassifies the concepts that it brings to bear (the concepts of the regional theories) not only in the theory that is to be rectified, but also in the theory that does the rectifying; not only in the theory worked on, but also in the theory that is put to work.

However, this effect brings a rather severe disadvantage in its wake if one fails to see that it is a question of the elaboration of a general theory, if one believes that what is involved is *simply* regional theories and their *simple* confrontation (as if everything were taking place between two regional theories, without the intervention of a third element, which, precisely, is not located at the same level, in other words, is not regional, but is a theory of a completely different kind, since what is involved is a *third* element, precisely the general theory). If this is not clear, and clearly conceived, one can be misled into thinking that what occurs in this confrontation is wholly due to one of the two regional theories. One might suppose that it is psychoanalysis which holds the keys to linguistics, or the other way round; one might suppose that one regional theory (that of psychoanalysis or linguistics) *is the general theory of the other*. This misperception will then give rise to an ideology that is either linguistic or psychoanalytic (as occurs frequently, because this is hard to avoid); it will lead one to say (and, worse, *to think*) that, for instance, linguistics is the mother-discipline of the human sciences, or that psychoanalysis is.

Despite all the precautions Lacan has taken, one cannot say that he – or, in any case, some of his disciples – is not tempted by this ideological misperception. Witness, for instance, the issue of *La Psychanalyse* on 'Psychoanalysis and the Human Sciences,'[9] and the positions Lacan has taken [vis-à-vis] the work of Lévi-Strauss, as well as certain themes that he develops in discussing the history of the Sciences [and] Descartes, or the (highly ambiguous) use to which he puts the thought of certain philosophers (Plato, Hegel, Heidegger). It is quite striking that the use to which Lacan puts linguistics in elaborating the concepts of the psychoanalytic regional theory is totally exempt from the effects of misperception which haunt these examples. This tends to prove that the general theory towards which Lacan is working, and for the elaboration of which he provides certain basic elements, is not perfectly *situated* in its status of general theory, since, for example, what Lacan withholds from linguistics with one hand, whenever he deals with it explicitly, he grants Lévi-Strauss with the other, and, as it were, surreptitiously – although it is obvious that Lévi-Strauss imports linguistics into his own field in an extremely summary, non-critical way that has nothing whatsoever to do with the kind of 'importation' that we find in Lacan (which is, precisely, critical, differential importation).

Although Lacan treats the relations between linguistics and psychoanalysis in a way that is epistemologically correct, he assigns the (incorrect) use of linguistics by Lévi-Strauss the task and responsibility of 'mediating' the relationship between psychoanalysis and the other Human Sciences.

This entails the following ambiguity: either linguistics is the general theory of the Human Sciences, or psychoanalysis (allied to linguistics, which it is supposed to have brought back to its origins) is the general theory of the Human Sciences. The existence and perpetuation of this ambiguity, whose effects are visible (the relations of psychoanalysis or linguistics to the Human Sciences), are the manifestation of the objective *limits* that Lacan has reached in his effort to elaborate a general theory, the necessity for which he lucidly perceives. It would be facile to explain these limits (and the effects of misperception to which they give rise) as the limits of an individual effort which, however brilliant it may be, is too 'caught up' in the labour of regional elaboration to attend as closely as it should to the labour of general elaboration whose absolute necessity Lacan nevertheless very clearly perceives. Such an explanation has to do with the personal history of Lacan's investigation. We need to examine this matter in the light of very different principles, and to say that the existence of these limits is in fact the sign of a limitation in Lacan's conception of the *nature* of *a general theory*. Going beyond these limits plainly calls for something other than an experience that is internal to the psychoanalytic regional theory and the linguistic regional theory: what is required is general epistemological views, that is, a well-defined, correct philosophical conception that effectively *embraces* the specific object known as a general theory.[10] Only if one has such a conception is one likely to take up and pursue the following *lead*: the idea that the general theory of psychoanalysis, the one which it requires and for which its regional theory calls, *cannot* be developed solely by means of the differential 'confrontation' (and its general-theory 'effects') between the regional theory of linguistics and the regional theory of psychoanalysis; that it must be developed *in a very different perspective*, by means of very different confrontations, through the intervention of very different regional theories and their differential relations, with the help of a very different reclassification which, precisely, calls into question the objects affected by the limitation described above – the famous Human Sciences.

I suggest that we look for the general theory of psychoanalysis in that which makes it possible to constitute the regional theory of the discourse *of the unconscious* as both a *discourse* and a discourse *of the unconscious* – that is, in not one but two general theories, whose articulation we need to think.

3. The character of the unconscious

To determine the nature of the theoretical elements that must be assembled in order to constitute the general theory of psychoanalysis, we have to set out from the characteristics of the object of the regional theory of psychoanalysis: the unconscious.

It is well known that this regional theory has been developed on the basis of observations and experiences provided by the practice of the cure as well as observations provided by other phenomena external to the cure (the effects of the unconscious in 'everyday' life, art, religion, and so on).

We can characterize the unconscious as follows:

(a) The unconscious is manifested, that is, *exists* in its *effects*, both normal and pathological:[11] these effects are discernible in dreams, all the various forms of symptoms, and all the different kinds of 'play' (including 'wordplay').

(b) This manifestation is not that of an essence whose effects are its phenomena. *That which exists* is the mechanisms of a system that functions by producing these effects. These mechanisms are themselves determinate. It may be said that, in the narrow sense of the word, *that which exists* is the formations of the unconscious – in other words, the determinate systems that function by producing certain determinate effects. 'The unconscious' designates nothing other than the theoretical object which allows us to think the formations of the unconscious, that is, systems functioning in accordance with mechanisms producing effects.

(c) The unconscious is a structure (or system) combining determinate elements subject to determinate laws of combination and functioning in accordance with determinate mechanisms.

(d) The unconscious is a structure whose elements are *signifiers*.

(e) Inasmuch as its elements are *signifiers*, the laws of combination of the unconscious and the mechanisms of its functioning depend on a general theory of the signifier.

(f) Inasmuch as these signifiers are the signifiers of the *unconscious*, not of some other system of signifiers (for example, language [*la langue*], ideology, art, science, etc.), the unconscious depends[12] on the general theory that allows us to think this specific difference. What this general theory is is a question we shall provisionally leave in abeyance, but it does not seem as if a general theory of the signifier can by itself produce (by deduction) the specific difference that distinguishes the discourse of science from the discourses of ideology, art, and the unconscious. It should make this difference possible through the play of the possible variations inscribed in the theory of discourse – but it cannot construct it.

(g) In order to determine which general theory will allow us to specify the difference that produces the characteristic form of the discourse of the unconscious as distinct from other forms of discourse, we must try to bring out this difference by a process of reduction, and then compare it to what the theory of the signifier is capable of producing as the required theoretical effect.

(h) If we compare the different existing *forms* of discourse – that is, the forms of unconscious discourse, ideological discourse, aesthetic discourse and scientific discourse – we can demonstrate the existence of *a common effect: every discourse produces a subjectivity-effect*. Every discourse has, as its necessary correlate, a subject, which is one of the effects, if not the major effect, of its functioning. Ideological discourse 'produces' or 'induces' a subject-effect, a subject; so do the discourse of science, the discourse of the unconscious, etc.

(i) The theory of the production of the subjectivity-effect falls within the province of the theory of the signifier.

(j) If we compare the various subject-effects produced by the different forms of discourse, we observe that (i) the relationship these subjects bear to the discourses in question is not the same; (ii) in other words, the subject position 'produced' or induced by the discourse vis-à-vis that discourse varies. Thus the ideological subject *in person* forms part of ideological discourse, *is present in person* in it, since it is itself a determinate signifier of this discourse. We observe that the subject of scientific discourse, in contrast, is *absent in person* from scientific discourse, for there is no signifier designating it (it is an evanescent subject which is inscribed in a signifier only on condition that it disappear from the [signifying] chain the moment it appears there – otherwise science slides into ideology). The subject of aesthetic discourse may be said to be present in aesthetic discourse *through the mediation of others* [*par personnes interposées*] (always in the plural). The subject of unconscious discourse occupies a position that is different from all those described so far: it is 'represented' in the chain of signifiers by *one* signifier which 'stands in' for it [*qui en tient lieu*], which is its 'lieu-tenant' [*son lieu-tenant*]. Thus it is absent from the discourse of the unconscious by 'delegation' [*par 'lieu-tenance'*]. The theory of the signifier, which must account for the subject-effect of every discourse, must also account for these different *forms of the subject* as so many *possibilities* of variation of the subject-form.

(k) The differential nature of the subject-effect, and the place (position) that the subject which it characteristically 'produces' as an effect occupies with respect to a given discourse, must be correlated with assignable *differences of structure* in the structures of that discourse. In other words, the structure of scientific discourse must differ from the structures of ideological discourse, aesthetic discourse, and the discourse of the unconscious. It is this difference of structure which allows us to characterize (and designate) the different discourses differently; in other words, it is this difference which makes it possible to talk about scientific discourse on the one hand and ideological discourse on the other, about aesthetic discourse and the discourse of the unconscious.

For example: ideological discourse, in which the subject-effect is present in person and is thus a signifier of this discourse, the main signifier of this discourse, possesses a structure of *speculary centring*; the subject induced is duplicated by a producing subject (the empirical subject is duplicated by the transcendental subject, the man-subject by God, etc.).

For example: scientific discourse, in which the subject-effect is absent in person and thus is not a signifier of this discourse, possesses a decentred structure [*une structure de décentration*] (that of a *system of abstract relations*, whose elements are concepts, none of which is 'constituent': as soon as a concept becomes 'constituent', we are in the realm of ideological discourse).

For example: aesthetic discourse, in which the subject-effect is present through the mediation of others (by way of a combination of *several* signifiers), possesses an *ambiguous structure of cross-references*, in which each presumable 'centre' is such only by virtue of the presence, that is, the negation of some other 'centre', which stands in the same relation of indecision [*indécision*] with regard to the first. When the work of art possesses a single centre, it lapses from aesthetic discourse into ideological discourse. When it evicts every subject from its domain, it lapses into scientific discourse.

For example: [in] the discourse of the unconscious, in which the subject-effect is absent by 'delegation', we are dealing with a pseudo-centred structure, subtended by a *structure of flight* or *'lack'* [*béance*] (a metonymic structure?).

(1) It seems that it is at last possible to establish a pertinent relation between the structures of these different discourses on the one hand, and, on the other, the *nature* of the *signifiers* comprising the characteristic elements of each of these structures.

The signifiers of language [*langue*] are morphemes (material: phonemes).

The signifiers of science are concepts (material: words).

The signifiers of aesthetic discourse are extremely varied (material: words, sounds, colours, etc.).

The signifiers of ideological discourse are also varied (material: gestures, modes of behaviour, feelings, words and, generally speaking, any other element of other practices and other discourses?).

The signifiers of the unconscious are fantasies (material: the imaginary).

(m) With the reservations required whenever one employs the concept *function*, it may be suggested that the reason for the structural specificities (and their subject-effects) has basically to do with the specific function of the formations of which these structures provide the concept. This function can be defined only by the place occupied by the signifying structure considered (i) with respect to other signifying structures; (ii) with respect to other, non-signifying structures, and by its *articulation* with these structures (place-articulation).

(n) Thus we can distinguish different functions:
  • of knowledge (science)
  • of recognition–misrecognition (ideology)
  • of recognition–perception (art?)
  • of a circulation of signifiers (language?) corresponding to the different structures.[13]

(o) We may, very cautiously, risk a suggestion as to which mode of articulation is at work in the case of the structure of the unconscious.

This mode could well be the following:

In every social formation, the base requires the support-[*Träger*] function as a function to be assumed, as a place to be occupied in the technical and social division of labour. This requirement remains abstract: the base defines the *Träger*-functions (the economic base, and the political or ideological superstructure *as well*), but the question of *who* must assume and carry out this function, and how the assumption of it might come about, is a matter of *perfect indifference* to the structure (base or superstructure) that defines these functions: it 'doesn't want to know anything about it' (as in the army).

It is ideology which performs the function of *designating* the subject (in general) that is to occupy this function: to that end, it must *interpellate it* as subject, providing it with the reasons-of-a-subject for assuming the function. Ideology interpellates individuals by constituting them as subjects (ideological subjects, and therefore subjects of its discourse) and providing them with the reasons-of-a-subject (interpellated as a subject) for assuming the functions defined by the structure as functions-of-a-*Träger*. These reasons-of-a-subject appear explicitly in its ideological discourse, which is therefore necessarily a discourse that relates to the subject to which it is addressed, and therefore necessarily includes the subject as a signifier of this discourse; that is why the subject must appear in person among the signifiers of ideological discourse. In order for the individual to be constituted as an interpellated subject, it must recognize itself as a subject in ideological discourse, must figure in it: whence a first speculary relation, thanks to which the interpellated subject can see itself in the discourse of interpellation. But ideology is not a commandment (which would still be a form of the 'I don't want to know anything about it'); this recognition is not an act of pure force (there is no such thing as pure force), not a pure and simple injunction, but an enterprise of conviction–persuasion: accordingly, it must *provide its own guarantees* for the subject it interpellates. The centring structure of ideology is a structure of *guarantee*, but in the form of interpellation, that is, in a form such that it contains the subject it interpellates (and 'produces' as an effect) in its discourse. Hence the *duplication of the subject* within the structure of ideology: God, in His various forms. 'I am that I am', the subject *par excellence*, Who provides the subject the guarantee that He is truly a subject, and that He is the subject Whom the Subject is addressing: 'I have shed this particular drop of blood for you'; 'God trieth the hearts and reins' (compare the speculary relations of the same order [between] the transcendental subject/ transcendental logic and the empirical subject/formal logic), and so on.

Ideology is articulated with the economic and political structures in that it enables the '*Träger*'-function to function by transforming it into a *subject*-function.

It would be interesting to examine the case of the *Träger*-function *of ideology*. A reduplication function of ideology exists which enables the *Träger* of the ideological as such to be transformed into a subject, that is, an *ideology of the ideologue*: we should try to establish whether Marx did not take this reduplication for ideology itself[14] (with all the illusions that that would involve), and whether this reduplication is not (at least under certain circumstances) one of the elements of the articulation of scientific discourse with the ideological (when an ideologue 'advances' in the direction of scientific discourse through the 'critique' of ideology, which is then conflated with the critique of the ideology *of* the ideologue, of the *Träger*-function of ideology).

I would propose the following idea: that the *subject-function* which is the characteristic effect of ideological discourse in turn requires, produces or induces[15] ... a characteristic effect, the unconscious-effect or the effect *subject-of-the-unconscious*, that is, the peculiar structure which makes the discourse of the unconscious possible. The latter function makes it possible for the subject-function to be guaranteed amid misrecognition.

4. On the 'unconscious'

To begin with, a comment concerning the term 'unconscious' itself: it will have to be replaced some day. It has its historical justifications: the only way to think the new object discovered by Freud was *to set out from* the categories in which the phenomena it designates had been either thought or ignored until then – that is, to set out from the vocabulary used for consciousness. The term 'unconscious' bears within it the marks of that which had to be jettisoned, that from which a distance, or more distance, had to be taken. The more Freud advanced in his theoretical thinking, the greater this distance grew; yet the 'original label' [*appellation d'origine*] remained. It is certain that the term 'unconscious' is to a large extent neutralized in Freud's work, that it has only negative connotations there, and that these negative connotations are drowned out by the positive connotations.[16] Yet we cannot be sure that this term did not have a deep influence on at least the first topography, and on certain elements of the second as well: on the articulation of the system *ucs* with the system perception–conscious, and so forth. In any event, it has had a particularly deleterious effect on the interpretation of Freud, especially by the philosophers of consciousness (Politzer, Sartre, Merleau-Ponty) who have attempted to appropriate Freud and draw him into their camp – on the philosophers especially, but on certain psychoanalysts too; let us mention only the school of Anna Freud and company, with its stress on reinforcement of the ego (identified with consciousness). One day this term will have to be changed, but it won't be easy. In any case, from now on, we have to be wary of all its resonances, which go well beyond the field of psychoanalysis: consider, for example, the use to which Lévi-Strauss puts the unconscious in ethnology – Lévi-Strauss and the 'structuralists'. We can no more talk about a psychoanalytic *unconscious* than we can, in the strict sense, talk about a social unconscious.

I take up the thread of my discussion again.

Ideological discourse (which is the discourse of everyday life, as Freud so perspicaciously noted, the discourse of 'experience' and the discourse in which the dream is narrated) – ideological discourse induces[17] an ideological subject-effect (as all discourse induces a subject-effect specific to it) inasmuch as ideological discourse interpellates individuals, is addressed to individuals in order to bring them to assume the *Träger* functions required by the various levels of the social structure. We have seen that the form in which ideological discourse interpellates individuals is a form of the kind that allows the interpellated subject to recognize himself[18] and recognize his place in this discourse,[19] even as it offers him the *guarantee* that *he* is truly the one being interpellated, and by *someone*, another Subject, that Name of Names (this is the definition of Man in Feuerbach, which takes up . . . whose definition of God – is it that of St.[20] Dionysius the Areopagite?), who is the centre from which every interpellation emanates, the centre of every guarantee, and, at the same time, the Judge of every response.

The interpellation of ideological discourse is such that it is destined to underwrite *recruitment* via the guarantee it offers the recruits. Recruiting ideological subjects, ideological discourse establishes them as ideological subjects at the same time that it recruits them. Thus, in one and the same act, it produces the subjects that it recruits as subjects, establishing them as subjects. The circularity of the ideological structure and its speculary centredness are a reflection of the duplicity (in both senses of the word) of this act. In ideology, all questions are thus settled *in advance*, in the nature of things, since ideological discourse interpellates–constitutes the subjects of its interpellation by providing them in advance with the answer, all the answers, to the feigned question that its interpellation contains. Hence the questions in it are feigned questions, mere speculary reflections of the answers that pre-exist the questions. Ideological discourse makes sense only as interpellation: it does not ask the question: *Do there exist* subjects to assume the functions of *Träger*? If it did so, it would risk not receiving an answer. It sets out from the already resolved question, that is, from an answer that is not the answer to a question, for the question does not by any means fall under the jurisdiction of ideological discourse. Ideological discourse 'sets out', if I may put it that way, from the premises that subjects exist – or, rather, it is that which makes these subjects exist, consenting to only one operation, which is, it must be said, essential to its economy: guaranteeing this existence for the subjects established by a Subject Who interpellates them and simultaneously summons them before the bar of His judgement. Only a 'subject presumed to exist' is ever interpellated – provided with[21] his identity papers so that he can prove that he is indeed *the* subject who has been interpellated. Ideology functions, in the true sense of the word, the way the police function. It interpellates, and provides the interpellated subject with/asks the interpellated subject for his identity papers, without providing its identity papers in return, for it is *in the Subject-uniform* which is its very identity.

That is why we may say that ideological discourse recruits by itself producing the subjects that it recruits. It solves the problem evoked in the old complaint of military men – what a pity soldiers are recruited only among civilians – because the only soldiers it ever recruits are already in the army. For ideological discourse, there are no civilians, only soldiers, that is, ideological subjects. The structure *requires Träger*: ideological discourse *recruits* them for it by interpellating individuals *as subjects* to assume the functions of *Träger*. The conscription carried out by the structure is blank, abstract, anonymous: the structure does not care to know *who* will assume the functions of *Träger*. Ideological discourse provides the who:[22] it interpellates individuals in the general form of the interpellation of *subjects*. Thus it is personal, 'concrete'; it is not blank, but, as the ideology of 'mass' industry explicitly says, 'personalized'.

I would like to put forward the following proposition: the *interpellation of human individuals as ideological subjects* produces a specific effect in them, the *unconscious-effect*, which enables these human individuals to assume the function of *ideological subjects*.

This thesis does not present itself in the form of a genesis. It is not a matter of demonstrating the *engendering* or *filiation* of the unconscious by the subject-effect of ideological discourse, any more than it is a question of demonstrating the engendering or filiation of the structure of the political by the economic structure, or of the ideological structure by the economic and the political. It is a matter (i) of observing the existence of an unconscious-effect that constitutes an autonomous structure; and (ii) of thinking the articulation of this structure with the structure of the ideological.[23] The type of reflection to which I appeal here is in every respect similar to the one by means of which Marx situates the different instances and thinks their articulation, without concerning himself with the genesis of one instance by the others. It is essential to make this clear in order to avoid straying into psychologism or 'sociologism', whether culturalist or of some other kind; they have nothing but geneses in mind.

We shall say, then, that we observe the existence of a specific instance, that of the unconscious; that the unconscious is 'structured like a language', and thus constitutes a discourse made possible by the existence of a certain number of signifiers of a peculiar kind (which, generally speaking, are not *words*),[24] a discourse which is subject to the general laws of discourse and which, like any discourse, produces or induces a *subject-effect*. We shall say that the discourse of the unconscious produces a 'subject' that is 'ejected' from the discourse of which it is the subject, and features in it by delegation (a signifier *representing* it there, in the Lacanian sense). We shall say that the existence of this discourse of the unconscious, and of the specific subject it induces, is essential to the functioning of the system thanks to which the individual assumes his 'role' of ideological subject interpellated as an ideological subject by ideological discourse.

We shall go no further, at least for the time being. And if we say, as I have just said, that the subject interpellated by ideological discourse 'produces' an effect, the unconscious-effect, this production is to be taken not in the sense of a genesis, but in the sense of a differential articulation. By the same token, if we say – as we may be tempted to, if only to facilitate matters – that the unconscious 'is essential to the functioning of the ideological subject', we do not lapse into functionalism, for functionalism is obviated by the simple observation that the unconscious is 'charged' (not in the sense of a 'mission', but in the sense of overdetermination: is *'overloaded'* [*surchargé*]) with several different functions. The terms 'production' and 'essential to . . .' represent nothing more than first approximations, introduced not in order to solve the problem of the constitution of the unconscious, but in order to think the determinations of its *articulation* with and in a particular reality.

We do indeed observe that the unconscious is articulated with the ideological subject, and, via this subject, with the ideological. This does not mean that the unconscious is articulated with the ideological and the ideological subject *alone*. The effects of the unconscious, or formations of the unconscious, exhibit other articulations with other realities: for example, a somatic symptom exhibits the articulation of the unconscious with the body [*le somatique*], even if this effect can[25] also be introduced into (be articulated with) the ideological. With this proviso – that articulation with the ideological is not the sole articulation of the unconscious – we observe that it exists, and that it plays a major role. (Among the other articulations: look into whether we should not also say that the unconscious is articulated with *other*[26] unconsciouses; this seems to be reflected in the observation which appears constantly in Freud, especially in connection with the cure, but which is also common in 'everyday life': that 'unconsciouses communicate'. But it would have to be determined whether this articulation of one unconscious with another does not pass by way of the effects of the unconscious *in* the ideological.)[27]

The articulation of the unconscious with and in the ideological is manifested in the following phenomenon, the *index* of this articulation. We may say, as long as we distinguish the effects of the unconscious from the mechanisms that produce them – or, rather, *from the* mechanism that produces them (the mechanism of the unconscious as a structure that 'functions') – that the unconscious is a mechanism which 'functions' massively *'on the ideological'* [*à l'idéologique*] (in the sense in which one says that an engine 'runs on petrol'. What does this phrase mean? It designates the *repetition* of the effects of the unconscious in '*situations*' in which the unconscious produces its effects, that is, exists in typical *formations* (symptoms, etc.). These 'situations' are observable and definable, just as the effects of the unconscious in them are observable and definable. The characteristic feature of these 'situations' is that they are intimately bound up with the formations of the unconscious realized in them.[28] In other words, we observe that the unconscious exists in the objective–subjective 'lived experience' (I employ these terms provisionally) and realizes certain of its formations there. What Freud says about the manifestations of the unconscious in the varied course of everyday life holds, strikingly, for the realization of the formations of the neurotic or psychotic unconscious in those 'situations' in which a typical effect of the unconscious, a typical formation (or one mode of the structure of the unconscious), is realized. This is the very principle governing 'repetition': the neurotic always finds a way to 'repeat' the same formations of his unconscious in 'situations' that are themselves repeated.

But what is a 'situation'? It is a formation of the ideological,[29] a singular formation, in which what is 'experienced' is informed by the structure (and specified modes) of the ideological; in which it *is* this very structure in the form of the interpellation received (and it cannot *not* be received). When someone 'tells the story of his life', describes his feelings in a 'situation he has experienced', recounts a dream, and so on, his discourse is informed by ideological discourse, by the 'I' who speaks in the first person and by the subject before whom he speaks, the Judge of the authenticity of his discourse, his analysis, his sincerity, and so forth. It is also informed by ideological signifiers (and their relations, which produce effects of ideological meaning), in the same act. In an 'experienced' situation (even if it is experienced without comment or analysis), ideological discourse always dominates (associating signifiers which, as we have already seen, can be something very different from words: 'feelings', 'impressions',[30] 'ideas', objects, images, open or closed orientations, etc.).

To say that the unconscious produces its formations, or some of them, in concrete 'situations' (of everyday life, family relations, workplace relations, chance relations, etc.) thus literally means that it produces them in[31] formations of ideological discourse, in formations of the ideological. It is in this sense that we can say that the unconscious reveals the principle of its *articulation*[32] with the ideological. It is in this sense that we can say that the unconscious 'functions' on ideology.

This formula may be construed still more precisely. As clinical experience goes to show, not every ideological formation allows the unconscious to 'take hold' [*prise*]; a selection is made among the available 'situations', or these 'situations' are inflected in a certain direction, or even precipitated, so that the unconscious can 'take hold' (in the sense in which one says that mayonnaise 'takes hold' [*prend*]). In other words, the unconscious (a given unconscious) does not function on just any formation of the ideological, but only on certain formations, those so configured that the mechanisms of the unconscious can 'come into play' in them, and the formations of the unconscious can 'take hold' in them. To go back to a metaphor used above: a given engine does not run on just anything, but on petrol if it is a petrol engine, and so on.

So constraints appear which can, on a first approach, be termed 'affinities'; they command the choice or precipitation of the 'situations' in which the formations of a given unconscious can 'take hold'. The articulation of the unconscious with the ideological can thus be described more precisely: it is never general, but always selective–constitutive, subject to constraints defined by the type of unconscious involved (here, the type of neurosis and its variations, the type of psychosis and its variations).[33] All of this can easily be shown to reflect the realities of the psychoanalytic clinic and the experience of the cure.

In very approximate language, it may be suggested that the ideological formations in which the formations of a particular unconscious 'take hold' constitute the 'material'[34] (informed in its turn) in which certain typical formations of this unconscious 'take hold'. Thus it would be by way of these ideological formations *among others* that, in the phenomenon described by Freud, unconsciouses 'communicate'; the situation of the transference would come about in this way as well. This point must obviously be developed, since it calls for careful conceptual definition and refinement: the category of 'material' is patently

insufficient. It has the major disadvantage of occulting the fact –
a very important fact – that the discourse of the unconscious is
produced in and through ideological discourse, the fragment of
ideological discourse in which the discourse of the unconscious
'takes hold', even while *it is absent* from this discourse. Indeed,
ideological discourse serves the discourse of the unconscious in
question as a symptom.[35] In the ideological discourse thus chosen, 'it speaks' [*ça cause*; *ça*, which means 'it or that', also means
'id'; *cause* can also mean 'causes'], that is, utters a discourse that
is different from ideological discourse, a discourse that displays
a crucial particularity: it does not have the same 'subject' as the
'subject' of ideological discourse.[36]

If the foregoing is correct, we may deduce from it the idea
that analysis of the elements comprising the formations of the
unconscious realized in ideological discourse cannot *not* show
that these component elements (or some of them) include not
only fragments of ideological discourse, but also its structure
and basic categories (for example, the centred speculary relation
and the categories of the Subject in the twofold sense of their
relation). Would it not be possible to reformulate the problem of
the status of certain categories that feature in the Freudian
topographies on the basis of this remark? The ego that says 'I' is
obviously closely akin to the 'subject' of ideological discourse;
the 'superego' is closely akin to the Subject who interpellates
every ideological subject in the form of a subject.[37] On the other
hand, the 'id' does not feature in the structure of ideological
discourse, since the id is what is realized there.[38] On the other
hand, the structure of the discourse of the unconscious is entirely
different from the structure of ideological discourse, since unconscious discourse is not centred, and since the 'subject' of the
unconscious does not appear in person in the discourse of the
unconscious, but by 'delegation'. The question we might ask –
although I do so only very cautiously – is whether something of
the structure of ideological discourse is not 'taken up' in the
structure of the discourse of the unconscious, with, however, an
utterly different status hinging, precisely, on the *structure* of the
discourse of the unconscious: this would be, in the form of the
radical absence whose presence in person in the structure of
ideological discourse marks the contrast that distinguishes the
two, Lacan's big Other, which is the true 'subject' [*qui est*

proprement le sujet] of the discourse of the unconscious. The big Other, which speaks in the discourse of the unconscious, would then be, not the *subject* of the discourse of the ideological – God, the Subject, and so on – but the *discourse* of the ideological itself, established as the *subject* of the discourse of the unconscious, and established in the specific form of the subject of the discourse of the unconscious, that is, as an *effect* of this discourse, present in the signifiers of this discourse as absent by representation in a signifier (present–absent by 'delegation').[39]

In all this, there is no question of genesis or the straightforward identification of categories. What seems to be in question is the articulation of one structure with another: and, in this articulation as in all others, the articulation exhibits the peculiar feature of bringing *certain categories of one structure into play in the other*, and *vice versa* (just as, in mechanics, certain parts of the apparatus [*dispositif*] 'overlap' or 'encroach on' the other apparatus).[40] The categories that overlap with the others, and the way they overlap, as well as the significance they take on as a result of the position conferred upon them in the new structure, must be thought with reference to this new structure, not the structure to which they belonged prior to or outside of this articulation. This would make it possible to understand how certain structural elements (or categories) can belong simultaneously to the structure of the discourse of the unconscious and the structure of the discourse of the ideological, and how certain structural relations (for example, centring) can belong simultaneously to the structure of the discourse of the ideological and the discourse of the unconscious – but, in each case, in a different position assigned by the structure with which these structural categories and relations 'overlap' (consider the ego, the superego, the big Other, etc.). Finally, this would allow us to understand *why* Freud was to some extent justified in bringing psychoanalytic concepts (not *all*, but only *some psychoanalytic* concepts; doubtless those, precisely, which 'overlap') to bear on ideological phenomena like religion, or even on certain effects of aesthetic discourse (although he did not reflect on the specific reasons for doing so).

Finally, this would allow us – not to solve, nor doubtless even to *pose*, the 'problem' that is thrown up again and again by most theoreticians of psychoanalysis (a few rare, remarkable exceptions aside): that of the establishment or irruption of the unconscious in the child. We have excluded any and all forms of the problematic of genesis, the other face of the ideology of filiation that dominates this concept. But everything that wears the appearance of a before and an after (the pre-Oedipal stages, the Oedipus complex) can lead us to replace the problem of the genesis of the unconscious with another, seemingly legitimate problem: the problem of irruption, the problem of the conjunction of the different elements that 'take hold' in the child in the form of the unconscious. I do not think that we can state this problem in the form of a problem; we can only *set out the elements* which are present and 'preside' over the conjunction that 'takes hold' in the form of the unconscious. But we have to employ the word 'preside' in the sense of the function exercised by a president – a function which, by definition, is always exercised at a certain distance. A president does not get his hands dirty.

The elements involved exist in the characters of the familial theatre, the familial situation: an ideological 'situation' in which are produced, as constitutive of this 'situation', the effects of the articulation of the mother's and father's unconscious with and in the structure of this ideological situation. Unconsciouses articulated with the ideological, unconsciouses articulated with each other by way of (in) their articulation with the ideological: this is what constitutes the 'situation' that presides over the establishment of the unconscious in the child. That very different forms can present themselves here is quite obvious: different unconsciouses articulated in different ways, different articulations with different sequences of ideological discourse – nothing could be more obvious. That there exists a relation between, on the one hand, the configuration of these articulations, which are articulations *of discourse* and subjects of discourse (the discourses being of different orders: the discourse of the ideological, the discourse of the unconscious; the subjects being of different orders: the subjects of each of these discourses), and, on the other hand, the way the different phases and their articulations are defined – this may be presumed. Showing it and proving it is another matter. The mechanism of the establishment of the unconscious cannot be observed, except in certain of its external effects (child psychology *à la* Spitz), which, as observable effects, can sometimes (only sometimes!) be brought [into relation] with a cause. This cause is, however, itself always a cause-effect – for instance, the behaviour of the mother, her presence–absence; we can never get at the nature of the cause in person. We have no choice but to proceed backwards from the results – from, precisely, the already constituted unconscious and the recognizable elements articulated in the play of this unconscious – bringing these elements into indicative relation with the *elements that are present*, the ones that I have just mentioned. It is unlikely that we will ever be able to go much further: we can analyse the elements at the two ends of the chain, as well as their articulation, with ever greater precision and rigour – the elements that preside over the establishment of the unconscious, and the elements that are combined and ordered in the unconscious once it is established – because all this is open to observation and analysis. I doubt, however, that we will ever be able to penetrate the mechanism by which the unconscious is established, except by dint of a theoretical hypothesis, which escapes observation and whose validity will depend on other theoretical elements.

5. *Once again: the general theory on which the regional theory of the theoretical object of psychoanalysis depends.*

(I shall use the abbreviations GT for 'general theory' and RT for 'regional theory'.)

To the extent that the theoretical object of psychoanalysis is the unconscious, and to the extent that this unconscious has the structure of a *discourse*, the general theory on which the RT of psychoanalysis depends is the GT *of the signifier*. The GT of the signifier should be distinguished from the RT of language [*la langue*]. In the case of language, we are dealing with a theoretical object whose elements are undoubtedly signifiers, but these signifiers are *morphemes*, the first storey of which consists of *phonemes*. Not all signifiers are *morphemes*; hence there exist signifiers whose minimal constitutive elements (the first storey) are something other than *phonemes*. The minimal signifying units of ideological discourse, scientific discourse, aesthetic discourse, or the discourse of the unconscious *can* be *morphemes* (for example, in scientific discourse, although mathematical algorithms are not morphemes; for example, in certain formations of ideological discourse or aesthetic discourse; or again, considered as elements *among others* in one and the same discursive formation – for example, in aesthetic discourse or the discourse of the unconscious), but these signifying units are not always or exclusively morphemes. The theory of language (linguistic theory) is thus an RT of the GT of the signifier, like the theory of the different types of *discourse*. This is very important, for it means that linguistics cannot be (since it is an RT) the GT of the RT of psychoanalysis.

To the extent that the theoretical object of psychoanalysis is a specific discourse possessing its own signifiers and structure (with a specific subject-effect), the specificity of analytic discourse does not come under the GT of the signifier alone. It comes under the GT that allows us to think the existence and articulation of the *different types of discourse*. (The specificity of each of these discourses can be conceived only on the basis of, and with regard to, the type of differential articulation that links each form of discourse to the others.) This articulation, the theory of this differential articulation, depends on the GT that enables us to think the place of the different discourses in their articulation: the GT of *historical materialism*. To which I should perhaps add that the GT of dialectical materialism also comes into play in the theoretical conditions required to think the articulation of certain discourses with others (for example, the articulation of scientific with ideological discourse) and, of course, articulation as such between discourses. But what is in question here is a GT of another kind, which we shall leave in abeyance for the moment.

Thus it would *seem* that we are dealing with a special case here. The GT on which the RT of the psychoanalytic object depends would be a specified form of combination of two GTs: the GT of the signifier and the GT of historical materialism, *with the second determining the first*, or, very precisely, with the second *intervening* in the first, that is, being articulated with the first (in the sense I have indicated: by providing the first with '*elements*', categories and structural relations that *overlap* with the first) in such a way as to make it possible to *characterize* the discourse of the unconscious as a discourse of the *unconscious*, which can be conceived as such (as being *of* the unconscious) only because of its articulation with ideological discourse, the concept of which comes under the GT of historical materialism.

Naturally, this case will seem 'special' to us if we cling to an idea of the GT mired in the Aristotelian categories of inclusion and subsumption. On this conception of 'generality', which it seems to us absolutely necessary to reject, the GT maintains relations of extension with its RTs (since every RT is *included* in *its* GT, one GT is enough to account for an RT). On this conception, an RT cannot depend on *two GTs;* it can depend on just one. There is a lingering echo of this conception, perhaps, in what one suspects is Lacan's temptation (and that of some of his disciples) to take linguistics (regarded as the GT of the signifier) for the GT of the RT of psychoanalysis. One would have to ask whether the principle of differential articulation does not also apply between GTs, *at least in certain cases* (there would be very many such cases in the sector known as the Human Sciences), and whether the case that seemed 'special' to us only a moment ago is not in fact quite common. In other words, if we do not think the possibility of an articulation between GTs, we will remain at the level of the *parallelism of the attributes* and of the temptation that constantly accompanies it, the *conflation* of the attributes. The parallelism of the attributes is tempered and corrected in Spinoza by the concept of substance: the different attributes are attributes *of one and the same substance*. It is the concept of *substance* which plays the role of the concept of the articulation of the attributes (it plays other roles, too, but that is one of them). The *distinction* between attributes is possible only on condition that they are articulated. Let us revert to our own terminology: the distinction between the GTs (which are our attributes) is possible only on condition that they are *differentially articulated*. We observe one instance of the existence of this differential articulation between the signifier-attribute and the history-attribute (that is, between the GT of the signifier and the GT of historical materialism) in the fact that the RT of the psychoanalytic object has as its GT a specified articulation of the GT of historical materialism with the GT of the signifier. Presumably there exist other instances where an articulation of the same kind between different GTs is required to account for an RT. Thus the case of the psychoanalytic RT is not a theoretical scandal or an exception: it appears that it is not an isolated instance.

I do not think I can take these considerations any further for the moment. But we can at least test our hypothesis about the nature of the GT of the RT of psychoanalysis with respect to *its possible effects*, some of which can be confronted with real objects.

First and foremost, this thesis would allow us to assign the object of the psychoanalytic RT its place in the objective field of scientificity in its current state. It would no longer be an isolated object, and the concepts used to think this object would no longer be isolated concepts – an isolation that tends to create, quite apart from the reasons for resisting psychoanalysis already noted by Freud (reasons that are articulated both with the discourse of the unconscious *and* with currently existing ideological discourse), the effect of an inexplicable strangeness that all those wishing to deny psychoanalysis any claim to scientificity hold against it, consigning analysis to the realm of magic or rejecting it as pure and simple imposture. The claims that the object of the RT of psychoanalysis has to scientificity would, this time, be manifest, because they would have been stated and substantiated, demonstrated by way of their theoretical relations with the objects of the neighbouring RTs, and also their relations with the GT on which they depend.

This thesis would justify the *core* of Lacan's theoretical enterprise: the idea that we have to look to the RT of linguistics for that which we require to explain what is at stake in the RT of psychoanalysis. But it would provide a way of avoiding what is still, perhaps, a temptation in Lacan's enterprise: either to take the RT of linguistics for the GT of the signifier, or to take the RT of psychoanalysis, as rectified by the RT of linguistics, for the GT of the signifier. The GT of the signifier is clearly present in the RTs of both linguistics and psychoanalysis, but on the same basis in each case, not in person, as a GT properly so called. What Lacan has given us is very important for the elaboration of the GT of the signifier, inasmuch as he was *the first to mobilize* a 'general theory' effect (GT-effect) when he saw the need to compare/rectify the RT of psychoanalysis with the RT of linguistics (and vice versa); but the fact remains that he has not clearly distinguished the GT from the effects of the mutual rectification of these two RTs. A GT-effect is not the GT in person, especially if this GT-effect is taken to be an effect of the RT, and especially when this RT is unjustifiably promoted to the rank of a GT. What Lacan has given us requires both that we dispel the ambiguities that continue to haunt his enterprise and that we constitute the GT, some of whose decisive, pertinent GT-effects he helps us to grasp.

This thesis would give us a better understanding of certain aspects of Freud's work that are disconcerting, and are turned to various apologetic ends, or dismissed out of hand: let us say, broadly, the 'cultural' texts (*Totem and Taboo*, 'The Future of an Illusion', *Group Psychology and the Analysis of the Ego, Leonardo da Vinci*, etc.; *Moses and Monotheism*, etc.). The articulation of the GT of the signifier and the GT of historical materialism would allow us to account for the legitimacy of Freud's undertaking, but also to criticize his theoretical *silences*, on which ideological discourses have been superimposed.

This thesis would allow us (I return to Lacan) to understand Lacan's predilection for the *Traumdeutung*, the *Witz*, and so on. That is, his predilection for those texts in which Freud alludes to the forms of the discourse of the unconscious inscribed in the forms of ideological discourse whose signifiers are morphemes (and the elements that constitute their first storey: phonemes). That Lacan brackets the fact that these forms of discourse are *ideological* (he can do so because the signifiers of the *Witz* are the same as those of an ideological discourse whose signifiers are, *in this case*, the signifiers of language) tends to create a kind of malaise, which is only intensified by the force of the reasons he invokes: why does he say so little about other texts by Freud, and so little about certain categories (such as the Superego)?

Finally, this thesis would allow us to arrive at a better conception of the relation between the real object of psychoanalytic practice (the cure) and the theoretical object of the psychoanalytic RT, as a particular relation among many other *possible* relations, these possible relations being defined by the investigation of the theoretical object of psychoanalysis (the discourse and subject of the unconscious). In this way we would know better what we know already: that the RT of psychoanalysis does not concern the cure alone, but a whole series of real objects, inasmuch as it is the theory of a theoretical, not a real object. This theoretical distance, which is what makes theory so fruitful, would be increased still further if we brought the RT into relation with the GT: this would not only allow us to understand the possibility of (and the conditions for) using certain concepts employed in the RT *outside* the cure and the effects observable in the psychoanalytic relation (for example, in the analysis of art or of such-and-such an ideology, as carried out by Freud), but would also allow us to shed light – something that is much more paradoxical, yet normal – on certain phenomena *observable in the cure itself*, phenomena that are the source of difficulties, or are quite simply impenetrable. What this appeal to the GT would also illuminate in the phenomena of the cure itself are *the elements* which, originating in ideological discourse, overlap with the discourse of the unconscious, the elements into which the discourse of the unconscious has to 'slip' (under which it has to 'slip') if it is to be realized: for example, the phenomenon of the transference, which cannot be understood if one neglects the fact that what is in question in it is a repetition of the discourse of the unconscious *in the structure of the discourse of the ideological*; for example, categories such as those of the superego or certain categories of the first topography such as the preconscious and conscious, and so forth.

Finally, this thesis would perhaps allow certain disciplines of the human sciences to recognize what they have so far stubbornly denied: that which ties them to the theoretical object addressed by psychoanalysis. Since this *tie* would no longer proceed *directly* by way of the RT of psychoanalysis but, rather, by way of the GT on which the RT of psychoanalysis depends, the resulting *rapprochement* would, instead of seeming to 'mutilate' the object or objects of the so-called Human Sciences, actually open their domain to two GTs combined in such a way as to serve as the GT of the RT of psychoanalysis: the GT of the signifier and the GT of historical materialism. Two kinds of effects would result from this as from any GT: first, effects of the *rectification* of concepts; second, effects of the *reclassification* of the RTs themselves (the drawing of new frontiers, a new status and new definition of the object of such-and-such an RT, even the elimination of one or another RT or the addition of a new RT), which would doubtless finally allow us to confer *theoretical* status on certain 'disciplines' that continue to wander about in the realm of ideological empiricism, or, at least, to confer such status on their subject matter – for example, on 'what is going on' in psychology or social psychology, and so forth.

This would be a way of confirming that the effect of the identification and constitution of the GT of psychoanalysis does not interest psychoanalysis *alone* but, rather, all the disciplines which, for one reason or another depend – as a result of overlapping and articulation, partially or not – on the GTs combined in the combination-GT of psychoanalysis. A little light would thus be shed on most of the disciplines of the Sciences qualified as 'Human'. In its turn, the philosophy that 'works' in the GTs – that is, dialectical materialism – would, without any doubt, derive from this the means to emerge and expand.

Note 2

The unconscious as a specific *discourse*.

(1) *The objection runs*: if we conceive of the unconscious as Lacan's formulation does, as 'structured like a language'; if we talk about the 'discourse of the unconscious'; in short, if we treat the unconscious as if it were a discourse, even if this discourse is said to be 'specific', do we not lose something that is encountered in the everyday practice of psychoanalysis, something that makes for the *irreducibility* of the unconscious and prevents us, precisely, from *reducing* it to the mode of a mere discourse: namely, the fact that what is in question is not a 'discourse' at all but, rather, drives, the libido, and the death instinct?

This *objection* occurs naturally to practitioners of psychoanalysis, who do not usually 'recognize' the object of their day-to-day practice in the theoretical designation of it as a 'discourse'. But since Freud's texts themselves oblige them to admit that there are indeed mechanisms in the unconscious that make it something like a discourse, and since Lacan has returned to these texts and systematically commented on them, their *objection* takes the following form:

- doubtless one can say that the unconscious is 'structured like a language', *but*, in stating this property of the unconscious, one does not state what is specific to the unconscious, one only states the laws of a mechanism, formal laws that leave out the very nature of *what* functions in accordance with these laws. What is more, one *reduces* the unconscious to these formal laws: one loses sight of what makes it, precisely, the *unconscious*: namely, the fact that it

is not just a discourse, and that that which 'speaks' in it and is therefore present in these formal laws is something *other* than these laws – the libido and the drives;
- hence one has to make distinctions. One has to distinguish, so the argument goes, the formal laws (which are essentially 'linguistic') from the *content*, the object of these laws. Thus we would have, on the one hand, the unconscious as *discourse* (that is, that which comes under these formal laws) and *something else* (the drives) which is manifested, which is expressed, which 'speaks' in the play of these laws, that is, in this discourse.

(2) At the heart of this objection, the arguments for which should not be taken lightly (for the objection rests on very powerful 'obvious facts' generated by analytic practice), we find the idea that what is designated by the concept of *discourse* applied to the unconscious cannot account for the specific *reality* of the unconscious. We also find the idea that conceiving of the unconscious as a discourse is a *reductive* operation. At the same time, we find a certain 'model' of intelligibility – deployed, doubtless, in the form of a *critical* argument – which suggests a distinction between the formal laws governing an object, on the one hand, and the essence of that object on the other.

(3) Confronted with these objections and the theoretical premisses on which they are based, we can proceed in various ways. I propose to take a short cut by throwing out a few random remarks about a different object, a different *discourse*. Take *Le Rouge et le Noir*. It is an aesthetic discourse. It comprises a series of statements presented in a certain order. Its elements are words, arranged in a complex order and obeying specific *constraints* that make this discourse an *aesthetic* discourse (not a scientific or an ideological discourse).

I maintain that this discourse quite simply *is* the existence of Julien and his 'passion'. We do not have the discourse of *Le Rouge* on the one hand and, on the other, Julien and his passion. Julien's passion, with all its emotional intensity (easily the equal of the intensity of the drives, for what is it if not those very drives, inscribed in a 'discourse' presented by the aesthetic discourse), does not lie behind or even between the lines of this discourse; it is not something other than this discourse, something that finds expression in its words, or slips in between them: it is nothing *but* this discourse itself, it is indiscernible from it. The *constraints* defining this *discourse* are the very existence of this 'passion'.

I suggest that we bring these remarks to bear on the proposition that designates the unconscious as a specific *discourse*.

In this case, the *constraints* characteristic of unconscious discourse, far from being formal laws external to *that which* functions when they operate, are, rather, the very forms of existence of *that which* exists in the form of unconscious discourse. There is no 'on the hither side of' and 'on the far side of' here. The *nature of the constraints* which define or constitute the discourse of the unconscious must be such that this discourse is *the very existence* of what the analyst encounters in his practice: the libido, the death instinct, the drives.

These constraints bear on

(a) the nature of the elements combined in the utterances of unconscious discourse;
(b) the specific syntax of this discourse (what may be called – should we verify this? – its specific structure, which is not the same as that of the other types of discourse: scientific, ideological or aesthetic).

(this is a way of saying that each type of discourse is defined by a *system of specific constraints*. It is the specific constraints which define the discourse. This level of the 'constraints' defining the different discourses should be distinguished from a more formal level, that of the laws of 'language' [*langage*], which come under the general theory of the signifier. One cannot *deduce* the specific constraints defining the different types of discourse from the general laws of the Signifier, a theory of which does not yet exist; the form of it that linguistics currently provides is the closest thing we have to such a theory.)

To come back to unconscious discourse, and to make it clear that the constraints defining unconscious discourse are not formal laws external to the specific object of psychoanalysis, the libido, we can say something like the following, without risk of serious error:

The constraints defining scientific discourse are such that it constitutes a 'machine' (or a mechanism) that 'functions' in such a way as to produce the *knowledge-effect*.

The constraints defining ideological discourse are such that it functions by producing another effect: the *recognition-misrecognition* effect.

And so on.

Similarly, the constraints defining the unconscious/unconscious discourse are such that it functions by producing *the libido-effect*.

These propositions, in order to be intelligible, presuppose that *the effect* is not *external* to the mechanism that 'produces' it. The point is not to repeat, in inverted form, what we have just criticized; the idea of the externality of the libido as a 'cause' that finds expression in formal mechanisms. The libido-effect is no more external to the unconscious/to unconscious discourse than the libido (as cause) is external and anterior to it. The effect is nothing other than the discourse itself. If I affirm that unconscious discourse 'produces the libido-effect', I do so *in order to show* that the libido is so far from being external, anterior or transcendent to the forms of 'its' discourse that we can conceive of it as the specific *effect* of that discourse!

On the one hand, the critique of the externality, anteriority and transcendence of the libido *vis-à-vis* the 'formal laws' that govern the functioning of the unconscious 'structured like a language' – and, on the other, the presentation of the libido as the libido-effect of a mechanism and its functioning – are simply two methods of theoretical/polemical exposition and exhibition which both aim to make people *admit* that we can conceive of the unconscious in terms of the category *discourse* without losing anything of that which constitutes the *specificity of this discourse*: namely, that it is unconscious discourse/the discourse of the unconscious, hence the discourse of the object that cannot 'function' without the libido, the death instinct, and the drive being *always and everywhere* in question in it.

If it is granted that we can apply the category of *discourse*, *defined as we have just tried to define it*, to the unconscious, then:

(1) We no longer risk 'losing the libido' in speaking of the unconscious as a discourse; we no longer risk relapsing into formalism of a linguistic type (the possibility of such formalism is sustained by the fact that linguistics alone is incapable of

producing a theory of the *different* discourses, although this inability is masked by its *claim* to provide that theory, on the pretext that it can provide a theory *of* discourse – but no theory *of* discourse can stand in for a theory of discourses, can replace it or deduce it from itself). What really does expose us to the risk of 'losing the libido' is a mistaken conception of the object, and thus of the claims of linguistics. If we interpret the phrase 'the unconscious is structured like a language' as one which presupposes *the deductive application* of linguistics to an object called the unconscious, then we are indeed dealing with a formulation that is *reductive* of its specific object, and with the loss of the libido. But if, in interpreting the same phrase, we bear in mind that that which defines the specific discourse known as the unconscious is a *definite* system of constraints (for which no other can be substituted) which *is* the existence of the libido itself (*or* implies the libido-effect, just as, in the example given above, Stendhal's novel *is* Julien's passion in person), then we do not 'lose the libido', the libido does not remain outside, external, different, transcendent – and, in that case, every enrichment of the libido, that is, every elaboration of the concept of the libido, can result only from theoretical work on the specific forms of the specific constraints that constitute unconscious discourse.

(2) We are in a position to attempt to think *the differential articulation* of unconscious discourse with its closest 'neighbour', the different type of discourse with which it is articulated: namely, *ideological* discourse. This second operation is essential to the first. It is closely tied in with the first, for the following theoretical reason.

All definition is differential; one can define an object A only through its difference from an object B. This object B, however, cannot be an arbitrary object with respect to object A. It must be A's other, A's 'neighbour'; to be very precise, the object *par excellence* with which it is articulated, the object whose articulation with A commands our understanding of A's articulations with other objects, C, D, and so on.

Rightly identifying the object B of an object A is a theoretical question of great importance, if by B we mean the object with which A must be articulated in order to exist as A; in other words, if by B we mean the object whose difference from A enables us to arrive at the definition of A.

It is this fundamental question that I propose to answer by identifying object B, so conceived, as *ideological* discourse – when I say that unconscious discourse is articulated with ideological discourse. Naturally it is articulated with *other* discourses as well – with all the other discourses, scientific discourse and aesthetic discourse. But the articulation of unconscious discourse with scientific and aesthetic discourse is not *the main articulation*, for these articulations do not enable us to give a differential definition of unconscious discourse. *The main articulation* of unconscious discourse (what we might call its *essential* articulation) is its articulation with ideological discourse, effected quite differently than in the form of verbal 'representations'.

If this proposition is granted, it becomes possible to understand the articulation of unconscious discourse with scientific discourse (the relation of Marx's or Cauchy's, etc., unconscious to their scientific work) or aesthetic discourse (Leonardo da Vinci . . .) as *secondary* articulations, that is, articulations that pass by way of the articulation of unconscious discourse with this or that sequence of *ideological* discourse. This enables us to think what Freud was trying to do in his discussions of the great works of art (with regard to their authors), and also to understand why it was literary examples and themes that so profoundly 'affected' him personally (Oedipus).

As for the relationship of articulation – not, this time, between a given author's unconscious and his work but between, on the one hand, a given Freudian concept whose object is the unconscious and, on the other, a given field of the ideological (morality, the ideological phenomena described in connection with mass psychology, the army, the Church, etc.) – this relationship would become intelligible in principle if we attributed a precise content to the articulation of unconscious discourse with ideological discourse (in the way I have very rapidly indicated, using the concept of *overlapping* or *encroachment*, in my Note 'On Psychoanalysis').

Note 3

The point on which I currently need enlightenment is the following:

(1) I (we) have come to the conclusion that it is absolutely essential to construct a theory of discourses in order to be able to provide a differential definition of the specific discourses known as

- scientific discourse
- aesthetic discourse
- ideological discourse
- unconscious discourse

(for the moment, I leave aside philosophical discourse, which should doubtless be distinguished from scientific discourse as such).

Our thinking about a number of theoretical problems has revealed the need for a theory of discourses:

(a) The problem of the specific *effects* of the different discourses, a problem first encountered in connection with the knowledge-effect (see the last part of the preface to *Reading Capital*, where there is a discussion of scientific discourse as productive of the knowledge-effect); then in connection with other effects, brought out, for example, by Badiou in connection with the fictional [*romanesque*] subjectivity-effect, and again in connection with the effect of ideological discourse (the effect of recognition–misrecognition). The identification of specific *effects* has revealed the existence of specific discourses as their condition.

(b) The problem of the 'nature' of the unconscious, which has appeared as a consequence of Lacan's work: the idea that the unconscious is 'structured like a language' necessarily leads to a conception of the unconscious as a specific *discourse*.

(c) The problem of the *articulation* between the different levels: between the scientific and ideological, the aesthetic and the ideological, and, finally (I have been working on this for several months), the articulation between the unconscious and the ideological. This articulation appears, in the light of initial research and reflection, to be an articulation between *discourses*.

(2) It then appeared that each of the discourses thus identified was endowed with a specific structure, different from that of the others.

It would seem that we can conceive of this difference in structure as a twofold difference: as a difference in the *elements* constituting the various discourses, and as a difference in the *constraints* governing the relationships in which these elements stand to one another.

As far as the difference between the *elements* is concerned, it seems that a path has already been cleared for an investigation, and that this investigation is possible.

We can say, for example, that the elements of scientific discourse are *concepts*. At the other extreme, we can say that the elements of unconscious discourse are *primal fantasies*. It is harder to designate the elements of *ideological* discourse with precision (I, at least, cannot), because we find different levels in it and also because, depending on the level, the elements are (at the most abstract levels) representations, or even concepts, and, at other levels, gestures, modes of behaviour, or, again, prohibitions and permissions, or, yet again, elements borrowed from other discourse, and so on. Similarly, the elements of aesthetic discourse seem to vary with the regions of the aesthetic involved. Nevertheless, despite the difficulties in each case, the principle that one should investigate the differential nature of the *elements* seems to be correct.

I find things more difficult when it comes to what I call the *constraints*.

I don't know exactly what the concept of *constraints* designates in the world of linguistics. Can someone tell me, and also let me know whether the linguistic use of the term is relevant to the research project we are pursuing?

With the term constraints, I would like to designate a number of structural laws characteristic of each of the discourses. For example, in the Note I entitled 'On Psychoanalysis', I tried to indicate, in connection with the 'subject', that it is possible to define the structure characteristic of each of the discourses (and therefore its constraints as well?) on the basis of the index provided by the place and role of the *subject* in each of them. Thus I tried to show that the subject of science is 'excluded in person' from scientific discourse, that the subject of aesthetic discourse is present in it 'through the mediation of others', and that the subject of unconscious discourse is absent from it by 'delegation' (Lacan). The 'place' of the subject in each discourse was thus defined with reference to the structure of each of the discourses. For example, ideological discourse is centred and speculary. For example, scientific discourse has no centre. For example, aesthetic discourse possesses a network of cross-references between ambiguous centres. For example, the discourse of the unconscious possesses a structure of lack, and so forth.

Since writing that note, I have come round to thinking that *the notion of subject cannot be employed unequivocally*, not even as an index for each of the discourses. Increasingly, the notion of subject seems to me to pertain to *ideological* discourse alone, of which it is constitutive. I don't believe that one can talk about a 'subject of Science' or a 'subject of the unconscious' without playing on words and opening the door to serious theoretical ambiguities. For example, the way Lacan talks about the subject of science in his lecture (*Cahiers pour l'Analyse*),[41] evoking Cauchy's tragic experiences, and so on, seems to me highly questionable. I think he takes the articulation of Cauchy's unconscious discourse with his scientific practice for the 'subject of science'.

That a scientist's unconscious discourse always comes into play (and that this is always a wrenching experience) when he establishes a new form of scientific discourse in a given discipline (discoveries) is one thing; it is a fact that no scientist can *pronounce* and then wrestle with a given scientific discourse without the discourse of his unconscious coming into play in his enunciation. But it is only at the price of an unwarranted conflation of two different things that one can evoke the discourse of science in a discussion of this *articulation* of the unconscious discourse of X with the enunciation of a scientific discourse. There is no such thing as a *subject* of science as far as scientific discourse, scientific statements, are concerned – which, precisely, are sustained by the fact that they can do without any kind of subject – any more than there are individuals 'who make history', in the ideological sense of that proposition. Similarly, it seems to me unwarranted to talk about the 'subject of the unconscious' in connection with the *Ich–Spaltung*. There is no *divided* or *split* subject, but something else entirely; alongside the

Ich, there is a *Spaltung*, that is, literally, an *abyss*, a precipice, an absence, a lack. This abyss is not a subject, but that which opens up *alongside a subject*, alongside the *Ich*, which is well and truly a subject (and falls within the province of the *ideological*; Freud, it seems to me, gives us the necessary grounds for thinking this on a number of different occasions). This *Spaltung* is the type of specific differential relation or articulation that binds (in the form of an abyss, a lack) unconscious discourse to the element or, rather, structural category of ideological discourse called the *Ich*. In a word, Lacan would appear to *establish the abyss or lack as a subject*, by way of the concept of the division of the subject. There is no 'subject of the unconscious', although the unconscious can exist only thanks to this abyssal relation with an *Ich* (the subject of the ideological). The lack of the subject cannot be called a subject, although the (ideological) subject is implied or reflected in Freud's second topography, in an original way, *through* this lack, which is not a subject, but something *altogether different*. That the shadow cast by the ideological should make itself felt even in the instances of the topography is one thing; but it doesn't authorize us to think this 'presence' of the ideological in the topography by means of *ideological concepts* such as the concept of the subject. (The same remark applies, in my opinion, to Lacan's way of using the *ideological* concept of *truth* in expressions invoking 'the truth as cause'.)

I am, then, very strongly inclined to revise what I have written about the *subject* of the different discourses in the light of this essential rectification. However, the approach I tried to take above still seems valid to me. The point is to define not only the elements characteristic of each discourse, but also the structure and the constraints (?) characteristic of each discourse. What I have in mind here is the fact that the elements are not only different in each discourse, but are also not arranged-ordered in the same way in each discourse. As a result of this arrangement-ordering, the categories (?) constitutive of each discourse (for example, the category of the subject in the case of ideological discourse) are not the same categories, and are not arranged in the same way. Thus we can say that ideological discourse mobilizes categories of its own (it is speculary with internal duplication, centred, and closed) – while scientific discourse mobilizes others, in a very different arrangement (non-speculary, without duplication, open-ended, etc.; all these structural concepts must be defined and made more precise).

I am constantly wondering which notions (borrowed from linguistics or any other discipline) should be brought to bear to account for these facts. There is, it seems, not only the difference between the elements (which, in principle, is not problematic), but also what I have just called the different *categories*, which can themselves be understood only in relation to their *arrangement*-ordering, or structure. Can we use the concept of *constraints* to designate this structure? Is the concept of category appropriate here? Is the distinction between the categories and the structure accurate and pertinent?

(3) If these questions can be clarified, one last question will remain.

Specific elements + categories + arrangements (constraints?) do indeed define the different discourses as *different*, and therefore irreducible. But the fact remains that they are all *discourses*, which we can define as discourses by virtue of their difference from *practices*.

The structure of a discourse is not that of a practice. Not only because a discourse produces only *effects* of, let us say, meaning, whereas practices produce *real* modifications–transformations in existing objects, and, at the limit, new real *objects* (economic practice, political practice, theoretical practice, etc.). This does not mean that the discourses cannot have effects [*exercer d'efficace*] on real objects, but they do so only by virtue of their insertion–articulation into the practices in question, which then make use of them as instruments in the 'labour process' of these practices. There is an entire field waiting to be explored here; we already have certain theoretical elements for the purpose at our disposal (consider what Balibar says about intervention in a practice, about the intervention of science in economic or political practice).

Once this essential difference between *discourse* and *practice* has been duly noted and defined, we find ourselves *ipso facto* faced with the task of defining what constitutes discourses as *discourses*, of defining what gives rise to the fact that they are all, their differences notwithstanding, *discourses*.

We can say some important things on this point. First, that these discourses, in order to exist as discourses, have to contain a 'twofold articulation'; their *elements* have to exist 'on two storeys' – a twofold articulation comparable to that which the linguists have shown to exist in language (phonemes–morphemes). In scientific discourse, for example, the first articulation is constituted by *words*; the second (I believe it is the other way round in Martinet's terminology) by *concepts*. In unconscious discourse, for example, the first articulation (or first storey) may be constituted by a whole series of units such as phonemes, words, images, sounds, smells, and so on; the second by fantasies, and so forth. We should be able to make this kind of inventory everywhere in order to bring out the fact that the existence of this *two-storey structure* is constitutive of all discourse as *discourse*.

In addition, we should be able to bring out the existence of a whole series of laws of combination, substitution, elision, subreption, accumulation, and so on – in short, what linguistics has thrown into relief and Lacan has used for his own purposes.

Can one distinguish these laws with precision, and if there are different types of laws, can one distinguish and define those different types and levels of laws? Certainly the linguists have already done some work on this question. Can someone help me to sum it up and spell out its implications in a way that is relevant to what we are looking for? (The laws of syntax, for example: at what level do they operate with respect to the laws of metonymy and metaphor? Where do we put tropes and stylistic devices? Information, please.)

If this question could be clarified, it would, it seems to me, throw up another, which is crucial. Precisely where, with respect to our attempt to found a theory of discourses, should we situate the discoveries and concepts of *linguistics*? Precisely where should we situate the laws whose existence has been demonstrated by linguistics with respect to our project to found a theory of discourses implying a theory *of* discourse?

Since *the* discourses with which we are concerned are not restricted to the forms of discourse that linguistics studies, and since we are studying discourses whose elements are not – or are not all, or are not always – *linguistic* elements, should we not consider linguistics to be a *regional* discipline that can serve as an epistemological 'guide', but only as a guide, for a general theory that is still lacking, and could be the *General Theory* of

Discourse (or of the signifier? but I am beginning to be suspicious of this term, which is too deeply involved in the idealism of the connotations of Saussure's signifier–signified). While the existence of linguistics is the index and the call for a General Theory of Discourse, it cannot, rigorously speaking, replace such a theory. What, then, are its own current *limits*, those that would allow us to think it as a regional theory, if that is how it should be thought? (But should it be thought that way, as I believe it should?)

The hypothesis I am suggesting would make it possible to assign, with respect to the specific laws defining each particular discourse (the discourses listed above), a status to the *general laws governing any discourse*, the laws that come into play in any discourse, but whose play or exercise is *constrained* by the *laws governing the constraints* characteristic of each particular type of discourse (those to which I have essayed an approach in my discussion of the specificity, for each discourse, of the system elements + categories + structures).

We would then have to establish an adequate *terminology*, which would doubtless no longer be quite the same as that used in linguistics – not only because our object goes beyond the limits of linguistics by virtue of the distinction we are drawing between the different discourses, but also by virtue of the fact that linguistics would not be the General Theory of Discourse it claims to be (or that one rather too hastily claims it is), even if, in the present conjuncture, linguistics alone can 'guide' us in going beyond linguistics in the two directions indicated. Terminological modifications would then become indispensable.

For example, the opposition *language/speech* [*langue/parole*] cannot be considered pertinent. *Speech* raises a very different problem, secondary with regard to the problem preceding it: that of the *discourses*. For a speech act [*une parole*] occurs only *in* a *discourse*.

The opposition language [*langue*]/discourse is theoretically pertinent, but it would no longer have the same status as the opposition *language/speech*; it may well be the concept of *a language* [*langue*] that will prove inadequate in our opposition, since we are assigning the concept of discourse a much broader meaning than the one authorized by linguistics in its current state. Perhaps the concept of *language* [*langage*] would become pertinent again: *language* would designate the structure of any discourse, and thus play vis-à-vis discourse (in the broad sense in which we use the term) the same role as the concept of *a language* [*le concept de langue*] played vis-à-vis 'linguistic' discourse in the narrow Saussurean sense (what Saussure has in mind when he pronounces the concept *speech*).

So many questions.

Are they relevant, and posed in the right way?

How can one answer them in the present state of affairs?

12 October 1966

Notes

1. As were Althusser's 'Letters to D.'. See Olivier Corpet and François Matheron, Introduction to 'Letters to D.', *WP* 33–4.
2. See 'Letters to D.', *WP* 70.
3. *LF* 711–12, 13 September 1966.
4. Ibid., p. 712.
5. 'Every' is underlined; a marginal note reads '? verify this'.
6. The two typed versions of the text read 'general', but the correct reading is undoubtedly 'regional'.
7. Handwritten addendum on the back of the preceding page: ' "reassigned" to the general theory or, rather, "temporarily reassigned" to the general theory (in the sense in which a teacher at a *lycée* is "temporarily reassigned" to a university post).'
8. 'Correct' [*juste*] is crossed out; the handwritten correction reads 'a certain concept'.
9. *La Psychanalyse*, no. 3: Psychanalyse et Sciences humaines, 1957.
10. Handwritten addendum in the margin: 'and its relation to regional theories'.
11. Handwritten addendum in the margin: 'or formations'.
12. Handwritten addendum in the text: 'as well'.
13. Handwritten addendum on a slip of paper attached to this page: 'The function of language [*langue*] is not at the same level = since there is no function of language! but only of the discourse for which it provides either signifiers or constitutive (first-storey) *elements* (segments) *of signifiers*. Thus there are no *functions* of language, in this sense, for language *does not exist*: only discourse*s* exist.'
14. Handwritten addendum in the margin: 'in *The German Ideology*'.
15. Handwritten addendum in the margin: 'cf. below (to be corrected)'.
16. The French is garbled, but the meaning is clear enough: the negative connotations of the word 'unconscious' in the sense 'not-conscious' are

outweighed by the positive connotations of the concept of the 'unconscious' in Freud. See 'On Lévi-Strauss', p. 26 above; *PSH* 76 [*Trans.*].
17. Handwritten addendum in the margin: 'watch out!'
18. Handwritten addendum in the margin: 'as a *selbst*'.
19. Handwritten addendum in the margin: 'as *his*'.
20. *Sic.*
21. Handwritten addendum in the margin: 'asked for', followed by a handwritten addendum on the back of the previous page: 'It is the Prefecture of Police which *provides* the individuals whom policemen *interpellate* with the identity papers that these policemen request (demand) that one *show*.'
22. Handwritten addendum on the back of the previous page: 'not the *who*, for this conscription is in any case obeyed – it provides the *subject-who*s (that is, *who*s to whom it offers the *guarantee* that they are the *subjects* of the interpellation to assume the functions of *Träger*)'.
23. Handwritten addendum in the margin: 'Yes! (*It's the same thing.*)'
24. Handwritten addendum in the margin: 'morphemes or even words'.
25. Handwritten addendum in the margin: '(or *must* simultaneously, in order to exist, pass by way of an articulation by *the ideological? the ideology of the body*)'.
26. Handwritten addendum in the margin: 'no'.
27. Handwritten addendum in the margin: 'yes'.
28. Handwritten addendum on the back of the previous page: 'the (some) formations of the unconscious are thus *inscribed in* (combined) modes of *ideological formations*'.
29. Handwritten addendum in the margin: 'a *mode* of an ideological formation'.
30. Handwritten addendum in the margin: 'gestures, minimal patterns of behaviour, etc.'.
31. Handwritten addendum in the margin: 'modes of'.
32. Handwritten addendum on the back of the same sheet: 'thus a discourse exists in the signifiers of another discourse – better, *in another discourse* – it 'avails itself' of the *signifiers* and of *certain structural relations* of the other discourse in order to exist *in* that other discourse [scientific discourse also makes use of the signifiers of *other* discourses, ideological, above all, but aesthetic as well] [there is no *pure* discourse: all of them *speak in one another* – communication of the genres – or, rather, *encroachment* of the genres on each other. That is what *articulation* is].' In the margin next to this handwritten addendum, the second of the two sentences that Althusser puts in brackets is preceded by an arrow that seems to point to the lines annotated here.
33. Handwritten addendum in the margin: 'mode'.
34. An arrow in the margin points towards the handwritten addendum reproduced in note 32 above.
35. Handwritten addendum in the margin: '? no'.
36. Handwritten addendum in the margin: 'or the same *structure*'.
37. Handwritten addendum on the back of the preceding page: 'Freud never made a secret of the fact that, for him, the Superego was the *moral*

Subject (the Ego Ideal, on the other hand, may well be of an entirely different nature) – find out why Lacan never discusses the Superego' – .

38. The French sentence is not particularly clear. Althusser may have meant to replace it with the sentence that follows [*Trans.*].

39. This sentence is preceded by an arrow that seems to point towards the handwritten addendum reproduced in note 32 above.

40. This sentence, too, is preceded by an arrow that seems to point towards the handwritten addendum given in note 32 above.

41. Jacques Lacan, 'La science et la vérité', reprinted in *Écrits*, Paris, 1966, pp. 855–77.

On Feuerbach

(1967)

One can mark off two major stages in Althusser's work on Feuerbach's philosophy; his archives contain a group of texts corresponding to each. Those in the earlier group, comprising nearly one hundred mostly typed pages, were originally intended for inclusion in a book on Feuerbach, and date from the period in which Althusser was completing the translations of Feuerbach that he published in 1960 under the title Manifestes philosophiques. *Two chapters and a few loose fragments have survived. The first chapter, entitled 'Why Elephants Have No Religion', is forty-three pages long and is written out in nearly finished form; the second, the title of which Althusser had not yet settled on – among the possibilities he was considering were 'On Alienation'; or 'God: A Bad Subject';[1] or 'Free the Attributes!'; or 'Give a Purer Meaning to the Word "Attribute"'! – runs to just twelve pages and is much rougher. Since Althusser summarizes the contents of these early analyses in his 1967 course on* The German Ideology, *we have opted not to include them in the present volume – not without a measure of regret, because certain passages in the first version of Chapter 1 are stylistically much more polished than the corresponding passages in the later version.*

The text published here has been culled from Althusser's course on The German Ideology, *one of the set texts for the oral examination in the 1967* agrégation[2] *in philosophy. Althusser outlined the structure of his course in an introduction to it: '1. The principles of Feuerbach's Philosophy; 2. A commentary on the basic theoretical principles of the* Manuscripts of 1844; *3. A commentary on the* "Theses on Feuerbach"; *4. A commentary on* The German Ideology.'

The documents preserved in his archives reflect this outline. However, only the first part of the course has been written out; the rest has been left in the form of notes which it would make sense to release only in a complete edition of Althusser's courses, lecture notes included. We have therefore chosen to publish only the section of the course on Feuerbach, omitting the introduction ('On The German Ideology'*), a straightforward presentation of Marx's and Engels's text tailored to the needs of students planning to sit the* agrégation.

There are two typed copies (an original and a carbon) of the 1967 course in Althusser's archives. Handwritten modifications have been made to each. Unfortunately, the modifications only rarely coincide. This is in large part explained by the different destinies of the two documents. The earlier copy of the text, the original typescript (called 'Document 1' in our notes), bears a large number of handwritten emendations. This is almost certainly the document to which Althusser referred in giving his course, at a time when he was planning to publish, in collaboration with Étienne Balibar, a book on Feuerbach, the early Marx, and Marx's 'works of the break'. The second text (the carbon copy, hereafter referred to as 'Document 2') bears a title in Balibar's handwriting ('Louis Althusser. Course 1967'); Althusser lent it to Balibar, who can no longer remember when he gave it back. Althusser's handwritten modifications to this text were almost certainly made after it was returned to him; thus they are more recent than the modifications to Document 1. The two sets of modifications are, moreover, completely independent of each other (it is highly improbable that Althusser had Document 1 in hand as he was revising Document 2; the opposite is even harder to imagine). Document 2 contains far fewer changes. Above all, they lack the systematic character of those found in Document 1, and do not seem to be motivated by any clearly defined project: the spaces left blank, usually for German quotations from Feuerbach, have not been filled in (as they are in Document 1). No modifications occur after page 57 of Document 2.

Thus the earlier document is, in a sense, more 'finished' than the later one. However, since it was impossible not to take Document 2 into consideration in preparing the present edition, we were left with no choice but to publish a text which, strictly speaking, is nowhere to be found as such in Althusser's archives. We have therefore adopted the following editorial policy. We have silently and systematically incorporated the modifications to Document 1 into the present text, whenever they do not conflict with those in Document 2; these changes are not flagged in the Notes. We have also adopted the modifications to Document 2, whenever they do not conflict with those made to Document 1; however, because of the peculiar status of Document 2, we have systematically flagged them. Finally, whenever the modifications to the two documents are incompatible, we have adopted what seemed to us to be the more carefully worked out version, while giving the other in the Notes.

The French translations of Feuerbach to which Althusser refers are those he published in his anthology of Feuerbach's early writings, Manifestes philosophiques; *his unpublished translation of 'The Concept of God as the Generic Essence of Man', preserved in his archives; and Joseph Roy's translation of* Das Wesen des Christentums *(L'essence du Christianisme, Paris, 1864). The English translations of passages from* Das Wesen des Christentums *have been taken from George Eliot's version, except in the case of the introduction, where they are taken from an anthology of Feuerbach's writings,* The Fiery Brook, *edited and translated by Zawar Hanfi. Translations of passages from all other works by Feuerbach have been taken from Hanfi's anthology and one other source, or provided by the translator of the present volume. Both Eliot's and Hanfi's translations have often been modified to bring them into conformity with Althusser's.*

François Matheron

Two restrictions:

1. I shall be dealing only with themes that bear directly on the theoretical problems posed by the *1844 Manuscripts* and *The German Ideology.*
2. To that end, I shall limit myself to those of Feuerbach's works which date from the period that interests us, the pre-1845 texts that I have collected and translated under the title *Manifestes philosophiques.*[3]

Before discussing Feuerbach's essential themes in detail, I would like to say a few words about the general character of his philosophy.

1. Feuerbach basically defines himself in relation to Hegel, whom he undertakes to 'invert', in the strict sense of the word. That is his intention, proclaimed and carried out. The critique of speculative philosophy does indeed constitute an inversion of

Hegel, in the proper sense of the word: putting what is on top at the bottom, and vice versa. This inversion, as we shall see, is expressed in various ways: inversion of the relationship between Thought and being, Idea and sensuous nature, Philosophy and non-philosophy; inversion of the relationship between subject and attribute, and so on. One and the same principle is at work in all these various forms of inversion of Hegel: the *sense* [*sens*] *is inverted* in order to restore an inverted sense.

Yet this critique of Hegel remains the prisoner of Hegel's problematic. For the most part, Feuerbach works on the Hegelian system and within that system, using its concepts. To the extent that the inversion he carries out bears only on the *sense* [*sens*] (which should be understood as both 'vector' and 'signification') internal to Hegel's conceptual system, he *adds nothing* to Hegel; he contents himself with rearranging the system and redistributing its concepts in order to obtain an *inverted, rectified* sense, an inversion that inverts the speculative inversion, and thus restores the truth in its authenticity.

2. However, if the inversion of Hegel *adds nothing* to Hegel, it has the interesting effect of *deleting*[4] something from him. The paradox of the Feuerbachian critique of Hegel is that it aims to go beyond Hegel once and for all in order to found a new philosophy, the philosophy of Modern Times, the philosophy required by the practice of modern Humanity, the philosophy of the practical atheism of Modern Times, the philosophy that fully corresponds to the development of *industry* and to the evolution and requirements of *political* activity – the paradox, I say, of this new philosophy which breaks with Hegel is that, to a certain extent, it brings us back to a *pre*-Hegelian position, to themes peculiar to the eighteenth century and a problematic that derives from both Diderot and Rousseau. The fact that Feuerbach's critique of Hegel takes the rigorous form of an *inversion* has the following consequence: it deletes from Hegel not only a whole series of concepts, but also something that constitutes an essential object of Hegelian thought – *history*, or culture, and that which Hegel situates at the origins of culture: *labour*. When, in the *1844 Manuscripts*, Marx attributes to the *Phenomenology of Mind* the inestimable merit of having 'grasped *labour* as the essence ... of man',[5] and reintroduces the Hegelian dialectic of history, he perceives what Feuerbach had eliminated from

Hegel, and tries to restore it. Feuerbach does, of course, occasionally talk about history in his work, but he never talks about culture in the Hegelian sense of *'Bildung'*, that is, as a product of labour (produced in its turn by the dialectic of the struggle unto death for recognition). When Feuerbach talks about history, what he usually has in mind is the history of religion and the history of philosophy. These are not true examples of history, not even in the Hegelian sense, but simple sequences of forms possessing a logic that proceeds from the Feuerbachian theory of alienation. We shall see[6] that on this point too, the theory of alienation, Feuerbach deletes something from Hegel, and that he is forced to do so by the theoretical effect of the principle informing his critique of Hegel: the principle of inversion. Very roughly, the measure of Feuerbach's retreat behind Hegel, the measure of what Feuerbach deletes from Hegel, may be taken from the type of criticism he makes of him: we may say that *Feuerbach replaces Hegel's absolute objective idealism with an absolute anthropologism or humanism; that he replaces the absolute idealism of the Idea with an absolute materialism of man.* One need only state the matter in this way to justify the schematic judgement made a moment ago. What remains of Hegel is the project of an *'absolute' philosophy*, a philosophy of infinity (we shall see what form these determinations take in Feuerbach). The result is that the project at the very core of Feuerbach's philosophy bears Hegel's stamp; that is why we do not find a full-fledged Feuerbach in the eighteenth century. On the other hand, what disappears from Hegel in Feuerbach is the content designated in Hegelian philosophy by the concept of the *Idea*, that is, *the dialectic of the object* called history. In that sense, Feuerbach relapses into the eighteenth century, into a pre-Hegelian position, retreating towards themes we can make out in various authors (Diderot's materialism, Rousseau's theory of human nature and origins, etc.); in his work, these themes take the form of anthropological or humanist materialism. Such, then, is the first paradoxical effect of the type of criticism that Feuerbach brings to bear on Hegel: a theoretical retreat with respect to Hegel. Engels clearly saw this in his *Ludwig Feuerbach*.[7]

3. The second paradoxical effect induced by the inversion of Hegel is an extraordinary anticipation of certain themes of modern philosophy: the philosophy of the *Welt* and *Umwelt*, the

philosophy of the *Weltanschauung* on the one hand, with its continuations down to Heidegger (see Karl Löwith's book *Von Hegel zu Nietzsche*),[8] and, on the other, the philosophy of the signification of consciousness as intentionality down to Husserl and his heirs in the contemporary hermeneutics of religious inspiration (whether theological, as in Karl Barth's Protestant theology, or philosophical, as in Ricœur).[9] I will give a few examples when I analyse Feuerbach's basic themes. We shall see that the anticipatory power of Feuerbach's theory stems above all from his retreat from Hegelian positions and his return to a philosophy of man that is simultaneously a philosophy of the origin; it stems, to be very precise, from the nature of his anthropology, which is an *anthropology of sense* rather than one of essence.

How did this influence, which modern thinkers have not acknowledged, come about? Between certain themes in Feuerbach's thought and certain themes of modern philosophy, is what we see the anonymous encounter of a rediscovery? Or is it, rather, the effect of an influence exercised through intermediaries, one transmitted by Nietzsche in particular? I am inclined to favour the second hypothesis. In any event, one could do an interesting piece of research in the history of philosophy on the subject, which I call to the attention of those who might be interested.

Here are the themes of Feuerbach's philosophy that I propose to discuss in very schematic fashion:[10]

1. the theory of the absolute horizon, or the theory of the object as the essence of the subject;
2. the theory of alienation as the inversion of sense and abstraction;
3. the theory of the species as the ground of theory and practice and also as the ground of the Revolution of Modern Times and the realization of the human essence;
4. the materialist inversion of speculative philosophy and the unity of humanism, of naturalism and humanism.[11]

I. The theory of the absolute horizon, or the theory of the object as the essence of the subject

The whole of Feuerbach's philosophy follows necessarily from a few very simple propositions, which I shall quote:

1. 'The *essence*[12] of man is not only the grounds, but also the *object* of *religion*.'[a]
2. 'God is ... the exteriorized [*entäußertes, aliéné*] self [*selbst*] of man.'[b]
3. 'But if religion, that is, the consciousness of God, is characterized as the self-consciousness of man, this does not mean that the religious man is directly conscious that his consciousness of God is the consciousness of his own essence, for it is precisely *the absence of such consciousness* that grounds the peculiar essence of religion.'[c]

In the first proposition, Feuerbach says that the essence of man is not only the grounds of religion. He thereby casts aside all the classical theories of religion since Epicurus, and, in particular, all the theories of religion to be found in Machiavelli, Spinoza, and the philosophers of the Enlightenment; these theories constitute so many ideologies of the anti-religious struggle, relating religion not to God and the various forms His revelation takes in human history, *but to man*. These theories differ from Feuerbach's in that, although they offer us *a genesis* of religion which sets out from man, that genesis involves only partial and, usually, *aberrant* effects of human nature – as a rule, a combination of partial and aberrant effects. What can be ascribed to man in religion is *fear, stupidity, imposture*, and politics or morals. When, for example, it is a question of politics or morals (see Spinoza or even Rousseau), the political or moral purposes served by religion are always concealed by the impostures of

---

[a] Feuerbach, Introduction to the *Essence of Christianity* [hereafter 'Introduction'], *FB* 98; translation modified.

[b] Introduction, *FB* 129. [Althusser includes the German words in brackets; *aliéné* is his translation of *entäußert*.]

[c] Introduction, *FB* 110; translation modified.

deceit or illusion – of, in a word, the imagination, whether that imagination reflects the workings of universal human nature or the deceptions concocted by a conspiratorial sect of priests or kings. Thus, the whole of this philosophical tradition of the critique of religion would find it impossible to endorse the Feuerbachian equation *'religion = the essence of man'*.

To bring out the novelty of his conception, Feuerbach says that religion is not only grounded in human nature, but that it is its *object*, its objectification, its *adequate* existence in the form of the objectivity of an object – precisely, religion as the *object peculiar to man* [*objet propre de l'homme*].

With the expression 'religion is the object proper to man', Feuerbach does not simply designate a specific *negative* difference setting man apart from the animals. Doubtless that is how things appear at first sight. Elephants[13] have no religion,[d] animals have no religion; man alone has a religion. But one must go further, and understand 'peculiar to man' not in the Aristotelian sense of 'peculiar to', but in the Cartesian sense of *the essential attribute* – in the adequate, positive sense in which religion is not only an index of the distinction between man and the animals, but that which constitutes man's humanity, the human essence in its adequation. In Spinozan terms, we would say[14] that *religion is the adequate idea* of man.

This is an important proposition, since it suffices to distinguish Feuerbach from Hegel. For Hegel, religion is the second moment of Absolute Spirit, which comprises three moments: art, religion and philosophy. Here I leave aside a very important matter, the fact that the 'essence of man' is not what is at stake in Hegel,[15] so that there can be no question of seeking, in Hegel, an answer to the non-Hegelian question of the 'essence of man'. Rather, at stake in Hegel is the Idea and its existence in *absolute* form. But even if we assume that Feuerbach substituted man for the Idea, and, with that reservation, put the question as transformed by Feuerbach to Hegel, we will not obtain the same answer. For there is something higher than religion, namely, philosophy, which in its turn 'supersedes' the first two moments of Absolute Spirit, art and religion; it is their 'synthesis' and expresses their 'truth', the unity of the in-itself and for-itself of

[d] Introduction, *FB* 97.

Absolute Spirit in the in-itself/for-itself of Absolute Spirit represented by philosophy. For Feuerbach, in contrast, we may say
that *nothing is higher than religion*. Religion is well and truly the
adequate idea of man, or, as Feuerbach says, the object of man,
in that it contains the whole of the human essence, *from the
beginning to the end of history*. When this thesis is rigorously
defended and developed, there naturally follow certain consequences as to the status of art and philosophy – philosophy in
particular. Feuerbach, precisely, presents philosophy not as
superseding religion but as a *religious effect*, an effect that can
either be alienated or, on the contrary, rendered adequate.
Indeed, it may be observed that philosophy emerges as a by-
product of theology in the history of humanity. The genesis of
philosophy thus proceeds by way of the filiation religion–theology–philosophy. This filiation is the site of an alienation: the
alienation of theology reduplicates the alienation of religion, and
philosophy only repeats, in its turn, this alienation of theology:
it culminates in Hegel's speculative philosophy. Ultimately, then,
philosophy is alienated religion: in philosophy, we do not get
beyond the limits of the essence of religion. What holds for the
alienated forms of philosophy also holds for the partially disalienated forms or the totally disalienated form of philosophy.
*In particular, the new philosophy founded by Feuerbach does not go
beyond the limits of religion:*[16] *it goes beyond the alienated forms of
philosophy, and thus the alienated forms of theology, in order to return
to the essence of religion* and *'disclose'* [*dévoiler*] the authentic
essence of religion in its very alienation. The new philosophy is
the truth of[17] religion – not in the Hegelian sense of supersession,
of a development of religion that supersedes it, but in the
Spinozan sense of an adequate idea of religion. The new philosophy adds nothing to religion: it simply strips it of its veils; it is
its *public avowal* or confession.

    That, moreover, explains why Feuerbach can say, in the third
of the propositions I have cited, that what constitutes religion as
religion, that is, as the alienation of man's essence, is 'the absence
of consciousness'. The new philosophy adds nothing to religion,
for what it gives it is this 'self-consciousness' that religion lacks.
Should we say that there is a relapse into a certain form of
Hegelianism here, in that philosophy adds the missing 'for itself'
to religion's in-itself? By no means; because, *in itself*, religion is

already consciousness, and because endowing religion with consciousness does not in fact consist in providing it with something
it lacks, but simply in *divesting it*[18] of what conceals from it what
it is, of what obstructs this consciousness. Far from adding
something to religion, then, philosophy *frees religion of, not a lack,
but a mask*, an obstruction, its blinkers, its veils. It is in this sense
that philosophy is a disclosure, *Enthüllung*: an unveiling of
religion, a visible manifestation of the pure essence of religion,
or, again, a confession and an avowal. Philosophy merely says
what religion says without saying it.[19] From this there follows a
fundamental thesis about the essence of philosophy as *unveiling
or disclosure*, the disappearance of philosophy in the object disclosed, and the nature of truth as what is manifested in this
disclosure. There also follows a fundamental thesis about the
unique source of disalienation, which is identical with disclosure
and the true, authentic realization of the human essence: it is
that everything hinges on the disclosure of that essence – to be
very precise, on bringing self-consciousness into full correspondence [*adéquation*] with consciousness. This, of course, has implications not only for the nature of ideologies, philosophy, and the
sciences, but also for politics, which is reduced to a critique of
the illusions of consciousness about itself, with the whole resting
on *the thesis of the practical and theoretical primacy of consciousness*.
We shall consider that point later.

For the moment, we shall confine ourselves to bringing out
the theoretical presuppositions of Feuerbach's thought by drawing the conclusions that follow from an equation which may be
written as follows: philosophy = the disclosure of religion =
man's self-consciousness = man's consciousness = man's essence
= man's object = religion.

We are dealing with a whole series of classical *concepts* in this
equation, but also with a term which, while it, too, figures among
the terms of classical philosophy, is nevertheless not a concept
of classical philosophy (except in certain Cartesian formulations):
the term *'object'*. This term sustains the entire edifice of Feuerbach's theory. We shall discuss it under the rubric of the 'theory
of the absolute horizon' or 'theory of the Feuerbachian object'.

The whole of Feuerbach's theory of the object is contained in
the following proposition: 'the object to which a subject *essentially and necessarily* relates is nothing but the subject's *own*

essence, but *objectified* [*vergegenständlicht*]',[e] a formulation that may be expressed in the following equation: a subject's *essential object* = that subject's *objectified essence*. This formulation admits of variants in which 'subject' is replaced by *being* or *species*, 'objectified' [*vergegenständlicht*] by externalized [*veräußert*] or alienated [*entfremdet*] or, again, by manifestation [*Erscheinung*], expression [*Ausdruck*], etc.

This equation expresses an – in principle – *perfect correspondence* [*adéquation*] between, on the one hand, the essence of a being or subject, and, on the other, his *peculiar* [*propre*][20] object, called his essential object. It is peculiar to him in the narrow, positive sense of the term, because it is nothing other than this being's or subject's *objectification*, externalization, or adequate manifestation. This immediately brings to mind a structure that is typical of the relationship between these concepts: a relation of subject to object (objects) or essence to phenomenon, a relation in which the centre is constituted by the constitutive subject, from which there emanates a space of objects concentric to this centre, objects objectifying the essence of this subject or being, who is thus the subject that constitutes them. This in the precise sense in which the term is anticipated in Kant and will later be reappropriated by modern philosophy, by *Geistesphilosophie* (*philosophy of Spirit*): a *Welt* if not an *Umwelt* (*Geistesphilosophie* or a certain biology or ethology), a *Welt* or, more precisely, an *Umwelt*. In suggesting these spatial images of centre and circular environment here, I am simply repeating the very terms used by Feuerbach, who speaks of the circle of essential objects surrounding the central subject as his '*horizon*'. That is why I speak of a theory of the object as a theory of the *horizon* (or the *Umwelt*); one can readily see the modern resonance of these terms. But I have yet to justify the other term in my phrase 'absolute horizon', the word 'absolute'. It, too, is in Feuerbach. Although he never speaks of an *absolute horizon*, both words are to be found in his text, and are employed in a sense that not only authorizes us to speak of an absolute horizon, but even requires us to do so.

In order to understand this 'absolute', we have to go into the details of Feuerbach's theory – that is, expose ourselves to the

---

[e] Introduction, *FB* 100; translation modified.

surprise of an astonishing 'transcendental biology'. It is, however, as is often the case in the work of innovators, merely a cover that provides an absolute anthropology with a terminology, and provides it with a terminology in order to justify this anthropology's twofold role as a foundation for the theory of knowledge as well as for morality and practice.

I say 'transcendental biology', but one might just as well say Philosophy of Nature in general, because, as we shall see, Feuerbach does not restrict himself to the animal world, but extends his theory to vegetables and minerals too, in order to provide it with a universal foundation and benefit from the ideological effects of this recourse to Nature.

Thus: 'the object to which a subject essentially and necessarily relates is nothing but the subject's own essence, but objectified'. And, astoundingly, Feuerbach immediately adds: 'In this sense the Sun is the object of the Planets . . .'. Later he will say that the leaf is the object of the caterpillar, and so on. Yet he is soon brought up short by an objection: the Sun is not the exclusive, unique, and thus peculiar object of one planet, but of several:

> The Sun is the common object of the planets, but it is not an object for the Earth in the same way as it is for Mercury [or] Venus . . . The Sun which lights and warms Uranus – and the way it does so – has no physical . . . existence for the Earth. Not only does the sun appear different, but it really is another Sun on Uranus than on the Earth. Hence, the Earth's relationship to the Sun is at the same time the Earth's relationship to itself, to its own being, for the measure of the magnitude and intensity of light which is decisive as to the way the Sun is an object for the earth is also the measure of the Earth's distance from the Sun, that is, the measure that determines the specific nature of the Earth. Each planet therefore has in its Sun the mirror in which its own essence is reflected [*Spiegel seines Wesens*].[f]

This altogether astonishing text brings out an essential characteristic of the subject–object relation: the mirror relation or *speculary* relation. This relation is identical to the relation of the objectification of essence that binds the subject to its object and the object to its subject. Once the equation has been correctly written, *one can approach matters from either end, subject or object; the result is the same*. This becomes clear from a hypothesis that Feuerbach

---

[f] Introduction, *FB* 100–101; translation modified.

makes about religion: if, after the extinction of the human race, an inhabitant of Uranus should one day land on Earth and discover a *theological treatise,* he could read the human essence in it at sight (assuming, of course, that he was a Feuerbachian), deducing from this treatise the fact that men had existed on Earth. To be sure, before one is authorized to treat the equation as reversible, it has first to be written, constituted. One then observes that what is reversibility at the level of effects is not reversible at the level of the cause; in other words, *the reversible speculary relation is possible only against the background of a centred structure* in which the essence of the subject occupies the centre, and the speculary objects the periphery formed by the *horizon.* This follows from the multiplication of the one and only Sun into as many particular suns as there are planets. Each planet does indeed possess, in the sun, the mirror of its own essence, on condition that one distinguish between *the* Sun, common to all the planets, living creatures and plants, and *its* Sun. This reveals the principle governing this differentiation, this *appropriation* of the Sun, that which establishes the Sun as the peculiar object of the essence of each planet: this principle is each planet's *central essence.*

One may, then, write the following modified equation: the essence of planet X = its *own* [*propre*] relation [*Verhalten*] to the one and only Sun = its Sun = the Sun in so far as[21] it is the planet's own [*propre*] object.

This modified equation is very important, for it concerns the *external* objects in the universe, common to a multitude of beings: mineral, vegetable, animal and human. In general, external objects are external in so far as different beings can take them as their peculiar objects within the *essential relation* in which these beings stand to them. If we succeed in identifying *this essential relation,* we may then consider it, in the specific sense, to be the *peculiar object* of the being in question, that is, that being's *objectified essence.* For all natural, non-human beings (we shall see the reasons for this restriction), this, of course, suggests the detour of science, whose function is to discover *this peculiar relation,* and, if possible, the complex *of peculiar relations* that make up the peculiar complex object constitutive of the objectified essence of a natural being, whether it be a species or an individual. Of course, this research programme for the natural sciences depends on the basic hypothesis that there is, by rights, a correspondence between the subject and its own essence which is objectified in its own object, a correspondence that is constitutive of all objective knowledge. One need hardly point out that this is a pure mythology inspired by Schelling, and that it in no way reflects the reality of the practice and concepts of the natural sciences. But this gigantic myth *is forged only in order to sustain, as we shall see, the theory of religion as man's peculiar object* and, with it, the whole theory of man's knowledge and activity.

Let us go straight to the heart of this problem, religion, postponing our consideration of the other facets of human activity.

What distinguishes religion as an object from external objects such as the Sun or, more generally, from the external objects found in nature, is, precisely, that they are *external*, that is, common to beings of various kinds, whereas religion, according to Feuerbach, is an *inner* object, which, for this reason, belongs to[22] *humankind* alone. The planets and plants have only an outer life. Animals have an inner life, but it 'is one with the outer' life, whereas man has a twofold life: 'an inner *and* an outer life'.[g] An outer life is a life that brings a species into relation with the outer world, hence with other species. An inner life is a life that brings the species into relation with itself – into relation with itself as its own essential object. This is the case with man. Thus the privilege of religion resides not in the fact that it distinguishes man from the animals as the index of an essential difference, but in the fact that it constitutes man's very essence, that is, the objectification of his peculiar essence, and therefore his peculiar object. Religion's immense privilege is that it is immediately, entirely, adequately, exhaustively,[23] just as it presents itself, in its objective existence, man's peculiar object, the essence of the human species. In this case, there is no need to look for the type of[24] *relation* essential to the human species which constitutes religion as man's peculiar object (as one had to with the Sun). Here, one does not need to make the detour of a scientific investigation in order to determine the peculiar *relation* that makes religion the religion of man, 'his' religion. Religion is, immediately, this very relation; it is, entirely, this

g Introduction, *FB* 98.

very relation; it is, adequately, this relation, and thus the human essence. It is clear that this thesis of Feuerbach's is the object not of a demonstration, but of a simple declaration. Or, rather, the Feuerbachian demonstration of this equation is provided, in *The Essence of Christianity*, by the endlessly *repeated* illustration of the speculary relation 'God's attributes/man's attributes'; this one simple *repetition*, which the speculary structure of the basic concepts of Feuerbach's theory makes inevitable, is the backbone of his pseudo-demonstration. I will not labour the point, except to say that Feuerbach gives us, in his theory, a model of the structure of a,[25] or of every, ideological discourse, a model which is particularly pure in its naivety; and that his philosophy is, perhaps, well and truly the *confession*, not of the truth of religion and the essence of man, but of the structure of all ideological discourse, and of the domination religious discourse exercises over philosophical discourse – at any rate, over the type of philosophical discourse that Feuerbach produces (which I, for my part, would not call a philosophical discourse, but an ideological discourse that comes under the heading of religious morality).

However that may be, one can draw an important conclusion from what has just been said. It is that if man enjoys the privilege of possessing his essence in an immediately given object peculiar to him, and in an adequate, immediately adequate form, it is because he takes *his own species*, his own genus, as his peculiar object, in the strict sense of the term. To say that man is the one being in the world to possess an inner life is to say that he possesses a life that unfolds entirely within his own essence, a life that is its own object, in the strict sense of the term: it is to say that he has the privilege over all other beings in nature of not having to *make the detour* through other, external beings in order to arrive at a definition of his peculiar object, in order to 'carve' his peculiar object 'for himself' out of the objects 'in-themselves' of the outer Universe by virtue of the essential *relationship* he maintains with them. It is to say that man does not have to make the detour through the sciences in order to arrive at the knowledge of his essence, but *that this knowledge is given to him in actu*, in its adequate content, in the form of the specific object known as religion. This calls an end to the infinite programme that the eighteenth century unfolded before the sciences of man and the social sciences after the idealism of the Cartesian Cogito had been rejected. Man no longer has to make the long detour through the sciences, the detour of that infinite quest in which the idea of man is, precisely, only an 'idea', serving as a regulatory, not a constitutive principle for empirical research; he possesses his own self-knowledge in the privileged object of religion, because, in religion, he possesses the ontological privilege of standing in immediate, adequate relation to *his own species*.

If we write out the equation that we are in the process of examining, we have: *inner life* (that is, man's inner life, since only human beings have an inner life distinct from their external life)[26] = *relation to his object = relation to religion = essence of man = essence of the human species*. This *inner relation* of the human species to itself in the form of its relation to its speculary object, religion – this inner relation has a specific name,[27] '*consciousness*'. To say that man distinguishes himself from the animals through religion, and to say that he distinguishes himself from them through consciousness, is to say one and the same thing – on condition that we take consciousness '*in the strict sense*': that is, that we take it to mean, not the sensation or perception of external things (common to both animals and man), or even individual consciousness, but something quite different. '*Consciousness in the strict sense is given only in the case of a being whose object is his own species, his own essence.*' This is what makes it possible to ground the difference between animal and human consciousness: '*Doubtless the animal takes itself as an object as an individual (that is what is meant by saying that it has a feeling of itself) – but it does not do so as a species (that is why it lacks consciousness, which takes its name from knowledge).*'[28h] It is here that the important difference between the individual and his species comes into play. We shall have to return to this point.

Let us say, then, that man is the one being in the universe who, as an individual, takes *his species* as his peculiar object, the essence of his species, which is given to him in the form of *consciousness* in the strict sense. This allows us to complete our equation of a moment ago by condensing it in the following formula: inner life = immediate relation to the essence of the

h Introduction, *FB* 97–8; translation modified.

species = religion = *consciousness* in the strict sense. This is not a casual proposition for Feuerbach. Concretely, we find in his work what we may call *concrete forms of existence of consciousness*, that is, objects and relations that directly express this full correspondence between individual and species: religion is their 'compendium', their summa and supreme realization. But we find the existence of this object in the form of all the activities and manifestations of the inner life in the narrow sense, that is, the individual's generic life. To speak, even to hold a monologue, that is, to speak with oneself, with oneself as if with another, is a form of consciousness in the strict sense, that is, a manifestation or realization of the human species. The same holds for loving, reflecting, thinking and knowing, of willing in the rational, ethical sense, or of participating in politics. These are all so many activities indistinguishable from consciousness in the strict sense, hence from man's inner life, hence from the immediate relation between the human individual and the human species.

> *The inner life of man is his life in its relation to his species, his essence. When man thinks, he converses, he speaks with himself. The animal, on the other hand, cannot perform any generic function without the aid of another individual external to itself. But man can perform the functions characteristic of his genre – for thought and speech are true generic functions – in isolation from another individual. Man is in himself both 'I' and 'Thou'; he can put himself in the place of another precisely because his object is his species, his essence – not only his individuality.*[i]

If we interpret the particular manifestations of man's generic functions narrowly, we may say that all of them are contained in the *religion-object*, which constitutes man's absolute object, his space and absolute horizon. *Man never goes beyond the limits of religion in any of his activities, even those that seem to be non-religious, because he never goes beyond the absolute horizon of his own essence.*[29]

When we correlate this thesis with that of the identity between consciousness in the strict sense and the essence of the species, we see that it requires us to specify the meaning of the Feuerbachian concept of '*consciousness* in the strict sense'. Consciousness in the strict sense means *self-consciousness* or *self-knowledge*, if we

---

[i] Introduction, *FB* 98; translation modified.

assign the word 'self' the following precise content: man's generic essence. The paradox of Feuerbach from the standpoint of the Cartesian tradition, although he is consistent here with certain theses of Hegel's, is that *self-consciousness* does not necessarily take the form of *consciousness* in the Cartesian sense of the transparency of self-presence. Man's self-consciousness in all the religious manifestations of his existence takes the basic form of the *opacity* of objects, gestures, institutions, practises, and even knowledge.[30] This opacity is the effect of alienation. This opacity has to do only with the *sense* expressed by these objects or gestures: they are manifestations of self-consciousness, and self-consciousness existing in the form of immediacy. One may say that, in alienation, what self-consciousness lacks is *consciousness*, not in the strict, but in the everyday sense: in religion and all his generic acts, man has to do with *self-consciousness*, but without consciousness, that is, without transparency. This does not mean that he lacks *consciousness* when he prays, acts, loves, speaks or knows. But in such cases the consciousness that accompanies his gestures and acts is a *subjective*, that is, *an individual* consciousness. It expresses nothing other than the relation of an *individual* who speaks, acts or loves to the object of his activity, perception, love and practices, the relation of an individual to his generic essence, his species; but it expresses it in opacity and misrecognition – a *non-transparent* relation. This is a consciousness that does not correspond to its object, a consciousness that expresses only the subjective, contingent, and thus limited or circumscribed relation of the individual to generic objects and activities, which are misrecognized as such. This misrecognition, this non-correspondence of the individual consciousness to generic objects and activities, is the effect of alienation. It results from the *form* in which alienation reveals to the individual the existence of his generic human existence. *Consciousness can* be rendered adequate *to self-consciousness* (that is, *self-consciousness* can become transparent) only through man's disalienation; through the inversion of alienated sense and the restoration of the original, true sense – through *disclosure*. This last consequence helps us to understand why Feuerbach affirms, in his definition of *self-consciousness*, that consciousness 'takes its name from knowledge'.[31] Self-consciousness as Feuerbach conceives it is in fact *Absolute Knowledge* of the essence of the human species – in other words, the essence of the human species revealed in an objective discourse that gives expression to it. We understand why it is possible for self-consciousness *not* to be conscious: the absolute knowledge constituted by religion can be either given in a consciousness that is adequate to Knowledge or in one that is not adequate to it.

This simple analysis makes it possible to see the sense in which Feuerbach is related to Hegel, and also why he relapses into a pre-Hegelian position. Feuerbach's philosophy is a *fictitious* Phenomenology and dialectic. The manifest aim, in both Feuerbach and Hegel, is to arrive at the identity of consciousness and self-consciousness, that is, *Absolute Knowledge* – not only in the theoretical sense of Knowledge, but in the practical sense of the immediate, adequate empirical existence of the truth in daily life. But whereas Hegel seeks to reveal the operations of the dialectic that engenders the identity of consciousness and self-consciousness *by setting out from consciousness*, and, in particular, to show that *self-consciousness is produced by the dialectic of the development of consciousness, something that presupposes all of history*, Feuerbach, in contrast, inverts the Hegelian relation between consciousness and self-consciousness, *treating self-consciousness as primordial and reducing the history of alienation to mere modes of consciousness*, that is, man's alienated relation to his generic essence. What Feuerbach must then produce is not, as in Hegel, self-consciousness and Absolute Knowledge *with consciousness as a starting point* but, rather, consciousness, with self-consciousness and Absolute Knowledge as a starting point. Even that formulation is inexact, for Feuerbach does not have to *produce* consciousness, since consciousness is not *the result of a process* but *the simple effect of a 'disclosure'*; hence he has no need for any theory of history as the process of the genesis of alienation and disalienation. If consciousness is thus reduced to *the disclosure of an originary self-consciousness*, an originary Absolute Knowledge, self-consciousness appears to be totally foreign to consciousness in the Hegelian sense: the word 'consciousness' does, it is true, appear in the expression 'self-consciousness', but this word, consciousness, merely designates the speculary reflection, the speculary relation, the specularity of universal existence and, in particular, of the existence of the generic essence of man in man's objects, in the human world.[32] Consciousness is thus merely the *'self'* *in* the speculary relation between man and *his world*. This speculary relation can be said to be *'consciousness' only* because the 'self' in question is the 'self' of the *human essence*, and because the word consciousness *has* to exist somewhere from the beginning if it is to appear at the end without itself requiring a genesis, without having to be produced – transparency plainly has to be designated as the *essence of opacity*.[j] In the expression *'self-consciousness'* as the speculary existence of the human essence in its objects, Feuerbach has thus taken the two words for granted: *'self'* on the one hand (= human essence) and *'consciousness'* on the other. This relieves him of the obligation to have any theory of history at all, even a Hegelian one. That is why he relapses into a pre-Hegelian position. What remains of Hegel in Feuerbach is merely the end product of the Hegelian theory of history: Absolute Knowledge on the one hand and, on the other, *the fact that Spirit does not have an adequate existence in* thought *alone, but also exists in the concrete and practical*[33] *in figures of history*, above all in the object known as religion, the human object *par excellence*. This object is clearly the *trace* of history, and clearly testifies that history has passed this way – history in the eighteenth century's sense as well as in Hegel's; yet Feuerbach treats religion as if nothing had happened since Descartes. His equation *'religion = self-consciousness = human essence'* can in fact be read as a *Cartesian Cogito whose object is no longer thought, but religion*.

Nor is that all. To the extent that the human essence is the essence of one natural species among others; to the extent that man's world, man's absolute horizon, is an *Umwelt*, one absolute horizon among others; to the extent that self-consciousness is assigned to the province of a biological species, Feuerbach regresses much further still, back to the Schoolmen and Aristotle. However, just as something has occurred since Descartes – namely, the recognition of the reality of *history and culture* – so something has occurred since Aristotle – namely, the rise and the recognition of *modern science*. That is why Feuerbach's tran-

---

[j] On opacity as transparency *except for itself*, see Feuerbach, 'Towards a Critique of Hegel's Philosophy', FB 91: 'Matter in itself is not darkness, but rather that which is illuminable [Althusser translates *'le transparent virtuel'*], or that which is unilluminated only for itself.'

scendental pseudo-biology may be called transcendental, to the extent that *he attributes to the human species an absolute privilege over all the other species, the privilege of taking as its object not merely its immediate environment, that of its 'practical'*[34] needs (which constitutes the absolute horizon for animal species), *but the whole universe itself,* the speculary object of the attribute of the human essence known as need, and of the *theoretical, contemplative, disinterested power.*

No doubt it is this paradoxical situation, anachronistic (philosophically speaking) in his own day, which confers upon Feuerbach's thought its ambiguous character: its regressiveness and impoverishment and, *simultaneously,* its profundity and powers of anticipation. When we compare Feuerbach's system of thought to others that are contemporary with their objects, we can clearly see that *it lags behind them every time*: it lags behind Hegel, and we relapse into the eighteenth century; it lags behind the eighteenth century, and we relapse into Descartes; it lags behind Descartes, and we relapse into Scholasticism and Aristotle. *But every time* Feuerbach falls back a period and refers to an earlier author, he gives the categories of the *earlier* author in whose terms he is thinking a *later* object to think. He gives the materialism and anthropology of Diderot/Rousseau, as well as the Cartesian Cogito, an object to think which he owes to Hegel: religion as a cultural object, as the actual existence of Spirit. He has Descartes's Cogito, again, think another object which he owes to Hegel: *the intersubjectivity of the 'we'.* He has the biologico-ontological concepts of the Schoolmen think an object which he owes to Descartes: modern science; and so on.

There is no end to these displacements and substitutions. The reason for them is of little concern to us. We want merely to consider *their effects*; especially, for the moment, *the effect of the profound ambiguity* that allows Feuerbach to equate the following terms: *species = essence = self-consciousness = absolute knowledge.* I say that this equation is *ambiguous*; that is plain enough, because it holds good only if we take each term, which simultaneously alludes to 'immediate' realities and to datable concepts drawn from the history of philosophy, sometimes in the sense of its historical or theoretical immediacy, and at other times in the skewed sense that makes it possible to force it into relation with the contiguous term. But I say at the same time that *this ambiguity is not a pure and simple wordplay of no consequence: this equivocation opens up a space* – or, rather, spaces – and produces *unprecedented meaning-effects*, which are, for this reason, effects of theoretical anticipation, effects that are themselves ambiguous and thus authorize modern readings of Feuerbach. We shall see this in a moment with respect to his historico-philosophical method. However, while indicating the reason for these effects, and the very special kind of dialectic that sustains it (a dialectic of surreptitious, theoretically anachronistic substitutions), I would also like to point out that the very spectacular effects produced by Feuerbach's stealthy substitutions always occur within certain absolute limits: those laid down, in the final analysis, by the common stock of theory that defines both the problematics and the objects he so unpredictably combines. This means, to put it plainly, that the Feuerbach who desperately wanted to have done with classical philosophy – as he himself says, and as Engels repeats after him – remained just as desperately its prisoner.

But let us return to our analysis. We have derived all the above considerations from Feuerbach's thesis of the identity of *man's inner life*, self-consciousness, and religion. The fact remains that man also has *an outer life*, a life that puts him in practical and theoretical relation, precisely, with external beings, that is, external individuals and species, that is, in the final analysis, with species external to him. In these outer objects he is not *bei sich*, at home. Whereas 'the religious object exists within' man, *the sensuous object* 'exists outside man'. This implies that, 'in the case of objects of the senses', that is, *in the case of the outer, non-cultural, natural world, one must 'distinguish between consciousness of the object and self-consciousness'*,[k] or again, '*the object in itself and the object for us*'. Is the theory of the absolute horizon compromised by this new type of relation, in which the external object is wanting or in excess with respect to self-consciousness, that is, with respect to the human essence? Or – to speak a different language, which is also to be found in Feuerbach – does not the relation that the human species maintains with the other natural species, which are intrinsically [*par essence*] different from the human species, project the human species *outside* its essence?

[k] Introduction, *FB* 109; translation modified.

Not at all, as we can see if we bring to bear on the human species the theory already developed with respect to the *relationship* [*Verhalten*] that each planet maintains with a Sun that all have in common, a relationship which, for each of the planets, converts one and the same Sun into 'its' Sun. Feuerbach himself says that his principle of the absolute horizon, 'far from holding only for intellectual objects, even applies to sensuous objects'. One need only bring the theory of *Verhalten* into play. 'Even those objects which are farthest removed from man are manifestations of the human essence because, and *in the sense in which*, they are objects for him.' Example: the moon. 'Even the moon, and the sun and the stars, say to man, "χνῶθι σεαυτόν" – know thyself. That he sees them, that he sees them the way he does, bears witness to his own essence.' This is a direct application of the theory of *Verhalten*, here formulated in the expressions '*in the sense in which* they are objects for him,' and 'that he sees them, that he sees them *the way* he does. . . .'¹ Thus it is spelled out here that *Verhalten*, the generic relationship existing between man and his external objects, is a *modal* relation ('that he sees them the way he does') and a relation of 'sense', both of which are in turn grounded in *the fact* that this relation exists ('that he sees them . . .'). Thus the speculary relation operates in the case of external objects as well, but bears only on the *relationship* man maintains with them. This thesis would accordingly seem to refer us, as in the previous case of the planet's relation to the Sun, to the infinite task of the sciences of nature, whose function would be, precisely, to distinguish, among the various relations between man and his external objects, those which have to do with the human essence from those which do not. However, a veritable theoretical *coup de force* spares us this endless quest. The short phrase '*that he sees them* [these objects: the moon, etc.]' 'bears witness to his own essence' is not there to acknowledge a factualness and a finitude in the Kantian sense:³⁵ in other words, to acknowledge that man is made in such a way that he sees *this* and *that*, and not something else. The 'seeing' in question here is not an 'empirical seeing' (man 'sees' the moon, but does not 'see' gravity), but a *theoretical 'seeing'*, the 'seeing' of reason, of objec-

---

¹ Introduction, *FB* 101; translation modified.

tive, scientific knowledge itself. This 'seeing' is an attribute of the human essence that distinguishes man from the animals:[36]

The animal is moved only by the rays of light, which are essential for its life, but man is also moved by the rays from the remotest star, which are indifferent to his life . . . Only man celebrates the theoretical feasts of vision. The eye that looks into the starry heavens, that contemplates the light that bears neither use nor harm, that has nothing in common with the earth and its needs, this eye contemplates its own nature, its own origin in that light. The eye is heavenly in its nature. Hence, it is only through the eye that man rises above the earth; hence theory begins only when man directs his gaze towards the heavens. The first philosophers were astronomers. The heavens remind man of his destination, remind him that he is destined not merely to act, but also to contemplate.[m]

Quite simply, this means, as Feuerbach literally says, that man's peculiar object is the Universe; not the object of the whole man (which is what makes science abstract in comparison with religion), but that of man *considered with regard to the attribute of reason.* And the Universe is that which is peculiar to man because it is the object of a theoretical need; because man is, in the proper sense, a 'universal being'.[n]

From this point on, things are simple. It is not only in the realm of feeling and the will that man is *'bei sich'*, in his own essence. Man also dwells in his own essence in 'vision', which is the ground for all perception of external objects, and thence for all scientific knowledge, and an attribute of the human essence. That is why the specific *Verhalten* that proceeds from the human essence in its relations with external species does not have to make the indefinite detour through science in order to be defined. It is immediately and adequately given by the *perception* of these external objects, by virtue of an immediacy and a pre-existent correspondence: the one that brings man and the whole

[m] Introduction, FB 101–2.

[n] 'Here too we need not go beyond the realm of sensuousness in order to recognize man as a being superior to animals. Man is not a particular being like the animal; rather, he is a *universal* being; he is therefore not a limited and unfree but an unlimited and free being, for universality, being without limit, and freedom are inseparable.' Feuerbach, *Principles of the Philosophy of the Future*, FB 242. See also Feuerbach, 'Towards a Critique of Hegel's Philosophy', FB 93: 'Human form cannot be regarded as limited and finite . . . [it is] the genus of the manifold animal species; it no longer exists as species in man, but as *genus*'.

universe itself into relation via the need for theory, the sense of the universal, reason. Science can then perfectly well be an infinite task: it is infinite because the attribute of reason is itself, like all the attributes of a species, infinite in itself – we shall see in what sense. *Religion bears direct and adequate witness to the nature of this attribute and its infinite character: in the omnipotence of the divine intelligence, man effectively has the definition of his reason, his theoretical 'seeing'.* That is why I think one has to say that if it is possible to *dispense* with scientific research when defining the sense in which the relation between man and external objects is a realization of the human essence, *it is owing to the existence of religion,* the fact that religion contains, *in principle, all the attributes of the human essence in a form adequate to their essence.* In other words, if Feuerbach can 'go beyond' the Kantian question, that is, fall back into a pre-Kantian position even while taking the Kantian revolution into consideration, and offer us noumenal *knowledge* of the human essence, knowledge of the Transcendental Subject, it is not *by realizing* the phenomenal object of the *sciences* in the form of what would be[37] a noumenal object, that is, by anticipating the development of the *sciences* and then confining it to a Subject by dogmatic fiat (Feuerbach's philosophy cannot be called dogmatic in this sense). *Quite the contrary: Feuerbach 'goes beyond' Kant by invoking the adequate existence of the human essence in the specific object constituted by religion* – an object which, unlike the 'objects' of the sciences in the ordinary sense, *is immediately the total speculary reflection of the human essence.* Hence it is in setting out from the privileged case of religion and religion alone that one can justify the utilization of the theory of *Verhalten* with respect to the relations between man and his external objects. 'The absolute being ... [of man] is his own essence. The power of the object over him is therefore the power of his own essence. Therefore, the power of the object of feeling is the power of feeling itself; the power of the object of reason is the power of reason itself; and the power of the object of will is the power of the will itself.'° Feuerbach illustrates these theses by showing that, in aesthetic emotion, the emotion has to do only with itself; in the emotion of love, only with love; in the will, with the will; and in reason, with reason.[38]

° Introduction, *FB* 102.

Let us sum up what we have just established. Man is the only species on earth that takes its own essence as its own object, in the Feuerbachian sense, because man's object is his own species. *Par excellence*, this essence is given to man in religion, in which man's three essential attributes – *reason, the will* and *the heart* – are realized in the form of an alienated object. This privileged object is the mirror of the human essence, the essence of the human species existing in the form of an object. Thus religion is self-consciousness, in the sense of Absolute Self-Knowledge of the human essence, whether that essence is experienced and intended [*visé*] in alienated form, in which consciousness does not correspond to self-consciousness, or in the adequate form of the new philosophy – materialist, humanist atheism – in which consciousness does correspond to self-consciousness. It is because the human essence is *thus given in its entirety somewhere, immediately present and visible*[39] *on condition that it is disclosed*, and, at the same time, because, among its attributes, this human essence includes reason, the universal power to 'see' and thus to know (universal because it takes the Universe as its object), that the objective, external existence of sensuous objects is not problematic for the theory of man. *This problem is solved in advance; its solution is always-already given in the essence of reason, which is, precisely, the faculty of the outer world, the attribute whose object is the Universe itself.* Thus the theory of the absolute horizon applies *without restriction* to man, whose *Umwelt* coincides with the (objective) *Welt* or Universe. This is how Feuerbach 'goes beyond' the pseudo-biological subjectivism of the absolute horizon of the species. Because the human species is a universal species, the only universal species, it escapes the *subjective* limitations of a particular horizon. The particularity and subjectivity of the absolute horizon are peculiar to animal, vegetable and mineral species. Universality and objectivity, on the other hand, are peculiar to the human species.

Thus it is easy to grasp the theoretical procedure that Feuerbach utilizes. He begins by constructing a theory of the absolute horizon that holds for all species; this theory has a biological cast and, taken literally, can obviously only lock him into a subjectivism of species, a relativism similar to that with which late-nineteenth-century German *Geistesphilosophie* wrestled. Within the framework of this theory, *it is not enough to grant man the privilege of self-consciousness*, of an inner object that adequately expresses, albeit in alienated form, his own generic essence; for, interpreted rigorously, this privilege does not suffice to save the absolute horizon of the human species from its subjectivism. It is at this point that Feuerbach *adds something* to the human essence, a faculty, a specific attribute which possesses the extraordinary property of transcending the subjectivity of the species: the faculty of theoretical 'seeing' – reason. It is at this point that Feuerbach's naturalism and biologism reveal themselves for what they are: a pseudo-naturalism and a pseudo-biologism that play their foundational role in order to sustain the thesis of the universality of the human species, that is, in order to ground a theory of the objective knowledge of the Universe. As I said a moment ago, Feuerbach's biology seems to take us all the way back to Aristotle; but this pseudo-biology is at the same time assigned responsibility for the object of Modern Times, the sciences of Nature and their rationality. However, this rationality is not, is no longer, the rationality of a Descartes, a Leibniz or a Spinoza: for *reason* is only *one of the three* essential *attributes* of man, along with the (ethical) *will* and the *heart*; and it is an attribute that exists in its plenitude only if it consents to acknowledge its intimate union with the other two.[40] Feuerbachian reason is simultaneously the heart and the will (or freedom), just as the heart in its turn is also reason and the will, and the will is reason and the heart. That is why religion enjoys the *exceptional privilege* that Feuerbach accords it, for *it is itself this unity from the outset*, whereas science is *merely* science, merely reason, and therefore abstract. Something has indeed happened since the Cartesians' day: precisely the recognition, which finds its consecration in Hegel's philosophy, that reason and freedom *truly* exist only in practice, can exist, in practice, in cultural objects[41] such as religion. Feuerbach adopts this Hegelian result and bends it to his own ends, proposing it to the Cartesian categories of the identity of the object and self-consciousness as well as to the Aristotelian categories of species and individual. From Hegel, he takes the form of Absolute Spirit constituted by religion, but he amends Hegel *by making religion Absolute Knowledge*. He thinks this cul-

ᴾ Introduction, FB 128.

tural object containing Absolute Knowledge in terms of the Cartesian categories of the identity of self-consciousness and the object. And he grounds this identity in an Aristotelian theory of species, the foundation for the theory of the absolute horizon. This is how the Hegelian theory of Absolute Knowledge becomes, in Feuerbach, the theory of the absolute horizon of the human species.

Let me point out an essential feature of this theory straight away: it is simultaneously a theory of knowledge and of practice. This unity is founded on the unity, evoked a moment ago, of the attributes of the human essence: the unity of reason, the will and the heart. It is owing to this unity that, within the field of man's absolute horizon, everything that is an object of reason simultaneously is, or can be, an object of practice, the will and love. *'Does not the aim determine the act?'* That is why man contemplates his own essence in religion, since, in God, he rediscovers his own reason, his own activity, and his own feelings. *'Thus in God man confronts his own* activity *as an object.'*ᴾ With this last conclusion, we see Feuerbach dissolving what he considers an abstraction in Kant's theory, the distinction between theoretical and practical reason, at the same time as he dissolves the distinction between reason and sensibility. He thus retreats behind Kant; however, he takes something of Hegel with him as he does so: the Hegelian critique of the distinction between nature and freedom – something that depends on Hegel's conception of the Idea, but shorn of the dialectic. A post-Kantian by dint of his conception of the unity of nature and freedom, theory and practice, Feuerbach nevertheless regresses to pre-Kantian positions, since, when all is said and done, he merely forges a new variant of rational theology. But, as we shall soon see, there exists a determining relation between the conjunction of this 'pre' and 'post' on the one hand, and, on the other, Feuerbach's 'discovery', his specific innovation: his theory of religion as the essence of man, his humanist atheism.

This innovation, precisely, produces astonishing effects of anticipation in the analytical method that Feuerbach applies to Christianity in *The Essence of Christianity*. I would like to pause over Feuerbach's method, for it anticipates certain effects[42] of Husserlian Phenomenology by elaborating a veritable philosophy of signification, a hermeneutics. As you will have noted in passing, this possibility is raised, if one is willing to disregard the letter of Feuerbach's text, from the moment he sets forth his theory of the object: in particular, the theory of the essential 'relationship' between an being and its object [*Verhalten*]. When Feuerbach tells us that the specific mode in which a being relates to an external object constitutes its peculiar object, in other words, its peculiar essence, and also reveals it, especially when he applies this theory of *Verhalten* to the *perception* of objects, it is impossible not to see in this an anticipation, couched in terms we may here treat as metaphorical, of a theory of the intentionality of consciousness. It is, indeed, the relationship within which the object is perceived by consciousness, a relationship that makes the object 'its' object, which reveals the nature of the being that intends [*viser*] the object in the mode peculiar to this intentional process [*visée*]. To be sure, Feuerbach speaks the language of being and object, but it is readily translated into another, that of the Cogito and its cogitatum, and that of the mode of intentional consciousness. It is this mode which determines the 'signification' (the word is to be found in Feuerbach himself) of the object intended in this relationship. Even better, we can say that there is in Feuerbach much more than a simple theory of *perception* as intentional consciousness; one finds in him a theory of *the intentionality of consciousness in general*. To be sure, he does not speak the language of Phenomenology here either: he speaks the language of the 'faculties'. But when he says that the human essence comprises three faculties, reason, the will and the heart, he puts great emphasis on the unity of these three attributes, which exist separately, in his view, only in the abstraction of alienation. Rather than of three faculties, then, one must speak of *three* modes *of the same essence, the same being*. And as these three modes are those of a *relationship to the object* that is identical with the relationship to the object of perception, one can legitimately and without strain translate Feuerbach's language to say that reason, the will and the heart are, in his work, the equivalent of different modes of one and the same underlying structure, which may be termed *the intentionality of the relationship to the object, that is, the intentionality of an intentional consciousness*. Feuerbach's attributes then become thinking consciousness, act consciousness, and consciousness of emotional fusion.[43] It is these theoretical implications which found the utterly novel method at work in the interpretation of religion – Christianity in particular.

Feuerbach reflects on this unprecedented method in the second Preface to *The Essence of Christianity*. It can most assuredly be said that he manages to define it only *in retrospect*, as if he had put it to work before grasping its specificity. This means, precisely, that it must in some way have been authorized as an effect by the theoretical concepts in which he thought. Thus we shall have the surprise of seeing Feuerbach himself proceeding exactly the same way we have: he will offer us, as one of the effects of his own theory, an equivalent of the translation that we have just presented.

This is how Feuerbach, replying to the critics who have misunderstood his interpretation of Christianity, describes his method: 'my work does not wish to accomplish anything more than a faithfully sense-oriented translation or, to put it non-metaphorically, an *empirical* or *historico-philosophical analysis* of the Christian religion designed to resolve its enigmas.'[q] This passage occurs in the Preface to the second edition of *The Essence of Christianity* (1843). It is the passage containing the crucial phrase: 'to discover rather than invent, to "disclose existence" [*Dasein zu enthüllen*], has been my only objective'. 'I let religion itself speak; I only listen to it and function as its interpreter rather than its prompter.'[r] The equivalence established between these concepts leaps to the eye: Feuerbach's philosophy is only a disclosure, and – for him, it amounts to the same thing – a disclosure of existence, of the factually existent, or, again, a *disclosure of sense* ('a faithful, sense-oriented translation', *sinngetreue Übersetzung*).[s] In the light of what we have already explained, we can write: *to disclose essence = to disclose the (factually) existent = to disclose sense*. Identifying essence, the factually existent, and sense by virtue of *its theory of the object*

---

[q] Feuerbach, Preface to the Second Edition of *The Essence of Christianity*, FB 251–2.

[r] Ibid., p. 254; translation modified.

[s] See ibid., pp. 259–60: 'We should not make the determinations and powers of reality, of real beings and things, into arbitrary signs ... symbols and predicates of a being that is distinguished from them ... rather, we should take them in the sense that they have *in themselves* [*in der Bedeutung nehmen und erfassen, welche sie* für sich selbst *haben* (Althusser's interpolation)].'

(and, to anticipate, by virtue of its materialist empiricism), Feuerbach's philosophy makes possible, through this series of inherently equivocal identifications, theoretical effects that give rise to an analytical method which, in the literal sense, anticipates the phenomenological reduction.

Let us state this more precisely.[44] Feuerbach shows that if his readers have misunderstood him, it is because they have sought in his work an answer to the vexed problem of the historical *existence*, the *historical* origins of the Christian religion or one or another of its components: Christ, to begin with, the miracles, this or that rite, and so on. That was the method of the historians and critics of the Christian religion. It is not Feuerbach's. His analysis is

> historico-philosophical as against the purely historical analyses of Christianity. The historian – for example, Daumer – shows that the Last Supper is a rite going back to the ancient cult of human sacrifice; that once real human flesh and blood instead of wine and bread were partaken. I, on the other hand, make only the Christian *signification*, or the signification sanctioned within the Christian position, the object of my analysis and *reduction* [*Reduktion* in German][t] in pursuance of the principle that the signification which a dogma or institution has in Christianity (naturally not in contemporary, but in ancient, true Christianity), no matter whether it prevails in other religions or not, is also the *true origin*[45] of that dogma or institution to the extent that it is Christian. Or, again, the historian – for example, Lützelberger – shows that the narratives of the miracles of Christ resolve themselves into contradictions and incompatibilities, that they are later concoctions, that, consequently, Christ was never a miracle worker, never that which the Bible has made him out to be. For my part, I do not ask what the real, natural Christ was or may have been in distinction from the fictitious or supernaturalistic Christ; taking the Christ of religion for granted, I rather show that this superhuman being is nothing else than a product and object of the supernatural human mind. I do not ask whether this miracle or that, whether a miracle in general *can* happen at all; I only show what a miracle is and, indeed, not a priori, but by referring to the examples of miracles narrated in the Bible as real events; in doing so, however, I answer the question as to the possibility, reality, or

---

[t] Feuerbach, *Sämtliche Werke*, ed. Wilhelm Bolin and Friedrich Jodl, Stuttgart, 1903–10, vol. 7, p. 290.

necessity of miracles in a way so as *to liquidate the possibility of all such questions*.[u]

If we read this passage closely, we see that it breaks with the *historical* interpretation of Christianity – that is to say, with an interpretation that proceeds by confronting the propositions of Christianity (communion, Christ, the miracles) with *reality*. Feuerbach rejects this problematic; indeed, he takes the opposite tack, posing the problem 'so as to liquidate the possibility of all such questions'. Now these questions all bear *on reality*, that is, on *theses of existence*. We may conclude that the historico-philosophical method[46] is based on the *suspension of the thesis of the existence of its object*. Feuerbach does not ask about the existence of Christ, miracles, and so on, or pose the theoretical questions that follow from the assumption that they exist (are miracles possible? can Christ, that is, the man-God, have existed?, etc.). He brackets such questions, and asks only about the *signification* immanent in the propositions or institutions of Christianity, with a view to disclosing that signification.

That is why he can describe his method as a *'reduction'*. His *'analysis'* is a *'reduction'*. This reduction bears on the *signification* of the object, without regard for its existence. It is the suspension of the assumption of existence that makes the reduction possible, by *isolating* the object of the reduction, signification, from all questions of existence.

The reduction that thus brings out signification is realized by way of an analysis of the available 'examples'. This suggests that Feuerbach effects a kind of eidetic variation, carried out across a range of the concrete variants of one and the same signification in the examples with which Christianity provides him.

The core of these variants is constituted by the *original* signification, not the subsequent distortions or alienations[47] it undergoes. That is why Feuerbach analyses Christian significations in their 'true origin', that of early Christianity. He does not examine just any origin, but the Christian origin of a signification; this means that he does not, when he looks at early Christianity, examine a *historical* origin, but an a priori origin that transcends any possible empirical history, an origin that is the very con-

---

[u] Feuerbach, Preface to the Second Edition of *The Essence of Christianity*, FB 260–61; translation modified.

dition of possibility of this history and its distortions. The early [*primitif*] Christianity that Feuerbach examines is thus original [*primitif*] not in the historical, but in the transcendental sense of the word. The origin is the relation represented by the equals sign,[48] the original signification, and that is why Feuerbach can as readily find examples of it in early Christianity as in the alienations of modern religion, theology, or even philosophy and politics.

If we draw up a balance sheet of these principles, we obtain the following system:

1. a suspension of the thesis of existence;
2. the method of reduction, which makes it possible to home in on signification;
3. the beginnings of an eidetic variation carried out through an analysis of *examples*;
4. the original nature of the signification.

Thus we have a set of theoretical principles strikingly reminiscent of the principles informing the method of the Husserlian reduction. Of course, in Feuerbach this transcendental reduction is everywhere sustained by a noumenal theory of the human essence, but this articulation of a transcendental reduction with a rational theology or anthropological dogmatism is itself, in his work, an ambiguous, shifting, unstable articulation, precisely because, if it is constantly affirmed and proclaimed by Feuerbach, it is not as rigorously grounded as it is loudly proclaimed. As a result, the body of principles that I have just listed, which *does* comprise a rigorous theoretical system, in contrast to the combination of transcendental reduction with anthropological dogmatism (or, again, of a philosophy of signification with a philosophy of the human essence), can function relatively *independently*, by virtue of its coherence and theoretical rigour. This relative autonomy of a body of principles founding a new method is undeniably one of the theoretical effects of the heteroclite nature (in the already defined sense) of the unstable theoretical combination that comprises Feuerbach's thought. It is because Feuerbach thinks in conceptual equations that are anachronistic, and thus lack any *overall* theoretical rigour, that he can produce regional theoretical effects which are at once rigorous and original. It is because he brings together *theoretical elements that cannot be thought in a single, unified whole* that he in fact opens up, in certain regions, new theoretical fields. His astonishing anticipation of the phenomenological reduction is an example. But one can also ask, in a wholly critical sense this time, whether this result is not, in the case to hand, an effect of these theoretically anachronistic combinations, these theoretically unstable unities. I mean, to be precise, that it is no accident that Feuerbach's historico-philosophical method (which he elsewhere calls genetico-critical) is predicated on an anthropological philosophy. The theory of the object, the theory of the intentionality of consciousness, the theory of reduction and original signification are all descended, in Feuerbach, from one fundamental thesis, that of the *Absolute Knowledge of the human essence in its objects; par excellence*, in the object *par excellence* known as *religion*, man's object of objects just as man is the name of names. This presupposition has the advantage of being explicit in Feuerbach; that is the positive side of his theoretical naivety. It is not irrelevant to the 'Theses on Feuerbach'⁴⁹ or to a possible critical examination of that Phenomenology which, as the example of its founder shows, seeks desperately to forge a transcendental philosophy that will not lapse into a transcendental or empirical psychology or anthropology.

Before summing up the elements of the theory of the absolute horizon, and drawing the consequences as far as the fate of the Feuerbachian concepts in Marx is concerned, we must develop one more point and give a more precise definition of one word: the adjective *absolute*,⁵⁰ of which I have already spoken.

The absolute horizon is absolute for each species because that horizon constitutes its world, beyond which nothing exists for it. 'Horizon' is, precisely, the concept that expresses the absolute limit on all possible signification for a given species, a limit beyond which nothing exists for that species. For a given species, there is nothing on the far side of its absolute horizon, which is defined by its essence, its faculties, its power. To affirm that the absolute horizon has its 'beyond' is to affirm that the object as it exists for a species exists in a form different *in itself.* But

> I can make the distinction between the object as it is in itself and the object
> as it is for me only where an object can really appear different from what it
> actually appears to me. I cannot make such a distinction where the object

appears to me as it does according to my absolute measure; that is, as it must appear to me.[v]

That is why theories of religion as anthropomorphic conceptions of God are nonsense. For they are based on the distinction between the in-itself of God, supposedly beyond man's compass, and the human representation of God, God for-us. The distinction between the in-itself and the for-the-species is possible for only one species, the one that has access to the in-itself of things, that is, objective knowledge of the Universe: the human species. For example, neither a planet, nor a caterpillar, nor a plant can distinguish between the Sun in itself and 'its sun'; *only man can,* by means of rational knowledge. But this very distinction, in so far as the human species is capable of drawing it, does not come into play for it as a species, since the distinction itself coincides with the generic essence of man. 'If my conception corresponds to the measure of my species, the distinction between what something is in itself and what it is for me ceases; for in that case this conception is itself an absolute one. The measure of the species is the absolute measure, law, and criterion of man.'[w]

What room does this absolute leave for the relative? The relative[51] constituted by the speculary relation between the essence of the species and its absolute horizon is, for the species, not relative, but absolute. Nor does the relative exist outside this absolute horizon, since [there] is no outside for the species. *The relative can accordingly exist only within the field of this absolute horizon,* as a *difference between the individual and the species.* That is why Feuerbach always speaks of *the relation between the species and itself* as constitutive of its peculiar object, its world of 'conceptions corresponding to the measure of the species,' and not of the *relation between the individual and the species,* or of conceptions that reflect only the individual's measure. Feuerbach declares that which reflects the essence of the individual to be subjective or imaginary, and thus relative. That which expresses the essence of the species he declares to be objective and absolute. The subjective and the relative merely express the *lack of correspondence between the individual and the species,* that is, once again, a misrecognition, since 'the essence of the species is the

---

[v] Introduction, *FB* 113.
[w] Introduction, *FB* 113–14.

absolute essence of the individual'.[x] This misrecognition is (?), in the final analysis, the foundation of alienation, as we shall see; in any event, it is one of the forms of *abstraction* (separating the essence of the individual from his absolute essence: that of the species) which constitutes alienation.

That neither the beyond nor the relative exists for the species has one last consequence: the *infinity* of the absolute horizon. Infinity is defined as the absence of limits:

> Every being is sufficient to itself. No being can deny itself, its own nature; no being is intrinsically limited. Rather, every being is in itself infinite; it carries its God – that which is the highest being to it – within itself. Every limit of a being is a limit only for another being that is outside and above it. The life of the ephemera is extraordinarily short as compared with animals whose life span is longer; and yet this short span of life is just as long for them as a life of many years for others. The leaf on which the caterpillar lives is for it a world, an infinite space.[y]

This is how this general principle is applied to man:

> Therefore, whatever the object of which we become conscious, we always become conscious of our own being; we cannot set anything in motion without setting ourselves in motion. And since willing, feeling, and thinking are perfections, essences, and realities, it is impossible that while indulging in them we experience reason, feeling, and will as limited or finite; namely, as worthless. . . . It is impossible to be conscious of will, feeling, and reason only as finite powers, because every perfection, every power, every being is the immediate verification and confirmation [*Bewahrheitung, Bekräftigung*][z] of itself. One cannot love, will, or think without experiencing these activities as perfections [*Vollkommenheiten*]; one cannot perceive oneself to be a loving, willing, and thinking being without experiencing an infinite joy in being so.[aa]

In the infinite faculties of God, it is this infinity of his faculties that man worships and hence acknowledges, unbeknown to himself. It is this infinity of the human faculties which opens up before man the infinite field of knowledge, freedom and love, in

---

[x] Introduction, *FB* 104; translation modified.
[y] Introduction, *FB* 104.
[z] Feuerbach, *Sämtliche Werke*, vol. 6, p. 7.
[aa] Introduction, *FB* 102.

particular the infinite field of the *natural sciences*, whose infinite development, far from being a transcendental obstacle to self-consciousness, that is, to man's absolute self-knowledge, becomes, rather, a manifestation of the infinity of the human essence. Feuerbach can, with perfect serenity, declare himself to be in favour of the natural sciences and their infinite development, without the slightest fear of the consequences as far as the knowledge of man's essence is concerned, for the very good reason that he possesses, in the Absolute Knowledge of man's essence, the infinite attribute of reason, which constitutes the absolute condition of possibility for the categories of any natural science.

Let us now try to sum up the basic propositions of the theory of the absolute horizon, and then examine the effects they have in Marx's early works.

1. The theoretical proposition on which everything depends is constituted by the equation: 'essence of a being (species) = its objectified essence = its object'. This can also be written: subject = *its* object.

This is a speculary relation, constitutive of a space defined by its centre and horizon. The subject occupies the centre and the object the horizon. The object is the mirror of the subject. This speculary relation may also be written: 'object = self-consciousness of the subject = absolute knowledge of the subject'. The remarkable thing is that these different equations rest on certain basic concepts, arranged in pairs by classical philosophy since Descartes: subject/object, consciousness/self-consciousness, essence/phenomenon.

2. Once this speculary relation has been established, it is reversible. Whether one is in the subject or the object, one is never anywhere else than in the essence of the subject; one never leaves it.

However, from the standpoint of the *genesis* of the object as well as from the standpoint of the knowledge of the essence of the subject, this relation is not reversible: it necessarily runs in only one direction.

3. From the standpoint of the genesis of the object, the relation runs from subject to object, from the essence to its phenomenon or manifestation.

The central position of the subject in Feuerbach's topography accounts for this direction/sense. The object emanates from the subject, and is nothing more than its objectification. Feuerbach utilizes the following concepts to express this direction/sense: objectification, realization, manifestation, and also production. He talks about the essence of the subject as constituted by powers or forces [*Kräfte*]; he even talks about the being's 'productive power' [*produktierende Wesenskraft*].[bb] All these concepts reappear in Marx's early works; one can see[52] the place the concepts of powers, forces, and the productive forces of individuals hold in *The German Ideology*.

Feuerbach also describes this objectification of the subject in its object as the affirmation, confirmation and self-satisfaction of the subject. He thereby expresses the *lived* adequation of the subject to itself in the form of its object. These concepts, too, reappear in Marx's early works and *The German Ideology*.

Without anticipating, let us say that the Feuerbachian concept of the speculary subject–object relation reappears in all its purity in the *1844 Manuscripts*, in the speculary form of the relation between *producer and product*. One can see[53] that the concept of product in the *1844 Manuscripts* stands in exactly the same relation to that of producer (or worker) as the concept of object to that of subject in Feuerbach.

4. From the standpoint of the genesis of knowledge of the subject, the relation runs from object to subject, from the phenomenon to its essence. It is in the object that one can come to know the subject. It is in the object that one must come to know the subject. What one finds in the object, one will find again in the subject; but one can decipher the essence of the subject only in its object.

This thesis finds its application in Feuerbach in the case of religion. It is in religion that man can attain self-knowledge.

We rediscover a trace of this thesis of Feuerbach's in Marx's first Feuerbachian works, especially in the form of the idea that all criticism has to set out from *criticism of religion*.[54] In Marx, however, there is a rapid shift in the point of application of this thesis. Marx passes successively from religion to politics and from politics to economics. The transition to politics is made in the *Critique of Hegel's Philosophy of Law*, *The Jewish Question*, and

[bb] Introduction, *FB* 104; Feuerbach, *Sämtliche Werke*, vol. 6, p. 9.

so on. The transition to economics is made in the *1844 Manu-scripts* and *The Holy Family*. The shift in the point of application, however, in no way alters the Feuerbachian schema. To begin with, it remains true that the human essence can be read or deciphered – that is, disclosed – in a specific object (politics and, later, economics); this presupposes that the basic speculary rela-tion between subject and object is maintained. Moreover, there still exists a privileged object, one that constitutes a compendium of the human essence: it is no longer religion but, initially, politics ('politics is man's religion, the heaven of his existence'),[55] and then political economy (in the *1844 Manuscripts*). Finally, the fact that the objectification of the human essence is condensed in a privileged object does not eliminate the other forms of exist-ence of the human essence; they are, however, merely phenom-ena of this primordial object. Thus, in the *1844 Manuscripts*, · politics, ethics and religion are merely subordinate aspects of the privileged object represented by the economy.

5. This has a fundamental consequence for the method that all knowledge of the human essence requires. Such knowledge is not research and production – that is, a labour of theoretical transformation – but pure and simple disclosure, pure and simple confession. The word may be found in the letters to Ruge.[56] The thing it refers to is everywhere in the Early Works, especially in the *1844 Manuscripts*. It is simply a matter of straightforwardly 'reading' [*herauslesen*] the great open book of man's specific object by revealing its text – simply a matter of reading the text without altering anything in it or adding any-thing to it. At the practical level, we can put this[57] to the test in the *1844 Manuscripts*: Marx does not modify a single one of the economists' concepts, but simply reads them by relating them to their hidden essence: the alienation of human labour and, by way of this alienation, of the human essence.

6. This has one final consequence: that one ultimately reads only texts, that one ultimately deciphers only texts or discourses, written or not. That is why, in the *1844 Manuscripts*, Marx merely pretends to talk about the reality of economic practice. In fact, he talks only about the discourses of the classical economists; he does not speak about any object that could be called a practise, he speaks of an object that is a discourse. That is what Feuerbach did as well: he talked about the object known as *religion*, which

also has the property of being a *discourse*; to be very precise, an ideological *discourse* in so far as it is *ideological*. By that I mean that the ideological exists in the form of a *discourse*, and that the only form of existence – or, at any rate, the form of existence which is equally privileged by Feuerbach and Marx at the time – is the form of *discourse*, since they talk only of discourse-objects and since it is only to discourse-objects that one can apply the correlative method of *disclosure* and confession. What is a confession? It is a discourse that rectifies a previous discourse by disclosing its true signification. Practically, this means that, at the level of what he actually does, the Marx of this period agrees with Feuerbach that *one should not talk about practice*, even in describing the producer's production of his product; one should talk only about *ideological discourses*, verbal or not, as constitutive of the human essence and reality. This means that Marx has not yet rejected the primacy of the ideological in history, even when he affirms, in the *1844 Manuscripts*, the primacy of economic production. It is only in the 'Theses on Feuerbach' that the theme of practice comes to the fore, for the first time, as a *concept*.

One more word about a quite spectacular – albeit involuntary – effect of the heteroclite, reactive conjunction of the theoretical components that go to make up Feuerbach's thought. I have already pointed to one such effect, the anticipation of the phenomenological reduction and hermeneutics; this may be considered an ideological effect. I would like to point out two others, positive this time.

First positive effect: ideological theory and theory of ideology

This effect is one of the products of the speculary theory of the object, an altogether paradoxical product. In Feuerbach, the speculary theory of the object – which is, moreover, sustained by and grounded in his materialist-empiricist theory of knowledge – can be regarded as the historico-theoretical source of three theoretical effects observable in the history of Marx and Marxism:

1. This theory survives in the *Marxist theory of ideology* as it is found in the *Manuscripts*, *The Holy Family*, and even the 'Theses on Feuerbach', but also, to a certain extent, in *The German Ideology*.

The essence of the speculary theory of the object is to be found in the equation 'object = essence of the subject'. Given

Feuerbach's empiricism, it is also possible to write object = religion, or real empirical object = religion. If we spell this out, we have: the mystery of such-and-such a speculative or religious construction = such-and-such an empirical fact.

Consider the Eucharist and Baptism:

> We give a true significance to Baptism, only by regarding it as a symbol of the value of water itself. Baptism should represent to us the wonderful but natural effect of water on man. . . . The profoundest secrets lie in common everyday things. . . . Eating and drinking is the mystery of the Eucharist. . . . One need only interrupt the ordinary course of things in order to given to common things an uncommon significance; *to life, as such, a religious signification.*[cc]

This is expressed in the equation: such-and-such an everyday act or empirical fact explains the 'mystery' [*Rätsel*] or enigma of such-and-such a practice or religious dogma.

This thesis has been taken over wholesale in the *1844 Manuscripts* (we shall see how), and is spelled out in the Eighth Thesis on Feuerbach: 'Social life is essentially practical. All mysteries which mislead theory into mysticism find their rational solution in human practice and the comprehension of this practice.' What we have here is the identity 'human practice = essence of the *enigma of mysticism*', an identity cast in the form of an adequation. It is cast in the form of the same adequation in *The German Ideology*.

This thesis is fundamentally Feuerbachian, and grounds the critique of Hegelian speculation as speculative empiricism: the recognition/misrecognition of fact and its presentation in travestied form as the essence of speculation. This misrecognition = alienation.[58]

Thus we have: empirical object, empirical fact, empirical practice, and so on = essence of its religious, speculative or ideological alienation. This paves the way for what has been incorrectly regarded as a *Marxist theory of the ideological*. Such-and-such an empirical given, empirical condition, empirical practice, empirical fact, and so on, is correlated, by way of an equation (with as many *mediations* as you like), with such-and-such a segment or formation of the ideological. Today this is the massively domi-

---

[cc] *EC* 275–8; translation modified.

nant theory of the Marxist conception of ideology (see Goldmann).[59]

The structure of this conception – or, rather, the structure *required* by this conception – can easily be broken down into the following theoretical elements:

(a) At one end, as *essence, an originary fact*, or a practice, or empirical conditions (which can even be class relations or relations of class struggle).

(b) *At the other end*, the corresponding ideological formation, or one of its segments, the *phenomenon* of this essence.

(c) Between the two, the necessity of producing the *genesis* of the phenomenon; in other words, the necessity of demonstrating the persistence of the originary essence down through the long line [*filiation*] of *mediations* that ultimately culminate in the phenomenon of this essence: ideology.

Origin, genesis, mediations: three concepts basic to this conception, all three of them included in the equation 'facts or empirical conditions = the essence of ideology'. This 'Marxist' thesis subsists even in *Capital*:[60] 'It is much easier to discover by analysis the earthly core of the misty creations of religion, than, conversely, to develop from the actual relations of life the corresponding celestial forms of those relations. The latter method is the only materialistic, and therefore the only scientific one.'[dd]

To rectify this ideological conception of ideology, one must obviously *abandon*, first, *the model it is based on, the theory of the speculary object*, and, second, *the concepts in which it exists*: origin, genesis, mediation, reflection.

The strategic point: everything is commanded by the concept of *genesis*, which is the conceptual translation of the equals sign. Hence the need for a radical critique of the ideology of genesis, as well as the need to elaborate a non-genetic theory of historical irruption, independently of a structural-functional theory of the ideological in its articulation with other instances.

2. Second effect: a theory of *reflection* as a theory, not now of

---

[dd] Karl Marx, *Capital*, trans. Samuel Moore and Edward Aveling, New York, 1967, vol. 1, p. 373.

the ideological, but rather of *knowledge*. Classic in Marxism since Engels,[ee] taken up again by Lenin.

The polemical, *negative*, and therefore ideological value of this conception should be distinguished from its theoretical value. From a critical-ideological standpoint, it represents a struggle against subjectivism, relativism, psychologism and sociologism (very clear in Lenin). The reflection theory is the theory of the *objectivity* of knowledge. As for its *positive* theoretical value, it is negligible, or even nil. One can derive nothing positive from an ideological theory that is polemical, and therefore negative. Complete theoretical sterility of a correct [*juste*] ideological defence when it is left to itself and as is. Right opinions, by themselves, produce nothing.

3. Here is the third effect, a veritable 'ruse of unreason' (ultimately, there are never ruses of reason, only of unreason).

In the classical Marxist tradition, the Feuerbachian theory of the speculary object served to found a Marxist pseudo-theory of ideology, an ideological theory of ideology. That is to say, we cannot regard the Feuerbachian theory of speculary reflection as the foundation of a (Marxist) theory of ideology. *However* – this is the ruse of unreason – it so happens that the Feuerbachian theory of speculary reflection does provide us with a remarkable *description of certain* essential features of the *structure of ideology*.

(a) First and foremost: the *category of the mirror*, or *speculary reflection*, or *reflection*. This category defines, not the relation between ideology and its real conditions of existence, which is *external* to ideology, but the relation, *internal* to ideology, between two categories constitutive of the ideological: subject and object (essence and phenomenon). We may say that the relation subject = object is typical of the structure of any ideology or ideological formation. Contrary to the claims of the classical Marxist tradition, which bears the stamp of a certain empiricism, the category of reflection – not in its polemical-critical-ideological sense, *but in its positive sense, as real determination*, is relevant not to the theory of objective knowledge but, without a doubt,

---

[ee] See Friedrich Engels, *Herr Eugen Dühring's Revolution in Science (Anti-Dühring)*, trans. Emile Burns, CW 25, *passim*.

to *the structure of the ideological*, in which a speculary reflection of correspondence between the subject or essence and the object or its phenomenon comes into play. All ideology is essentially *speculary*.

(b) Still better: this speculary structure appears as *centred* on the subject or essence. Hence: speculary structure = *structure of centring*.

(c) Still better: the structural effect of speculary centring is *reduplication*. This is what we have in the form of speculary reality. It necessarily follows that the object, which is the object of the subject, is also inevitably the subject of the subject. The centred speculary structure necessarily gives rise to this exchange of roles. That is why the object of the man-subject is God, who is the Supreme Subject. That is the sense of the Feuerbachian theory of religion. Specularity thus *reduplicates* the terms between which it operates. There is a subject only on condition that the subject is reduplicated by a subject who then becomes the Subject of the subject, who thereupon becomes the object of this subject. This inversion of sense/direction is typical of the structure of the ideological; but while Marx perceives it in his early works, *The German Ideology*, and even *Capital* as an inversion that inverts the relation between the outside and the inside of the ideological, this inversion is *in reality internal* to the structure of the ideological. The old formula, which comes from Spinoza, to the effect that religion is the world turned upside-down, or from Hegel, to the effect that philosophy is the world turned upside-down, a formula adopted by Feuerbach and then Marx in the form of the watchword: 'the inversion must be inverted so that ideology may be put back on its feet and destroyed as ideology' – this old formula has a merely *metaphorical* meaning as a theory of the relations between the real and the ideological; but it has a *positive, scientific* meaning as far as the internal structure between the elements constitutive of the ideological is concerned. However, if this characteristic of inversion is *internal* to the ideological, we can deduce from it no practical conclusion that can identify the transformation or elimination of the ideological through a counter-inversion, the inversion of the inversion. Or, rather, we may consider that *the practice of inversion does not affect the ideological, since it merely reinforces the structure of the ideological by acknowledging it* – that is, practically, by *making it work*. Yet this practice is at work in what is known as 'dialogue' as conceived by Garaudy:[61] to put religion back on its feet by recognizing its 'rational kernel', and so on; that is, by treating it as if it were *the inverted reflection of the real*, whereas this inversion is merely *internal* to religion itself. To put one's chips on the inversion internal to religion is by no means to call religion as such into question, but simply *to make religion work religiously*. Religion has never worked as well since finding functionaries in the ranks of the Communist parties who make it work much more effectively than the Christians themselves ever did. Christians are too often the prisoners of a rigid conception that misses the reality of the speculary relation as constitutive of religion. The Council[62] has finally realized this: it is never too late. To declare that the Church must open itself up to the world is to acknowledge that *if religion is to work well, its speculary relation must be put to work*: the speculary relation faith/world, internal to religion. A machine that is not used gets rusty and seizes up. To open religion up to the world – as Vatican II has set out to do by, for example, proposing bold liturgical reform – is to put the speculary relation to work right down to the level of the rite itself. It was high time. It has to be admitted in this regard that certain Marxists have, thank God, got a head start over the Fathers of the Council, not only opening up a path for them, but opening their eyes as well. Their merits have certainly been duly noted by the competent authorities, that is to say, by Providence. There are bishops *in partibus*[63] – but there are saints *in partibus* too.

(d) But still more is involved. This effect of the speculary relation with reduplication [*effet de relation spéculaire à redoublement*] leads to *a displacement, from the original centring to a centring that reduplicates the first*. There results a specific, *supplementary* effect whose functioning we saw when we discussed the ontological significance of the relation between subject and object, the centre and its horizon. This effect is now displaced on to the reduplicated Subject, here God. The relation subject = object, once it is caught up in the reduplication of this de-centring, takes on a new form, becoming a relation of the *absolute subordination of the first subject to the Second Subject*. The first subject becomes *accountable* to the Second Subject; the first subject is a subject subjected to the Second Subject, who is Sovereign and Judge. The speculary relation becomes a relation of moral accountability, that is, responsibility. On the other hand, the Second Subject serves the first as a guarantee. The couple submission/ guarantee (a highly provisional formulation) thus reveals itself to be basic to the structure of any ideology.

If this last determination of the structure of the ideological is accurate, then it looks as if the internal inversion produced under the effect of the speculary relation fundamentally modifies the relationship between the initial terms: *it is not the first subject, subject of the object, who is the true centre, but the second Subject who is the real centre.* Indeed, the couple submission/guarantee that I have just mentioned, and the reciprocal exchange that sustains it, begin to make sense when one sets out from this second Subject. This is, then, to say two things at once: *that the speculary relation is asymmetrical and unequal, and that its true foundation is this speculary inequality.*

As[64] we can see from this last remark, what Feuerbach contributes to our knowledge of the structure of ideology does not include the last of the consequences that we have drawn from him. This is because, first, Feuerbach *effectively denies* the functional validity of what he affirms: namely, the reduplication of the Subject. Second, it is because he is mistaken about what constitutes the centre; he inverts, within the speculary relation, the true domination, and quite simply ignores *its basic effect*: the couple submission/guarantee.

Thus there is, in Feuerbach's very important contribution to our knowledge of the structure of the ideological, a theoretical threshold he is incapable of crossing, quite simply because he takes religious ideology at face value; because, for him, religion is not an ideology, but merely the truth turned upside-down. For him, everything ultimately comes down to a question of sense, in the two senses of the word: signification and direction. (1) When he says that the whole of religion as such – as, that is, religion – turns on its *signification* (let us bear in mind what was said earlier about the anticipation of the Husserlian reduction and hermeneutics), he says that there is nothing to be learned from religion that does not come from religion. Thus he remains trapped within the self-consciousness of religion, without looking beyond it for that of which it is the symptom, and which operates in it without it. (2) When he says that the whole question of the demystification of religion as illusory form turns *on the reversal of sense* that makes it an illusion, he is still talking about an internal theoretical vector, and does not get beyond the limits of religion. This has a familiar consequence: that the knowledge of religion keeps us inside religion, since it is merely religion turned upside-down.

For us, things begin to look different as soon as we realize the necessity of certain *structural effects* about which Feuerbach says nothing, or which he denies the moment he mentions them: in particular, the effect of the *reduplication of the subject*, and the effect of *domination/guarantee* that follows from it. If we neglect this twofold effect, we too can put ideology to work in conformity with the pure schema of the speculary relation, but that is to follow ideology on to its own ground, and to consent to its characteristic illusion. If, on the other hand, we realize the *unprecedented* character, from the standpoint of the speculary relation, of *reduplication* and its effect of submission/guarantee, then we can treat these effects as precisely what is *mysterious* in the seeming transparency of the speculary relation, and as symptoms of what is at work in the ideological. We then discover, or can discover (this at any rate, is, the path I should like to take) that what we have so far called effects of the speculary relation, which can indeed be regarded as such within the field of the structure of the ideological, *is not merely an effect of this structure*, but the *symptom* of what commands its existence and very nature. We must therefore reverse the apparent order of the effects of the structure, and say that *the speculary relation is not the cause of the effects of reduplication and of submission/guarantee; quite the contrary, the speculary structure is the effect of a specific absence which makes itself felt, in the field of the ideological itself, in the symptom of the reduplication of the subject and the couple sub-*

mission/guarantee. This absence is an absence *in propria persona* in the field of the ideological, but a presence *in propria persona* outside it. This presence is ·that of the ideological *function* of recognition-misrecognition, a function that has to do with *what is misrecognized* in the form of the speculary relation of recognition: that is, in the last instance, the *complex structure of the social whole,* and its *class structure.*

If I have developed this remark in passing, this is because it is of the utmost importance *today,* because of the enterprises inspired not only by the development of religious hermeneutics or hermeneutics in general (ultimately, every hermeneutics is religious), but also by what is now generally called structuralism or structuralist interpretation, which is ultimately indistinguishable from hermeneutics (that is why Lévi-Strauss and Ricœur get along rather well). Take Sebag's essay, for example:[65] it shows what a 'structuralist' Marxist conception of ideologies can yield, or, rather, fail to yield. But one can go back to Lévi-Strauss himself, who ultimately does not disavow what Sebag forthrightly affirms.

Let me explain what I am driving at. As we have just seen in discussing what is interesting in what Feuerbach shows us about the structure of the ideological, it is quite possible to *make a structural analysis of an ideology work* while remaining entirely within the elements of its structure – while, that is, remaining the prisoner of what the ideology *says about itself,* or even while going much further than what it says, by analysing what it does not say about what it says, *its unsaid,* its latent discourse, which will then be called its *unconscious.* One never gets beyond the structure of the ideological when one proceeds in this fashion: bringing the structure of the ideological into relation with other, *isomorphic* structures does not undermine this structure, but has the opposite effect, inasmuch as this generalized isomorphism merely reinforces, merely *repeats,* the structure of the ideological. Indeed, there is every chance that it will put itself in the service of the ideological structure, repeating it at the level of objects and realities other than the ideological.

This is what happens in Lévi-Strauss's work, when he shows that the structures of language and of the exchange of goods, women and words repeat the structures of myths. The real question is: *who is repeating what?* If we know that repetition is a structure of the ideological, we have every reason to suspect that this isomorphism is itself an ideology of the relationship between the levels of social reality – that is, a negation of their differences under the dominance of the structure of the ideological, which has, among other functions (I am anticipating the results of work in progress), precisely [that] of *imposing differences under their denial, that is, under non-difference*. We come to the same conclusion when we observe, with Freud, that repetition can never be anything other than the *symptom* of something else, realized in repetition by way of the denial of the repressed that surges up in the symptom. Thus isomorphism is a repetition symptomatic of the ideological nature of structuralism. Far from providing knowledge of the nature of the ideological, the repetition of isomorphism is merely the symptom of structuralism's ideological nature.

This does not mean that structuralism has nothing new to teach us. It means that it comes to a standstill *at a threshold*, the one we have located in Feuerbach himself in discussing what he tells us about the functioning of the structure of religion. *This threshold is that of the misrecognition of the repressed*. Here, in the case of the ideological, it is the misrecognition of what operates in ideology in the speculary form of recognition: namely, the social or class function of the ideological structure itself. It is quite striking that we do not find a theory *of the different instances of* the *complex social whole* in Lévi-Strauss. This is obviously a result, in his case, of the ethnological ideological prejudice, the credo on which ethnology is founded; a few exceptions aside, it still dominates all ethnology and weighs heavy on it. The articles of faith of this credo are as follows: (1) a primitive society is not a society like the others; (2) the categories that are valid for modern societies are not applicable to it, for it is an undifferentiated society; (3) it is, fundamentally, an expressive society, each part of which contains the whole – a society one can recognize in its total essence by analysing one or another of these total parts (religion, kinship relations, exchange, etc.), since they all have an isomorphic structure; (4) this [expressivity] stems from the fact that social relations are human relations (whence the [ethnographic] way of listening, the ethnographic [experience], the ideology of 'fieldwork', of *Einfühlung*, of ethnographic understanding). The isomorphism of structures is the modern form of expressive causality. Structuralism is thus, in the last instance, a hermeneutics: the concept of structure is its theoretical fig leaf.

We can plainly perceive symptoms of structuralism's ideological limits at several exemplary points in its conceptual system: not only in the concept of *isomorphism*, but also in the couple *structure/unconscious*. The concept of the unconscious in Lévi-Strauss is highly symptomatic of his ideological limits. The unconscious is, for one thing, objective knowledge, unlike a society's self-conception – but then why call it the unconscious? We do not talk about the chemical unconscious, or the unconscious of physics. Lévi-Strauss talks about the unconscious, precisely, for a reason that has to do with the philosophical premises of his enterprise: the unconscious is *also* what is said without being said, it is the unsaid which is not external to the said, but *immanent* in it; it is therefore the knowledge that can legitimately be derived from the unsaid of the said, the unthought of the thought. The unconscious is thus the affirmation (the existence of the concept of the unconscious in the couple structure/unconscious) that *the knowledge of the ideological is immanent in ideology*. That is the basic thesis of any hermeneutics. It is this thesis that enables structuralist analyses to function without ever stopping to ask about the differential nature of the object they analyse. The consequence is that these analyses are quite likely to remain trapped in the categories of the ideology they analyse – that is to say, in their illusions.

We may find ourselves facing a similar temptation in our analysis of the structure of the ideological as given to us by Feuerbach. We can put it to work without stopping to inquire about the nature of the object it bears on. That is exactly how Feuerbach proceeds: that is why he merely gives us a penetrating but purely descriptive reproduction [*redoublement*] of the – or, rather of *certain* – categories of the structure of ideology, even while he remains the prisoner of religious ideology. In the same way, we too could yield to this temptation by pursuing the analyses of the ideological, and bringing all its categories to light; that would not, however, give us knowledge of the ideological. The risk is, precisely, that we will end up taking for effects of the structure what is only a symptom of that which is at work in it. The risk is that we will end up trapped in a hermeneutics which, while structuralist, remains a hermeneutics.

This is what happens to those who think that they can find a hermeneutics of meaning in Freud: when, as Ricœur does, they oppose a hermeneutics of meaning to an energetics of force in Freud, they miss the essence of Freud.[66] They treat the unconscious as the meaning immanent in the meaning, the unsaid of the said, the latent discourse contained in the manifest discourse, the latent discourse *of* the manifest content. They do not see that the structural effects which the hermeneutics of the dream manipulates are merely symptoms of an effect of the unconscious, which surges up in the field of these effects but is not immanent in them.[67] What they call biological energeticism is quite simply Freud's basic discovery: namely, that the unconscious is something other than the meaning-effects of the conscious mind; it is the effects of another mechanism, irreducible to the field of any hermeneutics whatsoever; it is another discourse. Recognizing this is merely the first, preliminary step towards recognizing what the unconscious is, but at least it indicates where we should not look for the cause of symptoms and where one should: outside the symptom itself.[68] There can be no Marxist theory of ideology in the absence of a radical break with all hermeneutics, existentialist or structuralist.

Second very interesting theoretical effect: theory of the ideological fact

This is an effect of the theory of the object; nothing leads us to expect it, it is even quite surprising: the theory of the ideological fact as the realization of desire – Freud's very words: *Wunscherfüllung*. Here Feuerbach anticipates not only Freud, with his terminology, but first and foremost Nietzsche, by way of the conceptual context. '*Thatsache ist jeder als erfüllt vorgestellte Wunsch.*' ['A fact is every desire which passes for a reality.']"

Feuerbach develops this theory in *The Essence of Christianity* in connection with the belief in miracles and the Eucharist. The religious imagination

> does not distinguish between subjective and objective – it has no doubts; it has been endowed with the five senses, not so as to see other things than we do, but to see its own conceptions changed into real beings outside of itself. What is in itself a mere theory is to the religious mind a practical belief, a matter of conscience – a fact. . . . O

" Feuerbach, *Sämtliche Werke*, vol. 7, p. 248; *EC* 205; translation modified.

ye short-sighted religious philosophers of Germany, who fling at our heads *the facts of the religious consciousness* ... do you not see that *facts are just as relative, as various, as subjective, as the representations of the different religions?* ... Were not angels and demons *historical persons?'*[88]

What is interesting here is that this theory of the ideological fact depends on the Feuerbachian theory of the object, whose *strict* consequence it is, and also on the Feuerbachian theory of religion as an inversion of sense and alienation in the object – an example of one of the effects of the consistency and coherence of a coherent component of Feuerbach's ideology.

Indeed, if we assume the following two propositions: (1) the object is the essence of an objectified subject; (2) the essence of the alienated subject is an alienated object; that is, if we assume the possibility of *a variation*, and thus of an inversion of sense in the very essence of the subject, we end up with a theory of the perception of the imaginary object as fact – in other words, a theory of *ideological hallucination* that anticipates Freud and Nietzsche, and is also of interest to any future Marxist theory of ideologies.

This theory is of still greater interest to Marxism in that it represents a serious challenge to all empiricist interpretations of Marxist philosophy. If what is perceived by the senses can be an ideological fact, the 'criterion of practice' is dealt an indirect blow. Whence the idea that the criterion of practice does not suffice to ground the Marxist theory of knowledge. Everything Lenin says about 'werewolves' in *Materialism and Empirio-criticism* falls short of the mark. The most interesting thing in Lenin's work is that the man who holds no brief for the belief in werewolves is the same man who, at the level of practice, forged a theory of ideological facts in his theory of spontaneity.

But what is much more interesting about the consequences of this theory of ideological hallucination (let me remind you in passing that the origins of it are to be found in Spinoza's theory of the image: the image is inherently hallucinatory – and, in Spinoza, the image is not, as in Taine, a state of consciousness, but the imaginary – that is to say, the ideological as a *systematic level*, a set, a system, or, we may say, a structured system) is that

[88] EC 204–5; translation modified.

we can bring the principle informing it to bear on those contemporary ideologies which *study facts* with extremely elaborate experimental apparatuses: for example, a number of human sciences [*such as*] psychosociology. The schema 'theory/verification by the facts' is perfectly valid when it comes to ideological facts. In science, we do not have verification by the facts, that is, by the facts of empirical consciousness, but a realization, in a theoretico-technical montage, of *theoretical facts*.[69]

II. THE GENUS
(THEORY OF THE SPECIES)

Species and genus: terminological ambiguity, a headache for translators. Should *Gattung* be translated 'species' or 'genus'? An Aristotelian reference, both logical and biological. 'Species' if we consider Feuerbach's transcendental biologism, but 'genus' if we consider his theory that the human species is the 'species of all the species'. 'Human form cannot be regarded as limited and finite ... [it is] the genus of the manifold animal species; it no longer exists as species in man, but as genus',[hh] – or, as he says somewhere, as 'nature's self-consciousness'.

At all events, when Feuerbach talks about the essence of man, or about man, he means not the human individual, but the human species. The human essence is the essence of the human species. This is a crucial point, for *Marx's break with Feuerbach* will be played out around the theme of the *human species*.

To talk about the human species is, by implication, to talk about individuals. The problem of the nature or the essence of the species implies the problem of the nature of the human individual, and of the relationship between the human individual and the species.

All of Feuerbach is contained in this definition: 'the essence of the species is the *absolute* essence of the individual',[ii] on condition that we assign the word 'absolute' the pertinent meaning. Its

---

[hh] Feuerbach, 'Towards a Critique of Hegel's Philosophy', *FB* 93.
[ii] Introduction, *FB* 104; translation modified.

pertinence is defined by the non-absolute, the *relative* – in other words, the limited or bounded: the *individual*.

The *individual* is the real being or individual subject whose absolute essence is the species, the essence of the species. A subject whose essential attribute is the essence of the human species. Practically speaking, this means that each human individual carries within him the essence of man, even if only in the form of the misrecognition of the human essence. But he does so within the limits of *individuality*.

What does the concept of the limits or bounds of individuality mean here? Two things:

1. Real, material limits. The limits of individuality as such, which are the determinations of empirical *existence* in the here and now. For example, having one or another determinate body: *a long or a short nose* ('it is true that the spirit or the consciousness is "species existing as species", but, no matter how universal, the individual and his head – the organ of the spirit – are always designated by a definite kind of nose, whether pointed or snub, fine or gross, long or short, straight or bent').[jj] For example, *having a sex*: male or female. For example, existing in such-and-such a historical period or century, and not another; hence existing in time, in a determinate time, not time in general. For example, existing in a certain place and not another.[kk]

Individuality = existence = finitude of existence = material determination = passivity. The whole of Feuerbach's materialist empiricism is based on the category of the determinate finitude of existence, the *primacy of existence*. Thus these material, empirical limits are not imaginary. They are *real*, and fundamental: they are the very limits imposed by *existence*.

2. But also *imaginary* limits. They are imposed, this time, on the essence of the human individual, not his or her existence. In itself, the essence of the human individual is the essence of the human species, existing within the limits of determinate individual existence. The imaginary limits stem from *confusing the necessary limitations of existence with the non-limit of essence*. The imaginary limits are those born of the individual's illusory belief

---

[jj] Feuerbach, 'Towards a Critique of Hegel's Philosophy', *FB* 57.
[kk] See ibid., and *Principles of the Philosophy of the Future*.

that his own individual limitations (existence) constitute the limits of the species (essence):

> Every limitation of reason, or of the human essence in general, rests on a delusion, an error. *To be sure, the human individual* can, even must, feel and know himself to be limited – and this is what distinguishes him from the animal – but he can become conscious of his limits, his finiteness, only because he can make the perfection and infinity of his species the object either of his feeling, conscience, or thought. But if *his own* limitations appear to him as the *limitations of the species*, this can only be due to his delusion that he is identical with the species, a delusion intimately linked with the individual's love of ease, lethargy, vanity, and selfishness.[ll]

The limits on individuality fall into two registers, *real* and *imaginary*. The paradox of Feuerbach is that, in the end, the only limits that constitute a real problem are not the real limits, those imposed by existence, but the imaginary limits. Those imposed, not by the nose and sex, but by the head. Not by the body and existence in the here and now, but by the imaginary confusion between individual and species.

The most characteristic illusion: that of the existence of the species in an individual: *incarnation*, or the reality of absolute knowledge:

> The incarnation of the species with all its plenitude into *one* individuality would be an absolute miracle, a violent suspension of all the laws and principles of reality; it would, indeed, be the *end of the world*. Obviously, therefore, the belief of the Apostles and early Christians in the approaching end of the world was intimately linked with their belief in incarnation. Time and space are *actually already* abolished with the manifestation of the divinity in a particular time and form, and hence there is nothing more to expect but the actual end of the world. It is no longer possible to conceive of the possibility of history; it no longer has a meaning and goal. *Incarnation* and *history* are absolutely incompatible; when deity itself enters into history, history ceases to exist.[mm]

Note what is interesting in these texts: the identification of an individual with the species is *the end of history*. Here Feuerbach reveals an idea that he has held in reserve. The problem of the

---

[ll] Introduction, *FB* 103; translation modified.
[mm] Feuerbach, 'Towards a Critique of Hegel's Philosophy', *FB* 57.

individual's relations to the species is in fact the problem of the possibility of *history*.

And its inversion: the existence of the individual in the species; also *speculative philosophy*, the destruction of the here and now, of determination, its negation, and so on. Compare Hegel and Neo-Platonic philosophy: the concept of the *concrete-universal* is precisely the existence of the individual in the species, that is, the end of the individual, the end of all determination, and therefore the end of all existence. The concept of the concrete-universal as *Unding* [non-sense]:

> Thought that *'seeks to encroach upon its other'* – and the 'other of thought' is being – *is thought that oversteps its natural boundaries*. This encroaching upon its other on the part of thought means that it *claims for itself that which does not properly belong to thought but to being*. That which belongs to *being* is *particularity* and *individuality*, whereas that which belongs to *thought* is *generality*. Thought thus lays claim to particularity; it makes the negation of generality, that is, *particularity*, which is the essential form of sensuousness, *into a moment of thought*. In this way, 'abstract' thought or abstract concept, which has being *outside itself*, becomes a 'concrete' concept. . . . Thought negates everything, but only in order to posit everything in itself. *It no longer has a boundary in anything that exists outside* itself, but precisely thereby it itself steps *out of its immanent and natural limits*. In this way reason, the idea, becomes *concrete*; this means that *what should flow from sense perception is made the property of thought* and *what is the function and concern of the senses, of sensibility and of life*, becomes the function and concern of thought. This is how the *concrete* is turned into a *predicate* of thought, and being into a mere *determination of thought*; for the *proposition 'the concept is concrete' is identical with the proposition 'being is a determination of thought.'* What is imagination and fantasy with the neo-Platonists, Hegel has merely transformed into the concept, or in other words, rationalized.[nn]

If we consider the relation thus affirmed: (1) on the one hand, existence and determination are associated with the individual; (2) on the other hand, his essence is associated with the species, what, then, is the theoretical status of the concept of species? Do we not relapse into *nominalism*? Are not the only existents individuals, and is it not then the case that the species is merely

---

[nn] Feuerbach, *Principles of the Philosophy of the Future*, FB 217–19; translation modified.

an abstract attribute, a universal in the sense the word had in the medieval debate over universals? In other words, is the species or the human essence or man not merely a name, *flatus vocis*, designating what is common to the individuals of one and the same period, or, in general, all periods?

This hypothesis is dangerous, for it paves the way for a critique of the human essence as a *name*, as an arbitrary, contingent formulation, bound up with history and the politico-ideological conjuncture. It opens up the path that Marx goes down when he says in *The German Ideology* that man is a myth that merely reflects the nostalgic ideology of the petty bourgeoisie. In that case, in the case of a nominalism, man or the essence of the human species is totally dependent on existing individuals, on their conditions of existence, and it becomes easy to denounce the idea of man or the essence of man as an artificial, inadequate notion that merely expresses the nostalgia or hope, etc., of certain individuals in a determinate period.

Feuerbach is not a nominalist: 'The species is not a *bloßer Gedanke*; it exists in feeling . . . in the energy of love.'[oo] No doubt he acknowledges that, for the individual, man or the human species is an *ideal*:

> The individual must be conscious of his limitation, and take man as such and the genus as his ideal. Our lives must be an ongoing realization of that ideal, an ongoing process of becoming-man. It is in the lower sense that everyone can say 'I am a man'; in a higher sense, however, one can only say, I must be, I want to be a man, but am not yet a man.[70][pp]

In other words, the interesting thing about Feuerbach is that he is not even momentarily tempted by a *neutral* nominalism. The human essence is not merely *the common remainder* proper to all individuals, the result of an inductive abstraction; for Feuerbach also describes it as an ideal. The human essence (species) is the supra-human, that towards which the individual tends, while recognizing or misrecognizing its superiority: *the supra-human*, that is, the supra-individual.

[oo] *EC* 268–9. [Where Althusser inserts *bloßer Gedanke*, Eliot translates 'an abstraction'.]

[pp] Feuerbach, 'The Concept of God as the Generic Essence of Man'.

But Feuerbach also affirms that the supra-individual is a real being:

> That there is something human in the supra-human is shown, for example, by the fact that a man places another man above himself and proposes to take him as an ideal. Thus a real creature is the ideal of a real creature. What is above me, above my individual powers, nevertheless belongs to the field of the human, to the genre, as it is developed in other individuals.[qq]

How are we to conceive the reality of the human species? How can the human essence be identified with an existence? How are we to conceive an existence which is not that of an individuality, that is, an existence which is not that of a finite material determination, of a finitude, but an absolute, infinite existence? How can we identify an absolute, infinite essence with an existence that is necessarily, like any existence, relative and finite?

A disarming solution: the real existence of the human species is *the whole set of men*, the totality of individual existences. Totality = the existence of all human individuals. What does 'all' mean? The answer is simple: the existence of all the individuals who have ever existed or will exist, who have existed or will exist in the past and the future – in short, in all of human *history*. The existence of the human species – that is, of the absolute, infinite human essence – is *human history* in its totality:

> All divine attributes, all the attributes which make God God, are attributes of the species – attributes which in the individual are limited, but the limits of which are abolished in the essence of the species, and even in its existence, in so far as it has its complete existence only in all men taken together, in the past and the future ... the future always unveils the fact that the alleged limits of the species were only limits of individuals.[rr]

But human history is not finished [*n'est pas fini; fini* also means finite]; Feuerbach does not defend the thesis of the end of history. Human history is, then, not finished [*non fini*], yet it is infinite [*elle est infinie*]. It does not yet exist in its entirety, but may none the less be anticipated as a totality, as an infinite totality. *It is*

[qq] Ibid.
[rr] EC 152–3; translation modified.

because it is not finished/finite [*elle n'est pas finie*] that it may be regarded as the *infinity of the essence* of the species; it is because it is not finite/finished [*elle n'est pas finie*] that it may be anticipated *as the absolute of the human essence.* And yet this infinity exists in the present finitude (unfinished, and therefore finite, because limited, human history); this absolute exists in the relative characteristic of the present [*le relatif actuel*].

In order to be able simultaneously to affirm the following two contradictory propositions: (1) Human history is the real existence of the infinite human essence; hence the infinite, unfinished character of human history is the existence of the infinite and the absolute of the human essence, of the human species; (2) But this human history is not finished, the totality does not yet exist; in other [words], the infinite exists only in the form of the finite; *it is necessary,* in order to resolve this contradiction – that is to say, in order to speak of this as yet non-existent totality, and know the essence of this totality while eschewing all nominalism – *it is necessary to assign this infinity a privileged locus of existence in the finite,* in *that which now exists,* in the *present.* One must go even further, and say that, from the very beginnings of human history, since one cannot wait for it to end, *the infinite of the species exists in the finite. It is necessary to have a theory of the present existence of the infinite, a contradictory concept.*

This theory, which is absolutely required by Feuerbach's premises, is the theory of the intersubjectivity of the I and the Thou. The species exists *in actu* in the I–Thou relation. This relation must exist in finitude itself (in order to be founded there), in empirical existence itself, precisely at the level of the determinations of the materiality of existence.

It is the theory of *sexuality* which founds the theory of intersubjectivity. Every individual is sexed: man/woman. The sexual relation is the empirical-material existence of the infinite essence of the species in empirical finitude: 'Where there is no *thou,* there is no *I;* but the distinction between I and thou, the fundamental condition of all personality, of all consciousness, is only real, living, ardent, when felt as the distinction between man and woman.'[ss] The thesis survives in Marx and the Marxist tradition. Take Marx in *The German Ideology:* the first degree of production

---

is the production of human beings (sexual production). Take Engels (*The Origins of the Family*), who takes up the same thesis again in connection with Morgan:

> According to the materialist conception, the determining factor in history is, in the last resort, the production and reproduction of immediate life. But this again is itself of a twofold character. On the one hand, the production of the means of subsistence, of food, clothing, and shelter and the implements required for this; on the other, the production of human beings themselves.'[tt]

Take the great classical thesis, a Feuerbachian thesis, which occurs in Feuerbach and Marx's early works, and is still faintly echoed in Bebel (*Die Frau und der Sozialismus*):[71] it is by the present state of man-woman relations – that is, by the degree of the *alienation*, servitude and exploitation of woman, and, accordingly, the degree of her *emancipation* – that one can judge the real state[72] of the human essence, of the alienation and disalienation of man. Woman's condition is the speculary mirror of the state of the human essence. It is from the state, alienated or not, of man–woman relations – hence from the condition, alienated or not, of woman, that one can judge the non-alienation or alienation of man (that is, of the human essence or human society). This idea is based on the theoretical premiss that *the essence of the human species and human society is wholly contained in the essence/existence identity of the man–woman relation*. This is plainly not a Marxist, but a petty-bourgeois humanist anarchist thesis, and it wreaks theoretical, aesthetic, ideological and political havoc. Take Aragon: 'woman is the future of man' (a specific variation on the Ponge-Sartre humanist thesis: 'man is the future of man'). The emancipation of woman is neither the absolute condition nor even the symptom of the emancipation of man. Not that the problem of woman's condition is not a real, objectively tragic problem; but this problem can obviously not be settled by the effects of the equation: 'woman's condition = man's relations to woman = the current state of the human essence'. And woman's condition cannot serve as a speculary index of the condition of the human essence. One can derive

---

[tt] Friedrich Engels, Preface to the first edition of *The Origins of the Family, Private Property, and the State, CW* 26: 131–2.

nothing, no strategy and no politics, from the equation that maintains this.

Feuerbach's thesis that the infinity of the human essence exists *in actu* in the finitude of intersexuality, the foundation of intersubjectivity, is prolonged in a veritable ideological delirium. Here are its essential moments:

1. The *sexual relation* is the recognition of the infinity of the species in the forms of finitude, determination and materiality – in short, of all the attributes of empirical existence. It is the paradigm of *all existence*. In the other sex, man confronts, in absolute fashion, existence as such in its original, raw state. Sexual love is the original and absolute experience of existence: of *Dasein*. This means recognition of the other-than-oneself as identical with existence, the other who exists outside me and is different from me. It is also the recognition of *submission to existence*: [*Copernican*] Inversion no. 2 of the primacy of the existence of the object over the subject. In love, I am not autonomous, not my own master, but am dependent on an external object, an object that is the true subject; I am its slave. This relation of existence, of determination by the other that exists outside me, this relation of heteronomy and submission to the existence of the empirical object external to me, this experience of the not-I, hence of *primordial passivity*, is not a purely intellectual way of looking at things, a conception arrived at belatedly; it is, from the outset, *a lived experience: the experience of passion–passivity, the experience of love.* It is not first known, it is first experienced. The species is experienced before being known, it is experienced from the beginning. Love is the originary experience of the radical origins of the species; love is the originary experience of the originary essence of the species. Love, primordially anchored in sexuality, is thus the recognition, experienced in the form of *feeling,* of the existence and infinite essence of the species, existing in the form of sexual finitude. The *predominance of religion* over all other natural or cultural objects of man and his world *also arises from the fact that religion is recognition* [*reconnaissance*] *in actu, which, throughout most of the course of history, goes without cognition* [*connaissance*]*, realizing all cognition by preceding it*; it is the recognition *in actu* of *the infinite essence of the species,* in the form of the relation to an *Other,* to the *Other: God.* This relation is *experienced* in religion; it is an origi-

nary existential relation, the originary relation that contains in itself the undeveloped truth of all other relations. When, in the course of its development, religion arrives, in Christianity, at the definition 'God is love', it attains the statement of what it is. *Whence a profound, originary relation between religion and sexuality* – although, of course, Feuerbach's conception of sexuality has nothing to do with Freud's, with the relation that Freud will later establish between religion and sexuality. In Feuerbach, sexuality is the originary existence of the human essence, of all the attributes of the human essence; it is not an autonomous *component* of this existence. Consequently, everything that Feuerbach deduces from what he indicates here remains – better, *is* – of no use whatsoever from a theoretical standpoint. Feuerbach was none the less, and this is yet another effect of the ruse of unreason – the first to establish a relation between *sexuality and religion*.

2. The sexual relation is the foundation and paradigm of every relation with the *Other* in general, that is, with an object different from the Subject. That is why this originary, intersubjective I–Thou relation is the condition of possibility for any relation with any object, taking 'object' here in every sense of the word, the external, natural object included:

> The first stone against which the pride of the individual, the *ego* stumbles is the *thou*, the *alter ego*. The ego first steels its glance in the eye of a thou before it endures the contemplation of a being which does not reflect its own image. My fellow-man is the bond between me and the world. I am, and I feel myself, dependent on the world, because I first feel myself dependent on other men. If I did not need man, I should not need the world. I reconcile myself with the world only through my fellow-man.[uu]

3. But in order for this individual sexed other, this or that particular man or woman, to establish the existence of the species with the other partner in the sexual relation, *this sexed other must be more than an individual*. For, as an empirical sexed being, he or she is an individual (nose, sex, here and now). More precisely, the other must, even while being a determinate and therefore limited individual, *function* as something other than a limited

[uu] *EC* 82.

individual. He or she functions, says Feuerbach, as a 'representative of the species':

> Between me and the *other* there is an essential, qualitative distinction ... he is for me the representative of the species, even though he is only *one*, for he supplies to me the want of many others, has for me a universal significance, is the deputy of mankind, in whose name he speaks to me, an isolated individual, so that, even if united only with one, I would have a social, a human life.[vv]

Is this to say that he is the representative of the species in the sense that he is the representative of the totality of human history: in other words, that he has the privilege – which inevitably leads, as we have seen, to the end of history – of being the species incarnate? Feuerbach cannot affirm this, although he comes close to putting it that way in many passages. In reality, the other, a finite individual, functions as the representative of the infinity of the species *in the* intersubjective *relationship* of sexuality and, more profoundly, of love. Thus it is *this relationship*, if we want to be rigorous in Feuerbach's stead, which itself functions as the infinite existence of the human essence. It is *this relationship* which is the existence *in actu* of the human species. Intersubjectivity is thus the foundation of every relation of human individuals to every object of the human species: theoretical objects (sciences) and practical objects (action). The Feuerbachian Cogito is a 'we'. But it is, as in Husserl – Feuerbach's terminology notwithstanding – a *concrete*, intersubjective Cogito, a theoretical and practical Cogito, and a historical Cogito. We are (see Thao) transcendental egos (and equals)[73] to the extent that we are equals in the originary exchange of constituent intersubjectivity.[74]

4. If the essence of the human species exists in this sexual intersubjectivity of the experience of love, *this is because the essence of the human species clearly exists in love*. The liberation of the human species from the limitations of its alienation is the realization of intersubjectivity *in actu*, its universal realization in non-alienated form. This means that the essence internal to all human relations *is love*; that the essence of hate is love; that the essence of social conflicts and wars is love. Men, as Christ said,

---

[vv] Ibid., p. 158, translation modified.

know not what they do: in reality, they love one another and think they hate one another; that is why they fight. Let them know what they do, let them know what they are, and they will love one another, thus realizing their human essence, the essence of the human genus. Love is thus the essence of hate; love is the essence of egoism. Men's political, economic and ideological conflicts are the quarrels of lovers who know not that they love. Let them realize it, let their eyes be opened, let the scales fall from their eyes, let the veils fall and their truth be unveiled, let them know the truth, and love will be realized, will become reality.

To love is to be a communist:

> Feuerbach is neither a materialist, nor an idealist, nor an identity philosopher. So what is he? He is in thought what he is in his actions, in spirit what he is in flesh, in essence what he is according to the senses – Man; or rather he is more, for Feuerbach only treats the essence of man in society – he is a social man, a *communist*.ᵂᵂ

Feuerbach is a communist. Feuerbach's communism is thus the communism of love, that is, the communism of the Christian religion 'taken at its word'. Examining this last conclusion, we see that what held earlier for the relationship between the first subject and the Second Subject in the speculary relation holds here as well. To understand the sense [*sens*] of that relationship, we have to reverse its direction [*sens*]. Feuerbach's deep reason – that is, the idea that he holds in reserve – is not what he presents as the foundation of his theory, namely, intersubjectivity, particularly sexual intersubjectivity – the true 'foundation' of his thought *is what he presents as its consequence*: his ideal of a communism of love and his conception of the revolution as disclosure, as 'the open confession of the secrets of his love'.[75] The revolution as confession (with the result that the sole means of political action is demystification; that is, disclosure, that is, books and articles in the press) – that is what he has in mind. To the question of the revolution, objectively posed by the class conflicts of his day, he answers with a theory of the communism of love, a theory of the revolutionary action of disclosure and

---

ᵂᵂ Feuerbach, '*The Essence of Christianity* in Relation to *The Ego and Its Own*', trans. Frederick M. Gordon, *The Philosophical Forum*, 7, nos 2–4 (1977), p. 91.

confession. Of course, in order to re-establish the true direction/ sense of his deductions, to re-establish this real order in the feigned order of his ideas, we have to take up a position outside the field of his ideas and the structural relation governing its elements.

5. Final consequence: *the conception of history*. History is necessary for several reasons. But, at the same time, the content of history in Feuerbach constitutes the resolution of the aporias of his conception of the relations individual/species.

History is, *first of all*, the resolution of the non-correspondence between individual and species, finite and infinite, relative and absolute, and so on. The existence of the human essence in its totality is the sum of individual existences in the totality of space and time, that is, in history. Thus the concept of history has *no* content *other* than that assigned it by the theoretical function which gives rise to it: *to make up the total, to be the total* – in other words, to fill in the gap between individual and species, or overcome the limitations of empirical individuality. History lodges itself, very precisely, *between* the individual and the species, in order to fill the vacuum separating them and transform the *species* from an abstract, nominalist concept into a *reality*: it is therefore nothing but the concept of this vacuum. The proof is that all the concepts which can be derived from it are vacuous. *There is absolutely no theory of history in Feuerbach.*

The fact that there is no theory of history in Feuerbach does not mean that the concept of history he mobilizes plays no theoretical role. On the contrary! It does nothing else. This explains *its second role*: to serve as a solution to the problem of alienation and the overcoming of alienation. History is accordingly the locus of existence of the events alienation/disalienation. But to say that it is their locus of existence is simultaneously to say that history is an empty place in which these phenomena exist. Yet it seems to be something more: it is the possibility of alienation and disalienation as the possibility of different states of human nature – thus there is a Hindu human nature, a Jewish human nature, and so forth, and one day there will be a fully realized human nature. But since these different forms of human nature *are not historical events except in so far as they are so many variations on the alienation and disalienation of the human essence,* we might as well say that calling them historical adds nothing to them –

except, precisely, the category of existence. History is accordingly the empty locus of the *existence* of the variations of the human essence.

Yet there is a privileged locus in history: the period in which the human essence will be realized and the originary essence will exist in the very form of authenticity. The whole theory of history as the locus of *existence* of the possible variations of the human essence is thus deduced from one particular form of existence, that of Absolute Knowledge, of the realization of the human essence – that is, the existence in which essence will be identical with existence. That is the negation of all history. *Thus, in Feuerbach, history exists only where history can no longer exist,* when its end realizes its origins. The identity of origins and end, an identity which is *to come,* is thus the negation of history. The concept negates itself in fulfilling its function. However, this particular period of history exhibits a special feature: it plays its privileged role in so far as this history, unlike past histories, does not exist and has never existed, or maintains an existence only in 'people's heads', in hope. I am a materialist in the sciences, says Feuerbach, but an idealist in history, a distinction that Marx and Engels adopted word for word – obviously a suspect borrowing (*The German Ideology* and Engels's *Ludwig Feuerbach*).[76] The concept of history thus reveals itself for what it is: the contradiction between existence and non-existence, or, more precisely, a type of existence required by its non-existence, by its existence *in the form of hope, as a wish.* History is the concept of the realization of a desire, or, rather, the phantasmagoric concept of the realization of a fantasy, the reduplication of a fantasy. If reduplication is typical of the structure of the ideological, then we are dealing, in the proper sense, with an ideology of history.[77]

Notes

1. *Un mauvais sujet* also means something like 'a bad apple'. Althusser makes the same play on words elsewhere; for example, *LP* 181. [*Trans.*]
2. The highest national competitive teachers' examination in France. One of Althusser's duties at the École normale supérieure was to help prepare students for this examination. [*Trans.*]

3. Feuerbach, *Manifestes philosophiques: Textes choisis (1839–1845)*, ed. and trans. Althusser, Paris, 1960.

4. Handwritten note in the margin of Document 2: 'effects of philosophical retreats different from mere deletions'.

5. Marx, *Economic and Philosophic Manuscripts of 1844*, trans. Martin Milligan and Dirk J. Struik, *CW* 3: 333.

6. This point is taken up in the third part of the course on Feuerbach, not enough of which has been written out to warrant publication here. See the Editors' Introduction above.

7. Here Althusser intended to quote an unspecified passage from Engels's *Ludwig Feuerbach and the End of Classical German Philosophy*.

8. Karl Löwith, *From Hegel to Nietzsche*, trans. David E. Green, New York, 1991.

9. See in particular Paul Ricœur, *Freud and Interpretation*, trans. Denis Savage, New Haven, CT, 1970, pp. 529–30: 'The same may be said of Feuerbach: the movement by which man empties himself into transcendence is secondary as compared to the movement by which he grasps hold of the Wholly Other in order to objectify it and make use of it; the reason man projects himself into the Wholly Other is to grasp hold of it and thus fill the emptiness of his unawareness.'

10. Here Althusser reverses the order of second and third parts of his course, not included in the present volume (see the Editors' Introduction to 'On Feuerbach').

11. Perhaps an error for 'humanism, naturalism, and sensuousness'. In 'The Humanist Controversy', Althusser talks about Feuerbach's impossible combination of Man, Nature, and *Sinnlichkeit*. [*Trans.*]

12. Handwritten note in the margin of Document 2: '*Wesen* (chez Hegel *Wesen ist was gewesen ist*).'

13. Althusser had planned to call the first chapter of an early text on Feuerbach 'Why Elephants Have No Religion' (see the Editors' Introduction above).

14. Document 1: 'we can say'.

15. See Althusser, 'Letter to Jean Lacroix', *SH* 207–8.

16. Handwritten note in the margin of Document 2: 'it goes down the same path the other way.'

17. Handwritten note in the margin of Document 1: 'not truth of, but admission, confession'.

18. Handwritten note in the margin of Document 2: 'to un-veil'.

19. Handwritten note in the margin of Document 2: 'Cf. Ruge/cf. book State/confession'.

20. Handwritten note in the margin of Document 2: 'the *Eigentum* of H[egel]/*bei sich* of F[euerbach]'.

21. 'In so far as' [*en tant que*] is a handwritten correction replacing 'as' [*comme*] in Document 2.

22. Handwritten note in the margin of Document 2: 'monopoly'.

23. These three adverbs are handwritten addenda to Document 2.

24. 'Type of' is a handwritten addendum to Document 2.

25. 'Of a, or' is a handwritten addendum to Document 2.

26. 'Distinct from external life' is a handwritten addendum to Document 2.
27. *S'appelle d'un nom spécifique*, which literally means 'calls itself by a specific name'. [*Trans.*]
28. Althusser translates 'consciousness/knowledge' in the second parenthetical phrase (which is not a parenthetical phrase in Feuerbach) with the words *conscience/science* (*Bewußtsein/Wissen* in the original German).
29. Handwritten note in the margin of Document 2: 'an absolute circle = without an outside'.
30. Handwritten note in the margin of Document 1: '*A knowledge* [savoir] *existing in the form of an object*, gestures, etc.'
31. See Note 28 above.
32. Here we have followed the wording of Document 2. Document 1 reads: 'but this word, consciousness, does not designate *transparency*, it merely designates the *speculary reflection*, the specularity of the existence of the generic essence of man in man's objects, in the human world'.
33. 'And practical' is a handwritten addendum to Document 2.
34. Handwritten note in the margin of Document 2: 'Theory/practice'.
35. 'And a finitude in the Kantian sense' is a handwritten addendum to Document 2.
36. Handwritten note in the margin of Document 1: 'this is why *the moon*'.
37. 'What would be [*qui serait*]' is a handwritten addendum to Document 2; the phrase originally read 'in the form of a noumenal object'.
38. The text indicates that Althusser wished to insert quotations here. He may have had the following passage in mind:

> Is it at all possible for the feeling man to resist feeling, for the loving man to resist love, for the rational man to resist reason? Who has not experienced the irresistible power of musical sounds? And what else is this power if not the power of feeling? Music is the language of feeling – a musical note is sonorous feeling or feeling communicating itself. Who has not experienced the power of love, or at least heard of it? Which is the stronger – love or the individual man? Does man possess love, or is it rather love that possesses man? (Introduction, *FB* 99–100)

39. Here we have followed the text of Document 2. Document 1 has 'immediately visible on condition that it is disclosed', and is emended to read: 'opaque by accident, but transparent on condition that it is disclosed'.
40. Handwritten note in the margin of Document 2: 'Why the privilege of religion?'
41. Here we follow the text of Document 2, which has been rendered uncertain by the fact that one correction has been written over another. Document 1 reads simply: 'that reason and liberty can exist in cultural objects'.
42. 'Certain effects' is a handwritten addendum to Document 2.
43. Handwritten note in the margin of Document 2: 'the same goes for the ant[eriority] of self-consciousness to consciousness and the antepredicative'.

44. 'Let me make this more precise' is a handwritten addendum to Document 2.
45. Handwritten note in the margin of Document 2: 'origin forgotten'.
46. Handwritten note in the margin of Document 2: '[genetico-critical?]'.
47. Handwritten note in the margin of Document 2: 'the subsequent covering-up.'
48. 'The relation =' is a handwritten addendum to Document 2.
49. 'For the "Theses on Feuerbach"' is a handwritten addendum to Document 2.
50. 'One word' is a handwritten addendum to Document 2.
51. Handwritten note in the margin of Document 2: 'primacy of the absolute'.
52. 'One can see' is written in over the phrase 'we shall see' in Document 2, but 'we shall see' is not struck.
53. See Note 52.
54. See especially the first sentence of Marx's 'Contribution to the Critique of Hegel's Philosophy of Law: Introduction', trans. anon., CW 3: 175: 'For Germany the *criticism of religion* is in the main complete, and criticism of religion is the premise of all criticism.'
55. See Marx, 'Contribution to the Critique of Hegel's Philosophy of Law', trans. Martin Milligan and Barbara Ruhemann, CW 3: 31.
56. Marx, Letter of September 1843 to Arnold Ruge, trans. Clemens Dutt, CW 3: 145. See 'The Humanist Controversy', Note 36.
57. 'One can put this' is written in over 'we will put this . . .' in Document 2. This is the last handwritten modification to Document 2.
58. Marginal note: 'blarney [*p. q.*] here on what Feuerbach calls his *genetico-critical* method'.
59. See especially Lucien Goldmann, *The Human Sciences and Philosophy*, trans. Hayden V. White and Robert Anchor, London, 1969 (1952), Chapter 2, A: 'The Problem of Ideologies'. Althusser's library contained a heavily annotated copy of this book.
60. From this point on, most of the quotations, a few very brief passages aside, are not directly incorporated in the text typed by Althusser; one finds only the page numbers of the passages mentioned or references to his notecards. We have included these quotations in the text, at the risk of including too much or too little.
61. Althusser is referring to the 'dialogue' between Communists and Christians, the theoretical justification for which was provided by Roger Garaudy, a member of the Political Bureau of the French Communist Party and the director of its *Centre d'études et de recherches marxistes* (*CERM*).
62. The reference is to the Second Vatican Council (11 October 1962 – 8 December 1965).
63. A prelate who bears the title of bishop but has no real jurisdiction of his own, since he is responsible for a purely nominal diocese in a non-Christian country.
64. Handwritten annotation in the margin: '*Watch out!*'
65. Lucien Sebag, *Marxisme et structuralisme*, Paris, 1964.

66. Ricœur, *Freud and Interpretation*, op. cit., Book 2, Part 1: 'Energetics and Hermeneutics'.

67. Handwritten note in the margin: 'They do not see that there are two different *discourses*, cf. the Freudian theory of the double inscription.'

68. At the end of this sentence, at the bottom of the page, there is a handwritten note: 'Lacan's str[ucturalism] is not hermeneutic.'

69. At the end of this sentence, there is a typed note: 'see the theory of the corresponding *organ* in Feuerbach (card)'. This notecard has not been found.

70. Althusser cites his own unpublished translation of this essay, preserved in his archives.

71. August Bebel, *Woman in the Past, Present, and Future*, trans. H.B. Adams Walther, New York, 1976.

72. Althusser's text reads 'the real relation'. [*Trans.*]

73. The two words [*egos, égaux*] are homonyms in French. See 'RTJL' 137. [*Trans.*]

74. Trân Duc Thao, *Phenomenology and Dialectical Materialism*, ed. Robert S. Cohen, trans. Daniel J. Herman and Donald V. Morano, Boston, MA, 1986 (1951). Althusser's library contained a heavily annotated copy of this book.

75. 'Religion is the solemn unveiling of man's hidden treasures, the avowal of his innermost thoughts, the open confession of the secrets of his love.' 'Introduction', *FB* 109–10.

76. See Marx and Engels, *The German Ideology*, trans. Clemens Dutt *et al.*, *CW* 5: 41: 'As far as Feuerbach is a materialist he does not deal with history, and as far as he considers history, he is not a materialist.' See also Friedrich Engels, *Ludwig Feuerbach and the End of Classical German Philosophy*, trans. anon., *CW* 26: 372:

> It was therefore a question of bringing the science of society, that is, the sum total of the so-called historical and philosophical sciences, into harmony with the materialist foundation, and of reconstructing it thereupon. But it did not fall to Feuerbach's lot to do this. In spite of the 'foundation', he remained here bound by the traditional idealist fetters, a fact which he recognizes in these words: 'Backwards I agree with the materialists, but not forwards.'

77. For the reasons indicated in the Editors' Introduction, we have not published the rest of Althusser's course, most of which he left in the form of notes.

The Historical Task of
Marxist Philosophy

(1967)

In April 1967, as the course from which 'On Feuerbach' is culled was getting under way, Althusser unexpectedly received a letter from Mark Borisovich Mitin, a pillar of the Soviet philosophical establishment. Mitin had launched his career with his contribution to a June 1930 Pravda *article unmasking Trotskyite sabotage of the materialist dialectic, gone on to play a key role, as 'Stalin's philosopher', in the 1948 triumph of Lysenkoism, and only recently, under Brezhnev, been named general editor of* Voprosy *filosofi [Questions of philosophy], the Soviet philosophical journal in the postwar era. He wrote to Althusser on behalf of the journal to solicit an essay for a special issue commemorating the fiftieth anniversary of the October Revolution. Althusser might submit a piece on 'developments in dialectical materialism' or 'the impact of the Russian Revolution on French philosophy'. The review 'would be equally happy', Mitin added, in what bore all the marks of a polite afterthought, to receive a 'summary' of Althusser's 'recent research'. The deadline was 1 July.*

Althusser harboured few illusions about the 'old fox' Mitin, to quote a letter of 23 April to his lover Franca Madonia. He harboured even fewer about the CPSU, whose right-wing revision of Marxist theory he regarded as the dominant factor in Soviet society's accelerating slide towards capitalism: the Russian 'fish', he wrote to his friend and former student Michel Verret on 1 March, was 'rotting from the head down'. It followed that the main task of Marxist philosophy was to promote, in what an unsigned article that Althusser had written the previous autumn euphemistically calls 'Yugoslavia', a revitalizing 'ideological revolution' like the one on the march in China.[1] It also followed that arriving at the 'correct conception of Marxist theory, of science, philosophy, and the relation between them' – ultimately the prerogative of the philosophers – constituted the task on which 'the fate of the socialist revolution' now hinged (p. 167 below). It did not by any means follow that the ideological state apparatus sustaining official Soviet Marxism–Leninism – the rotting head of the Russian fish, of which M.B. Mitin was a fairly representative incarnation – would help Marxist philosophy to accomplish its historical task.

Yet Althusser reacted to Mitin's letter as if he thought it might, doubtless because even the dimmest prospect of addressing a Soviet audience thrust all other considerations into the shadows. Working at the furious pace at which he usually turned out first drafts, he produced a 12,000-word 'summary of his recent research' in about two weeks, writing with an eye to 'getting by' the censors in Moscow, as he said in a May Day letter to Madonia, and, on the evidence of an undated letter to Étienne Balibar, 'sweating blood' in the process. He kept his other eye on the censors at home: if he enjoined the handful of associates to whom he sent his paper in April to maintain a 'total blackout' on Mitin's commission, it was not just out of a foible for the thrills of the clandestine, but also because he shared Verret's apprehensions (expressed in a letter of 2 May) that his enemies in 'the Party here' – beginning with the now beleaguered but still redoubtable Roger Garaudy – 'might succeed in stymieing publication there'. Thus Althusser most probably did not show his draft to anyone in the PCF leadership, although, as the letter that had prompted Verret's warning indicates, he did briefly contemplate clearing it with General Secretary Waldeck Rochet.

Althusser began revising his essay in late April. Since receiving Mitin's commission, he had been torn between providing an accessible summary of his work tailored to a Soviet audience and taking a fresh approach to questions he had been debating with himself since the appearance of For Marx *and* Reading Capital, *notably in a projected book on the union of theory and practice that had been expanding, to his own surprise, for the past year. In the event, he began by summarizing and ended by innovating. By the middle of May, ideas on the relation between philosophy and politics with which he had been grappling in the (never finished) book crystallized in a dense ten-page conclusion appended to the revised essay. They make 'The Historical Task', its pedagogical style notwithstanding, one of the pivotal texts in the Althusserian corpus. For 'Philosophy and Politics', as Althusser entitled his new conclusion, laid the groundwork for the thesis that informed everything he went on to produce, beginning with the critique of the 'theoreticism' that had informed everything he had produced so far: it argued that philosophy is not a Theory of theories which surveys the interrelations of all other discursive and non-discursive practices from a position above the fray, but a political practice representing, as Althusser would put it in a November interview, 'the people's class struggle in theory'.[2]*

Towards the end of May, Althusser submitted the revised and expanded version of his essay to a wider group of colleagues than he had the first draft, then had it put into Russian, so that – as he had written to Étienne Balibar on 17 April – the Soviets would not use the fact that they had to translate the text as a pretext for tampering with it. A week before the 1 July deadline, he wrote to 'Comrade Mitin' to say that the piece, which had ballooned to some forty-five single-spaced typed pages, would soon be expedited to Moscow. He added that he was also planning to publish it in France.

The rest was silence. In March 1968, long after the fiftieth anniversary of the Revolution and the commemorative issue of Voprosy filosofi *had come and gone, Althusser wrote to Mitin again to ask what had become of his manuscript, pointedly noting that he still intended to release part or all of it at home, that he could not decently delay French publication much longer, and that the resulting situation was 'delicate' for the Soviets as well. Unabashed, Mitin replied, after apologizing for his 'inexcusable' eight-months' silence, that Althusser's text was 'too long' (it was, in fact, double the length* Voprosy filosofi *usually allowed)[3] and that the Russian translation was 'less than brilliant'. He went on to say that, in a rare departure from 'usual practice', he had had the piece partially rewritten, retranslated, and pruned of the conclusion, which was 'absolutely independent' of the rest. The result of this operation, 'a success', would be published in a few months, once Mitin had Althusser's formal approval of the changes.*

Althusser's archives contain no trace of his response, which he may have given Mitin orally during his April 1969 visit to Paris. They do, however, contain a copy of a 26 August 1968 letter to the dissenting Soviet philosopher Merab Mamardashvili, in which, after noting that he had been hospitalized for a depression early in May, and again only recently, he reports that Mitin has sent him a 'remake' of 'The Historical Task', waxes indignant over the presumption involved in 'doing a rewrite', unbidden, of someone else's text, and complains that, stripped of its conclusion, his 'philosophical and political' essay appears unduly 'academic'. This suggests that he refused to authorize publication of the censored version of the piece. However, since the letter to Mamardashvili indicates that he was still weighing the pros and cons of bowing to Mitin, it is also possible that he did ultimately approve the expurgated version, only to see it, too, rejected on some new pretext. In any event, 'The Historical Task' never made its way into print in the USSR.

What might be called the non-publication history of the French text is more quickly related. In 1967, Althusser revived plans to found a theoretical journal that he had mentioned as early as 1963 in a letter to Pierre Macherey. As conceived in mid-1967, the first issue of Théorie, now slated for release by François Maspero's independent left-wing publishing firm on the fiftieth anniversary of the Russian Revolution, was to include some form of the essay that Althusser had submitted to Mitin, which – as Alain Badiou envisaged matters in a 24 June letter to Althusser – would serve as the new journal's 'real manifesto'. Meanwhile, Althusser had also decided to issue 'The Historical Task' as a book in a new, more broadly accessible sub-series of the series (also called 'Théorie') that Maspero had been publishing under his editorship since autumn 1965. Plans for this book almost reached fruition: Althusser's archives contain a full set of the page proofs. Yet it never materialized, any more than the review or the new sub-series in which it was supposed to appear. Perhaps because the new definition of philosophy proposed in 'The Historical Task' had been radically overhauled by autumn 1967, Althusser refused to pass the text for press.

He did not, however, suppress it outright, for an authorized Hungarian version, including neither sections I and II nor the concluding section on philosophy and politics, appeared in a collection of his writings released in Budapest in 1968. It is perhaps worth noting that this partial translation of 'The Historical Task' was the work of Ernö Gerö, who, after playing second fiddle for nearly a decade to Hungary's 'Little Stalin' Mátyás Rákosi, distinguished himself during his brief tenure as First Secretary of the Hungarian Party by begging the Soviet leadership to order the 1956 invasion of his country. Fallen upon evil days after a long exile in the Soviet Union, Gerö spent his last years in his homeland scraping a living as a freelance translator.

Many different versions of 'The Historical Task of Marxist Philosophy' have been preserved in Althusser's files, from the first draft through the handwritten Russian version sent to Moscow to the page *proofs of the projected French monograph. The present translation is based on the proofs, which were set from a typescript dated 18 May 1967. At some point before they were produced, Althusser intercalated a long passage in the typescript and added a long note; unlike the unmarked proofs, the typescript also bears many addenda and corrections in his hand. The typesetter's errors have been corrected after collation with this emended and expanded second draft. Such differences between the typescript and the proofs as show up in English translation have been flagged in the notes, minor modifications aside.*

G.M. Goshgarian

Today, in 1967, Communists the world over are celebrating both the fiftieth anniversary of the first socialist revolution and the one hundredth anniversary of the first volume of *Capital*: that is, in the full sense of these words, both the greatest *political revolution* and the greatest *theoretical revolution* of modern times, two revolutions that have changed the course of History.

On the occasion of this double anniversary, I would like to offer a few thoughts on the current situation, problems, and tasks of Marxist theory.

I.   TOWARDS A CORRECT UNION OF THEORY AND PRACTICE

To mention these two anniversaries in the same breath is to draw attention to something of crucial importance: Marx's theoretical revolution is one hundred years old; the Soviet revolution is fifty years old. Thus the revolution that Marx carried out in the realm of theory preceded, by fifty years, the revolution in Russian society carried out by the popular masses under Lenin's and the Bolshevik Party's leadership. For Marxists, there is nothing mysterious about the fact that the second revolution occurred so long after the first. The works of Marx, Engels and Lenin name the principle that allows us to understand why this should be so. It has to do with the nature of the workers' movement, the nature of Marxist theory, and the nature of the union of the workers' movement with Marxist theory.

1. 'Without revolutionary *theory*,' says Lenin in *What Is To Be Done?*, 'there can be no *revolutionary* movement.'

We need to pay very close attention to the wording of this famous dictum. Lenin does not say that 'without revolutionary theory, there can be no *workers'* movement'. For Marxist theory did not create the workers' movement. The workers' movement existed before Marxist theory, which would not have been possible without it.

On the other hand, the workers' movement did not produce Marxist theory by its own devices. Marxist theory is the product of a conjunction of theoretical elements (German philosophy, English political economy, French socialism) and political events (the class struggle, the first interventions of the workers' movement, etc.) in the ascendant phase of Western capitalism.

Lenin by no means affirms that Marxist theory is essential to the workers' movement; he says it is essential to the *revolutionary* workers' movement. He thereby indicates that, without Marxist theory, the workers' movement would have emerged and developed, but would not have become *revolutionary* in the objective sense of that term – that is, capable not merely of wishing or hoping for, but of *making* the socialist revolution.

This first thesis of Lenin's refers us to a second, well-known Leninist thesis on the objective limitations on the development of a workers' movement 'left to its own devices'. These limitations are the limitations of utopian socialism, anarchism and anarcho-syndicalism: in sum, of 'trade-unionism' and Social-Democratic reformism. They are the limitations of the 'spontaneous' ideology of the workers' movement. When Lenin calls this ideology 'spontaneous', he means that it is in fact dominated by bourgeois and petty-bourgeois ideology.

2. Only Marxist *theory* enables the workers' movement to transform itself and become objectively revolutionary, for this theory alone enables it to rid itself of the theoretical and practical effects of 'spontaneous' anarchist-reformist ideology.

Why is Marxist theory capable of ensuring this transformation and this emancipation? Because it is not one '*ideology*' among others, that is, a distorted [*fausse*] and therefore subjective representation of the history of societies, but a *scientific* and therefore objective conception of it.

Thus the workers' movement can become objectively revolutionary on the twofold condition that it (a) abandon the 'spontaneous' ideological theories which are an effect of the economic exploitation and political and ideological domination of the working class by the bourgeois class; and (b) adopt, as its own theory, the Marxist science of the history of societies.

It is this scientific theory which affords the workers' movement knowledge of the laws governing the structure and development of social formations, the social classes and their struggle, and the objectives, means, and forms of organization and action required to ensure the victory of the revolution. Only this scientific theory can bring about the transformation of the utopian workers' movement into a *revolutionary* workers' movement. Strictly speaking, then, Lenin's celebrated phrase should be amended to read: 'without (*scientific*) revolutionary theory, there can be no (objectively) *revolutionary* workers' movement'.

3. If we compare the following two statements: (a) the workers' movement existed before Marxist theory and independently of it; and (b) without a scientific theory of history, there can be no revolutionary workers' movement, we will grasp the theoretical and historical significance of the union of Marxist theory with the workers' movement, which is the great event of modern times.

Without this union, Marxist theory would have remained a dead letter; without this union, the workers' movement would not have become revolutionary.

History has, time and again, shown the correctness [*justesse*] of this principle. While the revolution has not triumphed wherever this union has been realized, it has triumphed only in places where this union has been truly realized: for the first time in the world in 1917 in Russia, and for the second time in China in 1949. On the other hand, in places where the workers' movement has not adopted Marxist theory and has not been transformed by it – for example, in England (on which Marx and Engels had nevertheless set great hopes in the mid-nineteenth century) – not only has the revolution not taken place, but the prospects for revolution remain remote. Again, in places where the workers' movement did adopt Marxist theory, but seriously distorted its principles in an evolutionist-economistic-reformist direction, as in the German Social-Democratic party before 1914, the revolution was rendered impossible; then, when it did break out in the aftermath of the First World War, it was crushed. Thus history clearly shows that the union of Marxist theory and the workers' movement is the necessary condition for the triumph of the revolution.

Yet it also shows that this necessary condition is itself subject to an absolute precondition: *this union cannot be just any kind of union*, it cannot be an unprincipled union or a union based on deformed or distorted principles. *It must be a correct union* based on correct principles, that is, on rigorously scientific principles and everything that follows from them, theoretically, ideologically and politically.

When the principles governing this union are not correct, or when correct principles are allowed to degenerate under the influence of bourgeois ideology – evolutionism, economism, empiricism, pragmatism, moral idealism, and so on – the practical consequences never take long to make themselves felt. They are always harmful, serious, or extremely serious.

The correct union of Marxist theory and the workers' movement can therefore only be the product of a long, hard struggle. History did not find this union ready-made; it required a struggle that lasted for decades, a struggle pursued in myriad, complex forms, in order to propose it to, and impose it on, the workers' movement via the First and Second Internationals. And we know how the Second International ended up: in a historic catastrophe. We know that a decisive intervention on Lenin's part was required to rectify the grave theoretical and practical errors of the Second International, and to propose to – and impose on – the workers' movement a correct form of the union of this movement with a correct conception of Marxist theory.

This struggle, then, is interminable: it is being pursued today as well, not only in the Communist Parties of the capitalist countries, but also in the socialist countries. It will be pursued tomorrow, too, throughout a very long period whose end cannot be foreseen.

Thus, if the union of Marxist theory and the workers' movement did not tumble from the skies of history, neither is it, for us, a *definitive result* that can simply be taken for granted. The experience of the past thirty years is proof of this. This union is a task that we must always accomplish anew, a result that we must constantly reinforce and rectify, defending it with the utmost vigilance against the many forms of pressure – visible and invisible, open or surreptitious – exerted by the bourgeois and petty-bourgeois ideology that is constantly reproduced, and constantly besieges and besets Marxist theory.

4. What does the *correctness* of this union depend on? Let us again take the example of Lenin's struggle against the distorted principles of the Second International.

What did Lenin do to rectify the erroneous forms of the union established by the Second International?

First, he struggled against deviations in the interpretation of Marxist theory in both historical materialism (the theoretical struggle against the revisionists and populists) and dialectical materialism (the struggle against the empirio-criticists and bourgeois philosophical ideology). In this way, he restored Marxist theory in its specificity and purity and treated it as a true science, developing it and using it to produce theoretical discoveries (for example, Imperialism).

Second, Lenin defined a new political line. At the same time, he defined new forms of organization (the Bolshevik Party, the Third International), leadership and political action. Lenin defined this new political line and these new forms of organization and action by analysing the concrete situation, mobilizing Marx's scientific concepts to do so.

In the process, however, Lenin did not only apply the then existing Marxist concepts. He produced, in rigorous fashion, *new* theoretical, scientific and philosophical concepts in order to solve the problems that history put before him; and he translated the results of his theoretical discoveries into political practice. We can draw important conclusions from this.

First conclusion

Without the existence and strength of the Russian workers' movement, the theoretical struggle and new knowledge produced by Lenin would have remained a dead letter, at least for an indeterminate period. But without Lenin's theoretical struggle and theoretical production, without his theoretical discoveries and their consequences (his analysis of the political situation, his definition of new forms of organization and action), a *correct* union of Marxist theory with the Russian workers' movement would not have been achieved; the proletarian revolution would perhaps have broken out, but it would not have prevailed.

Second conclusion

Lenin's actions clearly show us the *strategic objectives* of the struggle that enabled him to realize this correct union and made possible the triumph of the October Revolution. The strategic objectives of Lenin's struggle were the two domains of Marxist theory: the *science of history* (which commands the science of the political line, of organization, and of action) and *Marxist philosophy*, as well as the *articulation* between them.

Lenin struggled against bourgeois ideological distortions of Marxist science and philosophy and for the recognition of, cognition of and rigorous respect for both Marxist science and philosophy and the relation between them.

He struggled, as no one else ever has, to win recognition for the theoretically revolutionary nature (revolutionary, that is, in the theoretical realm) of Marxist philosophy and science; he struggled to win recognition for the specific nature of theory and theoretical work and the absolute requirement for 'purity', rigour, systematicity and fertility in this domain; finally, he struggled to win recognition for the decisive role that Marxist philosophy plays in theory, ensuring the existence, correctness, rigour and development of the Marxist science of history.

Third conclusion

Lenin did not content himself with defending Marxist theory and restoring it in its 'purity'. In practice, he treated it as a truly living, fertile scientific theory deserves to be treated: by developing it, that is, by producing not only new *knowledge* [*connaissances*], but also new *theoretical concepts*.

One can, of course, use existing scientific concepts to obtain new knowledge, and thus broaden the field of existing knowledge. That is what happens when – to use the consecrated expression – one 'applies' existing scientific concepts to new regions of reality or new concrete objects. In this way, it is possible to increase the stock of existing knowledge by analysing a particular concrete social formation in a particular conjuncture (Tsarist Russia before 1905, the new class relations after 1905, in 1917, and so on). If, in this case, one limits oneself to utilizing existing scientific concepts without producing new ones, then one can only be said to have increased the sum of existing *knowledge*, not to have developed theory.

But one can also – and this in fact occurs rather often, even when one sets out to do nothing more than increase the sum of what is known – develop theory, that is, produce new theoretical, scientific or philosophical concepts. To say that Lenin did not simply restore Marxist theory but also developed it accordingly means that he in fact produced new *theoretical concepts* in Marxist science and philosophy.

Thus to treat Marxist theory as a scientific theory is to enrich it in both senses of the word: to increase the stock of knowledge that it allows us to acquire, and to develop the theory itself: that is, to produce new theoretical concepts.

These results – knowledge on the one hand, theoretical discoveries on the other – are the product of that labour of criticism, elaboration, abstraction, combination of empirical givens with abstract principles, and so on, which comprises the specific form of practice that we may call *theoretical practice*.

The life of a scientific theory is therefore poles apart from mere contemplation of its principles, even if they are 'pure'. A scientific theory is not scientific – that is to say, living and fecund – unless it is the site of a veritable theoretical practice. Hence Marxist theory is not a dogma: it is a living entity only on condition that it produce new knowledge and theoretical discoveries. Its development is infinite, just as its object is 'infinite' (Lenin). A scientific theory is, therefore, an open-ended discipline. An ideology, in contrast, is a closed system that produces nothing new, never ceasing to repeat itself because it has only one goal: to legitimate certain prejudices, results or objectives established in advance. The kind of theoretical practice that characterizes a scientific discipline, on the other hand, constantly requires new *discoveries*.

The life of a theory does not consist, then, in contemplation of it, or commentary on it, or pure and simple repetition of it in 'examples' that merely illustrate the theory without in the least developing it; nor is it limited to 'applying' the theory to new concrete objects (an increase in the sum of knowledge). The life of a theory also consists in producing new theoretical concepts (it consists in the progress of the theory). The life of a theory is *theoretical practice, the production of new knowledge by means of the production of new theoretical concepts.*

Fourth conclusion

Lenin did not just engage in theoretical practice; he also deduced consequences for *political practice* from theoretical practice. Thus he brought theoretical practice into relation with the real practices (economic, political, ideological) which constitute the conditions of theoretical practice and provide it with its real-concrete objects; that is, he brought it into relation with the practice of the workers' movement. Yet if he was able to save the workers' movement from the deviations of its 'spontaneism', which overlapped with some of the deviations of the Second International, this was because he had scientific principles and scientific theoretical knowledge at his disposal. At the same time, Lenin demonstrated that political practice can – within determinate limits, and on condition that its results are subject to scientific analysis – not only verify or invalidate theoretical hypotheses, but even produce veritable *practical inventions* that are the equivalent of *theoretical discoveries,* inventions whose content theory then has to think, and from which it draws consequences (for example, the invention of the dictatorship of the proletariat by the Paris Commune, or the invention of the Soviets by the masses of workers during the 1905 revolution).

Such are the essential conclusions to be drawn from Lenin's and the Bolshevik Party's struggle to forge a correct union of Marxist theory with the workers' movement.

We can see that the *correctness* of this union depends on a correct conception of Marxist science and philosophy, and of their relationship; of theory as a theoretical practice that produces new knowledge; and of the relationship between theoretical practice and political practice. We can also see that if only one of these elements or relationships is distorted, the consequences will make themselves felt throughout this complex system and, ultimately, in political practice itself.

No doubt some of these deviations will have only limited effects, or effects that remain limited for a certain period, so that we have this period in which to rectify them. But it is equally clear – this explains certain major failures of the workers' movement, such as that of the Second International – that some of these deviations can be serious, and can affect too many elements in this complex whole to be rectified and brought under control in time, with the result that they end up producing historical catastrophes.

It is in this very precise sense that we can say that the outcome of the struggle for a correct union of Marxist theory and the workers' movement – that is, ultimately, the fate of the socialist revolution itself – will be determined not only by something that everybody can see – namely, *political practice* – but *also* and at the same time, and, in certain critical conjunctures, in absolutely *decisive* fashion, by the struggle for a correct conception of Marxist theory, of science, philosophy, and the relationship between them; the struggle for a correct conception of theoretical practice, and of the relationship between theoretical and political practice.

We should keep these conclusions constantly in mind when we are analysing the current tasks of Marxist theory. The struggle for the defence and development of Marxist theory, the struggle for its rigour and fecundity, is always a crucial factor in the revolutionary struggle. In certain critical conjunctures, it can even be, as it was in Lenin's day, the *determinant* factor in that struggle.[a]

[a] For example, in 1902, in *What Is To Be Done?*, Lenin pointed out the absolutely *determinant* character of theory for political practice at a critical moment in the history of the Russian and international workers' movement:

> *Without a revolutionary theory* there can be no *revolutionary* movement. *This cannot be insisted upon too strongly at a time when the fashionable preaching of opportunism is combined with absorption in the narrowest forms of practical activity* ... *In very recent times we have observed* ... *a revival of non-Social-Democratic* [that is, non-Marxist] *revolutionary tendencies. Under such circumstances, what at first sight appears to be an 'unimportant' mistake may give rise to most deplorable consequences, and only the short-sighted would consider factional disputes and* strict distinction of shades to be inopportune and superfluous. The fate of Russian Social-Democracy for many, many years to come may be determined by the strengthening of one or another 'shade'. (Lenin, *Essential Works*, ed. Henry M. Christman, New York, 1966, pp. 69–70; emphasis added, L.A.)

II. Towards a theoretical politics

How should we go about defining, in the light of these principles, the strategic tasks that are of vital importance for Communists in the field of Marxist theory today?

To define these tasks is to define what we must call a *theoretical politics*, that is, a general line on the action to be carried out in the realm of theory: a line that sets tactical and strategic objectives, and identifies the 'decisive links' in the present theoretical conjuncture, together with the corresponding means of action.

As with any kind of politics, in order to define the strategic and tactical tasks of a theoretical politics, we need to have the results of a twofold analysis:

1. an analysis of the general political, ideological and theoretical *conjuncture* in which Marxist theory must struggle in order to establish itself and develop. Such an analysis has to bring out the structure of this conjuncture, with its dominant and subordinate elements. It has to bring out the complex organic relationship between political, ideological and theoretical problems. It has to study the balance of ideological and scientific forces in the theoretical realm. Finally, it has to pinpoint the strategic problems in the ideological and theoretical struggle.

2. an analysis of the *present state of Marxist theory*, in both the capitalist and socialist countries; a balance sheet of its present strengths and weaknesses; a critical, historical and theoretical examination of the reasons for its results, successes, failures and shortcomings.

By combining the results of these two scientific analyses, we can define with certainty the strategic and tactical tasks of a theoretical politics, as well as the means required to carry it out.

There can obviously be no question of making such extensive analyses, even very schematically, within the narrow scope of this essay. I shall therefore take the liberty of using a direct method in order to draw the reader's attention to the problem I consider to be *strategic problem number 1* of Marxist theory: that of Marxist philosophy or dialectical materialism.

The thesis I propose is simple: *Marxist philosophy today repre-sents the 'decisive link' on which depend the future of Marxist theory and, consequently, the 'correctness' of the union of Marxist theory and the workers' movement.*

III.   Overcoming the lag between Marxist philosophy and Marxist science

I know that I risk doing violence to the convictions of a number of comrades, communist philosophers included, when I declare that, one hundred and twenty years after the *Manifesto*, one hundred years after *Capital*, and fifty years after Lenin, Marxist philosophy still objectively constitutes a *problem*. These comrades will certainly join me in acknowledging, in line with Lenin's theses, the importance of Marxist *philosophy* in the ideological and theoretical struggle. But they will not necessarily join me in affirming that Marxist philosophy is today the 'decisive link', and therefore the number 1 strategic task of Marxist theory. Above all, they may find it paradoxical, surprising and wrong to say that Marxist philosophy *still* constitutes a problem, and *our number 1 problem* at that.

I shall therefore explain what I have in mind, while anticipating possible objections as best I can.

Let me indicate the meaning of my thesis straight away.

In declaring that Marxist philosophy is the site of a very special problem for us, I obviously do not mean that we know nothing about the nature of Marxist philosophy. The opposite is true, since the texts of Marx, Engels and Lenin provide us, when they are read correctly, with the basic principles of Marxist philosophy. I mean, rather, to call attention to the genuinely paradoxical situation in which Marxist philosophy finds itself today:

(i) first, dialectical materialism objectively *lags behind* historical materialism in its theoretical development;

(ii) second, today, not just the solution to a number of very important theoretical problems, but also the way we pose them, depend on *dialectical materialism*. These problems fall to the province of historical materialism and other sciences.

If Marxist philosophy is the site of a problem, and a special problem at that, it is because of this *objective paradox*. Let us therefore say, using a metaphor of Lenin's, that although dialectical materialism should stay 'one step ahead' of historical materialism in order to play its appointed role in the theoretical conjuncture, it has in fact fallen several steps behind.

Let us first examine the lag between Marxist philosophy and historical materialism.

This is an objective fact; no one who is familiar with Marxist theory can deny it. To give non-specialists a sense of it, we might begin by pointing out that the classic authors have bequeathed us infinitely fewer texts on philosophy than on economic, political or historical theory. Marx offers the most striking example: in philosophy, he has left nothing even remotely comparable to *Capital*. But it is not only a question of the quantity of the texts available to us; it is also a question of the quality of what they contain.

One can perfectly well situate the qualitative difference between the texts on dialectical materialism and those on historical materialism available to us: it lies in a difference in *theoretical elaboration* – to be very precise, in a difference in conceptual precision and rigour as well as in theoretical systematicity. In a word, it is a difference in what Marx calls the abstract (or conceptual) 'forms' and the 'order of exposition'. *Capital* displays exceptional conceptual precision, intellectual rigour and theoretical systematicity. The philosophical texts available to us are a very long way from possessing these qualities; moreover, they by no means claim to. Engels warns us, in the preface to *Anti-Dühring*, that his book is a 'polemical work'; thus it is not a rigorous, systematic exposition of Marxist philosophy. The same holds for Lenin's *Materialism and Empirio-criticism*. These are books of ideological and political combat, not rigorous, systematic expositions of dialectical materialism comparable to *Capital*. In the last instance, then, the lag between Marxist philosophy and historical materialism is a difference in conceptual rigour and precision as well as theoretical sytematicity.

We can explain this lag by adducing, first, diverse *historical* reasons. Engels himself says that he and Marx did not 'have the time' to develop philosophy as fully as everything else. And it is true, from a practical standpoint, that for a long time historical materialism represented the 'decisive link', and that it was critically important that progress should be made in this field, given the imperatives of the class struggle.[b] Indeed, if most of the philosophical texts handed down to us by our classic authors are texts of ideological struggle, that is because these authors felt a pressing need to reply to the attacks of the enemy, to 'follow him on to his own ground',[c] and, often, to fight him with his own weapons, which were simply *turned against* him. Hence the relatively improvised and, in any event, limited nature of the reasoning and concepts deployed, and their relative lack of rigour when compared with those mobilized in *Capital*. We could adduce many more historical reasons, such as the evolutionism and empiricism of certain theoreticians and leaders of the Second International and, in the 1920s, the historicism of the 'ultra-left' theoreticians, succeeded by the pragmatism and dogmatism of the period of the 'personality cult'. Evolutionism, empiricism, historicism, pragmatism and dogmatism are ideological tendencies that run counter to not only the development of Marxist philosophy but even, under certain circumstances, its very *existence*, by virtue of both their theoretical and practical effects.

We need only examine these so-called historical reasons with a modicum of attention to see that they are not just historical, but also *theoretical*.

For example, the ideologies that Engels and Lenin had to combat on philosophical grounds (Dühring's humanist idealism, the empirico-criticist idealism and historicist subjectivism of Lenin's adversaries, etc.) most certainly were historical obstacles to the development of Marxist philosophy; but they were at the same time theoretical obstacles, revisionist ideological interpretations of Marxism that Marxist philosophy had to combat – that is, to refute theoretically – if it was itself to survive and progress.

---

[b] On this point, see Engels, Letter of 21–22 September 1890 to Joseph Bloch, in Marx and Engels, *Selected Correspondence*, ed. S.W. Ryazanskaya, trans. E. Lasker, Moscow, 1975, pp. 394–6; Lenin, *Materialism and Empirio-criticism*, trans. anon., Moscow, 1970, pp. 230, 318–19.

[c] Engels uses this formula in *Anti-Dühring*, as does Lenin in *Materialism and Empirio-criticism*.

Similarly, the evolutionism, empiricism, historicism, pragmatism and dogmatism of a later period constituted historical and political obstacles to the development of Marxist philosophy only to the extent that they were simultaneously theoretical obstacles to it.

Thus it is not enough to adduce simple historical facts to explain why Marxist philosophy lags behind historical materialism. One must also adduce *theoretical* reasons, which, as we have just seen, involve the struggle that Marxist philosophy inevitably had to wage against various forms of bourgeois philosophical ideology in order to secure not only the right to develop, but also, quite simply,[4] the right to exist. The unity of the historical and theoretical reasons that can be evoked in this connection – in other words, the reasons for the lag between Marxist philosophy and historical materialism – is to be found in this struggle against bourgeois philosophical ideology and for the existence and development of Marxist philosophy.

If this thesis is correct, we must go much further. It was not just 'because they did not have the time' that Marx and Engels did not raise Marxist philosophy to the theoretical level of *Capital*. It is no accident that Engels only belatedly joined the philosophical battle against Dühring, who had been wreaking havoc in the socialist party for ten years. It is no accident that Engels was merely reacting to the attack of an adversary who had stolen a march on him, on the ground chosen by this adversary, philosophy. In a certain sense, Marx and Engels learned something from Dühring, something whose importance they had previously underestimated: the fact that the existence of Marxist philosophy was *vital* to the Marxist science of history itself.

Thus the lag between dialectical and historical materialism goes back much further than the historical events just mentioned and, consequently, involves more than the individuals Marx and Engels. This lag is not just the consequence of certain political or ideological events, nor even of the time constraints or personal preferences of the founders of Marxism; in the final analysis, it is the consequence of a law of the history of the production of knowledge. To be very precise, it is the effect of *the law governing the emergence of a new science in its relationship to the new philosophy required by the new science.*

We can roughly formulate this general law as follows: when a radically new science is founded in a great 'continent' as yet unexplored by scientific knowledge, yet dominated by theoretical formations of an ideological kind, the new philosophy that the new science requires can emerge and develop only *belatedly* [*après coup*]: inevitably, then, it lags behind the new science.

I mean a radically new science founded in a new, previously unexplored 'continent': for example, Geometry, founded by the Greeks (Thales and others); Physics, founded by Galileo; or History, founded by Marx. In each of these three instances, the new sciences opened up a new 'continent' of reality to knowledge – a continent that was independent of the other, already explored continents. Once this new 'continent' is opened up by the new science, other sciences can appear in it, one after the other: they explore 'regions' of this 'continent', but do not open up new 'continents'. For example, experimental chemistry, founded by Lavoisier, is clearly a new science, yet it does not open up a new 'continent', but merely occupies a 'region' within the 'continent' of physical nature opened up by Galileo's discovery, a 'region' hitherto unexplored by scientific knowledge. In the case of these *regional sciences*, the law which states that philosophy lags behind the new science does not apply if the essentials of the philosophy called for by the new regional science were produced after the foundation of the science that opened up the new 'continent'.

The empirical history of theories verifies this law.

The philosophy required after the Greeks opened up the 'continent' of mathematics – strictly speaking, the first philosophy in human history – emerged *belatedly*: it began with Plato and was developed by Aristotle, Epicurus, the Stoics, and others. The philosophy required after Galileo opened up the 'continent' of physical nature also emerged *belatedly*: it began with Descartes and was developed by Leibniz, Malebranche, the eighteenth-century philosophers, Kant, and others. In contrast, Lavoisier did not induce the emergence of any truly new philosophy by founding chemistry: the principles of this philosophy already existed when Lavoisier made his discovery.

Marx's and Engels's scientific discovery, in its turn, was subject to the same law as the discoveries of Thales and Galileo: since it opened up a new 'continent' to knowledge, the philosophy which it carried within it and for which it called, arrived *belatedly*, that is, lagged behind the new science.[5] The chronology of Marx's works in itself provides confirmation of this. The first (albeit still highly ambiguous) formulation of the theoretical principles of the science of history appears in *The German Ideology*. Yet, in *The German Ideology*, Marx declares in no uncertain terms that philosophy must be purely and simply abolished – not so that it may be 'realized', as he had maintained in his earlier philosophical works, but in order to make it possible to 'undertake the study of positive things'. This hardly means that there is no philosophy at work in *The German Ideology*. The philosophy found there is, precisely, a dialectical positivist empiricism accompanied by a historicist philosophy of the subject (individuals are conceived as the 'subjects' of history) unrelated to the dialectical materialism elaborated later; it eventually disappears. This, however, does mean that dialectical materialism is absent from *The German Ideology*; the positivist-empiricist thesis about the abolition of philosophy ratifies its absence. Thus the fact that dialectical materialism *lags behind* historical materialism makes itself felt in *The German Ideology* in the form of the absence of dialectical materialism. Yet this absence is simultaneously a presence: the presence of the idealist-empiricist philosophical ideology still at work in *The German Ideology*.

We can draw an important conclusion from this 'absence' and 'presence': the place of philosophy is never *empty*. If this place is not occupied by the new philosophy required by the new science, it is occupied by an earlier philosophy foreign to that science – one that, in this case, does much more than simply lag behind it; it contradicts it. The contradiction can be resolved only when the new philosophy begins to emerge, and is then developed and reinforced.

We can see this very clearly in Marx. The idealist philosophy still at work in *The German Ideology* gradually yields to a new philosophy as a result of the conceptual progress made by the new science.[d] But this new philosophy necessarily lags behind the theoretical state of the new science for a long time – not only

---

[d] *The Manifesto; The Poverty of Philosophy; Wages, Price, and Profit; A Contribution to the Critique of Political Economy; Capital.*

quantitatively, but also qualitatively: its concepts lack the precision, rigour and systematicity of those of the new science.

For example, this lag makes itself felt in the continuing, objective theoretical gap between (1) philosophy as it is explicitly recognized and defined in *Capital*; and (2) the same philosophy as it is practiced and put to work by Marx in the scientific analyses of the mode of capitalist production in *Capital*.

I have, for example, demonstrated the existence of this gap between the formulation and the reality of the philosophy in *Capital*; that is to say, I have demonstrated, with respect to the famous phrase about the *'inversion'* of Hegel, that the theoretical definition of philosophy in *Capital* lags behind Marx's own philosophical practice in it. This phrase is extremely important, since, in defining Marx's relationship to Hegel as one of 'inversion', it *ipso facto* proposes a definition of Marxist philosophy. But the phrase about 'inversion' is not the *concept of*, but a *metaphor for*, the solution of the problem it raises. 'Inversion' is undoubtedly a concept in Feuerbach's philosophy, from which Marx borrows; it is the concept of the actually existing relationship between Feuerbach's philosophy and Hegel's. But it is not the concept of the relationship between Marx's philosophy and Hegel's; it is merely a metaphor, and this metaphor merely indicates that, between Hegel and Marx, a theoretical revolution took place. In order to know what kind of revolution it was, we have critically to compare the metaphor of 'inversion' with the reality of the revolution accomplished by Marx in his scientific work. This comparison reveals that that revolution consisted not in an 'inversion', but in *replacing* an ideological problematic with a new, scientific problematic.[e]

This conclusion allows us to go still further by raising the following question: how can we account for the general law according to which philosophy lags behind science in the case of sciences that open up new 'continents' to knowledge? Here we find ourselves facing a problem we are not yet in a position to solve, or perhaps even to pose, if it is true that there is a crucial difference between stating the existence of a difficulty (as we have done) and posing this difficulty in the (scientific) form of a problem. Let us nevertheless advance a provisional explanation.

[e] See *FM* 87 ff.; *RC* 145 ff.

It may be said that the lag between philosophy and science is, in the type of example under consideration, a 'particular case' of the 'lag' between theory and practice, if it is clearly stipulated that, since what is involved is a science, the practice in question is a theoretical practice. Philosophy's lag behind science would thus be one instance of a fundamental principle of materialism: the primacy of practice. Without a doubt, we need to search in this direction. But a general principle yields knowledge only if it is specified in the forms required by its singular object. How can we specify this general principle? I shall confine myself to bringing out one aspect of the specific conditions under which it takes effect.

Whenever a new science is constituted, opening the way to knowledge of a new 'continent', a veritable theoretical revolution occurs in the domain in which the object of that science is to be found. The new science broaches a *'continent'*, that is, an *absolutely new* object. Yet this field is already occupied by ideological theories which, although they treat of this object (in our case, the 'philosophies of history' that preceded Marx), make it the object of a discourse that is necessarily and massively distorted.

The theoretical revolution that intervenes in this 'continent' consists in rejecting these ideological theories and replacing them with a scientific theory. However, since it does not explore one region of a continent whose major principles are already known but, rather, 'opens up' a new 'continent', how can this new scientific theory come into existence?

It cannot borrow its theoretical concepts from the *ideologies* occupying this 'continent', because they are profoundly distorted representations of reality. Nor can it simply 'apply' to this new 'continent' theoretical concepts that hold for other 'continents', since this 'continent' is completely new. Finally, it cannot directly [and] immediately extract its theoretical concepts and their system from the empirical reality of its new object: that is an empiricist, ideological, and hence distorted conception of the practice and history of the sciences.

The new science resolves this contradiction in the following way: it *imports* a number of theoretical elements (concepts, categories, methods, etc.) into its field, borrowing them from existing scientific or philosophical disciplines outside that field.[6] It puts these theoretical elements to work on the reality of its new object and, in performing this labour, it also *rectifies* these imported theoretical elements in order to adapt them to the reality of their new 'continent'.

This importation is indispensable, but it comes at a high price.

To begin with, it comes at the price of an inevitable discordance [*écart*] between the imported concepts and their object in the field of the new science. This discordance is corrected and reduced in the practice of the science as it develops: the imported concepts and their system are rectified one step at a time.

But the rectification of this discordance within the science sooner or later generates philosophical counter-currents. When it is a question of a science that actually opens up a new 'continent', there finally comes a moment in which the radical novelty of this object calls into question, not the imported *scientific concepts*, but the grand *philosophical categories* in which these concepts had previously been thought. Let us take a classic example. Galilean science not only borrowed and rectified imported concepts in order to think the laws of physical movement: there came a moment in which it challenged the existing philosophical categories, such as the concept of *causality*. This was the Cartesian moment; it was then, after the scientific revolution, that a philosophical revolution took place. It bore on basic philosophical categories – or, to be more precise, on the system or a segment of the system of the existing philosophical categories, which it replaced with new ones.

Experience shows, however, that if science needs time to rectify the scientific concepts it imports, we also need time: first, to perceive the need for new philosophical categories, and, second, to produce them. Indeed, what holds for all revolutions holds for this philosophical revolution as well: it does not begin by fiat, as soon as the need for it makes itself felt. The tools for accomplishing it must also be available. But they are not always available. In the history of philosophy and the sciences, as in the history of human societies, it is sometimes necessary to wait a very long time for a favourable conjuncture to offer the theoretical tools adapted to the solution of a long-pending problem. To say that it is necessary to wait for these tools is to say that the science or philosophy in question cannot produce them all by itself; it needs outside help, needs to import new theoretical elements to solve its critical problems. But these theoretical elements are not delivered by fiat: it is necessary to wait until they are produced by developments internal to other disciplines.

This holds for *the sciences*. It sometimes happens that they remain stymied for a long time in the face of an insoluble problem: then progress in another science, or in philosophy, suddenly provides them with the theoretical tools they lacked. As we know, this law came into play in the foundation of the Marxist science of history: the encounter of three different disciplines (English political economy, German philosophy, and French utopian socialism) was needed to bring it into the world.

The same law also holds for the *new philosophy* for which a new science feels the need in its own practice. The need is not enough: the theoretical tools indispensable for the production of new philosophical categories are also required. These tools may not exist for a certain period of time, in which case it becomes necessary to wait for a favourable theoretical conjuncture (progress in some other science, etc.) to produce them. Until a favourable conjuncture comes about, the philosophical revolution objectively called for by the development of a new science is left pending, as is the rectification of its concepts: philosophy lags behind science.

This holds for Marxism, all historical problems and ideological struggles aside. In the most systematic, rigorous Marxist work, *Capital*, there are a great many signs of the pressing need for new philosophical categories that fully correspond to the theoretical practice of its scientific analyses. Together with this need, which everywhere strives to 'break through' to the surface, we observe, in *Capital*, the existence of objective theoretical limits that this need could not transcend, given the state of the tools available at the time.

It can be shown, for example, that Marxist science calls for a new category of *causality* and the *dialectic*, and that it simultaneously calls for a revolution in the old universe of the philosophical categories of subject and object, essence and phenomenon, inside and outside, and so on. At the same time, however, it is apparent that this need comes up against insurmountable theoretical limits in *Capital*: the fact that the means capable of producing these new philosophical categories are lacking.

That, profoundly, is why Marx is literally compelled, even as he takes the greatest possible distance from Hegel, to invoke Hegelian categories. This is why the metaphor of 'inversion' is so important. It is not a slip or an oversight on Marx's part, a mere linguistic failing. It is the rigorous symptom of his contradictory philosophical situation, which, at the time, necessarily remained unresolved. Marx could think his total emancipation from Hegel's philosophy only as a function of Hegel's philosophy. That is why he could rid himself of Hegel only with the help of a *metaphor*.*

It is immediately obvious that the lag between philosophy and science induces ideological and theoretical effects that are potentially quite serious, for they are effects of distortion. Today it is clear that a whole series of *distortions* of Marxist theory were and still are based on this metaphor of Marx's 'inversion' of Hegel – that is to say, on a false conception of the Marx–Hegel relationship: for example, the *'evolutionist'* distortion of the Second International, the *'voluntarist'* distortion of the ultra-left theoreticians and movements of the 1920s, and so on. Obviously I am not claiming that the nature and historical destiny of the Second International, or the ultra-leftism of the 1920s, can be attributed wholly to theoretical deviations that are due, in the final analysis, to the inadequacy of the formula of 'inversion'; in the last instance, class relations and the forms of the class struggle were the determining factors. But precisely because it was also a question of the forms of the class struggle, these forms were to a great extent dependent on the social-democratic and, later, communist organizations; on their theory, organizational and operative methods and political line – and, therefore, on their interpretation of Marxist theory.

Hence it can be said that, in large measure, a measure dependent on theory alone, the evolutionist (Second International) or voluntarist (the 1920s) distortions of Marxist theory were based on a mistaken conception of the Marx–Hegel relationship,[7] a conception that masked the revolutionary specificity of Marxist theory in philosophy. I limit myself to these two old, familiar examples, but one could mention a great many others, contemporary examples among them, to show how and why the lag between Marxist philosophy and Marxist science can generate

---

* See the passages in *FM* and *RC* cited above.

effects of distortion that are not merely theoretical but also ideological and, ultimately, political.

One more word relevant to our own situation. If, in the last analysis, Marxist philosophy lags behind historical materialism for the reasons just cited, two consequences follow.

First consequence

Philosophy is not condemned to lag behind science for ever; such a lag is characteristic of the first phase of a new scientific revolution. The length of this phase varies, but, when the time is ripe, it becomes possible to move beyond it. The lag that is inevitable at the outset can, then, be overcome in a *later* phase. Today, precisely, we find ourselves in this later phase; our task is to overcome this lag. The law governing the history of scientific and philosophical theories, which explains why this lag is necessary, also helps us to understand the conditions that allow us to overcome it. Thus it is a law which encourages not fatalism, repetition and resignation but, rather, labour, research and discovery. Such labour is indispensable if we are to rectify the theoretical distortions, both ideological and practical, produced by this lag.

Second consequence

We have every reason to believe that the new tools now available to us are appropriate for carrying out this crucial, urgent theoretical work.

I have in mind, first, the effects of the new *political and ideological conjuncture*. Not only can the problems posed by this conjuncture stimulate theoretical research; it is *this conjuncture itself* which allows us to pose, openly and clearly, the problem of the lag of Marxist philosophy.

I also have in mind the contemporary *theoretical conjuncture*. Emerging before our very eyes is a theoretical *conjunction* of several disciplines external to Marxism, which on their own ground, in their own fashion, and from their own particular angles of approach, raise philosophical problems that are undeniably related to the new philosophical problems posed by Marxist science.

Among these disciplines, let me mention, in particular, (i) the beginnings of a true history of the sciences, a truly historical epistemology; (ii) the beginnings of critical and theoretical reflection on Freud's work; and (iii) the modern linguistics that derives from Ferdinand de Saussure.

I shall take only one example: on its own ground, and in its own fashion, each of these scientific disciplines also poses the problem of the definition of a new category of *causality*. It poses it in terms such that the conjunction of its problem with the Marxist philosophical problem of causality can help us to take a decisive step forward in philosophy.

I do not think I am mistaken in saying that dialectical materialism's backwardness vis-à-vis historical materialism is a phenomenon we shall be able to master in the years ahead. It can already be predicted that this theoretical lag will, for the most part, soon be overcome.

But, if we are to overcome it, we will have to work seriously in philosophy: we will have to pinpoint the problems confronting us, pose them clearly, making judicious use of the theoretical tools available in both the works of Marxism and certain important works produced by non-Marxist scholars and pioneers – and arrive at a solution to them.

It was with all these reasons in mind that I said that Marxist philosophy is the site of a *problem* – not only because of its backwardness, but also because we must treat this backwardness as a problem to be solved, precisely in order to overcome it. In the final analysis, to treat Marxist philosophy today as a problem is to treat it, in a Marxist perspective, as if it were a truly scientific discipline; it is to take the conjuncture in which it finds itself into account, to take into account the law of unequal development that explains its backwardness, precisely in order to overcome it. It is also to home in on all the effects of distortion that this backwardness spawns in theory, ideology and practice. Thus it is to understand the great lesson that Marx, Engels and Lenin have handed down to us, and to continue their work – not by contenting ourselves with mechanically repeating everything that they have given us, but by taking up everything that is theoretically advanced with a view to developing it, and by rectifying whatever is theoretically backward so that we can overcome this backwardness and correct the distortions it produces.

If Marxist philosophy is the site of a problem, it is so in this sense.

IV. THE TWO STRATEGIC TASKS OF MARXIST PHILOSOPHY

If Marxist philosophy is not just a problem, but *the number 1 problem*, the reason is, above all, the current conjuncture – not just the political and ideological conjuncture, but the theoretical conjuncture as well.

That is the thesis I shall now go on to develop.

If it is a matter *of extreme urgency* that Marxist philosophy overcome its theoretical backwardness, that is because this backwardness blocks or retards its intervention in critical areas of the ideological and theoretical conjuncture, where such intervention is urgently required and critically important. Marxist philosophy must consequently overcome its backwardness in order to be equal to its historical tasks in three areas:

1. First of all, it must struggle against all the ideological *distortions* of Marxist theory; that is to say, in the final analysis, against the effects of bourgeois and petty-bourgeois ideology on the interpretation of Marxist theory. The struggle against these distortions is a crucial, pressing task today.

2. It must contribute to the progress of the sciences that come within the purview of *historical materialism*. The development of historical materialism today depends on the solution of crucial theoretical problems, both scientific and philosophical, which can be posed and resolved only with the help, and through the intervention, of dialectical materialism.

3. It must subject the disciplines that have developed under the rubric of 'Human Sciences' or 'Social Sciences' to a radical critique, setting their houses in order. In their current state, most of these disciplines are in the hands of bourgeois ideology. They must be thoroughly overhauled and established on the basis of their only authentic prin-

ciples: those of historical materialism and dialectical materialism.

It is not hard to see that the third task largely depends on the second, since what is at stake is the existence of historical materialism and its consequences.

In principle, these three tasks ultimately come down to two:

Strategic task number 1: the defence of Marxist philosophy and science against bourgeois ideology.

Strategic task number 2: the development of historical materialism and the regional sciences that depend on it, by way of the reconquest and overhaul of the disciplines now dominated by bourgeois ideology.

I shall now proceed to examine these two tasks. Obviously, my analysis can only be extremely schematic.

V. STRATEGIC TASK NUMBER 1:
THE DEFENCE OF MARXIST THEORY AGAINST
BOURGEOIS IDEOLOGY

Bourgeois ideology attacks Marxist theory not only from the outside, but also *from the inside*, finding support in the various forms of 'spontaneism' of the working class, the petty bourgeoisie, and the intellectuals. These 'spontaneous' forms are, essentially, petty-bourgeois legal and moral *idealism* (humanism, whenever it is presented as the *theoretical foundation* of Marxism); the empiricism and positivism of scientists; and the pragmatism of those charged with practical tasks (politicians, technicians, and so on). These 'spontaneous' forms of the ideology internal to the working-class movement reflect bourgeois ideological forms external to the workers' movement.

For deep-seated historical and theoretical reasons, these ideological forms common to bourgeois ideology and the 'spontaneism' of the workers' movement comprise a system whose elements are complementary. Thus positivism, empiricism and technicism go hand in hand, at a very general level, with moral idealism. To go straight to the point: the form that holds the greatest threat for Marxist theory today is the pair *'humanism/ technicism'*. It appears in broad daylight in the capitalist countries in the present ideological conjuncture, dominated by technocracy and humanism. It also makes itself felt even within the Communist parties, and in both capitalist and socialist countries, in the form of a tendency to interpret Marxist philosophy as a *theoretical humanism*, and also in the form of a tendency to put uncritical, mechanistic faith in the development of the *sciences and technology*, while underestimating the role of politics, ideology, and philosophy.

On these matters, however, we must once again trace things back to a point that considerably antedates present-day phenomena. We can find a *historical* explanation for these two tendencies in the contemporary events of the twentieth century: the reaction against the effects of the 'personality cult' (the tendency towards theoretical humanism) or the 'impetuous development' of technology and the sciences (the tendency towards technocracy or technicism). Or we can seek the source of these temptations in the past history of the workers' movement: technicism is associated with the mechanistic economism of the Second International; theoretical humanism with certain forms of theoretical revisionism (a moral or Kantian interpretation of Marxism by certain theoreticians of the Second International). And we can explain these older forms in terms of the influence of bourgeois ideology.

But the truth is that we must also give *theoretical* reasons connected with the law we stated above, the law that explains why Marxist philosophy inevitably lags behind Marxist science.

We have seen that the place of philosophy is never empty. The place left unoccupied by historical materialism is therefore occupied by a totally different philosophy: by, first, a properly ideological philosophy, and then by the various forms in which the new philosophy strives to express its revolutionary specificity, although they remain for a long time subordinate to the dominant forms of bourgeois ideological philosophy. We should not close our eyes to the fact but, rather, look it square in the face: *empiricism* and *evolutionism* (which is, as it were, the vulgar form of Hegelianism) have left their stamp on the history of Marxist philosophy, particularly under the Second International.

Marxist philosophy has not yet rid itself of them for good and all. And there is a danger that its current attempts to rid itself of them will send it plunging headlong into another ideological philosophy: the form of idealism represented by *theoretical humanism*.

The terms empiricism, evolutionism and theoretical humanism call for a few words of explanation. The great Marxist leaders have always struggled against empiricism and pragmatism (the practical effect of empiricism): Marx (the 1857 Introduction), Engels (*Anti-Dühring; Dialectics of Nature*), Lenin (*Materialism and Empirio-criticism*), and others as well. They have also waged a vigorous struggle against the interpretation of Marxism which makes it a form of moral idealism: Marx's struggle against the 'true socialists', against Proudhon, Weitling and Kriege; Engels's struggle against Dühring's moral spiritualism; Kautsky's struggle against Bernstein's Kantianism; Lenin's struggle against the populists' moralism; in France, Maurice Thorez's struggle against Léon Blum's humanism, and so on. The struggle against *evolutionism*, on the other hand, did not give rise to philosophical works: it remained a practical struggle of a political kind, revolving around political problems (the conception of the revolution, the organizational forms of the class struggle, the political line on the First World War) as well as problems of strategy and tactics. Lenin is the incomparable representative of this practical struggle against evolutionism.

It is rather well known, at least in principle, why *empiricism* is an ideology and, consequently, why the empiricist interpretation of Marxism is a theoretical distortion of it. Empiricism, as a theory of knowledge, neglects or underestimates the role of the properly theoretical elements that come into play in all knowledge, even 'empirical' knowledge.[8] Empiricism does not take into account the specificity and nature of the practice that produces knowledge – that is to say, theoretical practice. It reduces theoretical practice to other forms of practice. It speaks of practice in general, without distinguishing the levels and specific differences that distinguish the various practices: economic practice, political practice, ideological practice, scientific and philosophical practice. That is why it produces both a false

---

[8] *RC* 94–100; 'OTW' 43–67.

idea of theory and a false idea of practice. The practical consequence is practicism or pragmatism, which Lenin very clearly
condemned.

Today, one of the most dangerous forms of empiricism is
historicism – in other words, the idea that it is possible to know
the nature of history directly, immediately, without first producing the theoretical concepts indispensable to acquiring knowledge of it. A historicist interpretation of Marxism (visible, for
example, in some of Gramsci's writings) consists in affirming
that Marx simply 'historicized' the results of classical political
economy, that he simply injected 'process' or the 'dialectic' into
the old philosophical categories, and so on. Historicism neglects
a fundamental theoretical fact: Marx's discovery of absolutely
new theoretical concepts with which to think the reality of what
we call, and experience as, 'history'.

Theoretical[8] *humanism*, or the moral-idealistic interpretation of
the theoretical foundations of Marxist doctrine, should be precisely defined. This interpretation consists in substituting *ideo-*
logical notions for the scientific concepts and philosophical
categories[9] that provide the real theoretical foundation for Marxism. The Marxist *science* of history takes as its theoretical foundation a system of concepts: mode of production, infrastructure
(productive forces and relations of production), superstructure
(juridico-political and ideological), social class, class struggle,
and so forth. For these scientific concepts, which constitute the
theoretical foundation of the science of history, theoretical
humanism substitutes ideological notions: man, alienation, the
disalienation of man, the emancipation of man, man's reappro-
priation of his species-being, 'the whole man',[10] and so on. In
Marxist *philosophy*, the basic theoretical concepts are the concepts
of materialism and the dialectic, the distinction between being
and thought, between the real object and the object of thought,
the primacy of practice, and so forth. Theoretical humanism
substitutes for these concepts the ideological notions of subject
and object, consciousness, activity, act, creation, and so on.

Of course, *after* making these substitutions, theoretical humanism rediscovers the classic concepts of Marxism; however,
because it interprets them in the light of these ideological notions
that stand in for a theoretical foundation, the meaning of the
classic concepts is distorted. For example, Theoretical humanism

reduces the concept of 'social relations' (relations of production, political relations, ideological relations) to 'human' or 'intersubjective' relations. The concept of 'practice', for example, is assimilated to the notion of the activity or act of a subject, and so on. Thus theoretical humanism distorts – to a greater or lesser extent, depending on the case, but always to some extent – the concepts of Marxist theory.

Even when this interpretation takes its distance from bourgeois humanism, even when it declares[11] that Marx conceives the essence of man in a new way (practical, social and historical), it remains the prisoner of moral ideology. The concept of the human essence of man is denounced as ideological and religious as early as *The German Ideology*, in terms devoid of all ambiguity. This concept is completely absent from the basic theoretical system of historical and dialectical materialism. The science of history and Marxist philosophy are based on very different concepts that have nothing to do with the ideological concept of man.

This does not mean that communists do not have a political and moral 'ideal'. In struggling to establish the socialist mode of production, communists struggle to abolish the exploitation of the working class, together with its effects. In the long term, they struggle for the establishment of the communist mode of production – that is to say, for the abolition of all classes and the 'emancipation of all men'. Their ideal is inseparable from their struggle, but, like their struggle, it is based on historical necessity, the need to make a revolution, the need to establish a socialist mode of production, and so forth. This historical necessity is not, however, *intelligible* in terms of the notions that express communists' political and moral ideals. This means, to be very precise, that the notions of 'the emancipation of all men', 'freedom' and 'man' are ideological notions, not fundamental theoretical concepts of Marxist theory (science and philosophy).

Again, to reject an interpretation of Marxism as a form of theoretical humanism does not mean that the problems of 'individuality' or 'subjectivity' are foreign to Marxist theory, or are imaginary problems. However, to the extent that they do feature in it, they are subordinate to the (scientific) concepts and (philosophical) categories of Marxist theory. *They* are subordinate to Marxist theory; Marxist theory is not subordinate to them. This simply means that the concepts of individuality, subjectivity, the human person, and so on, and, *a fortiori*, the notions of man, the moral subject, 'creative labour', creation, freedom, creative freedom,[12] the 'creation of man by man', and so forth, have no legitimate claim to being the theoretical concepts on which Marxist theory is based. When one presents them as the theoretical basis of Marxism, one inevitably lapses into a petty-bourgeois moral or religious ideology that is anterior and foreign to Marxism – the very ideology with which Marx had to break in order to found his theory, beginning with the 'settling of accounts' he undertook in *The German Ideology*.

The *evolutionist* interpretation of Marxism is less well known; it is no less serious for that.[13] Basically, it consists in applying to Marx the finalist, teleological schemas of the Hegelian dialectic, Darwinian biology, Spenserian 'philosophy', and so on. We have an example of it in Plekhanov's interpretation of Marxist philosophy, and in the mechanistic, economistic, fatalistic interpretation of historical materialism defended by certain theoreticians and leaders of the Second International. 'Marxist' evolutionism holds, for example, that the modes of production follow one another in an inevitable, immutable order: we find a trace of this in Stalin's famous list, contained in his short book *Dialectical and Historical Materialism*. Evolutionism also holds, like Hegelian idealism and all the philosophies of history (which, in this respect, are religious), that there is a 'meaning' to history, conceived as a *finality* governing it: we find traces of this in the formulas that effectively identify historical necessity with fatality, speak of the *inevitable* triumph of socialism, and so on.

'Marxist' evolutionism is incapable of accounting theoretically for the possibility and necessity of the political activity of the Communist parties, for the possibility of the failures of the workers' movement, and even for some of its successes, whenever they are unexpected and paradoxical in the sense that they fail to conform to its mechanistic schemas or the immutable order of the modes of production (the Cuban revolution, the possibilities of revolution in the 'backward' countries, etc.). Evolutionism breeds technicist and economistic illusions and political passivity; it systematically underestimates the adversary's capacity to react; it underestimates the role of class struggle, politics, ideology and philosophy in the class struggle.

When it is translated into practice on a massive scale, it leads to historical catastrophes, from which, moreover, it learns no 'lesson' (the 'bankruptcy of the Second International'). Lenin's political practice represents an exemplary struggle against 'Marxist' evolutionism. But the struggle against evolutionism has not yet been waged openly in theory. And it is obvious that this struggle cannot be waged in theory for as long as the problem of the theoretical relations between Marx and Hegel has not been clarified and settled once and for all.

I said a moment ago that there is also a *theoretical* reason for these ideological distortions of Marxism. What has long exposed interpretations of Marxism to the influence of empiricism, evolutionism, or 'humanist' idealism from within the workers' movement itself is, from a theoretical standpoint, *the unprecedented nature of the theoretical revolution carried out by Marx.*

If Marx himself experienced great theoretical difficulties in defining the *philosophical* categories required by his *scientific* discoveries, if he had to appeal to the existing philosophical categories, Hegel's, it is not surprising that, *a fortiori,* Marxist militants – and even excellent theoreticians – should have found themselves in the same predicament – or, rather, in a still more difficult one. If they have often put forward interpretations of Marxism contaminated by empiricism and evolutionism, and, today, by humanist idealism, that is also because Marxist science needed a philosophy, whereas Marxist philosophy was not yet strong enough theoretically to settle accounts with the dominant philosophical ideologies and impose itself at the theoretical level by dint of its rigour and systematicity.

Today, we have gained sufficient perspective on all these effects to be able to understand their causes and measure their consequences.

Today,[14] we can and must say that it is not only the avowed adversaries of Marxist theory (science and philosophy), the bourgeois ideologues, who loudly proclaim that it has contributed nothing new, or is 'outmoded'; it is also its partisans, when they read Marx's texts and 'interpret' Marxist theory through the established self-evident truths, those of the reigning ideological philosophies.

To take only three examples: Marxists who read and spontaneously interpret Marxist theory – without difficulties, scruples or hesitation – within the schemas of empiricism, evolutionism, or 'humanism' *in fact declare that Marx contributed nothing new* to philosophy and, by implication, to science. These Marxists reduce the prodigious philosophical novelty of Marx's thought to existing, ordinary, 'obvious' forms of thought – that is, to forms of the dominant philosophical ideology. In order clearly to perceive and grasp the revolutionary novelty of Marxist philosophy and its scientific consequences, it is necessary lucidly to resist this ideological reduction, to combat the bourgeois philosophical ideology that supports it, and to state what distinguishes the specificity of Marx's thought, what makes it revolutionary not only in political practice, but *also in theory*.

That is where the ultimate difficulty lies. For it is not easy to break with the 'self-evident truths' of theoretical ideologies such as empiricism, evolutionism or 'humanism', which have dominated all of Western thought for two hundred years. It is not easy to say that Marx was not an empiricist, that Marx was not Hegelian (Hegelianism is the 'rich man's' evolutionism) or evolutionist, that Marx was not theoretically 'humanist'; it is not easy to show positively how Marx, because he is not Hegelian, evolutionist, 'humanist' or 'empiricist', *is something else entirely*, something which must then be defined. And when one does try to show this, it is not easy to make people acknowledge and accept it, for the 'resistances' are extremely powerful.

Marxist theory, because it is *theoretically revolutionary*, inevitably contains this fundamental difficulty. Unless we are to cede to the false 'self-evidence' of the dominant theoretical ideologies (whether by that we mean empiricism, evolutionism, humanism or other forms of idealism), and thus betray what is most precious in Marx's thought – that is to say, what makes it theoretically revolutionary – we must confront this difficulty, and struggle against the ideologies that continually threaten to suffocate, reduce and destroy Marxist thought. This is no imaginary difficulty; it is an objective historical difficulty, as real in its way as the difficulties of revolutionary practice. The earth, or the structure of society, does not rise on new 'foundations' as easily as might be supposed; neither does the system of thought.

We know that a revolution has to take place before the social structure can 'rise on new foundations'. But, after the revolution, an extremely long, arduous struggle must also be waged in politics and ideology, to establish, consolidate and ensure the victory of the new society. The same goes for the system of thought. Following a theoretical revolution, another extremely long and arduous struggle is required in theory and ideology to establish the new thought, gain recognition for it, and ensure its victory, especially if it is a form of thought that founds a new science and philosophy serving as the basis for a new ideology[15h]

h The scientific theory of Marxism (philosophy, the science of history) is not an ideology. An ideology is a *distorted* representation of reality: it is *necessarily* distorted, because it is not an objective but a *subjective* representation of reality – let us say, for the sake of brevity, a social (class) representation of reality. Science, in contrast, exists only on condition that it struggles against all forms of subjectivity, class subjectivity included (consider Lenin's struggles against the 'spontaneous' ideology of the proletariat); science is objective. Science provides knowledge of reality independent of 'subjective' class interests. Ideology, in contrast, provides a representation of reality that is not knowledge in the strict sense of the term, since it is subordinate to class interests.

We can nevertheless legitimately maintain that Marxism has 'produced a new ideology' in the working class, and that this ideology, even while remaining ideological in *form* (it does not have the form of a science), becomes increasingly scientific in *content*. We can legitimately talk about an *ideology* of a scientific character or, for the sake of brevity, a *scientific ideology*.

But this new ideology is a *transformation* of the previous ideology of the working class. This transformation draws the ideology (moral, political, philosophical) of the working class towards a new *content* that is more scientific because it is increasingly informed by the scientific principles of Marxism – or, at any rate, by the results of Marxist science and philosophy.

This transformation is possible because Marxist theory, which is objective, offers the working class scientific knowledge of its *interests*, as well as the means of realizing them: it is the scientific, objective character of Marxist theory that allows it to 'serve' the interests of the working class without being distorted by the subjective representation of these class interests. Thus it is the scientific objectivity of Marxist theory which produces this *historically utterly unprecedented* result: the emergence of an ideology whose *content* has been transformed, an increasingly *scientific* ideology.

But the ideology of the working class, even if its content has been transformed in a scientific direction, nevertheless remains an ideology as far as its *form* is concerned: for example, a transformed proletarian moral ideology continues to take the form of a moral ideology, and proletarian political and philosophical ideology continues to take the form of ideology.

This is because ideology has a *form of its own*, resulting from its social function, from the fact that it constitutes one level of the superstructure of any society. Hence the *form* of ideology necessarily subsists as one of the levels constitutive of society; the form of ideology reflects, precisely, this social function of ideology, which distinguishes it from science. That is why, even if it is becoming increasingly scientific, proletarian ideology, or the ideology of a socialist society, can never be confused with science. That is why, if we assign and political practice. Prior to the success of this long struggle, the revolution in society, like the revolution in thought, runs a very great risk: *that of being smothered by the old world and, directly or indirectly, falling back under its sway.*

It will be understood why, even today, we have to make a real effort accurately to represent the theoretical revolution accomplished by Marx in science and philosophy, against the old ideologies that tend constantly to subject this revolution to their own law – that is, to smother and destroy it.

The task of defending Marxist theory is, in the final analysis, incumbent on Marxist *philosophy*. This defence involves an ideological and, simultaneously, theoretical struggle against bourgeois ideological tendencies both inside and outside Marxism. If this theoretical struggle is to be successful, we cannot content ourselves with denouncing and criticizing the hostile ideologies and ideological forms that exercise an influence over Marxism. We must also – this is the absolute condition for theoretical victory – make Marxist theory an *impregnable fortress*.

If we have an impregnable theoretical fortress at our disposal – that is to say, a rigorous, exact, systematic theory that is well and truly alive – we will have a powerful force of positive scientific demonstration, capable of sweeping away the fallacious arguments and concepts of the ideologies, and compelling recognition for the plain truth. We will then be in a position to sally forth from our 'fortress' to attack our adversaries with our own weapons, on grounds of our own choosing. *Ideological struggle* will then become a natural consequence of theoretical strength. We will then be able to define a theoretical and ideological strategy and defeat our adversary, since we will no longer be vulnerable to his initiatives, forced to 'follow him on to his own ground', and reduced to engaging in mere 'polemics'. *We* will have the ideological initiative, because we will have the requisite theoretical strength.

Let there be no mistake: the word 'fortress' is an *image*. The point is not to *shut ourselves up* in a stronghold: that would be dogmatism.[16] The strength of Marxist philosophy consists in

---

these concepts a rigorous meaning, it is not possible to say that Marxist theory as science is a *'scientific ideology'*. Marxist science is based not on a 'scientific ideology', as is too often said, but, like any science, on a *scientific theory*.

rigorously solving the problems before it, and investing its solutions with the force of scientific – that is, irrefutable – proof. Thus its strength consists in showing that it can rectify deficient concepts, make still vague concepts precise, and produce new concepts where they are lacking, in order to explore and conquer those domains that belong to it by rights. Its strength consists in investing the system of its concepts with a rigour that can find expression in an 'order of exposition' (Marx) comparable to that found in *Capital*: the irrefutable order of a *scientific proof*.

Simply as an indication of the fundamental problems that it is urgent for Marxist philosophy to explore, let me mention the following: the problem of the specificity of philosophy as opposed to science; the problem of the nature of theory; the problem of practice and the specificity of the various practices (economic, political, theoretical); the problem of the specificity of the Marxist as opposed to the Hegelian dialectic; the problem of the Marxist conception of 'causality', the nature of ideology, and so on. Long arguments would be required to show in what sense each of these themes constitutes a still unsolved problem whose solution requires us to produce or rectify theoretical concepts. I cannot undertake that task here.[i] But we can gain some sense of its importance and urgency from a rapid examination of just one problem, that of *the union of theory and practice*.

This problem is central to Marxist philosophy and practice. Yet, to my knowledge, we do not possess a systematic, rigorous theory on this question, but have only a general orientation, inscribed in the classical thesis about the need for the union of theory and practice and the primacy of practice. We also have a few theoretical elements involving practice as the 'criterion of truth'. Above all, we have a large number of political texts, by both Lenin and other great leaders of the workers' movement, which sum up and critically assess a vast range of practical experience in which the realization of the union of theory and practice is exemplified. All this is quite rich, but it does not yet constitute a theory of the union of theory and practice.

A correct general orientation does not make a theory; nor do isolated elements, or even the richest imaginable records of practical experience.[17] We need to think what exists 'in the

---

[i] See *FM* and *RC*, which touch on some of these themes.

practical state' in the experience of scientific and political practice. To do so, we need to produce the concepts that reality
demands, organizing them in a rigorous demonstrative system.
This is an immense theoretical task; we can find a model and
resource for it in the work Marx did in order to produce the new
concepts and theoretical system of *Capital*. We will not, strictly
speaking, possess a true philosophical theory of the problem of
the union of theory and practice until we have treated this basic
philosophical problem with a rigour comparable to that of
Capital.

Yet we saw, in the opening pages of this essay, the importance
that the *correct* conception of this problem has not only for
Marxist theory, but also for the practice of the revolutionary
Parties. On a more positive note, it can be said that, when this
theory has at last been established, we will be able to bring
vastly increased theoretical power to bear in the struggle against
bourgeois ideology (the number 1 strategic task for Marxist
philosophy) and the rigorous, productive elaboration of the
practical and theoretical problems falling within the purview of
historical materialism.

Let me sum up what I have said so far. The *number 1 strategic
task* for Marxist philosophy is to become a *true theory*, in the
strong sense, so that it can struggle and prevail against bourgeois
ideology and its influence on the revolutionary workers' movement. Marxist philosophy cannot become the impregnable 'theoretical fortress' that it must be unless it undergoes the kind of
profound theoretical development needed to overcome the still
extant lag between philosophy and Marxist science, and to
endow philosophy with the conceptual precision and rigour, as
well as the theoretical systematicity, that it still lacks. It is
imperative that Marxist philosophers go to work with, first and
foremost, this specific goal in mind.

VI.   STRATEGIC TASK NUMBER 2:
DEVELOPING HISTORICAL MATERIALISM

If it carries out its number 1 task, Marxist philosophy will
acquire the tools that can help it carry out *strategic task number 2*.

Most of the scientific disciplines that fall within the scope of historical materialism are, today, in great need of help from Marxist philosophy: this holds not only for the disciplines known as the 'Human Sciences', but also for certain regions of the Marxist science of history.

1.   Historical materialism

Here, too, I must be schematic; I will content myself with rapidly citing just a few examples in order to make myself understood.

We have, in *Capital*, a theory of the capitalist mode of production – but we still have nothing comparable for the other modes of production, pre-capitalist or socialist (even if important work has been done here),ʲ or for the phases of transition between these modes.ᵏ

As far as the capitalist mode of production itself is concerned, if we possess an impressive conceptual system for thinking the reality of its economic level (*Capital*), we have no comparable theory for thinking the reality of its political and ideological levels.

As far as the *political* level is concerned, we do, it is true, have general theses on the state, the class struggle, and their development, [as well as] the concrete analyses found in a number of historical and political works; we also have analyses of the rich experience of the class struggle (for example, all of Lenin's speeches and writings), and so on. But we have no rigorous, developed theory, in the strong sense of the word, of the nature of social classes, the state and state power, the state apparatus and bureaucracy, the various forms of the capitalist state, the 'bloc of social forces in power', the Leninist distinction between a class and its representatives, and so forth.

ʲ On the Asiatic, slave, and feudal modes of production, important work has been done in the Soviet Union, Czechoslovakia, Hungary, Democratic Germany, France, etc.

ᵏ However, on the politically very important problem of transitional phases, there are some remarkable texts about the first phases of the transition between capitalism and socialism (Lenin and Bukharin). Yet the general theory of the transition has yet to be worked out. Let us mention, in France, the work of Charles Bettelheim.

This theoretical lacuna is infinitely more striking when it comes to the nature of *ideologies*: the relationship between, on the one hand, the ideological level and, on the other, the economic and political levels; the difference between ideology and science; the double – social and theoretical – determination of the ideologies, and so on. If we had a theory of ideology and the political (the juridico-political superstructure) for, at least, the capitalist mode of production, we could extend its concepts (transforming them in accordance with their object) to cover other modes of production; we would then have a theory of the political and the ideological specific to these productive modes. But we are a long way from possessing such theories. This lacuna has both theoretical and political consequences.

Historians, who work on the past (the slave-holding and feudal social formations, etc.), like the ethnographers and ethnologists who are today working on primitive social formations, suffer from the effects of this theoretical inadequacy in their own work. They encounter them in the form of problems involving the nature and role of the 'institutions' and ideologies of these social formations, or the determination of the dominant element in the dialectic of their history or 'non-history'.

Political leaders and parties, for their part, come up against the practical consequences of this theoretical deficiency. For the solution of important political and ideological problems in the construction of socialism and the transition to communism depends on the availability of theoretical knowledge about the state form of the dictatorship of the proletariat and the ideology of a socialist social formation. But we lack, precisely, a theory, in the strict sense, of the political and the ideological in the socialist mode of production, and of the transitional phases between capitalism and socialism.

This lack is still more conspicuous when it comes to the transition of pre-capitalist social formations to socialism. If we had a theory of the political and the ideological in pre-capitalist modes of production, it would be easier to pose the problem of the state, the political Party, and the forms of political action required to ensure the success of this transition.

To mention one last, still controversial example: it is undoubtedly because we lack a theory of the juridico-political and ideological superstructure that, concerning the phenomenon of the 'personality cult' which arose within the superstructure of a social formation in the phase of the dictatorship of the proletariat, we have not produced anything more than hypotheses that are far more descriptive than theoretical, and therefore threaten to block the solution of the problems involved. One simple indication among a dozen others will help to bring this fact home: of the many works of Soviet empirical sociology, virtually none deals with the sociology of political or ideological social relations.[1]

At a still more abstract level, we still do not have, however improbable this may seem, a truly satisfying general theory of what a mode of production is, although *Capital* gives us all we need to construct such a theory. In this connection, I will mention only one point, which has major consequences from a practical point of view: it involves the concept of *productive forces*. The general concept certainly is available to us, but, as its very formulation suggests ('forces', in the plural), the term quite often stands for a mere empirical list: material resources and sources of energy, instruments of production, labour-power, and the 'technical experience' of this labour-power. This was Stalin's definition of the term; to my knowledge, it has not been modified since. An empirical list, however, is not a concept, even if the expression 'productive forces', as it is currently formulated, does indeed designate one specific reality while distinguishing it from another, the relations of production. If we are truly to possess the concept of productive forces, we need something more: we need to discover and describe the specific relations which, for each mode of production and each of its phases, organize the empirical elements on the list into organic unities that are specific and original.[m] It is obvious that if, in defining the productive forces, we do not go beyond drawing up a simple quantitative list of their elements, we are highly likely to put the emphasis, indiscriminately, on the technical element, and thus to lapse into economism or its contemporary technicist variants, as the Second International did.

[1] See *La Sociologie en URSS. Rapports des membres de la Délégation soviétique au Congrès d'Evian*, 1966, especially Ossipov's paper.
[m] On this point, see Balibar's important contribution to *Reading Capital, RC* 225 ff.

If, on the other hand, we bring out the organic relations that combine these elements in original wholes [*unités*] corresponding to the different modes of production and each of their phases, we can see that the dominant element can be displaced. It may be technology in the narrow sense (the instruments of production), or the organization of labour (the forms of co-operation), or the technical level of the labour force which represents the dominant element in the specific original wholes constituting the essence of the productive forces in a particular case. These distinctions are obviously important, because they determine the type of action required to develop the productive forces in a given instance: depending on whether one should act on this or that constitutive element of the productive forces, because it is, in the prevailing conjuncture, the 'decisive link', the emphasis must be put on the economic (or on one or another aspect of it), the political, or the ideological.

At a still deeper level, we do not have a theory, in the strict sense, of either '*determination in the last instance by the economy*' or the specific type of causality that governs the modalities of this determination, and so constitutes the articulation of the different levels of a mode of production (economic, political and ideological). We do not have a theory, in the strict sense, of the *displacement* of dominance among the various levels, within determination in the last instance by the economy. We do not have a theory to account for the *variations of the conjuncture*, although the everyday political practice of the Communist parties carefully takes these variations into account, and Lenin's writings (to cite only Lenin) constantly point to the displacement of dominance as that which defines the conjuncture.[18n]

Of course, the theoretical elaboration of all these questions is not the sole responsibility of Marxist philosophy, nor, in consequence, of the philosophers. It is, first and foremost, the task of the many different theoreticians working in the field of historical materialism: theoreticians of the economy and of politics, theoreticians specializing in the ideologies, historians, and so on. Yet

---

[n] This theory of the conjuncture, of the displacement of dominance among the various levels, etc., is directly relevant to the theory of the dialectic. The most remarkable formulation we have of it may be found in Mao Zedong, 'On Contradiction'.

the work of these theoreticians needs the help of Marxist philosophy, especially today. Here, too, I will give only one example.

In my view, it is not an accident, nor even a circumstance due
to historical causes alone, that we still do not possess a true
theory, in the strict sense, of *social classes, the political,* or *the
ideological.* There are also *theoretical* reasons for this shortcoming;
to be quite precise, philosophical reasons.

Let us go back to what I said above about the lag between
philosophy and science in the case of a science that opens up a
new 'continent' to knowledge (as Marx did). The 'need' for
philosophy that the new science feels at a later stage in its
development does not have to do only with the attacks or
ideological philosophical deviations that threaten it; it is also,
fundamentally, an inner need that the science perceives when it
tries to overcome the theoretical limits it encounters in its own
work and field. But some of these theoretical limits depend, in
the final analysis, on the *philosophical categories* in which the
science must think its new objects. For there comes a moment in
the progress of a science when certain old philosophical categories objectively constitute a theoretical obstacle to the solution of
new problems. It is this properly philosophical obstacle which
then stands in the way of the development of the science, by
preventing it from solving certain precisely identifiable scientific
problems. I am convinced that this has long been the case for the
theory of social classes, the political and the ideological.

In order to think the nature of a social class, it is indispensable
to take *conjointly* into account the determination of the economic
base, juridico-political superstructure, and ideological superstructure. It is also indispensable to take into account the *'play'*
that occurs within this joint determination, in order to explain
the possible displacements of the dominant instance among these
different determinations.°

° Lenin's and Marx's historical analyses (Lenin's great political texts, Marx's
The Eighteenth Brumaire) clearly attest to the 'play' that makes displacements
possible. We can say that a social class is determined, in the last analysis, by the
relations of production – but it is simultaneously determined by the structure of
the political and the ideological. It may or may not possess its own political
organization, or find its political 'representatives' among politicians who belong
to another class (for example, Napoleon II and the small peasants); in other
words, it may be either present or absent in person in the struggle between
political classes, possess its own ideology or not, and so on. We must account

In order to think, all at once, the conjunction of several different determinations and the variations of their dominance, the classical philosophical category of 'causality' is inadequate – as is even the category of 'reciprocal causality' between cause and effect, or that of the 'resultant of forces'. These may well allow us to 'describe' phenomena, but they do not help us to think their mechanisms. On this precise point, it may be said that the classical concept of causality, even 'improved' with the help of the concept of reciprocal causality or concepts borrowed from cybernetics, today constitutes a philosophical obstacle to the solution of a scientific problem. This is why the theory of social classes, the class struggle, and so on, has now reached an impasse.[p]

To remove this obstacle, we must endeavour to produce a new philosophical category capable of accounting for the specificity of a dialectical reality that has been identified by Marxist science: the conjunction of different determinations on the same object, and the variations of the dominant among these determinations, within their very conjunction.

I have, for my part, tried to take account of the existence of this problem, and sketch a theoretical solution to it, by proposing two new philosophical categories: *structural causality* and *overdetermination*. I cannot analyse them in detail within the narrow confines of this essay.[q] Let me merely indicate the general *raison d'être* for each of these categories.

'Structural causality' is meant to draw attention to the fact that the classic philosophical category of causality (whether Cartesian linear causality or Leibnizian 'expressive' causality) is inadequate for thinking the scientific analyses of *Capital*, and must be replaced by a new category. To give some sense of this innovation, we can say that, in structural causality, we find something that resembles the problem (often invoked by biolo-

---

theoretically for all these possible variations. The distinction between the 'class in itself' and the 'class for itself' that we find in *The Poverty of Philosophy* (1847) clearly designates one aspect of this problem, but is not yet the theory of it.

[p] The fact that theory has reached an impasse does not always mean that political practice also has. As we have seen, political practice can be in advance of theory in certain cases. In other cases, however, the fact that theory has reached an impasse also blocks or checks political practice. The theory of the possibility of these variations has yet to be developed.

[q] See *FM* 87–116, 200–18; *RC* 29 ff., 182–93.

gists) of the causality of the 'whole upon its parts', with the difference that the 'Marxist' whole is not a biological, organic whole, but a complex structure that itself contains structured levels (the infrastructure, the superstructure). Structural causality designates the very particular causality of a structure upon its elements, or of a structure upon another structure, or of the structure of the whole upon its structural levels.

As for 'overdetermination', it designates one particular effect of structural causality – precisely the one I evoked a moment ago in connection with the theory of social classes: the conjunction of different determinations on the same object, and the variations in the dominant element among these determinations within their very conjunction. To go back to the example of social classes: we may say that they are overdetermined, since, in order to grasp their nature, we have to mobilize the structural causality of three 'levels' of society, economic, political and ideological – with structural causality operating in the form of a conjunction of these three structural determinations on the same object, and in the variation of the dominant element within this conjunction.

I do not claim that these formulations (structural causality, overdetermination) are satisfactory. They have to be tested, developed and rectified. My only claim is that they point to the existence of an undeniable philosophical problem that is of decisive strategic importance when it comes to removing the properly philosophical obstacle with which all true theories of social classes, class struggle, the political, and the ideological are confronted today.

The theory of the nature of the *ideological* presents, moreover, a particular philosophical problem that has in fact prevented us from elaborating it to date. It is not enough to say that ideology, too, is subject to 'structural causality' in order to account for its specificity. Nor is it enough to say that ideology represents the case of the conjunction of two different determinations: one having to do with cognition [*connaissance*] (which confers representational value upon the ideological), the other involving the division of society into classes (which explains why ideological representation is distorted [*faussé*]). We must also account for the reality we are calling a 'distorted representation'; that is to say, we must account for the paradoxical unity of a discourse that states something false [*qui énonce le faux*] even as it claims to state the truth. It is not enough to invoke the old philosophical concept of error: it merely names the difficulty, without posing or solving the problem. Nor is it enough to say that this duplicity of ideological discourse is a particular case of 'overdetermination'; we must also account for the fact that this overdetermination is that of 'the true' and 'the false', by virtue of the fact that it exists within the specific object known as a 'discourse'.

Clearly, then, if we are to remove the theoretical obstacle that is currently standing in the way of all theories of ideology, we have to bring into play not only the new philosophical concepts of 'structural causality' and 'overdetermination', but also what we can call the *theory of discourses*, which will require contributions from structural linguistics if it is to emerge. This theory of discourses has not yet been born, and it cannot be elaborated without the help of philosophy. I do not pretend to be able to offer results here, either: it will be a long time before any appear. I only claim to have posed a real, important problem. In so far as the solution of this problem concerns the Marxist science of the ideological instance of productive modes, any theory of ideology today requires the decisive intervention of Marxist philosophy.

2. The 'Human Sciences'

What is true of the theoretical regions within historical materialism is still more true of the disciplines known as the 'Human Sciences'.

Ours is the age of the 'Human Sciences', which include, besides history and political economy, sociology, ethnology, demography, psychology, psycho-sociology, linguistics, and so on. Most of these disciplines have developed outside Marxism, and it is blindingly obvious that they have been profoundly marked, in their 'theory', 'methodology', and research 'techniques' – ultimately, in their object – by bourgeois ideology.

The extensive methodological and technical apparatus that these disciplines put to work is by no means proof of their scientific nature. It is well known that there can exist highly technical disciplines (utilizing, for example, mathematical methods) which are nevertheless *'sciences' without an object*, or, if one likes 'sciences' whose object is altogether different from the one they declare to be theirs. I cannot provide a detailed demonstration of this here, but there are irrefutable reasons for maintaining that, as far as many of their subdivisions are concerned, several of the 'Human Sciences' are not sciences which provide theoretical knowledge of a real object, but (highly elaborate) *techniques of social adaptation or readaptation*. Psycho-sociology almost in its entirety, as well as most of the work that has been done in empirical sociology, contemporary political economy, and even in much of psychology fall into this category.

At the practical level, one becomes aware of the imposture of these disciplines 'without an object' when one observes that they are incapable of providing a rigorous, precise, unequivocal definition of their object, and that, in practice, they all fight over an 'object' to which none can lay indisputable claim. It is common knowledge not only that the *'problems of the boundaries'* separating political economy, sociology, psycho-sociology and psychology are highly controversial, but also that the disciplines in question are incapable of resolving them. When a 'science' endlessly disputes its 'object' with one or more neighbouring 'sciences', it is quite likely that what is at stake is the nature of this 'object' itself and, consequently, the nature of these would-be 'sciences'. Indeed, within one and the same discipline (for example, political economy, sociology, psychology or psycho-sociology), disciplines are proliferating before our very eyes (a good dozen disciplines exist within political economy, psychology, etc.), so that the 'problem of boundaries' is posed anew within political economy and sociology, psycho-sociology, psychology, and so on. These divisions do not by any means correspond to a theoretical division of labour grounded in their object; they reflect divergent conceptions of the same 'object'.

It can be shown that this disorder, this anarchy within 'sciences' that often boast an impressive methodological and technical apparatus, ultimately stems from a basic ambiguity surrounding the putatively 'scientific' nature of these 'sciences' (which are often mere 'techniques') and their *'object'* (which is often not an object, but an *objective*: social adaptation or readaptation).

Part of the reason for this ambiguity, no doubt, is the fact that these disciplines are still young; in the last analysis, however, it is owing to their domination by not only bourgeois ideology but also, and in some cases directly, bourgeois politics. It is bourgeois ideology which imposes on these 'sciences' the distorted ideological categories in which they set out to define their 'object', with the result that they miss their real objects; and it is ultimately bourgeois politics and ideology which impose on them the *objectives* that these sciences dependent on the bourgeoisie then spontaneously take for their 'objects'.

This situation is extremely serious – not only for Marxists, but for all the scholars and technicians working in the field of the existing 'Human Sciences'. Many scholars in the 'human sciences' are uncomfortable with a practical and theoretical situation whose deplorable consequences they must put up with even in their day-to-day professional activity. More or less confusedly, they feel the need for a theoretical clarification that would free them from the contradictions and dependencies in which they live and work.

But the greatest danger in the present situation is that Marxists themselves may be taken in by the deceptive prestige of these 'sciences', succumbing to them in the hope that they will provide knowledge that they do in fact need. With a few exceptions, the conclusion holds that *to succumb to the existing 'Human Sciences' today, without subjecting their theories, methods, techniques and, finally, their 'objects' to radical criticism, is in fact to succumb to one of the most dangerous (because least perceptible) forms of bourgeois ideology.*

This danger is especially great today, when, after decades of isolation and stagnation in certain fields, communists feel the need to resolve certain problems posed 'by life'; in throwing themselves upon the 'Human Sciences' without taking the precaution of subjecting their foundations and methods to rigorous criticism, they risk falling prey to the illusion that they are 'solving' their real problems, when the contemporary 'Human Sciences' in fact often represent the chief obstacle to their solution.

To get to the bottom of the matter, we must, rather, come to understand that most of the Human Sciences, although they have developed outside Marxism, fall *in principle* under the jurisdiction of Marxist theory. Political economy, sociology and 'social psychology', and even, for the most part, what is called 'psychology,' can exist only on the theoretical basis of the principles of historical materialism. All these disciplines are simply regions of the new 'continent' (the history of human societies and their effects on the individuals subjected to their structures) opened up to knowledge by the new science founded by Marx. Only on condition that these regional sciences are situated where they belong, in this 'continent', can they be assigned their true object (as opposed to a mere objective), a correct [juste] theory of this object, and the appropriate [correcte] methodology corresponding to it. It is on this condition that it will become possible to put an end to the 'border conflicts' raging both within and between contemporary disciplines.

There is every reason to believe that this labour of critical transformation and foundation will produce significant results, some of which will constitute real discoveries. By dint of this labour, Marxist theoreticians will overcome the backwardness that has left historical materialism lagging behind in areas of[19] research which, for the most part, depend on its own principles. They will take back entire regions occupied by by-products of bourgeois ideology, for the greater good of Marxist theory and politics. This reconquest of what rightfully belongs to historical materialism represents a major form of struggle against bourgeois ideology.

Of course, we cannot promote criticism and thoroughgoing reorganization of the 'Human Sciences' by straightforward 'application of' or, a fortiori, 'deduction from' the principles of historical materialism. Quite the contrary: we will arrive at this result only at the cost of a major effort of criticism, research, and theoretical production. We need to work on both existing Marxist method and the Human Sciences in their present state; in a word, we need to make use of all the theoretical resources and empirical raw material at our disposal. We must also learn to discern, among the existing Human Sciences, those that already provide theoretical guarantees strong enough to justify the affirmation that they possess an object their title to which is not disputed by a host of other disciplines: for example, linguistics and psychoanalysis. Again, we will have to undertake a critical examination of the present state of the last-named disciplines[20r] in order to

---

[r] It particular, it is crucial that we free Freud's discovery from all the idealist

determine how far they have developed and, finally, to discern what they contain that might be of use as a theoretical resource for solving some of the problems thrown up by other disciplines. It follows that historical materialism cannot accomplish this task alone: it will need the help of dialectical materialism, which is indispensable not only for criticizing the effects of bourgeois ideology in the field of the 'human sciences', but also for recognizing the positive results achieved by some of them, and for redefining the theoretical regions of the 'continent' that Marx opened up to knowledge.

The reader will have understood that, in setting out this programme, I am by no means calling for a return to 'dogmatism'. The point is not that all problems have been solved in advance by Marxist theory, so that we can 'retreat' back to Marx. There do indeed exist new problems about which Marx said nothing; new disciplines, such as linguistics and psychoanalysis, founded since Marx's time, have begun to broach them. These regions do not belong either directly or exclusively to historical materialism; they also seem to belong, at least in part, to other 'continents', or perhaps to one other 'continent': the question remains open. On the other hand, in all the regions that belong to historical materialism, Marxism has things to say. It can say them only if it sets out from Marx, the true Marx, in order to progress, and in order to become the strategic centre of, and the general theory on which, research in the Human Sciences depends.

If Marxism remains open to all that is new and authentically scientific, open to all real problems, while at the same time remaining constantly alert to the danger represented by the temptations and traps of bourgeois ideology and its effects, it

---

bourgeois ideology under which it has been buried, not only in the United States, but also in Europe, rigorously distinguishing its object from the 'object' of psychology. Psychoanalysis is not a psychology or a branch of psychology. Its specific object is not behaviour or the 'personality', but the unconscious and its effects. A great deal of work must be carried out in order to give Freud's discovery the scientific form that it calls for. This task has been undertaken by researchers working, above all, under the impetus provided by the œuvre of Lacan, who, setting out alone, was the first to open up this path. Modern linguistics also raises critical problems of the same kind, but it exists, and has a real object: it has produced remarkable results (the Soviet school, Danish school, American and French schools, etc.).

can acquit itself of this historical task, whose theoretical and practical – and, therefore, political – importance is obvious. But, in order to accomplish it, Marxists have to stick to the positions of Marxist theory, without retreating behind Marx into bourgeois or petty-bourgeois idealist ideologies, as is all too often the case with those of them who go hunting for the solution to the problems of the 'Twentieth Century'[21] in the *works of the early Marx*.

To develop historical materialism while reconquering and reorganizing, on the right theoretical bases, the disciplines occupying the field of the 'Human Sciences': *this strategic task number 2 today depends, in the last analysis, on the progress of Marxist philosophy, that is to say, on strategic task number 1.*

VII.   Conclusion: philosophy and politics

In conclusion, I would like to reply to a final objection that my readers may bring up.

In spite of all the explanations I have provided, and even the arguments and examples of Marx, Engels and Lenin, the reader may have the impression that the emphasis I have put on philosophy's decisive role in the present conjuncture threatens to compromise the grand principle of the primacy of practice and the *primacy of politics*.

To meet this objection, we need to go back to the Marxist conception of the union of theory and practice. For it is in the context of the union of theory and practice that it becomes possible to resolve the contradiction, apparent or real, between theory or philosophy on the one hand and practice or politics on the other.

The union of theory and practice implies that every political practice contains a philosophy, while every philosophy contains a practical signification, a politics. That is why it is essential, under certain circumstances, to go all the way back to philosophical principles in order to combat the ideological distortions of political practice, and why it may be crucial under other circumstances – not only for the Marxist science of history, but also for the practice of the revolutionary parties – to rectify and develop existing philosophy. It is the way the union of theory and practice is realized, the distortions of which it is the locus, the threats that hang over it, and the theoretical needs that arise when the attempt is made to solve the problems it entails (whether scientific or political) which require us to put the emphasis on either politics or theory, depending on the circumstances, and, within theory, on either historical or dialectical materialism. For the reasons that I have very rapidly set out, I think it is clear that the present theoretical conjuncture, considered against the background of the general conjuncture, requires that we *put the emphasis on Marxist philosophy*.

But we must go further still. The union of theory and practice must also appear within Marxist theory (the articulated ensemble of Marxist science and Marxist philosophy), and even within Marxist philosophy itself. To make my meaning absolutely clear, I would say that the primacy of politics must be expressed in forms that are specific to Marxist theory, and that *it is by definition the responsibility of philosophy to ensure the primacy of politics in theory*.

It is not enough to say that the primacy of politics is ensured by the fact that every philosophy contains a practical signification and a politics. Of course, this politics must first be correct. But the primacy of politics in theory has also to be realized *in theoretical forms*; politics must, in short, have precise, perceptible consequences within theory itself. The primacy of politics manifests itself in theory in two essential forms, both of which depend on philosophy.

1. The primacy of politics is manifested, first, in the call for the kind of *theoretical politics* defined in Part II of this essay. Both knowledge supplied by historical materialism (analysis of the ideological and political conjuncture) and also the direct intervention of dialectical materialism are required to define this theoretical politics. For only dialectical materialism can identify the deviations that have to be fought, the errors that have to be corrected, the theoretical needs that have to be satisfied, and the deficiencies in the theoretical domain that have to be made good. Only dialectical materialism can define a theoretical strategy and tactics, and establish theoretical objectives in a hierarchical order

that reflects the imperatives of the theoretical conjuncture (task number 1, task number 2, etc.).

2. The primacy of politics in theory appears directly and decisively in *the nature of Marxist philosophy itself.*

To grasp this, if only in principle, we need to say something about the great theoretical problem at stake in this thesis: the problem of the specificity of Marxist philosophy, the problem of *the difference between science and philosophy.* Even when we demand that philosophy exhibit the formal characteristics of a science – precision, conceptual rigour and demonstrative systematicity – we have to affirm, at the same time, that it is not a science. *What radically distinguishes philosophy from the sciences, the science of history included, is the internal, intimate, organic relation that philosophy maintains with politics.*

The Marxist science of history, like any other science, stands in an *external* relation to politics. Political conditions are part of the ensemble of objective social conditions that condition both the existence of the sciences and their development. These political conditions also appear in a particular form: that of the ideologies which constantly besiege all the sciences, acting on them from the outside while seeking to take advantage of the philosophical difficulties internal to their theoretical practice. In so far as they give expression to the balance of forces in the class struggle, the ideologies refer us to the science of the class struggle, which is part of the Marxist science of history. In so far as these ideologies state philosophical theses, represent philosophical tendencies, and exploit the difficulties that the sciences encounter in their theoretical practice, they refer us to the Marxist philosophy that can provide an understanding and a critique of them.

Thus that which, in the political intervention of the ideologies, is internal to the sciences pertains to *philosophy*, not to the sciences themselves. To the extent to which the interference of ideology in the life of the sciences does not involve philosophy, this interference may be considered external to the sciences; it is part of the objective social conditions for the existence and development of the sciences, but it is not part of what constitutes the scientificity of the sciences. This conclusion holds for all the truly constituted sciences, and thus for the Marxist science of history as well.

But it will be objected that the Marxist science of history should not be so hastily conflated with the other sciences: mathematics, the natural sciences, and so on. For the real difficulty, it will be said, lies in the fact that the objects of these sciences have nothing to do with politics, whereas the Marxist science of history takes politics as its object, and consequently stands, as a science, in an intimate relation with politics.

This argument is important, but wide of the mark. To refute it, it is not enough to say that the Marxist science of history takes as its object not only politics (the class struggle), but *other* objects as well: the political (the juridico-political superstructure, that is, law [*le droit*] and the state), the economic, the ideological, their articulation in the various modes of production, the combination of several modes of production in concrete social formations, and so on. In other words, it is not enough to say that politics is only one object of Marxist science among others. One must also show that the fact that Marxist science takes politics as one object among others clearly distinguishes Marxist science from the other sciences, but does not affect, internally and intimately, its scientific character as such, that is, the *scientificity* of this science.

The relationship of the science of history to politics is, in principle, identical to the relationship that any science has to its object. This relationship is one of scientific *objectivity*, and concerns the general forms of the scientificity of any science, the fact that a science can produce knowledge of its specific object only by mobilizing a theory and a method in a determinate theoretical practice; this includes, in certain cases, an experimental practice (the political practice of the Communist parties is part of the theoretical practice of Marxist science, on condition that it is treated scientifically). The nature of the object of a science only determines certain forms of this relationship of objectivity, but not this relationship itself, which is the same no matter what object a science studies.

To bring out the objectivity of this relationship – that is, the fact that it is independent of the specific nature of any particular object – we may say that the specific properties of the object do not affect scientific knowledge of it. Spinoza observed that the concept of a dog does not bark; similarly, we might say that the concept of sugar is not sweet, that the knowledge of atoms is not atomic, that the knowledge of life is not 'a living thing', that the science of history is not 'historical', and so on. In the same way, it may be said that the science of politics is not political. This is a way of expressing the fact that the qualitative nature of the object of a science does not affect – internally, intimately, organically – the intrinsic nature of a science, which is its scientificity. Politics or 'ideology' is therefore not the determining principle of the Marxist history of science *qua* science.[s]

[s] This point is crucial. Yet it is not always clearly understood by those Marxists, philosophers included, who work in the disciplines that come under the jurisdiction of historical materialism, such as political economy, sociology, history, etc. This can be seen in the papers on the problem of the relations between sociology and 'ideology' delivered by the Soviet participants in the 1966 Conference at Evian (see the papers by Konstantinov, Kelle and Chesnikov).

The Soviet participants' thesis is that sociology cannot do without ideology – not only because it must, like any science, struggle against ideology with the help of philosophy, but also because there is, so the argument runs, a close, organic link between sociology and 'ideology' by virtue of the very special nature of the object of sociology and the situation of the sociologist. This is said to distinguish sociology and the other social sciences from the natural sciences. The object of the natural sciences is the different modes of existence of matter; the natural scientist remains external to his object, is not conditioned by his object, is not an organic part of his object. In the social sciences, the Soviets argue, the situation is fundamentally different: the object of these sciences is not matter, but human societies and the different modes of human existence. The sociologist is himself determined by the object he studies, human society; he is an organic part of his object, is engaged in social struggles and the transformation of society, and must, ideologically, take sides. For all these reasons, it is claimed, there is an intimate link between sociology (the social sciences) and ideology.

The Soviet participants cite, in support of their thesis, arguments that certain American sociologists use against others who advocate the 'de-ideologization' of sociology.

In fact, the Soviet participants use the same concept, the concept of ideology, to designate three fundamentally different realities:

1. the ideological theory that serves as the basis for bourgeois sociology (here ideology means 'a representation that is false' because subjective class interests have made it false);
2. the scientific theory on which a scientific sociology should be based; here the term 'ideology', to which the Soviets append the term 'scientific', simply designates the scientific theory that serves as the basis for a science;
3. the philosophical theory of dialectical materialism (they use the term 'ideology' to designate this third theory as well).

Sound theoretical method rules out the use of a single concept to designate three objectively distinct realities, for this inevitably sows confusion and leads to ambiguities.

The term 'ideology' *tout court* is appropriate when what is in question is the ideological (false) theory of bourgeois sociology. In this case it adequately designates its object. Ideology (or politics) is clearly an organic part of philos-

It is a very different matter when it comes to *philosophy*. Politics is naturally part of the objective social conditions for the existence and development of philosophy, and politics, in the form of ideologies, also acts on philosophy – but *politics* concerns philosophy in a wholly different sense, because *it is organically and intimately bound up with the nature of philosophy* qua *philosophy*. It is philosophy's intimate, organic relationship with politics that distinguishes it from all the sciences.

One can form a schematic idea of the specific nature of philosophy as opposed to all the sciences by noting, for example, that it does not take as its object, as all the sciences do, a region of reality, or even the whole set of regions comprising a 'continent' of reality, in the sense I gave that word earlier. Quite the contrary: philosophy takes as its object what is traditionally, and improperly, called the 'totality' of the real. To put it more precisely, and to escape the religious-dogmatic effects of the concept of 'totality', let me say that philosophy takes as its object the tendential law of the transformation of a *complex ensemble*

---

ophy, but the concept of ideology does not suffice, precisely, to define Marxist philosophy. Marxist philosophy is not an ideological theory in the sense in which bourgeois sociology is based on an ideological theory.

The term 'ideology' is, on the other hand, an altogether inadequate designation for the theory of a science.

By using three distinct concepts to designate these three distinct realities – ideological theory, scientific theory, and philosophical theory – we avoid ambiguity and confusion. Moreover, we do away with the distinction that is the source of this [confusion]: the distinction that the Soviet participants draw between the natural and the social sciences on the grounds that they are sciences of different kinds.

To be frank, I think that this distinction represents a return – doubtless in attenuated form, but undeniably a return – to a distinction that idealist bourgeois philosophical ideology draws between the object of the natural sciences and that of the human sciences. For bourgeois ideology, only the natural sciences are sciences in the strict sense; the 'human' or 'social' sciences are not true sciences, because they derive from philosophy and treat of man. Marx's whole scientific *œuvre* is a refutation of this characteristic distinction of bourgeois ideology. Marx says again and again that *Capital* is a scientific, not an ideological work, whatever meaning one may assign the term – even if the term 'ideology' were, in this case, to designate Marxist philosophy. For we know, thanks to Marx, Engels and Lenin, that Marxist philosophy is by its nature distinct from the science of history. Like any science, the science of history, and therefore Marxist sociology as well, need philosophy. However, it is as a science that the science of history needs philosophy: the science of history is distinct from philosophy. This confusion is a confusion that is typical of the bourgeois ideology of science.

constituted by the articulation of two great systems that are themselves internally complex and articulated:

1. *the system of theoretical practices*, or the system of the regions and continents explored by scientific knowledge: in other words, the system of the sciences, in their relation to the ideologies, which they must combat in order to exist and develop;
2. *the system of the different social practices* (economic, political,[22] and ideological) which condition the existence, practice, and development of the sciences.

The nature of this complex ensemble and the tendential law of transformation governing it constitute the specific object of philosophy. This is the object of which philosophy provides knowledge [*savoir*] in the form of philosophical knowledges [*connaissances*]: the philosophical categories, which are distinct from all possible scientific concepts (the categories of materialism and the dialectic, together with all the categories subordinate to these two major, basic categories).

When we talk about this complex ensemble, we do not exclude philosophy: at every moment in the transformation of this ensemble, the existing philosophy *itself also* features in it – in the system of theoretical practices.

In stipulating that philosophy takes as its object not only the nature of this complex ensemble but also the tendential law of transformation governing it, we are not merely adding a detail; we are stating an essential thesis: namely, that this ensemble is caught up in a process of development, with the result that *historical* events, in the full sense of the word, occur there, affecting sometimes the first system, at other times the second, and at still others the link between them, etc. We thus affirm that knowledge [*connaissance*] of this ensemble is knowledge of *the historical law governing it*.

To produce knowledge of this ensemble, then, philosophy cannot just draw up a balance sheet. It cannot be a mere *encyclopaedia*, as certain of Engels's formulations might lead us to think, a *summa* of the scientific knowledges [*connaissances*] existing at a given moment, even if these knowledges are conceived in terms of the laws of the dialectic.

Philosophy has to take into consideration the fact that it, too, is included in this *summa*, included in the guise of an active force of intervention within this ensemble. It must recognize the significance of its own presence in any possible *summa* – the fact that the presence of philosophy in any *summa* of scientific knowledge is the proof *in actu* of the unstable – that is, historical and dialectical – nature of this state of the sciences, of which philosophy can speak only by intervening in it, by taking an active part in it – that is, in the broad sense of the term, by intervening in it *politically*.

To say that philosophy has to provide us knowledge of the tendential law governing the transformation of the complex ensemble that comprises its object, and to observe that philosophy itself makes up part of the ensemble of which it must provide knowledge, is therefore to say one and the same thing. It is to say that this complex ensemble cannot be the object of an *Absolute Knowledge*; that philosophy cannot be the *Science of the sciences*; that the law of the transformation of this complex ensemble is never given in advance, *but has to be deciphered step by step*.

This is the point at which politics intervenes directly in philosophy, and in decisive fashion. Not only because the existence of politics has always, in whatever form it takes, come down to intervening actively in the complex ensemble that constitutes its own object, or because this intervention can be termed, in the broad sense, a political intervention; but also because it is *politics* in the narrow, strict sense of the term that constitutes, as the *pertinent index par excellence*, the starting point from which it becomes possible, at the practical level, to undertake this deciphering. There are two reasons for this; they have to do with the privileged position that politics occupies in each of the two systems whose complex ensemble comprises the specific object of philosophy.

1. *The system of social practices* (economic, political and ideological).

Politics is indeed, as Marx, Engels, Lenin, and all the leaders of the Marxist workers' movement repeatedly observed, a *'summary'* or *'digest'* of all the social practices. The state of the class struggle provides, in the form of a 'summary', a theoretical and practical view of the state of the relations between the practices that condition the system of the sciences, its current existence, and its development. However, the role of pertinent index that politics plays in the system of social practices does not, in this form, concern philosophy as such, because politics in this sense is the object of the Marxist science of history. What directly concerns philosophy is the articulation of the system of theoretical practices with the system of social practices. It is at this precise point that philosophy is, in the strong sense, the pertinent index for the deciphering of the tendential law of transformation governing this complex ensemble.

2. *The system of theoretical practices* (science, philosophy, ideology).

Here, politics is directly present in the form of the *ideologies*. It is in the ideologies that the class struggle figures in person in the conjuncture of the theoretical system. The ideologies are, in the theoretical conjuncture, the form in which the class struggle, and therefore politics, intervenes in the theoretical system. There can be no sciences and no philosophy that do not take up a position vis-à-vis the ideologies, that do not stage theoretical (scientific and philosophical) counter-interventions against the ideologies. Consequently, the state of the *ideological struggle in the domain of the theoretical system is the basic pertinent index* from which one can set out to decipher not only the state of the theoretical conjuncture, but also – and this is determinant – the relationship between the theoretical system and the social system, which represents the tendential form of the articulation between the two systems.

Thus ideology enjoys a very special sort of privilege that allows it to play the role of pertinent index. It can play this role because it belongs to the two systems at the same time: as an expression of the class struggle, it belongs to the system of the social practices; but it belongs to the system of the theoretical practices in so far as this expression of the class struggle takes the form of *theoretical* ideologies comprising an organic part of the system where the sciences and philosophy reside; these can exist only on condition that they define themselves in contradistinction to the ideologies, and constantly combat them.

Thus politics, in the form of *politics* in the proper sense of the word, and also in the form of its *ideological* expression, is the pertinent index *par excellence* when it comes to deciphering the tendential law governing the complex ensemble, because it is the index of the state of the articulation between the two systems. Hence philosophy must above all be guided by politics in attempting to decipher this tendential law, which forms its specific object. When philosophy takes politics into account in posing its own problems, it truly takes its own object into account. It can thereby ensure – in its own domain, which is philosophical, and in the philosophical mode (utilizing a rigorous theory and a method of a scientific kind) – the primacy of politics. It does not have to respect the primacy of politics for reasons stemming from the nature of politics, but for reasons stemming from its own, philosophical, nature.

Ultimately, we find that which distinguishes philosophy from all sciences whatsoever here. No science concerns itself, as science, with the articulation of the two systems (the system of social practices and the system of theoretical practices) and the tendential law governing it; indeed, no science concerns itself with the state of the theoretical system as a whole. That is not the object of any science, whether it be mathematics, physics, biology, or even the science of history. It is, however, the specific object of philosophy. This is because philosophy is directly concerned with politics, by virtue of its nature, theory (materialism), method (the dialectic) and categories.

I am not putting forward unprecedented theses. It is Lenin's extraordinary philosophical merit to have understood this, and to have stated it with astounding clarity and boldness in *Materialism and Empirio-criticism*.[23] No doubt we do not find a theory developed from this hypothesis in Lenin, but we do find in him proof that he considered this thesis to be absolutely essential to Marxist theory. It is enough to recall the insistence with which he proclaimed that *'partisanship' in politics* is an intimate part of any philosophy, and that this partisan position must become, for communist philosophers, a conscious taking of sides, based on a rigorous theory of philosophy and its relationship to politics.

Consequently, to say that the development of Marxist philosophy is a task which, objectively, has priority in the prevailing conjuncture is not to contradict the principle of the primacy of the political. We contend, on the contrary, that philosophy, if it is to be a truly Marxist philosophy, must be approached in accordance with its own peculiar nature, which is political. The primacy of philosophy today is therefore the contemporary form of the primacy of the class struggle at the heart of the political nature of philosophy.

We must straight away point out the very great difficulties and risks associated with this task. Of course, *the thesis of the political nature of philosophy is*, as it must be, *quite the opposite of a pragmatic thesis*. For centuries, philosophy was the 'handmaid of religion', and in the guise of modern idealism, still is today. There can be no question whatsoever of perpetuating this idealist tradition by making philosophy the 'handmaid of politics', even if what is involved is correct politics; that is to say, there can be no question of reducing philosophy to the rank of a commentary on the political decisions of the day, or even of a correct political line. That would be to make philosophy a political ideology, and to reduce it to the existing *political ideology*. Political ideology has its rights: it is indispensable to the political struggle. But *philosophy is not a political ideology*. It is a discipline which, at the theoretical level, is absolutely distinct from political ideology, and it has *the autonomy* of a discipline of a scientific character;[24] its development is subject to specific imperatives – precision, conceptual rigour and demonstrative systematicity. It meets a requirement that is fundamental to any theoretical discipline of a scientific character, which must provide the knowledge of its object in person, not of another object that is not its own. *The object* of philosophy is not politics, but philosophy is *political by nature*. Philosophy cannot be faithful to its own object and nature unless it thinks its object (the tendential law governing the articulation of the complex ensemble of social practices/theoretical practices) philosophically, and assumes its nature philosophically: that is, *unless it ensures the primacy of the class struggle within philosophy itself, in forms that are rigorously and specifically philosophical*.

Without a twofold awareness of (1) the primacy of the political in philosophy itself; and (2) the specifically philosophical theoretical requirements that this primacy be treated philosophically, Marxist philosophers run the risk of lapsing into either (a) theoreticism, which completely ignores the class struggle; or (b) pragmatism, which completely ignores the specificity of theory and philosophy, as well as its scientific requirements.

To develop Marxist philosophy is therefore an extremely arduous task, because it requires a very high level of political consciousness in philosophical work: it requires that one respect philosophically, in philosophy, the primacy of the class struggle, while avoiding the pitfalls of theoreticism on the one hand and pragmatism on the other.

That the tasks of Marxist philosophy are demanding ones, that they call for deep awareness of the class struggle and its effects, great critical lucidity, great scientific sureness of touch, years of hard study, reflection and analysis, and unyielding rigour combined with the greatest possible theoretical inventiveness and audacity – none of this can intimidate us; on the contrary, it shows us what we have to do. Any political[25] activist who has an experience of *scientific* practice in one capacity or another, a political capacity included,[26] is aware of this challenge, and of the necessity and fecundity of this task. Marxist philosophers must meet the same challenge, if they wish to produce a Marxist philosophy equal to its historical task in the present conjuncture.

They would do well to recall Marx's words: 'at the entrance to science as at the entrance to hell . . .', where 'every beginning is difficult', one must, as Dante says, 'abandon all suspicion and fear'.[t] We can make no 'concession to the prejudice of public opinion', but must 'welcome every judgement based on scientific criticism'.[u] They would also do well to remember Lenin's phrase: 'Marx's theory is all-powerful because it is true'.[v]

Notes

1. 'SRC' 10.
2. 'PRW' 21.
3. Vladislav Lektorsky (editor-in-chief of *Voprosy filosofi*), personal communication, 25 June 2002.
4. The last eight words are contained in the typescript from which the proofs were set (hereafter 'the typescript'), but not in the proofs. This

---

[t] Preface to *A Contribution to the Critique of Political Economy* (1859).
[u] Preface to *Capital* (1867).
[v] 'The Three Sources and the Three Component Parts of Marxism' (1913).

and similar omissions are doubtless due to oversights on the typesetter's part.

5. The words 'the new science' are contained in the typescript but not in the proofs.

6. In the proofs, this sentence is followed by another that is absent from the typescript and probably extraneous: 'It puts these existing theoretical or philosophical elements to work.'

7. Both the proofs and the typescript read 'Marx's relationship to Engels'.

8. This and the following paragraph represent a late intercalation in the typescript.

9. Althusser substituted the words 'scientific concepts and philosophical categories' for 'concepts' in a handwritten addendum to the typescript.

10. 'The whole man' is a handwritten addendum to the typescript. The notion of 'the whole man', which the Marx of the *1844 Manuscripts* and *The German Ideology* takes from Ludwig Feuerbach, holds a central place in the work of the PCF's then 'official philosopher' Roger Garaudy, as well as in that of Maximilien Rubel, Henri Lefebvre, and others (see, for example, Lefebvre, *Dialectical Materialism*, trans. John Sturrock, London, 1968; Garaudy, *Perspectives de l'homme*, Paris, 1959, pp. 1, 315 and *passim*; *Qu'est-ce que la morale marxiste*, Paris, 1963, p. 217).

11. The proofs read: 'Even when this interpretation tries to take its distance from bourgeois humanism. Even when this interpretation takes its distance from bourgeois humanism, even when it declares . . .'.

12. 'Creation, freedom, creative freedom' is the reading of the typescript; the proofs read 'creation, creative freedom'.

13. The words 'no less' are a handwritten addendum to the typescript, which originally indicated that the evolutionist interpretation of Marxism was *less* serious than the humanist interpretation. The Hungarian translation ('A Marxista filozófia történelmi feladata', in *Marx – az elmélet forradalma*, trans. Ernö Gerö, Budapest 1968, p. 289) has it that the evolutionist 'deformation' of Marxism' is 'no less serious' than the humanist deformation.

14. The following six paragraphs represent the revised version of a passage from a manuscript on the union of theory and practice that Althusser intended to publish in book form in the mid-1960s. The chapter containing this passage was published in *La Pensée* in April 1967 and translated as 'OTW' 55–6; I have followed the existing translation closely here.

15. The footnote that follows is an intercalation in the typescript.

16. See Jorge Semprun, 'Marxisme et humanisme', *La Nouvelle critique*, no. 164, March 1965, p. 30: 'We cannot restore the vigour and rigour . . . of Marxism by shutting ourselves up in the besieged fortress of an abstract, ahistorical Marxism.'

17. This sentence, only part of which is contained in the proofs, is translated from the typescript.

18. Althusser introduced the second sentence of the following note in a handwritten addendum to the typescript.

19. The preceding ten words are contained in the typescript but not in the proofs.

20. In distinguishing the object of psychoanalysis from the 'personality' in the note that follows, Althusser was doubtless thinking of Lucien Sève, who was working on a project that would issue in the voluminous *Marxism and the Theory of Human Personality* (trans. David Pavett, London, 1975), the first edition of which was released by the Communist Party's publishing house Éditions sociales in 1969. Althusser commented on this project in a 27 June 1966 letter to Sève:

> what some people *call psychology*, or, in any case, what you are going to treat under the rubric 'theory of the development of the personality', using concepts that are 50% Garaudyist (humanism, the individual in your sense of the word, labour, etc.) essentially belongs to (1) psycho-physio-biology, and (2) *sociology*. . . . The third term, the unconscious and its mechanisms, belongs not to what is *called psychology*, but to psychoanalysis.

21. An allusion to Roger Garaudy, *Marxism in the Twentieth Century* (trans. René Hague, London, 1970 [1966]), which concluded with a sharp attack on Althusserian 'dogmatism'.

22. Both the typescript and the proofs read 'practical'.

23. The typescript contains the following addendum, written in Althusser's hand and then crossed out: 'albeit in philosophical categories dominated by a *sensualist*-materialist ideology'.

24. The typescript originally read: 'It is a rigorous theoretical discipline'; the sentence has been crossed out and replaced by the one translated here.

25. 'Political' is a handwritten addendum to the typescript.

26. The preceding eight words are a handwritten addendum to the typescript.

The Humanist Controversy

(1967)

Althusser's archives contain two different versions of this text, some ten pages of which were published, with minor modifications, in 'Marx's Relation to Hegel' (in Lénine et la philosophie, *Paris, 1972;* English translation in Montesquieu, Rousseau, Marx: Politics and History, *trans. Ben Brewster, London, 1982). The author probably typed the first draft of the text himself. Only thirty-eight pages of it survive; they are unpaginated and covered with countless handwritten modifications, most of which were incorporated into the last part of the second version of the text. Doubtless because he found the first draft relatively satisfactory, Althusser had a secretary at the École normale supérieure retype it, and then made a few handwritten modifications to her typescript: whence the second and, this time, full version of the text. Full, but most probably unfinished: all indications are that Althusser abandoned an originally much more ambitious project en route. In particular, the second part of the text includes the beginnings of a first subsection which, however, stands alone. Here we publish the text of the second version, without indicating where it has been modified. The numbering of the chapters is, however, based on the first version. This poses certain problems, which are discussed in the endnotes.*

The second typed version of the text comprises two distinct parts. The body of the work, numbered from page 1 (initially page 17) to page 103, is preceded by a brief introduction numbered from page 1 to page 16. Editing 'The Humanist Controversy' was complicated by the fact that these first sixteen pages do not read as a continuous whole, despite the continuous pagination, but, rather, fall into two separate parts. The first constitutes a true introduction to the work: we publish it as is. The existence of the second is explained by the kind of book that Althusser initially planned to release under the title La Querelle de l'humanisme; *it was to contain, in addition to the text included in the present volume, two texts that he had initially published in journals and then collected in* For Marx – *'Marxism and Humanism' and 'A Complementary Note on "Real Humanism"' – together with several representative essays from the debate these two texts sparked off. (See the Introduction to the present volume.) The second part of the introduction thus comprises a group of short individual texts in which Althusser presented and commented on the essays he intended to bring together in* The Humanist Controversy. *If this book had seen the light, then, short introductions by Althusser would have preceded each of the essays included in it. Since it makes little sense to publish these introductions in the absence of the essays they were intended to introduce, the reader will not find them below. Thus we hear the voice of only one of the disputants in the humanist controversy.*

François Matheron

Amid the detail of trifles and quarrels, even if only for or against humanism, one must bow to the evidence: history loves little flaps [*l'histoire adore les histoires*].

The 'humanist controversy' began as peacefully as could be imagined. One summer day in 1963, at a friend's house, I happened to meet Dr Adam Schaff, a leading member of one of our Communist parties. (Charged by the leadership of the Polish Communist Party with responsibility for the 'intellectuals', Schaff is both a philosopher known for his books on semantics and the problem of man in Marxism,[1] and a high-ranking party leader esteemed for his cultivation and open-mindedness. He was on his way back from the United States, where he had given talks on Marx to large, enthusiastic academic audiences.) Schaff told me about a project under the direction of Erich Fromm, whom he knew well and had recently met in the USA. Before the war, in the 1930s, Fromm had been connected with a German Marxist group with ultra-left tendencies that aired its views in an ephemeral journal, the *Zeitschrift für Sozialforschung*.[2] It was in this journal that Adorno, Horkheimer, Borkenau and others first made a name for themselves. Nazism drove Fromm into exile, as it did many others. He has since become famous for his essays on modern 'consumer' society,[3] which he analyses with the help of concepts derived from a certain confrontation between Marxism and Freudianism. Fromm had just released, in the United States, a translation of selections from texts by the young Marx; eager to gain a wider audience for Marxism, he now had plans to publish a substantial collective work on 'socialist Humanism', and was soliciting contributions from Marxist philosophers from countries in the West and the East.[4] Doctor A. insisted that I participate in this project. I had, moreover, received a letter from Fromm a few days earlier.[5] Why had Fromm, whom I did not know, written to me? Doctor A. had brought my existence to his attention.

I pleaded the conjuncture, and the solemn title under which this much too beautiful international orchestra had been assembled: the only thing that could come of it, I said, was a *Missa Solemnis in Humanism-Major*, and my personal part could only spoil the Universal Harmony of the score. But it was to no avail that I made the conversation ring with all the capital letters that Circumstance obliged me to use; to no avail that, out of arguments, I gave him my arguments, called a spade a spade, said, in brief, that my music would not be appreciated. A. (Schaff) sealed my lips with an impeccable syllogism. Every Humanist is a Liberal; Fromm is a Humanist; therefore, Fromm is a Liberal. It followed that I could play my instrument in peace, after my own fashion. I let him coax me about as long as was seemly – to savour the situation, but also because I was plagued by a nagging doubt. I may have been wrong, after all: with a good theory of the displacement of the dominant, which I was trying hard to profess, one could, after all, imagine a Humanist who was *also* a Liberal, the conjuncture notwithstanding. Everything was a matter of the conjuncture.

I wrote my article immediately. Just in case, and with an eye to the public that would be reading it, a public I did not know, I made it very short and too clear, and even took the precaution of subjecting it to a 'rewrite', that is, of making it even shorter and clearer. In two lines, I settled the question of the early Marx's intellectual development with no ifs, ands and buts, and, in ten, wrapped up the history of philosophy, political economy and ethics in the seventeenth and eighteenth centuries; I went right to the point, with tolerably unrefined arguments and concepts (a sledgehammer opposition of science and ideology) that would, if they did not quite manage to convince, at least hit home. I went so far as to indulge in a bit of theoretical mischief – flattering myself that it would fall into the category of Anglo-Saxon humour and be perceived as such – by putting forward, in all seriousness, the preposterous concept of a 'class' humanism.[6] I had my article translated into English by a competent friend[7] who, I knew, would be all the more meticulous because his ideas were as far from mine as they could possibly be; and I posted this short *ad hoc* text without delay. Time was of the essence: deadlines.

I waited. Time passed. I kept on waiting. It was several months before I received an answer from Fromm.[8] He was terribly, terribly sorry. My text was extremely interesting; he didn't question its intrinsic value; but, decidedly, it had no place in the project – in, that is, the concert of the others. Professions of gratitude, excuses. My law of the displacement of the dominant had failed to come into play. The same went for the Humanist-therefore-Liberal syllogism: all a matter of the conjuncture. One more reason for thinking that between Humanism and Liberalism on the one hand, and the conjuncture on the other, there existed something like – as, moreover, my article said, in black and white – a non-accidental relation.

This was one more reason to publish my text. To publish it where, *at the time*, it could be published: all a matter of the conjuncture. Thanks to the liberalism of *Critica Marxista*, a new theoretical journal of the Italian Communist Party, and of the philosophical section of the *Cahiers de l'ISEA* (with Jean Lacroix as its general editor), it was possible to publish the essay in Italy and France (spring/summer 1964).[9] I continue to be sincerely grateful to these two journals: they deserve credit for accepting my text, for it ran counter to all or part of their explicit ideology. Months followed in which nothing happened. That, too, is a prevailing law in intellectual work.

Then, one day in January 1965, I was surprised to read, in the monthly *Clarté*, the organ of the UEC [*Union des Étudiants Communistes*] of the day,[10] a courteous but very spirited critique of my text. It was the work of Jorge Semprun, a writer known for a very fine novel about the deportation.[11] His refutation was based on what may be called an 'Italian' line of Marxist argument. I beg the pardon of our Italian comrades: contrary to what one might suppose, neither Italy, nor the Italian Communist Party, nor Italian Marxism is in question here – 'Italian' is not, then, a simple adjective of physical geography, it is an adjective of *political* geography, by which certain French intellectuals, or intellectuals who are French by culture, were in the habit of designating the particular position on the French political map that they intended to occupy.[12] The relationship between this so-called 'Italian' position and the real Italy (the true relationship and the mythical version of it) is another story, which will make a curious subject of study some day. None the less, I had reason to believe, on the strength of reliable information I received later, that certain intellectuals in the Italian Party had expressed a wish that someone reply to the article I had published in *Critica Marxista*: out of consideration for me, a Frenchman and a member of the French Communist Party, they had preferred that the rejoinder appear in a French political organ. Various random factors, no doubt, had led to the choice of *Clarté*.

The pace of events now quickened. With Jorge Semprun's and my authorization, *La Nouvelle critique* published a 'dossier' on the debate and opened the discussion (March 1965). It went on for months. Francis Cohen, Michel Simon, Geneviève Navarri, M[ichel] Brossard, Michel Verret, Pierre Macherey, and others took part. The discussion was rekindled when François Maspero published *For Marx* and *Reading Capital* in the series 'Théorie' [autumn 1965]. It was pursued at a general assembly of Communist Philosophers at Choisy-le-Roi[13] in January 1966. Some of those who took the floor at this conference – Roger Garaudy, for example – fiercely attacked my essays. At a meeting held at Argenteuil in March 1966,[14] the Central Committee deliberated upon Humanism and, directly or indirectly, took a stand on the theses and counter-theses under 'discussion', even while declaring that this discussion was, in every sense of the word, 'open'. It is now obvious that it will not be 'closed' any time soon.

Thus it was that a decidedly minor event (a few pages on what seems to be a purely theoretical or even doctrinaire question), an event which one (I most of all) would have had every reason to consider a mere 'accident' of a more or less autobiographical kind (the chance encounter between Fromm's project and a few studies that I had been pursuing), acquired dimensions out of all proportion to its beginnings. This is a sign that, even in the very rough form it took, the essay that I had written for an American audience must have touched an extremely sensitive spot in the present ideological, if not theoretical, conjuncture. Let us say that, in a certain sense, it 'entered' this conjuncture by forcing open a door that some people doubtless had an interest in holding stubbornly shut – and by closing another door that the same people doubtless had an interest in regarding as the only one open to the public. A door, open or shut: the conjuncture had made it, in its way, one of the Doors of the Hour, one that no one could ignore or that everyone had to notice. I am not about to claim that, as I was writing my text, I was entirely unaware of the effect it would have in an important conjuncture, since, on the contrary, I insist, in a dozen different places, on the *conjunctural* significance of the 'Humanist' tide in certain contemporary Marxist circles. But the 'consciousness' one has of what one is doing in defending a Thesis is one thing; the relationship that that 'consciousness' bears to the real world is quite another. The little 'stories' [*histoires*] I told and the effects that followed from them are, in some sort, the experimental record of a confrontation between a thesis (or diagnosis) and reality: that is how little 'stories' go down in 'history' [*c'est par là que les petites 'histoires' entrent dans l'histoire*]. Nor would I ever have described their mechanism in detail if it were not now clear that this mechanism, the stuff of anecdote, was itself the effect of a necessity in which all of us taking part in the debate were caught up. To tell the truth, if history is forever bringing little stories into the world [*si l'histoire fait toujours des histoires*], it doesn't love them all: it loves only those that concern it in one way or another. And it assigns no one, not even its victims, the task of 'sorting them out'. Let us say that, as far as the 'humanist controversy' is concerned, the sorting out has been done – or, rather, is now under way. And all of us sense that, riding on the small change of a few concepts or words that are now being sorted out, is the outcome of a game in which we all have a stake, of which this 'discussion' of Humanism by a few philosophers is an echo, close to hand and infinitely remote: the way we should understand Marx, and put his ideas into practice.

It is time to recall – when, in view of the enormous problems forced on us by the redoubtable conjuncture that assails us, so many people are wondering 'what is to be done?' – it is time to recall a warning of Lenin's drawn from the work which bears that title. . . .[15]

I. Marx's Theoretical Revolution

1

I take up, then, one more time, *the* question of the history of the development of Marx's theoretical thought: the question of the 'epistemological break' between the ideological prehistory and the scientific history of his thought; the question of the radical theoretical difference that forever separates the works of Marx's youth from *Capital*.

Let the reader be forewarned: I make no apologies for returning to this question. We shall return to it as often as we have to, for as long as we have to – as long as this key question has not been settled, both in and of itself and in its effects. To call things by their true names: as long as a fundamental ambiguity is not resolved, an ambiguity which today objectively provides, in its domain, a theoretical basis for (philosophical and religious) bourgeois ideology even within certain organizations of proletarian class struggle, in our country and elsewhere. Something extremely serious is at stake in this ambiguity: it is a question of the struggle to defend Marxist theory against certain tendentially revisionist theoretical interpretations and presentations.

On the theoretical and historical problems of the history of the formation of Marx's thought, on the crucial period of the *1844 Manuscripts*, the 'Theses on Feuerbach' and *The German Ideology*, the detailed studies for which this question calls are in progress. We shall publish them in due course. Here I want to consider just a few of the provisional, but essential, conclusions that we have come to.

It is not scholarly fetishism to 'return to Marx' and follow the development of his thought word for word through his texts. Nor is it the fetishism of a historian to go back to work on the *1844 Manuscripts*, *The German Ideology*, and *Capital*. It is not a question of 'fleeing' the present for the past, however illustrious that past. It is a question of our present itself: of Marx's theory. It is by no means a question of taking up residence, as some have seen fit to put it in a singularly demagogic phrase, in the 'fortress' of an ahistorical Marxism, the 'eternity of concepts' or 'pure abstraction', in order to issue, from on high, doctrinaire decrees about the practice of others who are wrestling with real, complex historical problems.[16] It is, rather, a question of arming ourselves with the only available theoretical principles for mastering the real problems, immense and difficult, that history has today put before the International Communist Movement. We can master these practical problems only if we grasp their mechanisms: we can grasp their mechanisms only if we produce scientific knowledge of them. Charges of 'doctrinaire abstraction', exaltation of the 'concrete', and denunciations of 'neo-dogmatism' are not merely the arguments of a vulgar demagogy, both ideological and political; they are also, when they are not simply isolated slips of the pen, the perennial symptoms of theoretical revisionism in Marxism itself.[a]

[a] Lenin, *What Is to be Done?*, trans. anon., in Henry M. Christman, ed., *Essential Works of Lenin*, New York, 1971, p. 54n, pp. 68 ff.:

At the present time (this is quite evident now), the English Fabians, the French Ministerialists, the German Bernsteinists and the Russian 'critics' – all belong to the same family, all extol each other, learn from each other, and are rallying their forces against 'doctrinaire' Marxism.

'Dogmatism, doctrinarism', 'ossification of the Party – the inevitable retribution that follows the violent strait-lacing of thought', these are the enemies against which the knightly champions of 'freedom of criticism' rise in arms in *Rabocheye Dyelo*. We are very glad that this question has been brought up . . . [but] who are to be the judges . . .? thus we see that high-sounding phrases against the ossification of thought, etc., conceal carelessness and helplessness in the development of theoretical ideas. The case of the Russian Social-Democrats strikingly illustrates the fact observed in the whole of Europe . . . that the notorious freedom of criticism implies, not the substitution of one theory for another, but freedom from any complete and thought-out theory; it implies eclecticism and absence of principle. . . .

We can judge, therefore, how tactless *Rabocheye Dyelo* is when, with an air of invincibility, it quotes the statement of Marx: 'A single step of the real movement is more important than a dozen programs.' To repeat these words in the epoch of theoretical chaos is like wishing mourners at a funeral 'many happy returns of the day'. Moreover, these words of Marx are taken from his letter on the Gotha Program, in which he *sharply condemns* eclecticism in the formulation of principles: If you must combine, Marx wrote to the Party leaders, then enter into agreements to satisfy the practical aims of the movement, but do not haggle over principles, do not make 'concessions' in theory. This was Marx's idea, and yet there are people amongst us who strive – in his name! – to belittle the significance of theory. . . .

If we go back to Marx, and, in the present conjuncture, deliberately put the emphasis on theoretical problems and especially the 'decisive link' in Marxist theory, namely, *philosophy*, it is in order to defend Marxist theory against the theoretically revisionist tendencies that threaten it; it is in order to delimit and specify the field in which Marxist theory must at all costs progress if it is to produce the knowledge the revolutionary parties urgently need in order to confront the crucial political problems of our present and future. There can be no equivocating on this point. Marx's past, which we shall be discussing here, is, whether we like it or not, a direct road to our present: it *is* our present and, what is more, our future.

2

I shall go straight to the point, in a few pages and a few necessarily schematic distinctions.

We are doubtless still too close to Marx's monumental discovery to measure its exceptional importance in the history of human knowledge. Yet we are beginning to be able to describe Marx's discovery as a momentous theoretical event which 'opened up' a new 'continent', that of History, to scientific knowledge.[17] As such, there are just two other great discoveries in all of human knowledge to which it is comparable from a theoretical point of view: Thales', which 'opened up' the 'continent' of mathematics to knowledge, and Galileo's, which opened up the 'continent' of physical nature to knowledge. To the two 'continents' (and their differentiated internal regions) accessible to knowledge, Marx added, with his fundamental discovery, a third. We are only just beginning to explore it.

Not only are we just beginning to explore this 'continent', whose riches we as yet hardly suspect; we are just beginning to measure the unprecedented import and range of this scientific discovery. It is more than a merely scientific discovery, for it bears within it, like all the great 'continental' scientific discover-

---

These people who cannot utter the word 'theoretician' without a disdainful pout, who call their worship of unpreparedness and development for the realities of life a 'sense of life', in fact demonstrate their ignorance of our most urgent practical tasks.

ies, incalculable *philosophical* consequences; we have not even taken their true measure yet. This last point is crucial. Marx's scientific revolution contains an unprecedented philosophical revolution which, by forcing philosophy to think its relationship to history, profoundly alters the economy of philosophy. We are still too close to Marx truly to appreciate the import of the scientific revolution he precipitated. *A fortiori*, we are much too close to him even to imagine the importance of the philosophical revolution that this scientific revolution carries within it. If we are today confronted, in many respects cruelly, with what has to be termed the *backwardness* [*retard*] of Marxist philosophy vis-à-vis the science of history, it is not only for historical, but also for theoretical reasons of which I have elsewhere[18] attempted to give a preliminary and very summary idea. This backwardness is, in the first stage of things, inevitable. However, in a second stage, which now lies open before us, it can and must be overcome, at least in its essential aspect.

3

It is against the general background of the double theoretical revolution induced by Marx's discovery (in science and in philosophy) that we can pose the problem of the history of the formation and theoretical transformation of Marx's thought.

If we are to pose this problem clearly enough to hope to be able to resolve it, we have clearly to distinguish its various aspects. To begin with, we have to distinguish the political from the theoretical history of the *individual* named Marx. From a *political* standpoint, the history of the individual Marx, who entered the political and intellectual arena in the 1840s, is the history of a young German bourgeois intellectual's transition from radical liberalism to communism. A radical-liberal in 1841–42 (when he wrote the *Rheinische Zeitung* articles), Marx went over to communism in 1843–44. What did 'go over to communism' mean at the time? It meant taking up a position, first subjectively and then objectively, at the side of the working class. But it also meant espousing certain profoundly ideological communist conceptions: utopian, humanist, or, in a word, idealist conceptions – whose idealism was marked by the central notions of religious and moral ideology.

This explains why Marx's *theoretical* development lagged behind his *political* development. This lag [*décalage*] is one of the keys to the question at hand: if we fail to take it into account, we fail to understand how the *1844 Manuscripts* can be the work of an author who is politically a *communist*, but theoretically still an *idealist*.

The *theoretical* history of the young philosopher Marx, which must be considered in its own right, is the history of a double transition. We have, to begin with, the transition from an ideology of history to the first, revolutionary principles of a *science of history* (whose premises are contained in *The German Ideology* in what is still extremely confused form). Secondly, there is the transition from neo-Hegelian rationalist idealism (a Hegel reinterpreted in terms of a philosophy of Practical Reason, and thus 'read' through a philosophical ideology of a Kantian cast) to, initially, the humanist materialism of Feuerbach (1842), then the historicist empiricism of *The German Ideology* (1845–46), and finally, in 1857–67, when Marx wrote the works that were to culminate in *Capital*, a radically new philosophy (what we call dialectical materialism). If we compare Marx's theoretical to his political history, we observe an unmistakable *lag* between the events of the theoretical and the political history. A double lag: a lag between the scientific and the political 'breaks'; and an additional lag between the philosophical and scientific 'breaks'.

Of course, we cannot conceptualize all these 'events' and their dialectic, with its complex 'lags', as so many 'acts' of an individual engaged in 'inventing' or 'creating' a new theory in the pure world of his 'subjectivity'. As Lenin has clearly shown, to understand the historico-theoretical necessity of Marx's discoveries (their possibility and their necessity), one has to conceive them as the events of a specific theoretical history of which the individual Marx was the 'agent' – a theoretical history that unfolds, in its turn, against the backdrop of a social and political history.

When we think Marx's discovery within the field of this *history of theories*, it emerges as the revolutionary effect produced by the *conjunction* of German philosophy, English political economy and French socialism in a determinate theoretico-ideological *conjuncture*, against the background of a determinate sociopolitical *conjuncture* (the class struggles sparked off by the expansion of capitalism in the Western world). It is in the field of this *history of theories* that the epistemological 'breaks' whose reality we can observe in the intellectual history of the individual Marx become intelligible ('breaks' between the philosophy of history and the science of history, idealism and humanist materialism, historicist materialism on the one hand and dialectical materialism on the other).

One hardly need add that while Lenin's remark is extremely valuable, and while we are convinced that it is necessary to develop this *theory of the history of theories*, we are very far from possessing its specific concepts. The theory of the history of theories – ideological, scientific and philosophical – is still in its infancy. This is no accident: the theory of the history of theories rightfully belongs to the 'continent' of history to which Marx has only just provided us access. It is not far-fetched to hope that, with the help of a number of valuable works by specialists in the history of the sciences (Bachelard, Koyré, Canguilhem, etc.), we shall some day be able to propose – starting out, for example, from the history of the formation of Marxist theory – a few concepts of the type needed to produce the rudiments of such a theory.

4

At all events, it is against the general background of this history that we can bring out our carefully considered reasons for defending the thesis of Marx's *theoretical anti-humanism*.

I have said elsewhere,[19] and will repeat here, that we should, in the strict sense, speak of Marx's theoretical *a*-humanism. The reason that I earlier used the phrase 'Marx's theoretical *anti*-humanism' (just as I propose to speak of the anti-historicism, anti-evolutionism, and anti-structuralism of Marxist theory) was to emphasize the relentlessly polemical aspect of the break that Marx had to effect in order to think and articulate his discovery. It was also in order to indicate that this polemic is by no means behind us: we have to pursue, even today, in the face of the same ideological prejudices, the same *theoretical struggle*, with no hope of seeing it end any time soon. We are not labouring under any illusions: theoretical humanism has a long and very 'bright future' ahead of it. We shall not have settled accounts with it by next spring, any more than we shall have settled accounts with evolutionist, historicist or structuralist ideologies.

To[20] speak of Marx's rupture with Theoretical Humanism is a very precise thesis: if Marx broke with this ideology, that means he had espoused it; if he had espoused it (and it was no unconsummated marriage), that means it existed. There are never any imaginary wives in the unions consecrated by the history of theories, even in that particular field of theories represented by the imaginary field of ideologies. The Theoretical Humanism Marx espoused was that of Feuerbach.

Marx, like all the Young Hegelians, 'discovered' Feuerbach in very special conditions, which I have said something about, following Auguste Cornu.[21] For a time, Feuerbach 'saved' the Young Hegelian radicals theoretically from the insoluble contradictions induced in their liberalist-rationalist 'philosophical conscience' by the obstinacy of the damned Prussian State, which, being 'in itself' Reason and Freedom, persisted in misrecognizing its own 'essence', persevering much longer than was proper in Unreason and Despotism. Feuerbach 'saved' them theoretically by providing them with the reason for the Reason–Unreason contradiction: by a theory of the *alienation of Man*.

In my essay, admittedly, I spoke of Humanism as if it had directly sustained the entire problematic of classical philosophy. That formulation is too crude to serve as anything more than a general indication; it has to be corrected and made more precise, as can be done in later works, which some of us have already undertaken. Since our aim is to be a bit more precise, we shall narrow our focus here, and speak only of Feuerbach.

Obviously it would be impossible – on whatever basis, even a Marxist one – to think that the matter of Feuerbach can be settled by a confessional note of the kind: a few quotations from him, or from Marx and Engels, who *had* read him. Nor is it settled by that adjective of convenience and ignorance which none the less resounds in so many disputes: a *speculative* anthropology. As though it were enough to remove the speculation from the anthropology for the anthropology (assuming one knows what that word designates) to stand up by itself: cut the head off a duck and it won't go far.[22] As though it were also enough to pronounce these magic words to call Feuerbach by his name (philosophers, even if they are not watchdogs, are like you and me: for them to come, they must at least be called *by their names*). Let me therefore try to call Feuerbach by his name – even, if need be, by an abbreviation of his name.

Of course, I shall discuss only the Feuerbach of the years 1839–45, that is to say, the author of *The Essence of Christianity* and the *Principles of the Philosophy of the Future* – not the post-1848 Feuerbach, who, against his own earlier precepts, 'put a lot of water in his wine' (in his prime, he maintained that everything had to be savoured in its unadulterated, pure, 'natural' state – coffee *without sugar*, for example).[23]

The Feuerbach of the *Essence of Christianity* occupies a quite extraordinary position in the history of philosophy. Indeed, he brings off the *tour de force* of putting an 'end to classical German philosophy', of overthrowing (to be quite precise: of 'inverting') Hegel, the Last of the Philosophers, in whom all its history was summed up, by a philosophy that was *theoretically retrogressive* with respect to the great German idealist philosophy. Retrogressive must be understood in a precise sense. If Feuerbach's philosophy carries within it traces of German idealism, its *theoretical foundations* date from *before* German idealism. With Feuerbach we return from 1810 to 1750, from the nineteenth to the eighteenth century. Paradoxically, for reasons that would make a good 'dialectic' derived from Hegel giddy, it was by its retrogressive character that Feuerbach's philosophy had fortunate progressive effects in the ideology, and even in the political history, of its partisans. But let us leave this point aside.

A philosophy which carries *traces* of German idealism but settles accounts with German idealism, and its supreme representative, Hegel, by a *theoretically retrogressive* system – what are we to make of that?

The *traces* of German idealism: Feuerbach takes up the philosophical problems posed by German idealism. Above all, the problems of Pure Reason and Practical Reason, the problems of Nature and Freedom, the problems of Knowledge (what can I know?), of Morality (what ought I to do?), and of Religion (what can I hope for?). Hence Kant's fundamental problems, but 'returned to' by way of Hegel's critique and solutions (broadly, the critique of the Kantian *distinctions* or abstractions, which for Hegel derive from a misrecognition of Reason reduced to the role of the Understanding). Feuerbach poses the problems of German idealism with the intention of giving them a Hegelian-type solution: indeed, he tries to pose the *unity* of the Kantian *distinctions* or *abstractions* in something resembling the Hegelian Idea. This 'something' resembling the Hegelian Idea, while being its radical *inversion*, is *Man*, or *Nature*, or *Sinnlichkeit* (simultaneously sensuous materiality, receptivity and sensuous intersubjectivity).

To hold all this together – I mean, to think as a *coherent* unity these three notions: Man, Nature, and *Sinnlichkeit* – is a dumbfounding theoretical gamble, which makes Feuerbach's 'philosophy' a philosophical velleity, that is to say, a real theoretical inconsistency invested in a 'wish' for an impossible philosophical consistency. A moving 'wish', certainly, even a pathetic one, since it expresses and proclaims in great solemn cries the desperate will to escape from a philosophical ideology against which it ultimately remains a rebel, that is, its prisoner. The fact is that this impossible unity gave rise to an *œuvre* which has played a part in history and produced disconcerting effects, some immediate (on Marx and his friends), others deferred (on Nietzsche, on Phenomenology, on a certain modern theology, and even on the recent 'hermeneutic' philosophy which derives from it).

It was an impossible unity (Man–Nature, *Sinnlichkeit*)[24] which enabled Feuerbach to 'resolve' the great philosophical problems of German idealism by 'transcending' Kant and 'inverting' Hegel. For example, the Kantian problems of the distinction between Pure Reason and Practical Reason, between Nature and Freedom, and so on, find their solution in Feuerbach in a *unique* principle: Man and his attributes. For example, the Kantian problem of scientific objectivity and the Hegelian problem of religion find their solution in Feuerbach in an extraordinary theory of *speculary* objectivity ('the object of a being is the objectification of its Essence': the object – the objects – of Man are the objectification of the Human Essence). For example, the Kantian problem of the Idea and History, transcended by Hegel in the theory of the Spirit as the ultimate moment of the Idea, finds its solution in Feuerbach in an extraordinary theory of the intersubjectivity constitutive of the Human Genus.[25] As the principal term in all these solutions, we always find Man, his attributes, and his 'essential' objects (speculary 'reflections' of his Essence).

Thus, with Feuerbach, Man is the unique, originary and fundamental concept, the *factotum*, which stands in for Kant's Transcendental Subject, Noumenal Subject, Empirical Subject and Idea, and also stands in for Hegel's Idea. The 'end of classical German philosophy' is then quite simply a verbal suppression of its solutions which respects its problems. It is a replacement of its solutions by heteroclite philosophical notions gathered from here and there in the philosophy of the eighteenth century (sensualism, empiricism, the materialism of *Sinnlichkeit*, borrowed from the tradition of Condillac; a pseudo-biologism vaguely inspired by Diderot; an idealism of Man and the 'heart' drawn from Rousseau), and unified by *a play on theoretical words* in the concept of Man.

Hence the extraordinary position and the effects Feuerbach could draw from his inconsistency: declaring himself in turn and *all at once* (and he *himself* saw no duplicity or inconsistency in this) a materialist, an idealist, a rationalist, a sensualist, an empiricist, a realist, an atheist and a humanist. Hence his declamations against Hegel's speculation, reduced to *'abstraction'*. Hence his appeals to the concrete, to the 'thing itself', to the real, to the sensuous, to matter, against all the forms of alienation, whose ultimate essence is for him constituted by *abstraction*. Hence the sense of his 'inversion' of Hegel, which Marx long espoused as the real critique of Hegel, whereas it is still entirely trapped in the empiricism of which Hegel is no more than the sublimated theory: to invert the attribute into the subject, to invert the Idea into the Sensuous Real, to invert the Abstract into the Concrete, and so forth. All that placed under the category of *Man*, who *is* the Real, the Sensuous and the Concrete. An old tune, whose worn-out variations are still served up for us today.

There you have the *Theoretical Humanism* which Marx had to deal with. I say *theoretical*, for Man is not just an Idea in the Kantian sense for Feuerbach, but the theoretical foundation for the *whole* of his 'philosophy', as the Cogito was for Descartes, the Transcendental Subject for Kant, and the Idea for Hegel. It is this Theoretical Humanism that is overtly at work in the *1844 Manuscripts*.

5

But before turning to Marx, one more word on the consequences of this paradoxical philosophical position which claims radically to abolish German idealism, but respects its problems and hopes to resolve them through the intervention of a jumble of eighteenth-century concepts, gathered together within the theoretical injunction of Man, which stands in for their 'philosophical' unity and consistency.

For it is not possible to 'return' with impunity to a position *behind* a philosophy while retaining the problems it has brought to light. The fundamental consequence of this theoretical retrogression accompanied by a retention of current problems is to induce an enormous *contraction* of the existing philosophical problematic, behind the appearances of its 'inversion', which is no more than the impossible 'wish' to invert it.

Engels and Lenin were perfectly well aware of this 'contraction' with respect to Hegel. 'Feuerbach is small in comparison with Hegel.'[26] Let us go straight to the point: what Feuerbach unforgivably sacrificed of Hegel is History and the Dialectic – or rather, since it is one and the same thing for Hegel, History *or* the Dialectic. Here too, Marx, Engels and Lenin made no mistake: Feuerbach is a materialist in the sciences, but . . . he is an idealist in History. Feuerbach talks about Nature, but . . . he does not talk about History – since Nature stands in for it. Feuerbach is not dialectical. And so on.

With the perspective we have on the matter, let us try to make these established judgements more precise.

Of course, history certainly is discussed by Feuerbach, who is capable of distinguishing between 'Hindu', 'Judaic', 'Roman' (etc.) 'human natures'. But there is no *theory* of history in his work. And, above all, there is no trace of the theory of history we owe to Hegel as a *dialectical process of the production of forms*.

Of course, as we can now begin to say, what hopelessly distorts the Hegelian conception of history as a dialectical process is its *teleological* conception of the dialectic, inscribed in the very *structures* of the Hegelian dialectic at an extremely precise point: the *Aufhebung* (transcendence-preserving-the-transcended-as-the-internalized-transcended), directly expressed in the Hegelian category of the *negation of the negation* (or negativity). To criticize the Hegelian philosophy of History because it is *teleological*, because from its origins it is in pursuit of a goal (the realization of Absolute Knowledge), hence to reject the *teleology* in the philosophy of history, but, *at the same time*, to take up the Hegelian dialectic again *just as it is*, is to fall into a strange contradiction: for the Hegelian dialectic, too, is *teleological* in its *structures*, since the key structure of the Hegelian dialectic is *the negation of the negation, which is the teleology itself*, identical to the dialectic.

That is why the question of the structures of the dialectic is the key question dominating the whole problem of a materialist dialectic. That is why Stalin can be taken for an extraordinarily perceptive Marxist philosopher, at least on this point, since he struck the negation of the negation from the 'laws' of the dialectic.[27] But to the extent that it is possible to abstract from the teleology in the Hegelian conception of history and the dialectic, it is still true that we owe Hegel something which Feuerbach, blinded by his obsession with Man and the Concrete, was absolutely incapable of understanding: the conception of History as a *process*. Indisputably – for it passed into his works, and *Capital* is the evidence – Marx owes Hegel this decisive philosophical category, *process*.

He owes him even more, which Feuerbach, again, did not so much as suspect. He owes him the concept of a process *without a subject*. It is fashionable in philosophical conversations, which are sometimes turned into books, to say that, in Hegel, History is the 'History of the alienation of man'. Whatever people have in mind when they utter that phrase, it *states* a philosophical proposition which has an implacable meaning, which one can find in its offspring, if one has not already discerned it in their mother. What it states is this: History is *a process of alienation which has a subject*, and that subject is man.

Now nothing is more foreign to Hegel's thought than this *anthropological* conception of History. For Hegel, History is certainly a process of alienation, but this process does not have Man as its subject. First, in the Hegelian history, it is a matter not of Man,[28] but of the Spirit, and if one must *at all costs* (which in respect of a 'subject' is false anyway) have a 'subject' in History, one should talk about 'nations', or, more accurately (we are approaching the truth), the *moments* of the development of the Idea become Spirit. What does this mean? Something very simple, but, if only one takes the trouble to 'interpret' it, something *extraordinary* from the theoretical point of view: History is not the alienation of Man, but the alienation of the Spirit, that is to say, the ultimate moment of the alienation of the Idea. How should we interpret this? For Hegel, the process of alienation does not 'begin' with (human) *History*, since History is itself no more than the alienation of Nature, which is itself the alienation of Logic. Alienation, which is the dialectic (in its final principle the negation of the negation or *Aufhebung*), or, to speak more precisely, the *process of alienation*, is not, as a whole current of modern philosophy which 'corrects' and 'contracts' Hegel would have it, peculiar to Human History.

From the point of view of Human History, the process of alienation has *always-already begun*. That means – if these terms are taken seriously – that, in Hegel, History is thought as a *process* of alienation *without a subject*, or a dialectical process *without a subject*. Once one is prepared to consider just for a moment that *all* of Hegelian teleology is contained in the expressions I have just stated, in the category of alienation, or in what constitutes the master structure of the category of the *dialectic* (the negation of the negation), and once one agrees to *abstract* from what represents the teleology in these expressions, then there remains the formulation: history is a *process without a subject*. I think I can affirm that this category of *a process without a subject*, which must of course be torn from the grip of Hegelian teleology, undoubtedly represents the greatest theoretical debt linking Marx to Hegel.

I am well aware that, *finally*, there is in Hegel a *subject* for this process of alienation without a subject. But it is a very strange subject, one which calls for extensive commentary: this subject is the very *teleology* of the *process*, it is the *Idea* in the process of self-alienation, which constitutes it as Idea.

This is not an esoteric thesis on Hegel: it can be verified at each instant, that is, at each 'moment' of the Hegelian process. To say that there is no *subject* to the process of alienation, whether in History, in Nature or in Logic, is quite simply to say that one cannot at any 'moment' assign as a 'subject' to the process of alienation any 'subject' whatsoever: neither some being (not even man), nor some nation, nor some '*moment*' of the process, neither History, nor Nature, nor Logic.

The only *subject* of the process of alienation is *the process itself in its teleology*. The subject of the process is not even the End [*Fin*] of the process itself (a mistake is possible here: does Hegel not say that the Spirit is 'Substance becoming Subject'?), it is the process of alienation considered as a process in pursuit of its End, and hence the process of alienation itself as teleological.

Nor is 'teleological' a determination which is added *from the outside* to the process of alienation without a subject. The teleology of the process of alienation is inscribed in black and white in its definition: in the concept of *alienation*, which is the teleology itself *in the process*.

Now perhaps it is here that the strange status of *Logic* in Hegel begins to be clearer. For what is Logic? The science of the Idea, that is to say, the *concept of the process of alienation without a subject*, in other words, the concept of the process of self-alienation which, considered in its totality, is nothing but the Idea. Thus conceived, Logic, or the concept of the Idea, is the dialectic, the 'path' of the process as a process, the 'absolute method'. If Logic is nothing but the concept of the Idea (of the process of alienation without a subject), then it is the concept of this strange subject we are looking for. But the fact that this subject is only the concept of the *process of alienation itself* – in other words, this subject is the Dialectic, that is, the very movement of the negation of the negation – reveals the extraordinary paradox of Hegel. The process of alienation without a subject (or the dialectic) is the only subject recognized by Hegel. There is no subject of the process: it is the process itself which is a subject *in so far as it does not have a subject*.

If we want to find what, finally, stands in for 'Subject' in Hegel, it is in the teleological nature of this process, in the *teleological* nature of the dialectic, that it must be sought: the End is already there in the Origin. That is also why there is in Hegel no *origin*, nor (which is never anything but its phenomenon) is there any beginning. The origin, indispensable to the teleological nature of the process (since it is only the reflection of its End), has to be *denied* from the moment it is *affirmed* for the process of alienation to be a process without a subject. It would take too long to justify this proposition, which I advance simply in order to anticipate later developments: this implacable exigency (to affirm and in the same moment *deny* the origin) was consciously assumed by Hegel in his theory of the *beginning* of Logic: Being is immediately non-Being. The beginning of Logic is the theory of the non-originary nature of the origin. Hegel's Logic is the Origin affirmed–denied: the first form of a concept that Derrida has introduced into philosophical reflection, *erasure [rature]*.[29] But the Hegelian 'erasure' constituted by the Logic from its first words is the negation of the negation, dialectical and hence teleological. The true Hegelian Subject resides in the teleology. Take away the teleology, and there remains the philosophical category that Marx inherited: the category of a *process without a subject*.[30]

It might seem that these considerations take us a long way from Feuerbach and the problem before us, Marx. In fact, they lead us straight to it, for the following reason: they make us see the extraordinary contraction to which Feuerbach subjected Hegel's problems and objectives.

Everyone knows that Feuerbach 'took over' the concept of alienation from Hegel. Man and alienation are Feuerbach's master-concepts. But once History has been reduced to Man, once Man has been made the subject of what stands in for history, once man is declared to be the subject of alienation (religious or otherwise), then, whether or not one continues to use the Hegelian *word* 'alienation', one still falls a hundred leagues behind Hegel, into the very conceptions that he rejected with all his lucidity. Hence it is no surprise that the Feuerbachian concept of alienation should in its turn be a pathetically contracted version, and a caricature, of the Hegelian concept of alienation.

In Feuerbach, there is no theory of history as process; thus there is neither a dialectic nor a theory of the process without a subject. What stands in for history in Feuerbach (let us say, the cultural objects of the human world: religion, science, philosophy, art, etc.) is reduced to the level of the shallowest anthropology. *There is alienation only of Man*, not of Nature – there is no dialectic of Nature. The prodigious Hegelian conception of History as the alienation of a process that has always-already begun (Logic and Nature) is reduced to the theory of an arbitrary essence whose claim to playing that role remains unknown: the human essence, objectifying itself in its objects in the immediacy of a speculary relation that draws around itself the circle of an Absolute Horizon (the Horizon of the human species: in the same way, every species – the dragonfly, the rhododendron, this or that planet, etc. – has its absolute horizon). The Human Essence objectifies itself in its objects immediately – *without a process* [*sans procès*, which also means 'without further ado']. Nothing is said in Feuerbach about the process by which the objects of the human 'world' are produced; nothing is said about *labour*, to which Hegel had assigned the crucially important role of producing the Works of Culture [*Bildung*]. The Human Essence is endowed with generic attributes, realized by way of their objectification in objects that are the 'mirror' in which man only ever has to do with his essence and nothing but his essence, even when he thinks he has to do with God. Alienation is thus reduced, within the speculary equation 'subject = Object', to the *mode of the meaning/direction* [*sens*] of this identity – to be precise, to a *reversal* of this *meaning/direction*. Man thinks that he is the object of a Subject, God, whereas he is the true Subject of his generic Object, that is to say, God, in whom he never discovers anything other than his own essence; simply, he discovers it in the form of a *reversal of meaning/direction* (in both senses of the word *sens*: direction = signification).

Just as history as dialectical process disappears, to be replaced by the closed field of the absolute horizon of the speculary relation between the Human Essence and *its* objects (religion, *par excellence*, but also the sciences, art, philosophy, politics, the state, etc.), so, as a consequence, the dialectic too disappears, since it is superfluous. Because Man's generic essence is 'attributed' to the set of all men, past, present and future, all of them individuals constituted by the 'absolute' essence of Man, History has to seek refuge in the difference between individuals and the 'genus': the attributes of the Human Essence that have *not yet* been realized *will* be in the centuries to come. Feuerbachian history is an eternal present that needs an eternal supplement: the Future. With this sleight of hand, a 'bad infinity' in the Hegelian sense, Feuerbach makes short work of such history as remains for him and, by the same token, of the dialectic.

Alienation, too, is distorted by this procedure. Alienation comes into play only in the speculary relation between the Human Subject and the Objects in which its essence is

adequately objectified – in the 'reversal' of their meaning/
direction [*sens*]. Alienation is no longer a *process* involving real
transformations, but an abstraction involving only *significations*.
The disalienation of man is accordingly a mere 'reversal' of the
'reversal' of the meaning/direction that binds Man to his
Essence, alienated/realized in his Objects. This 'reversal of the
reversal' thus affects meaning/direction alone: it derives, in sum,
from a new, rectified *awareness* of what already exists *in actu*; it
is, in sum, 'the right reading' of an already written text that
people have been reading the wrong way. It is *hermeneutic* in its
very principle. If it has revolutionary overtones which suggest
that the earth shall 'rise on new foundations', it nevertheless
takes place entirely within *consciousness*, which has merely to be
rectified: all the evils [*maux*] of humanity, said Feuerbach, to
justify his total silence during the terrible years of the 1848–49
revolutions, are ultimately only 'headaches' [*maux de tête*]. The
destiny of humanity – and, *a fortiori*, of the working class – is
decided not on the barricades but in a reform of consciousness
and a recognition that the religion of God has from time immemorial been nothing more than the religion of a Man ignorant of
who he is. Thus Theoretical Humanism showed, in practice,
what it had 'in its head': a petty-bourgeois ideology dissatisfied
with Prussian despotism and the imposture of established
religion, but frightened by the Revolution that its moral concepts
had disarmed in advance.

6

We may now turn back to Marx, in order to see what came of
his encounter with Feuerbach.

Feuerbach liked to call himself a 'communist' (the reign of
love among men reconciled among themselves because reconciled with their Essence). He seemed to furnish the Young
Hegelians with all they needed to break out of the theoretical
dead-end into which history had driven them, offering them a
theory that explained the reason for existing Unreason[b] (the
contradiction between reality and right, between the state of the

---

[b] The original title of *The Essence Christianity* was *Critique of Pure Unreason*.

world and Man). He gave them, as if by magic, a *purchase* on existing Unreason, demonstrating its necessity as the alienated Essence of Man. In pathetic, prophetic tones, he announced the New Age of Freedom and Human Brotherhood.

We can readily understand what Engels meant when he recalled, fifty years later, this immense hope of having *at last secured a purchase* on the world: 'We were all Feurbachians'[31] – and they were enthusiastic Feuerbachians at that. The history of Marx's early works, between 1842 and 1845, is the history of this hope and this enthusiasm; then, after 1845, of a bitter disillusionment and an irreversible break.

I would like to scan the essential moments of this history by simply commenting on a few key sentences that serve all our modern 'humanists' as alibis:

1. Before the *1844 Manuscripts*, Marx is, theoretically speaking, a Feuerbachian – with no qualifications. 'To be radical is to grasp the root of the matter. But for man the root is man himself.'[32] That sentence sums up his whole position.

To which the usual objection runs: 'But Marx is no Feuerbachian, *because* he discusses not just religion but also politics, law and the state, about which Feuerbach rarely speaks.' And our opponents hurl this famous sentence from the 'Contribution to the Critique of Hegel's Philosophy of Law' (1843) at us: '*Man* is no abstract being encamped outside the world. Man is *the world of man*, the state, society.'[33]

I reply: this sentence is one hundred per cent Feuerbachian. Feuerbach does nothing else, from one end of *The Essence of Christianity* to the other, but describe the following equation: man is the world of man, the Essence of Man is the *world of his objects*, precisely by virtue of the speculary relation: Essence of the Subject (Man) = objectification of this Essence in his Objects, his human *world*, which includes the state as well as religion and a good deal else besides.

In principle, then, Feuerbach says nothing other than what Marx repeats in 1843: man is not an abstract being (standard Feuerbachian fare), but a concrete being. If you want to know the essence of Man, look for it where it is to be found: in his Objects, his world. Only those who have not read Feuerbach, but have manufactured a cosy little idea of him for the purposes of their 'demonstrations', can imagine that there is in Marx's sentence so much as the trace of a trace of a theoretical *innovation* – never mind a theoretical revolution.

To which the usual objection runs: but Feuerbach did not, as Marx does, put the emphasis on society, law, politics and, soon afterwards, the proletariat. This objection raises a question of principle about which we need to be perfectly clear.

What is truly new in Marx's texts of this period is political interests and a political position of which Feuerbach was altogether incapable. But the fact that Marx took a new position has to do with his *political* development; for the moment, it has no effect whatsoever on his *theoretical* position, and changes not a single one of its terms. This new political position does, of course, shift the point of application of Feuerbach's Theoretical Humanism: we move from religion to politics. But what matters *from the theoretical point of view*, which is the only decisive point of view when one sets out to produce a history of the transformations of a *theory*, is not the fact that *one more object* is subjected to a given theoretical treatment, and thus to a given theory. What matters is the *theoretical treatment* and the theory themselves. In certain cases, treating one more object can precipitate changes in the theory, but then one must be able to *show* what those changes are, and to demonstrate that they are indeed real changes in the theory, not merely a change in the object to which one and the same theory is applied. No one has been able to identify such changes *in the theory* in 1843, and for good reason. Thus the present case falls under the general law. A theory no more changes its nature by treating an additional object than a capitalist who makes aeroplanes becomes a socialist by adding refrigerators to his product line.

In the 'Critique of Hegel's Philosophy of Law', as well as 'On the Jewish Question', Marx merely *extends one and the same theory from religion to politics*: the Feuerbachian theory of Man and alienation. Who would deny that this investigation produces novel effects (a distinction between the rights of man and the rights of the citizen, a critique of the state as the alienated existence of man's generic being, even a theory of the proletariat as the existence of the alienation of the Human Essence as Inhuman Essence)? But the fact remains that these new effects depend, in the final analysis, on Feuerbach's humanist theory, which they do not modify one iota. For example, Marx avowedly treats the state and politics as the 'heaven' of earthly existence[34] that is to say, precisely in the categories of Feuerbach's theory of religion. And even when he talks about revolution, he conceives it in the Feuerbachian terms of disalienation: the public recognition of a *meaning* that has been misunderstood because it was alienated, and thus as the 'confession' of what had been shrouded in silence.

After proclaiming, in the famous letter to Ruge of September 1843: 'thus nothing prevents us from tying our criticism to the criticism of politics and to a partisan position in politics, and therefore from tying it to *real struggles* and identifying it with them', Marx clearly indicates the sense of this *critique*:

> We can formulate the trend of our journal[35] as being: self-clarification (critical philosophy) to be gained by the present time of its struggles and desires. This is work for the world and for us. It can be only the work of united forces. It is a matter of a *confession*, and nothing more. In order to secure remission of its sins, mankind has only to declare them for what they actually are [Marx's emphasis].[36]

'Tying our criticism ... to real struggles' is the effect of adopting a new *political* position. That this step forward in politics *could* bear within it theoretical consequences which would one day be taken into consideration is for us, *now*, certain. But the fact is that these potential theoretical consequences do not find expression anywhere in the theoretical positions that Marx adopted at the time. They do not change his theoretical positions in the slightest. We cannot avoid the difficulty with the argument of all the apologetics which explain *ad nauseam* that 'the seeds' of these theoretical transformations are contained in Marx's announcement of the shift in his political position, and that the only thing these 'seeds' lack is, in sum, that they have not yet sprouted, that is to say, have not yet found *explicit* theoretical expression. For we have to go so far as to say that these changes in Marx's political position did not induce any change at all in his *theoretical* positions, because his theoretical positions radically *prevented* him from even suspecting the *possible* theoretical consequences whose 'seeds' were supposedly contained in his change of political position. What appears to be the 'seeds' of a possible theoretical transformation to us, who know what Marx later made of them, was for Marx, at the time, *nothing at all*. The theory dominating his thinking ruthlessly repressed anything that could even remotely affect it: it reduced what is for us 'seeds', or a possibility, to nothing. But it would be better to say that it did not have to eliminate that possibility: the theory was such that, for it, *nothing was happening*. That is why Marx, after evoking those 'real forces', can placidly serve up to us without any qualifications, or a moment's hesitation, his definition of revolutionary criticism as a public confession by Humanity of Humanity's sins. In Marx's *political* history, something important has plainly happened: he has rallied to the real forces to which he aimed to 'tie' his critique, and with which he aimed to 'identify' it. In Marx's *theoretical* history, nothing has *yet* happened: therefore nothing happens.

2. The situation is seriously transformed in the *1844 Manuscripts*. Marx's *political* position is now openly avowed: he is a communist. But his *theoretical* position, too, is marked by an event that is genuinely new and important.

This event is not, as is usually supposed, the 'encounter' with Political Economy. For, from this standpoint, we relapse into the situation just mentioned. Feuerbach's theory of Man and alienation is extended to one more object: after religion and politics, the economy. To be sure, the economy is not just the first object that happens to come along. Feuerbach had discussed the state and politics only hastily, but he had, after all, discussed them. He doubtless talked about the economy, if that is the word, in connection with the Jewish people, but only in order to repeat commonplaces about the 'practical needs' that dominate 'Jewish man'.[37] In the *1844 Manuscripts*, the Political Economy that is 'added' to the previous objects is no longer an absurdity: it is the Political Economy of Smith and his successors (minus Ricardo: a symptomatic omission) – in short, the Political Economy of the Economists, and, with it, all their categories: capital, labour, wages, profits, rents, the division of labour, the market, and so on.

However, as we have already shown[c] – but we will have to

---

[c] See *Reading Capital*, I, Rancière's text, Chapter 1 [Jacques Rancière, 'Le concept de critique et la critique de l'économie politique des *Manuscrits de 1844*

come back to this point – Marx, in the *1844 Manuscripts*, brings off the theoretical feat of *criticizing* the categories of the Economists and Political Economy itself by subjecting them to the theoretical principles of Feuerbachian Humanism: Man and alienation. The speculary relation 'Essence of Man = Essence of his objects as objectification of his Essence', which is characteristic of Feuerbachian Humanism, dominates the whole theory of *alienated labour*. Through labour, Man objectifies his essence (his 'essential forces', his 'generic forces'), which is externalized in the form of the products of his labour. Of course, we are dealing here with the production of real, material objects, not, as before, of spiritual objects, such as God or the State. But the principle of alienation remains the same. It comes into play within the speculary relation: the worker (Subject) = his products (his Objects), or Man = the world of his objects. The effects that Marx derives from this application/extension of Feuerbachian theory to the objects of economic production and the categories of the Economists (which he considers, at this time, to be the categories of the economy, without for a moment calling them into question as he will later, in *Capital*) are, of course, *new* with respect to earlier discourses on religion and politics. But these effects *do not affect* the principles of the Feuerbachian theory of Man and alienation, or Man's Generic Essence (which Marx 'rediscovers' in, for example, the division of labour), and for good reason: they are its direct and necessary product. Thus the 'encounter' with Political Economy (or, rather, with the categories of the Economists) does not in any way alter Feuerbach's theoretical system.

The theoretical event specific to the *1844 Manuscripts* is of a very different sort. It may be summed up in a phrase: *the intervention of Hegel in Feuerbach.*

I say '*in* Feuerbach', that is, within the theoretical field defined by Feuerbach's basic concepts, which are taken over as they stand, and which this intervention does not modify, since it takes place *within* the theoretical field delimited by them. Let us examine this a little more closely.

What, of Hegel, is introduced into Feuerbach? *Part* of what

au *Capital'*, in Althusser *et al.*, *Lire le Capital*, ed. Étienne Balibar, Paris, 1996, pp. 85–110 – *Trans.*].

Feuerbach had eliminated from Hegel, and an important part at that: *history as a dialectical process or process of alienation*. This introduction of history has the effect of considerably altering the forms in which the Feuerbachian category of *alienation* operates.

What is the Feuerbachian theoretical field into which history in the Hegelian sense is introduced? The field of the speculary relation 'subject = Object', or 'Generic Essence of Man = objects of the human world as objectification of the Essence of Man'. This theoretical field is left as it is: it is dominated by a *Subject*, Man, whose essential forces are objectified in the alienation of his Objects (in the *1844 Manuscripts* this means, by virtue of what we have just said about the displacement of politics on to the categories of the Economists, in the *products of human labour* above all).

Because we know what, of Hegel, is thus introduced into what we recognize to be Feuerbach's theoretical field, we can clearly state the *result* of this intervention. Once Hegelian History, *as a process of alienation*, has been inserted into the speculary theoretical field 'subject (Man) = Object' (products of the human world with its various spheres: economics, politics, religion, ethics, philosophy, art, etc.), it inevitably takes the following form: History as *the process of alienation of a Subject, Man*. History in the *1844 Manuscripts* is, in the strict sense this time – to repeat a phrase which, as we have already noted, cannot be Hegelian – *'the history of the alienation (and disalienation) of man'*. This phrase rigorously expresses the effect of Hegel's intervention *in* Feuerbach, because the Hegelian concept of history as a process of alienation (or dialectical process) is *theoretically subjected* to the non-Hegelian category of the Subject (Man). Here we are dealing with something that makes no sense at all in Hegel: an anthropological (or humanist) conception of history.

This effect represents a considerable modification of the previous Feuerbachian schema. History enters it, and, with history, the *dialectic* (the negation of the negation, the *Aufhebung*, and negativity all function comfortably in it). With history and the dialectic, the Hegelian conception of *labour* enters the schema as well, realizing, as Marx sees it, the miraculous theoretical encounter between Hegel and Political Economy with the blessing of the Feuerbachian Essence of Man. Marx celebrates the harmony prevailing at this Summit Conference of the Concept in terms that are touching in their naivety; or, if you prefer, in their profundity. What has modern Political Economy (read: the Economists) accomplished? It has, says Marx, reduced all the economic categories to their *subjective* essence: labour. What extraordinary exploit has Hegel achieved ('in the *Phenomenology*')? He grasps, says Marx, '*labour* as the *essence* of man'.[38] Subject, Man, Labour. Subject = Man = Labour. Man is the Subject of history. The essence of Man is Labour. Labour is nothing other than the act of objectification of the Essential Forces of Man in his products. The process of alienation of man externalizing his essential forces in products by means of labour is History. Thus everything enters into Feuerbach again, for a very good reason: we have not left Feuerbach for a single second.

There is nothing surprising about this. Feuerbach is the host. Political Economy and Hegel are his guests. He greets them and introduces them to each other, explaining that they belong to the same family (Labour). Everyone takes a seat, and the conversation begins: *at Feuerbach's place*.

Is it seemly to disrupt this family reunion by pointing out that it is only thanks to a play on words that one can identify Smith's concept of *labour* with 'subjectivity', with Man as Subject, so as to make Smith 'the Luther of Political Economy'?[39] Is it decent to disrupt it by pointing out that if the concept of labour has its place in Hegel, it is never declared to be the essence of Man (even assuming that one can find a definition of the essence of Man in Hegel, whose definition makes man a 'sick animal', not a 'labouring animal'), for the very good reason that, labour being a moment in the process of the alienation of Spirit, it is no more the origin or subject of History than Man is? But no matter. What counts is not the plays on words, but the theoretical functions they fulfil. Their function is to seal the union of Political Economy and the Hegelian dialectic in a Humanist theory of History, as the alienation (and disalienation) of Man, the Subject of History.

The upshot is the most extraordinary piece of theoretical ideology that Marx has bequeathed us, a text of exceptional density and rigour: his *only* Hegelian text (in which the purest of Hegelian dialectics is turned loose to go to work, to its heart's content, upon the categories of Political Economy). But it is a Hegelian text *in* Feuerbach: this means, since Feuerbach is Hegel turned upside down, that it is the one text in which we have a Marxian 'inversion' of Hegel.

Thus, if we want a sense of what has been termed the *Theoretical Humanism* with which Marx broke, we have to go back to *Feuerbach*. If we want to understand just how far the reign of Feuerbach's Theoretical Humanism extends in Màrx, we have to recognize that, contrary to the self-interested opinions making the rounds in certain circles, the *1844 Manuscripts* is the text in which this conception culminates and triumphs, reaching the height of its power, inasmuch as it proves capable of subjecting the Hegelian dialectic and Political Economy in person to its law.

No slick theoretical manoeuvring will allow us to avoid facing up to these observations, which, though elementary, have far-reaching consequences. In particular, people must, for good and all, stop telling us tales about Marx's break with *speculative* anthropology,[40] while making believe that that term designates Feuerbach's theory. For the break with *speculative* anthropology, the credit goes not to Marx, but to Feuerbach, who, from beginning to end, never ceases to proclaim the merits of the concrete, real, corporeal, whole man, his feet firmly planted on solid ground, exercising all the powers of his nature, and so forth – as opposed to abstract, speculative (and so forth) man. The true question is not that of *speculation* (denouncing speculation does not get us very far: it rids us of certain myths, but does not yield, as such, any *knowledge*; the serious questions begin to emerge only afterwards), but that of *anthropology*: a term which masks the ideological enterprise we have discussed under the rubric Theoretical Humanism (History as the process of the alienation of a subject, Man), and the corresponding philosophical presuppositions.

In this perspective, notwithstanding all its 'concreteness' and all the 'human' 'richness' of its analyses, the *1844 Manuscripts* is, theoretically speaking, one of the most extraordinary examples of a total theoretical *impasse* that we have. If we take from Gaston Bachelard the idea that certain concepts, or certain ways of posing a problem, can constitute '*epistemological obstacles*' that block, in whole or in part, the development of a theory, and if we examine, from this point of view, the proposition that epitomizes the *Manuscripts* (History is the process of alienation of a

Subject, Man), we arrive at a highly edifying result. Alienation, Subject, Man: three concepts, three 'epistemological obstacles'. Three concepts that will have to be *cleared away* so as to open up a path for the one positive concept imprisoned in this imposing conceptual system, that of *process* (which, freed of the trammels of the subject and Man, will become '*the process without a subject*'). It will be granted that a proposition comprising four concepts, three of which are epistemological obstacles, represents a by no means ordinary ideological concentration and 'blockage'. It is, precisely, the *extraordinary* character of Marx's undertaking in the *1844 Manuscripts* which constitutes the interest, and also the *critical* character, of the text.

By that, I do not mean to say that the *Manuscripts* has even the beginnings of objective critical value. I mean that it is the expression of a *critical* situation of extreme gravity, and that this critical situation of Theoretical Humanism is precipitated by Marx's undertaking itself, by his desire to think out to its logical conclusions the miraculous unity of this *three-way encounter*: Hegel and Political Economy in Feuerbach. *Officially*, everything comes off marvellously at this Summit Conference: Brother, behold thy Brother, says their common Father; be seated, and let us break the bread of the Concept. A Conference of Mutual Recognition and Unity, with full agreement about the World Revolution. In reality, this 'unitarian' conclave can only be *explosive*. For, as we have seen, the whole thing is rigged. Identities have been falsified: the Brother is not the Brother. As for the Father, who seems to have everything under control, he is in reality barely able to keep on his feet. At the moment in which Marx is delivering the extraordinary Discourse of Unity known as the *1844 Manuscripts*, the extreme theoretical tension of his discourse itself proves that it is a discourse not of criticism, but of crisis. Everything is too beautiful; it can't be true. But this encounter, like this impossible Project, had to take place so that the irresolvable crisis could come to a head and explode, and, this time, rock everything to its foundations. One might say, parodying the well-known sentence: it is no longer a critique, but a radical crisis. To be radical is to grasp things by the root: the root of the crisis is the crisis of Man.

After the *Manuscripts*, it is all over with Feuerbach. It takes time, a long time. But it is over. Theoretical Humanism has shown itself for what it is: an imposture – not even a theory, but an ideological makeshift. At the theoretical level, nothing: hot air. Or, rather, a major obstacle to theory, one that will have to be cleared away. On the ideological plane: an idle wish, unarmed but dangerous. The idle wish of the petty bourgeoisie, which would like to see things change, but doesn't want the change to be called – or, rather, *be* – the Revolution. Theoretical Humanism (and everything resembling it) is the theoretical disguise of run-of-the-mill petty-bourgeois moral ideology. Petty-bourgeois in the worst sense of the word: counter-revolutionary.

3. The rupture commences. It will be a long time before it is, as they say, 'confirmed'. For it is one thing to proclaim a rupture (which dates from the 'Theses on Feuerbach' and *The German Ideology*); it is quite another to 'consummate' it. The 'rupture' will be consummated one step at a time over the long years that intervene between *The German Ideology* and *Capital*: a period punctuated in different ways by mutations that lead to the rise of the concepts of the new science and the categories of the new philosophy it bears within it.

Let us single out and briefly gloss the essential moments of this punctuation, the history of the break with Theoretical Humanism. The 'Theses on Feuerbach', however brief (a few hastily scrawled, but deeply meditated sentences), show us what comes about [*advient*], and how it comes about. Feuerbach is directly challenged, *in propria persona*, and in two respects which (this is a new phenomenon) are, for the first time, sharply *distinguished*: with respect to his conception of Man, and with respect to his basic *philosophical* categories.

Man. Let us recall the Sixth Thesis: 'The essence of Man is no *abstraction* inherent in the isolated *individual*. In its reality, it is *the ensemble of social relations*.'

In the history of Marxism, this brief dictum has met and continues to meet, every day, the most edifying and the most absurd fate imaginable. Calling it obscure and unintelligible would create a scandal. Everyone considers it clear – clear because it is comprehensible. Not only does Marx say, in black and white, that man is not abstract, is not an abstract essence of which the 'isolated individuals' would be the subjects (in the Aristotelian sense), but he says something that 'rings true': the human essence is *the ensemble of social relations*. We are on familiar ground: at the heart of historical materialism.

Yet we need only compare the interpretations of this sentence which are at all precise to convince ourselves that it is by no means clear; worse, that it is literally incomprehensible, and *necessarily* so. The reasons for this have to do with the fact that Marx *could not* state what he was trying to say – not only because he did not yet *know* how to say it, but also because he prevented himself from saying it by dint of the simple fact that he began his first sentence with the phrase 'the *essence of Man*'. When, with the first word one utters, one obstructs, with a gigantic 'episte-mological obstacle', the path that one is opening up with the intention of striking out on it, one can only come to a standstill, or make singular detours to get around the obstacle. These detours are inscribed in this sentence, which necessarily goes uncomprehended, because it is incomprehensible.

An example – a famous one, because we find a trace of it in Engels himself (the parallelograms of forces),[41] and, in black and white, in Gramsci.[42] 'The essence of man is . . . the ensemble of social relations' has been read and interpreted as follows: the essence of a human individual is constituted by the sum of social relations that he maintains in the society he lives in. The individual is at, or *is*, the point of intersection of 'multiple social relations'. If you want to know the essence of Mr X, add up and collate his familial, professional, political, ideological, sporting, ornithological, etc., relations; Mr X is at their intersection, *qua* their result. I am not joking: much of contemporary sociology and psychosociology puts forward categories of this kind. Let us leave the absurd aspect of this interpretation to one side. It is interesting despite this, because it reveals one of the *meanings* covered by the term Man: that of *individual*. The kind of interpre-tation I have just evoked draws the Sixth Thesis in the direction of what we shall call the problem of the *theory of individuality*.

It is clear, however, that in the sentence that constitutes this Sixth Thesis, Marx has something completely different in mind: another *meaning*, a very different one, which is also covered by the term Man. This meaning throws up what we shall call the problem of the *theory of society* and the History of societies.

Now Marx does not say: in order to produce a *theory of society*, it is necessary to consider, in their distinction, articulation and unity, 'the ensemble of the (various) social relations'. Marx says: in order to produce a theory *'of the essence of Man'.* . . . The theoretical obstruction is to be found here, beginning with and in these first words. Once one has pronounced them, one can no longer say anything that, *taken literally,* makes any sense whatsoever. To give this theoretically contorted sentence a meaning, one has to retrace, in reverse, the detour it had to make simply in order to be pronounceable. This is the detour I mean. It is necessary to have done with Feuerbach, and therefore with what he includes in the human essence. It is not enough to say, as in 1843: Man is the world of Man, society, the state. The world of man is not the objectification of his essence; it is not mere Objects; it consists of altogether astounding realities: *relations,* taken in their 'ensemble'. However, something of Feuerbach remains even in this innovation: namely, that which Feuerbach called the *generic* essence of man, the 'ensemble' of men, which the *1844 Manuscripts* showed to be at work in the 'relations' of the division of labour and other practical categories of Political Economy. It is on account of this concept, which is *absent* from his sentence (the human *genus*), that Marx can write this impossible sentence: 'The *human essence* is no abstraction inherent in the isolated *individual,* but the *ensemble* of social relations.'[43] 'The human essence' clearly *aims at* (since it avoids the individual) the problem of the structure of society, but by way of the Feuerbachian concept of *human genus.* Unless this concept of *human genus* (which is itself a fine example of an epistemological obstacle) has been eliminated, it is only possible to produce contorted sentences that are literally incomprehensible.

But we have gained something here: we have learned to *distinguish* two problems:

(i) the problem of a theory of society (and history);
(ii) the problem of a theory of individuality (of that which is usually called the human individual).

We have also gained something from seeing that the access route to these two problems was blocked by two epistemological obstacles: the concept of *Man* and the concept of human *genus.*

But something else happens in the 'Theses on Feuerbach': the basic philosophical categories defining the field of Theoretical Humanism as that of the speculary Subject–Object relation are called into question. Theses 1, 2, 5, 8 and 9 explicitly call into question the nature of the concepts that sustain this field: Subject and Object.

The Object: Feuerbach's failing is to have 'conceived sensuousness (*die Sinnlichkeit*) only in the form *of the object* . . . but not as concrete human activity . . .' (First Thesis); '. . . he does not conceive the sensuous world as man's concrete practical activity' (Fifth Thesis).

The Subject: it must be conceived as historical and social *praxis*.

The couple constituted by the categories Subject–Object is thus no longer originary. The Theses bring into play, at a deeper level than this couple, the category of *historical praxis*.

Philosophically, this transformation is important. It effectively means that Marx is drawing certain conclusions from his break with Feuerbach's Theoretical Humanism, bearing on both the typical categories constitutive of the field of the speculary relation and the operation essayed in the *Manuscripts*: Hegel *in* Feuerbach. Indeed, to go beyond the Feuerbachian couple 'subject = Object' by means of historical praxis is to extricate Hegel from the narrow constraints of the couple 'subject = Object'; it is to set the Hegelian dialectic to work on the Feuerbachian concepts of Subject and Object themselves. Historical praxis is the concept of a theoretical compromise, in which, this time, the previous relationship is modified: historical praxis is what remains of Feuerbach *in* a certain Hegel; it is, very precisely, the transformation of the Subject into praxis, and the *historicization of this subject* as subject.

This transformation is very important, for it provides the key to the *philosophy* that dominates the whole of *The German Ideology*: the *historicism* of the Subject. The category of the Subject is maintained. There is a subject, or there are several subjects, of history. *The German Ideology* will say: it is individuals, it is 'men' – read, real men – who are the subjects of history. *But* they are not abstract subjects standing outside history; they are themselves *historical in nature*, and are affected by the historicity of the history whose subjects they are. This is a very special sort of theoretical compromise: history is no longer contained *within* the field delimited by Subject and Object; it transcends these limits (Subject–Object) and invests them with historicity, while respecting their status of Subject and Object. What holds for the subject also holds for the object. Every object is historicized in its turn: nature is thoroughly historical, transformed by human praxis.[44] Not only nature, but also science itself; not only the subjects of history, but also the subjects of the knowledge of history, and the knowledge of history itself.

The *historicism* of *The German Ideology* would later weigh very heavy on the history of Marxist theory. It is no historical accident that this historicism is always associated, wherever it is professed in Marx's name, with a Humanist Ideology. For, in the formation of Marx's thought, the historicism of the 'Theses on Feuerbach' and *The German Ideology* is nothing other than a new relationship between a so-called 'Hegelian' conception of history and the Feuerbachian Humanist categories of Subject and Object. This new relationship is a modification of the old one (that of the *Manuscripts*). Hegel *in* Feuerbach becomes, in the Humanist Historicism of the 'Theses' and *The German Ideology*, (what is left of) Feuerbach *in* (a certain) Hegel.

4. Thus we can readily see which *philosophical* conception, still haunted by concepts which originate in the enterprise of the *1844 Manuscripts*, presides over *The German Ideology*.

I mean, of course, the conception (not made explicit as such) that reigns in *The German Ideology*, not the conception of philosophy that *The German Ideology* puts forward in black and white. For *The German Ideology* makes no bones about the matter: it radically suppresses all philosophy as sheer ideological illusion, dream, chimera, bred by the alienation of the division of labour; and, in the space thus cleared, it installs *science* alone.[45] All that remains of what is declared to be philosophy comes down to the spontaneous ideology of science: that is to say, an empiricism of the given, facts, the 'real', the 'concrete' (it is still doing quite well, thank you), baptized 'materialism' in *The German Ideology*. We shall conclude from this that if *The German Ideology* is interesting from the standpoint of *historical materialism*, whose basic elements it expounds, albeit in what is still an extremely confused form, it is distinguished by the total absence of what will be called, in the Marxist tradition, *dialectical materialism*, the new philosophy that Marx's great scientific discovery bears within it.

Indeed, what is to be said of the scientific concepts which, in

The German Ideology, announce the scientific discovery that consists in the opening up of the 'continent' of History to knowledge? What is their state here, in a situation dominated by the absence of any new philosophy whatsoever?

Between the *1844 Manuscripts* and *The German Ideology*, there occurred a small event whose importance has been appreciated by only a small handful of specialists:[d] the publication of Stirner's *The Ego and His Own* (1845). What interests us about this text? The fact that it helped *shatter the Hegelian*[46] *category of Man*, breaking it down into two component elements: on the one hand, an empirical concept, the real, singular, concrete, etc., individual; and, on the other, the *religious* Idea of Man. Stirner arrives at this result by categorically accusing Feuerbach of never getting beyond the limits of religion, but simply replacing God with Himself in calling Him Man. In *The Ego and His Own*, this accusation takes the form of an argument which it is hard to refute; it shows that Feuerbachian Humanism (if not all humanism), and therefore *atheistic Humanism* (all atheistic humanism), is merely a form of religious ideology, the modern form of religion. Marx and Engels were deeply affected by this charge.[47] With Stirner's demonstration as a starting point, something new was acquired at the theoretical level: Man and Humanism were now seen to designate something which, contrary to what Marx and Engels had previously supposed, was the very opposite of the real, concrete, and so on; Man and Humanism were the stuff of priests' tales, a moral ideology of an essentially religious nature, preached by petty bourgeois in laymen's dress.

Man was thus dealt a mortal blow. The murder exposed the presence, under this old term constitutive of Theoretical Humanism, of *three* realities, or problems, or indices of problems:

(i) the individual (the problem of a theory of individuality);
(ii) society (the problem of a theory of society and history);
(iii) an ideology (the problem of a theory of ideology – in particular, of the ideological concept of Man and of Humanist Ideology, that is, of Humanism as Ideology).

---

[d] In France, Henri Arvon [Arvon, *Aux sources de l'existentialisme: Max Stirner*, Paris, 1954].

It is against the background provided by the first stages of the grand 'settling of accounts' [*Abrechnung*] now under way,[48] and by these now established distinctions, that we must try to see the elements of the concepts of historical materialism produced by *The German Ideology*.

I have said that the subject of history was historicized in *The German Ideology*. Strikingly, it is no longer Man who, in *The German Ideology*, is the Subject of History, but real, empirical *individuals*, endowed with certain *forces*, living in concrete socio-historical conditions, and producing, by putting 'their productive forces' to work in 'relations of mutual commerce'[49] [*Verkehrsverhältnisse, Verkehrsformen*], that with which to satisfy their own vital needs in their material-life-process [*Lebensprozeß*].

Over against these real, empirical, concrete, etc., individuals, who are the basic 'premises' for the new conception of history (which is not 'devoid of premises'),[50] and are thus the always present origin, the always contemporaneous [*actuel*] subjects of a history that is their very *production*, in which they objectively externalize their 'essential forces' in a process of alienation that, as a result of the division of labour (instrument and name of alienation), separates them from their products and their conditions of existence, which then dominate them as an alien force (alienation effect) – in a word, standing over against these *individuals*, we no longer find *Man*.

Man, in *The German Ideology*, is an Ideology pure and simple. He is the 'slogan' and 'rallying-cry' [*mot d'ordre*] of an impotent moral protest, that of the German petty-bourgeois intellectuals who, incapable of making anything at all that looks like History, gain a form of verbal assurance over it and take verbal revenge on it in the name of what they dream of being: Man, the essence of History. In short, Man has ceased to be a fundamental, rational category that renders History intelligible; on the contrary, Man is an irrational, derisory, hollow notion, which, because it is ideological, is by its very nature incapable of explaining anything whatsoever, but has itself to be explained, that is, reduced to what it is: the religious impotence of a ridiculous 'wish' to take part in a History that does not give a damn[51] about the petty bourgeois who want to lay down the law in it. A vain, empty discourse, Man is, in essence, the diversionary tactic of a reactionary ideology.

Of course, things are not that simple – by which I mean that this does not yet settle the most important questions. *The German Ideology* does not say that the individual (a category at last divested of the ideology of Man) is the index and the name of a theoretical problem that must be posed and resolved. For the empiricism of *The German Ideology*, the individual is not a problem for a single second; on the contrary, it is the solution itself, but *its own solution*. The individual is *that which one sets out from*, the commencement, the given, the subject, that 'which goes without saying', since he is a 'sensuously perceptible reality'. What does one '*see*' in History? Individuals. 'Individuals have always started out from themselves [*von sich ausgegangen*].'[52] One need only do the same. Let us, then, start out in our turn in the theory of individuals, and show 'what arises' when we follow their tracks [*quand on les suit à la trace*], in an empirical genesis worthy of them – when we track the products of the utilization (externalization/alienation) of their 'productive forces' in their 'life-process'. When we do this, we observe the *genesis*[53] ('genetico-critical', 'genetico-empirical' – Feuerbachian expressions) of the *Productive Forces* and the *Relations of Production*, whose unity constitutes the *mode of production* of the material life of the aforementioned individuals; we observe the genesis of property forms (relations of production), followed by that of social classes, the state, and Ideology (their 'consciousness').

Despite these genuinely new *words*, which are the first elements of the concepts of historical materialism, we are still caught in a *transcription* of what still subsists of Feuerbach. If the Productive Forces are so often said to be the 'productive forces *of the* individuals', this is because they are still bound up with the Feuerbachian concept of the essential Attributes or essential Forces of the Human Essence, which has become the *individual*, the individuals. If the Relations of production are conceived only within the concept of *Verkehrsverhältnisse*; if, therefore, this relation is conceived within the category of 'mutual commerce' [*Verkehr*], and thus of an *inter-individual relation*, it is because the individuals are still vaguely or explicitly conceived as the subjects constitutive of all social relations.

Indeed, Man himself haunts even the extraordinary final theory of communism,[54] in which the individuals, at last freed of the alienation whose historical authors (subjects) they are, will for the first time become truly 'free', non-'contingent' individuals, constituted by pure inter-individual relations – that is, delivered from the Social Relations (of production, and other relations as well) in which they had heretofore made and, simultaneously, been subjected to their history.

There is further reason to believe that Man continues, despite everything, to weigh heavy on the *individual*, even the historicized individual, of *The German Ideology*: it appears when we observe that the notion of *alienation* is still present and active in this text in the guise of the *division of labour*. In order that the individual may be free at last, in order that the communist revolution can set him free, all the labour of History is required – that is to say, all the labour of the *process of alienation*. In the diffuse Hegelianism of *The German Ideology*, we remain the prisoners of a notion of the necessity of alienation, hence of a *teleology* of the process, hence of a *process with a subject*. This subject is the individuals. They are, on the one hand, declared to be empirical and historical, and the definition of them proclaims that it can do without the idea of Man altogether. But because, on the other hand, the individuals are the *subjects* of a process of alienation, and thus of a teleological process, it is once again a question, necessarily, of History as the history of the alienation of a subject: the individuals. Man is, to be sure, condemned in the broad daylight of criticism. But he lurks behind the theoretical scenes, constituting individuals as *subjects* of the process of alienation of their 'forces'. Thus he is waiting at the End of this process to welcome the individuals to the freedom whose concept he has been from the very start.

Ultimately, the individuals cannot escape this discrete but terribly effective control by Man until Marx abandons his empiricist convictions in order to think the individual, not as a subject or principle of explanation of the social structure that is *in itself clear*, but as an obscure object that needs to be defined and a *problem* that has to be resolved – to begin with, a problem that has to be properly posed. In order to understand the individual – and, *a fortiori*, the social structure – one must start out now, not from the individual, but from the social structure. The notion of individual is therefore in its turn an epistemological obstacle of no mean proportions.

That is why *The German Ideology* is such an equivocal work.

Something new is certainly going on in it; Marx was not mistaken when he identified it as the place where his discovery was born, amid his rupture with 'his former philosophical conscience'. The novelty of *The German Ideology* finds expression in concepts which, it is true, are christened with new names (mode of production, productive forces, social relations, etc.), yet are still governed by *philosophical categories* that have remained basically unchanged: after those of the Hegel–Feuerbach theoretical compromise (Feuerbach and a certain anthropological Hegelianism), after the major crisis of the *1844 Manuscripts* in the 'Theses on Feuerbach', a historicist – that is to say, *still humanist* – empiricism.

In the light of this conclusion, one can doubtless readily *see* what is meant by what I have called the *absence* of dialectical materialism in *The German Ideology*. In *The German Ideology*, the break with the past begins on the terrain of the science of history. But the break with the past on the terrain of philosophy *has yet to begin*. Presence, for the first time, of historical materialism; absence of [dialectical] materialism:[55] one sees the effects of this in the confusion of the concepts I have analysed. But the most pertinent effect of this unstable conjuncture is the theory of *ideology* that *The German Ideology* gives us.

The German Ideology talks incessantly about ideology; that is its subject *par excellence*. And it proposes a theory of ideology: ideology is an effect of alienation (of the division of intellectual labour separated from manual labour). Ideology is literally *nothing*, the empty (and inverted: the *camera obscura*), exact reflection of what takes place in the real world. Once again, a reversal of meaning/direction [*sens*], with this little supplement: this meaning is perfectly *superfluous*. Prior to the division of labour (manual and intellectual), there was no ideology. Nor will there be any ideology under communism (the end of alienation, thus the end of ideology and all the 'idealistic humbug').[56] The proof? We already have it in the proletariat, which long ago threw all ideology, religion, philosophy, etc., overboard. In this respect, it is already, in itself, communism. Like the proletarians who have rid their lives of Ideology, *The German Ideology* proclaims the elimination of philosophy. The end of all ideologies, the end of all abstractions: the real, the concrete, the empirical – there you have truth, the only truth there is. No wonder there is no theory of science in *The German Ideology*: a theory of science can be produced only in a philosophy. In all of this, with the modification effected by a radical historicist empiricism which declares that Man is mere ideology, and that ideology is *nothing*, we are still within the philosophical legacy of Feuerbach.

The break with Feuerbach has been announced and initiated. But this break, too, is a *process*, which is only just beginning. It has not yet been consummated.

We can follow the stages of this process in *The Manifesto, The Poverty of Philosophy*, the *Contribution*, and *Capital*. I shall not go into detail; I shall go straight to the end of the process.

5. To present Marx's break with theoretical humanism, one can, as I have just done in broad outline, scan the essential moments in its history. But one can also, after first clearly establishing the theoretical contents which Marx took as his starting point, turn to the end of this history, and take an *inventory* [*constat*: literally, a bailiff's report] of the new theoretical contents, noting the presence or absence of the concepts that originally featured in the system characteristic of Theoretical Humanism.

It then becomes easy to show that – apart from a few isolated and isolatable, and in any case highly localized, survivals – the categories constitutive of Theoretical Humanism have *in fact* disappeared from *Capital*. This is a relatively simple question: all that is involved is a theoretical inventory. Obviously, it calls for the sort of bailiff who is thoroughly familiar with the special kind of object of which he must make an inventory, and can therefore be relied on not to take mere words for scientific concepts or philosophical categories, as often occurs in polemics.

Let us sum up the results of this inventory; anyone can verify them for himself.

A. *The science of history.* The science of history does not take as its object the essence of man, or the human genus, or the essence of men, and so forth. The object of the science of history is the history of the forms of existence specific to the human species.

The[57] specific difference that distinguishes the forms of existence of the human species from those of animal species is (1) that human beings live exclusively in social formations; and (2) that these human social formations have specific histories, which, as such, are governed not by the biological and ecological laws of the species, as 'animal societies' are, but by the 'social' laws of the *production*, and the *reproduction* of the conditions of *production*, of the means of existence of these social formations.

If we consider the theoretical system of its fundamental concepts, the science of history is no more based on notions like man, human species, men, individuals, and so on, than its object is the essence of Man, and so forth. The fundamental concepts of the theory of the science of the history of social formations are the concepts of mode of production, productive forces and relations of production (and their unity), juridico-political superstructure, ideological superstructure, determination in the last instance by the economy, relative autonomy of the instances, and so on and so forth.

We are plainly on a completely different 'continent' and in a completely different theoretical universe, one that no longer has anything to do with the ideological universe of the *1844 Manuscripts*, or even *The German Ideology*, in which some of these new concepts do feature. It is no longer a question of saying that Man is the root of Man and the essence of all the Objects of his human world. It is no longer a question of 'starting out from individuals' who 'have always started out from themselves', as in *The German Ideology*, and tracing the effects of an empirical, constitutive genesis with a view to 'engendering', with 'the forces of individuals' as one's point of departure, Productive Forces, Relations of Production, and so on. It is no longer a question of starting out from the 'concrete' in theory, from the well-known 'concrete' concepts of Man, men, individuals with 'their feet firmly planted on solid ground', nations, and so on. Quite the contrary: Marx *starts out from the abstract*, and says so. This does not mean that, for Marx, men, individuals, and their subjectivity have been expunged from real history. It means that the *notions* of Man, etc., have been expunged *from theory*, for, in theory, no-one has yet, to my knowledge, met a flesh-and-blood man, only the *notion* of man. Far from being able to found and serve theory, these ideological notions have only one effect: they *foreclose* theory. These notions of Theoretical Humanism have been eliminated from Marx's scientific theory, and we have every right to eliminate them, root and branch – for the simple reason that they can act only as *'epistemological obstacles'* there.

To put it plainly: we need to say once and for all to all those who, like Feuerbach and the Marx of the *Manuscripts*, and even, all too often, the Marx of *The German Ideology* (the most contrary of these texts, because it is the hardest to handle and to quote *with total legitimacy* [*de plein droit*]), are constantly harping about man, men, the real and the concrete, and hope to impose the use of these notions in theory as the basic concepts of the science of history – we need to tell them once and for all that this idealist blackmail and unbearable, if not criminal, demagoguery have gone on long enough. For their jeremiads will never provide even the beginnings of the kind of knowledge that is useful to real men, with whom Marx continued to concern himself throughout his life; it was in order to provide them with real and not merely verbal services that he forged the concepts that are indispensable for producing the means of understanding their real existence, and really transforming it. For if these humanist discourses do not yield any knowledge, they certainly do have the catastrophic effect of dragging us back to *pre-Marxist positions* and a petty-bourgeois ideology which, in our day and age, cannot be anything but revisionist and reactionary.

B. The same holds for *Marxist philosophy*. Its basic philosophical concepts are not Man, the Subject, the Cogito (even in the plural – the 'we'), the act, the project, praxis and creation – all notions that people, communist philosophers included, are today hauling out of the old reserves of idealism: not of *critical* idealism (which at least had its grandeur, for it modelled itself on science), but of *spiritualist* idealism (the most reactionary form of idealism, because it is craven enough to model itself on religion).[58]

The basic categories of Marxist philosophy (dialectical materialism) are materialism and the dialectic. Materialism is based, not on the ideological notions of Subject and Object, but on the distinction between matter and thought, the real and knowledge of the real – or, to put it differently and more precisely, the distinction between the *real process* and the *process of knowledge*; on the primacy of the real process over the process of knowledge; on the knowledge-effect produced by the process of knowledge in the process of correlating [*dans le procès de mise en correspondance*] the process of knowledge with the real process.

As Lenin said, materialism studies the history of the 'passage from ignorance' (or ideology) to 'knowledge' (or science), and, to that end, has to produce the theory of the different practices: those that operate in knowledge, those that serve as a basis for theoretical practice, and so on. The dialectic determines the laws which govern these processes (real process and process of knowledge) in their dependence (primacy of the real process) and their relative autonomy, and so forth.

Given what has been said about the *lag* of Marxist philosophy with respect to the science of history, every informed Marxist philosopher is well aware that the danger of theoretical revisionism always has been, and still is, greater in philosophy than in the science of history. Ideology abhors a vacuum, and since every 'lag' is a vacuum, it rushes to fill it. This is one more reason to struggle against ideology with lucidity and resolve, and to take back, inch by inch, in the face of all idealist and spiritualist inanities and the eclectic makeshifts and *bricolages* currently in fashion – compared with which Feuerbach's incoherence is a high point of thought and a model of rigour – the ground that, by all rights, belongs to Marxist philosophy. Our primary theoretical, ideological and political (I say political) duty today is to rid the domain of Marxist philosophy of all the 'Humanist' rubbish that is brazenly being dumped into it. It is an offence to the thought of Marx and an insult to all revolutionary militants. For the Humanism in Marxist philosophy is not even a distinguished form of the bourgeois *philosophy* that has taken up residence in Marx: it is one of the vilest by-products of the most vulgar modern religious ideology. We have long been aware that its effect, if not its objective, is *to disarm the proletariat*.

These, then, are the results of the method of taking an inventory. Nothing for it: as Hegel himself said (but he had the consolation of saying it as he stood looking up at the mountains): that is how it is.

6. Before examining the theoretical consequences of this inventory, I should like to consider once again the principles that command, or are suggested by, my very brief analysis of the moments punctuating the theoretical history of the formation of Marx's thought.

I said, before embarking on these analyses, that in order to carry them out with certainty, we should have to have at our disposal the principles of a theory of the history of theories that does not yet exist. But the conditions for producing this theory cannot be reduced to extending to the history of theories (ideologies, sciences, philosophy) the conceptual system at our disposal for thinking the history of social formations. Of course, because what is involved is in every case a theory of history, we shall have to borrow, from what we already have by way of a theory of the *history* of social formations, all that it can furnish us for thinking the *history* of theories. Yet this work, pursued on the existing theoretical bases, can in no case provide us, by itself, the knowledge of our *specific* object. We must study this specific object *for itself*, in its concrete formations; that is to say, we must work on the concrete data of the history of theories, giving preference to the examples and segments of this history which we have good reason to consider *pertinent*, that is, inherently rich in determinations that will provide us with the key to other phenomena. It is reasonable to suppose that those moments in the history of theories when new sciences irrupt, especially when these sciences are 'continental', are relevant to our purposes. That is why I believe that the study of the formation and transformations of Marx's thought can also be of direct relevance to the development of this theory of the history of theories that we require.

I therefore propose very briefly to reconsider a few of the concepts that I have used in the analyses in which I have attempted to scan the history of Marx's thought: the opposition science/ideology, the 'break', and so on. I believe that I can, in this way, begin to respond to some of the often legitimate criticisms that have been addressed to me.

To begin with, a word on the science/ideology opposition, which gives the concept of 'epistemological break' its meaning. Even when it is hedged round with all the precautions that rescue it from contamination by the 'Enlightenment' opposition between truth and ideology,[e] the opposition between science and ideology, crudely formulated, cannot *not* be generally understood as Manichaean and, therefore dogmatic. From the *ideologi-*

[e] See *Reading Capital*, vol. 1, p. 56 [RC 43].

cal point of view, this opposition effectively fulfils its role: that of drawing, in the present conjuncture, a clear, authoritative *line of demarcation* between the scientific demands that Marxists should make and the easy options and demagoguery of eclecticism and theoretical revisionism.[59] Drawing this line of demarcation was an urgent necessity and there can be absolutely no question of repudiating it. From a *theoretical* point of view, however, it is essential that we do not content ourselves with a formulation that is ideological in nature but, rather, advance more precise propositions that are appropriate for thinking this opposition, in that they provide a more specific account of it.

Let us again take the example of the ideological nature of Theoretical Humanism. To begin with, it is clear that that which characterizes the fundamental notions of Theoretical Humanism as *ideological* can be stated only *retrospectively* [*après coup*]. If Marx had not produced the new concepts appropriate for thinking the object of his discovery, we would not be able to pronounce the Judgement of ideology that we apply to the notions with which he had to break. The ideology/science opposition is thus always based on a *retrospection* or *recurrence*. It is the existence of science itself which establishes the 'break' in the history of theories which can then serve as grounds for declaring the prehistory of science *ideological*.

This break and this retrospection are, however, the correlatives of a real process, that of the constitution of science (born in ideology) through theoretical work that leads up to a *critical* point which explodes in a break, instituting the new field in which the science will establish itself. Whence a paradox: science is plainly born of ideology and in ideology – yet the ideology of which science is born as it tears itself away from ideology can be given the *name* of ideology only by the science born of it and separated from it.

A long train of important consequence follows. I will mention just two:

(i) The first has to do with the nature of the 'break'. Certain pertinent signs that manifest both the extreme tension of a desperately sought, impossible synthesis (the *1844 Manuscripts*) and the sudden release of tension due to an unprecedented conceptual mutation (the 'Theses on Feuerbach' and *The German Ideology*) make it possible to assign the break something like a *date* (1845); but the break is never anything more than the beginning of an event of very long duration which, in a sense, never ends.

Here, then, I would like to rectify what was obviously too cut-and-dried in the indications I gave in my essay, for which I have quite rightly been criticized. Of course, the corrections I make here remain descriptive: they do not constitute even the rudiments of a theory of the break, on which one of us will soon publish an essay.[60] However, what I have too briefly said about the 'Theses' and *The German Ideology* does show that if the 'liquidation' that Marx consciously announces is plainly set in motion in these texts, it is *only just* set in motion; the work essential for truly clearing the theoretical space in which, twenty years later, *Capital* will unfold has yet to be carried out. The 'break' is therefore itself a process of very long duration comprising dialectical *moments*; a detailed study of them, and comparison with studies of the other great 'breaks' that we have enough documentation to broach (for example, the break effected by Galileo), will perhaps bring out what is typical of all of them, and what is specific to each. The study of the moments constitutive of a 'break' of this kind (the kind that inaugurates the opening of a new 'continent') could constitute a theory of the process of the 'break'; it could also bring out the *necessity* of the successive reorganizations (moments) or secondary breaks which, via the appearance, definition and resolution of a series of new problems, lead a science from its beginnings to its maturity by way of its maturation.

This conception of the 'break' as process is not a backhanded way of abandoning the concept of the break, which certain critics are only too happy to invite us to do.[f] That it takes time for the 'break' to be consummated in its process by no means prevents it from being well and truly an *event* in the history of theory, one whose *beginnings*, like those of any other event, can be *dated* with precision. In Marx's case, the date is 1845 (the 'Theses', *The German Ideology*).

This event is an event of long duration, and if in one sense it clearly has a beginning, in another it has no end. For science, which is born in and of the ideology from which it tears itself

---

[f] Semprun, Bottigelli, etc.

away, is not, once born, securely established in its domain, as if it inhabited some pure, closed world in which it had to do only with itself. For as long as it lives, it works unceasingly on a raw material that is always affected, in one way or another, by ideology; and it expands only by conquering 'areas' or 'objects' designated by notions which its conquest makes it possible to describe, *retrospectively*, as *ideological*. Thus the work of criticism and of the transformation of the ideological into the scientific, which inaugurates any science, never ceases to be the appointed task of established science. *No science is ever anything more than a continuing Break*, punctuated by further, internal breaks.

(ii) If this is correct, then we can turn back to the period 'before' the break, and study the specificity of the process that produced it. Here, too, we come up against a very important theoretical problem; we can make progress towards solving it only at the price of meticulous investigations. What type of necessity produces, in the history of theories, the rise of a science?

Permit me simply to call attention to a singular 'coincidence'. I have cited Lenin's thesis to the effect that historical materialism came about as an effect of the encounter of three disciplines: German philosophy, English political economy, and French socialism. This thesis may perhaps be related to the triple *theoretical* encounter which occurs in the *1844 Manuscripts*, in the way I have described. Let us recall the names of the three theoretical personages present at this encounter: Hegel, Political Economy, Feuerbach. The one item on Lenin's list that is missing here is *French socialism*. But, in the light of the insistence with which Feuerbach proclaimed that the Human Revolution would be born of the union of revolutionary French materialism and German idealism, and in the light of the fact that he regarded himself as the philosopher of the heart (which is French and revolutionary) and declared himself a 'communist', it is not impossible to consider him, at least *to some extent*, as the symbolic representative of French utopian socialism in the Encounter of the *Manuscripts*.[61] One day, perhaps, we will be able to derive from this figure of the encounter certain elements for a theory of the process by which the 'break' was produced.

II[62]

I should now like to begin to examine some of the *real problems* that Marx's rupture with Theoretical Humanism has brought to light. This examination will concern not only Marx but also, as we shall soon see, most of the 'theoretical' arguments advanced by most of my critics.

What justifies the parallel? The fact that some modern 'Humanists' have *once again taken up* precisely those notions that Marx had to eliminate from the field of his reflections as so many *epistemological obstacles*: Man, the Human Genus, the individual, the subject, and so on.

To avoid all ambiguity (experience proves that one can never take too many precautions in these matters), we need to be perfectly clear about the object and bases of this examination, as well as the justification for it.

The examination I shall proceed to make is a purely *theoretical* one. I do not propose to examine the nature and social function of Humanism as an *ideology*, or to question Humanism's 'right' to exist as an *ideology*. I simply propose to examine, from a *theoretical* standpoint, the *justification* that the ideologues of Theoretical Humanism (the Young Marx, our moderns, etc.) invoke for assigning a theoretical role to *ideological* notions like Man, the Human Genus, and so on. It is, then, from the *theoretical* standpoint, and from that standpoint alone, that I shall be treating these notions as so many *epistemological obstacles*.

To make this more precise, I must add two important stipulations.

To say *obstacle* is to suggest a concept that is meaningful only in terms of a theoretical metaphor that can be formulated roughly as follows. Theory has struck out on a *path* that it must travel in order to attain knowledge of its real object or objects. At some point, this path is blocked by an *obstacle* that prevents the theory from approaching and attaining its object. Thus the metaphor of the epistemological obstacle signifies two things: (1) the theory comes up against an obstacle that prevents it from advancing; (2) this obstacle blocks a path and hides objects *that are in some sense behind it*. To eliminate the obstacle is to clear the path and perceive the objects that were hidden by it. Thus there is a twofold relationship between the obstacle and the path (or the objects): on the one hand, a relationship of opposition [*contrariété*], but also, in a certain way, a relationship of correspondence [*affinité*] which, albeit hard to define, is unmistakable. It is not just any obstacle that blocks just any path or 'hides' just any object. The history of theories shows that there is a certain relationship between the way of handling (eliminating) the obstacle and therefore the nature of the obstacle, on the one hand, and the path it blocks or the objects it 'hides' on the other.

In this commentary, I am merely stating a proposition that I will develop later. It concerns one of the two aspects of the function of ideology: its function of *allusion*, invested in its function of *illusion*. It is because an ideological notion is always, to a certain extent, *allusive* – in the very form of the illusion it imposes – that such a notion, which is an epistemological obstacle from the theoretical standpoint, corresponds to some extent [*possède quelque affinité*] to the real problems it recognizes in misrecognizing them. I shall do nothing more than apply this theory of allusion–illusion, or the recognition–misrecognition of ideology, to the epistemological obstacles I shall be discussing. This will make it possible to reveal the real theoretical problems concealed (when such is the case) by these epistemological obstacles by *removing* them from our path.

Second remark. The work of removing obstacles that we shall undertake below will not be, in most cases, a real labour of theoretical production, but a simple labour of critical *repetition*. For the most part, at least in principle, the work has already been done by Marx. We shall limit ourselves to *going over the same ground*. Although, on one or two points, we may find that we have to remove an obstacle which Marx did not have occasion to remove himself, we shall not, for the most part, find ourselves in the characteristic situation of a living science (which has to discern and eliminate epistemological obstacles that had previously gone unnoticed). We shall simply have to repeat Marx's operation and to comment, if possible, on certain of its consequences.

Now that these methodological principles have been clearly defined, we can begin our examination. It will lead us to identify the *epistemological obstacles* that the notions of Theoretical Humanism place in the way of scientifically posing and solving real problems, of identifying *these real problems*, and of thinking the theoretical conditions for posing and solving them.

Our analyses of these epistemological obstacles and real problems will also intersect most of the criticisms, objections or questions that have been addressed to me in the debate about Humanism.

I shall not be dealing with all the real problems involved in the dialectic 'epistemological obstacle/real problems', but, broadly, with those of direct interest to *historical materialism*, postponing the bulk of the problems that fall to the province of dialectical materialism.

The general theme that will guide us in our analyses may be described as follows. The essential epistemological obstacles in the basic system of the ideology of Theoretical Humanism (i.e. Humanism with theoretical pretensions) are constituted by a number of notions that I have identified in the preceding analyses:

1. the notion of Man (the essence or nature of Man);
2. the notion of the human species or Human Genus (Man's generic essence, defined by consciousness, the heart, inter-subjectivity, etc.);
3. the notion of the 'concrete', 'real', etc., individual;
4. the notion of the subject ('concrete' subjectivity, the subject constitutive of the speculary relation, the process of aliena-tion, History, etc.);
5. the notion of consciousness (for example, as the essential defining feature of the human species, or as the essence of the ideological);
6. the notion of labour (as the essence of man);
7. the notion of alienation (as the externalization of a Subject);
8. the notion of dialectic (in so far as it implies a teleology).

These are basic notions. It is not hard to match them up with their contemporary variants, traces of which appear in the objec-tions to the thesis of Marx's theoretical anti-humanism: for example, the derivative notions of 'subjectivity', 'subject' or 'act', 'creation', 'project', 'transcendence', 'social labour', and so forth.[63]

It should be recalled that the scientific pretension of these ideological notions resides in the presentation of them as something they cannot be: scientific concepts that allow us to pose and solve scientific problems in the open-ended theoretical field of scientific research, which produces discoveries. It should be recalled that the scientific pretension of these fundamental ideological notions is an imposture that hides their *real function*: their anti-scientific ideological function. It should be recalled that the ideological function of these notions with theoretical pretensions does not consist in *posing* real *problems*, and thus in opening up the theoretical field in which real problems can be scientifically posed; it consists, rather, in *imposing in advance* – masked by fictitious problems devoid of scientific content – ready-made *solutions* that are not *theoretical* solutions, but merely theoretical *statements* of 'practical' solutions, social solutions that exist in the form of realities which have been, or are to be, brought into existence [*faits accomplis ou à accomplir*] in a class society, and correspond to the 'problems' of the economic, political or ideological class struggle in that society.

To put it schematically, the ideological notions in question here are merely transcriptions, with theoretical pretensions, of *existing states of affairs*. In the final analysis, they depend on the balance of power in the class struggle: they are ideological *prises de parti* in favour of certain moral, religious and political 'values', and, by way of those values, certain political institutions, certain moral and religious prejudices, and the prejudice of morality and religion.

Therefore, far from *opening up* the theoretical field in which it would be possible to pose real problems scientifically, these ideological notions, which are basically nothing but theoretical transcriptions of actually existing social *solutions*, have the function of preventively *closing off* the field they pretend to open up, thus making it impossible to pose any real problems or, consequently, make any pertinent discovery. Diderot demonstrated clear insight into the basic nature of ideology when he declared that he would believe in theology when someone showed him its 'discoveries'.

We could, with no trace of irony, ask those who have today resolved to defend and propagate these shopworn ideological notions to be so good as to show us the scientific 'discoveries' that the philosophies of Man, the Subject (in all its avatars,

Phenomenology included), the Act, Labour, Praxis, Alienation, and so on, have yielded or sparked *in any field whatsoever*, or the research that their miraculous 'categories' have made more fertile. Even a nodding acquaintance with what is currently going on in the 'Human Sciences', in which these categories find their field of predilection, will suffice to confirm not only the *entire sterility* of their intervention, but also the *retrogressive* effects it provokes. Far from contributing to the 'progress' of the disciplines in which they 'take an interest', these philosophical ideologies merely seek to 'domesticate' them and harness them to the apologetic service of the Great Causes whose agents they are. Bringing out real problems is thus not merely the last of their concerns; it is that which it is their function, precisely, to *preclude*.

Hence it is necessary to identify and then remove these epistemological obstacles in order to clear the path they block and then open up the theoretical field in which *real problems* can be identified, posed and examined.

What real problems can we discern behind the notions of *Theoretical Humanism*, once their impostures and theoretical pretensions have been challenged? Let me mention the essential ones, correlating them with the main epistemological obstacles that 'correspond' to them:

1. The problem of the definition of the *human species* – or of the specific difference that distinguishes the forms of existence of the *human species* from those of animal species (obstacles: the notions of man's generic essence, of consciousness, etc.).

2. The problem of the structure of *social formations* (obstacles: the notions of Man, Man's generic essence, the 'heart' or intersubjectivity, consciousness, the subject, etc.).

3. The problem of the dialectic of *history* as a process without subjects (obstacles: the notions of Man, Genus, subject, alienation, the teleological-dialectic).

4. The problem of the forms of *individuality* (obstacles: the notions of Man, Genus, individual, subject, the concrete, etc.).

5. The problem of the nature of the *ideological* (obstacles: the notions of Man, consciousness, subjectivity, etc.).

Each of these 'real problems' is said to be a *'real problem'* in a precise sense that needs to be made clear.

These problems are not said to be 'real' in the empiricist sense of the word, as if it were enough to *open one's eyes* to identify them – as if it would have been enough, *from time immemorial,* to have opened one's eyes to identify them. Most of our good 'Humanists' incessantly invoke, in incantatory fashion, the 'real', which for them is the 'concrete', 'life', 'richer and more vibrant than any concept', in order religiously to contrast it with 'theory', which is, as everyone knows – ever since the famous *bon mot* that, though it contains its grain of truth, can also be used to justify all kinds of resignation – 'always grey'. It is not *that* 'real' that we mean, but the *scientific* 'real', which – as Marx compellingly demonstrated – has nothing to do with the 'concrete' or the 'real' of the obvious facts of everyday life, which are given and imbued with the self-evidence of ideology.

These problems are *real* because they are posited as real *in the theoretical field* conquered by the long theoretical labour that has culminated in the present state of scientific knowledge. Thus we are talking about the *theoretical reality* of theoretical problems, which as such pertain to the process of knowledge, and appear as such only within the process of knowledge, as a function of a given historical state of the theoretical concepts that constitute the problematic of a theory.

Of course, the real (theoretical) problems generated by the process of knowledge have to do with *realties* that exist independently of the process of knowledge, and pertain to the *real process* or process of the real; the establishment of this correlation [*cette mise en correspondance*] constitutes, precisely, the knowledge-effect produced by the process of knowledge.

This distinction explains what empiricism cannot explain: the transformation in the *way problems are posed,* and the transformation of the objects of knowledge within the process of knowledge; in other words, the appearance of *new objects not seen* previously. Empiricism thinks that knowledge is an act of vision [*une vue*]: it is incapable of explaining the appearance of new objects in the field of 'the seen' [*le champ de la 'vue'*], and thus the fact that these new objects were not 'seen' [*vus*] earlier. It does not 'see' that the seeing [*la vue*] of what one sees in science depends on the *apparatus* of theoretical vision, and therefore on the history of the transformations of the theory within the process of knowledge. Thus what are called *real* problems derive from the *reality* of the process of knowledge, its apparatus of theoretical vision at a given time, and its *theoretical criteria of reality*. *Reality* is, in the precise sense in which we are using it, a category of the process of knowledge itself.

The same holds for the category '*problem*' in the expression '*real problem*'. In the everyday sense, the term 'problem' designates any kind of *difficulty*. Everyone has his 'problems' – so does History, so do the Communist parties. In this sense, all problems are 'real' or 'concrete', as so many obstacles that the various 'projects', whatever they are, come up against. We need to set aside this vague sense of the word, which is much too broad and confused, in order to specify the precise sense in which we are employing it.

Not every difficulty is a *problem* from the scientific point of view. Only those difficulties identified in the theoretical field of scientific research and susceptible of being *posed* as problems are scientific problems. The posing [*position*] of a difficulty as a problem must be understood in a precise sense that we can illustrate with the spatial metaphor of *position*. To pose a problem is to find, within the field of the existing theory, the precise *place* that rightfully falls to it, and so allows it to be conceived and treated as a problem. To assign it its place is simultaneously to *identify* it and to call it by its name. Assigning it its place, identifying it and stating it are of a piece. These three linked operations are made possible only by reference to the theoretical concepts constitutive of the existing theoretical field. To pose a problem, then, is to assign it its place, give it its name, and so on, by confronting a difficulty that one has pinpointed with the concepts constituting the field of the theory that has enabled one to pinpoint it.

This *confrontation* does not always allow one to pose in the form of a problem every difficulty one encounters: there are difficulties that remain in the state of difficulties, and cannot be posed as problems: they subsist in the state of *remainders*. As a rule, one talks in this case about 'problems without a solution', but this expression is not exact. It would be better to talk about difficulties that cannot be posed in the form of *problems* whenever the arsenal of existing scientific concepts *does not yet make it possible* rigorously to pose these difficulties in the form of problems. It also happens that certain problems can be posed theoretically, although one does not possess all the theoretical instruments required to produce their solution. These are problems that (for the time being) have no solution. Finally, it can happen that certain problems are 'posed' (and even resolved) in practical fashion without being posed and resolved theoretically: this holds for what we may call *practical inventions*, which are in advance of the corresponding theoretical solutions (discoveries). Political practice offers some striking examples.

All these 'problems' relative to the conditions for posing difficulties as problems deserve to be *posed* correctly in their turn. That task falls to philosophy.

I have said enough about this to make my meaning clear. When I talk about the list of *real problems* discernible behind the epistemological obstacles created by the notions of Humanist ideology, I am referring to scientific *problems* in the strict sense, that is to say, difficulties that can be assigned a place, identified, and stated in function of the theoretical concepts of science in its present state: in the case to hand, in function of the existing concepts of historical materialism. Thus each of these problems can legitimately stand as the object of a *theory*.

We shall see that, of the real problems I have listed, some can be posed rigorously in conditions that enable us to state the principle of their solution, on condition that serious theoretical research is carried out. Others, in contrast, can for now merely be correctly posed, while we wait to acquire the theoretical elements *which we do not yet possess, and without which we cannot envisage their solution.*

First problem: the definition of the human species[64]

In order to state this problem and take its exact scientific measure, as well as to evaluate its ideological and scientific import, we have first to remove the epistemological obstacle blocking access to it. This epistemological obstacle depends on a notion fraught with ideological determinations, on account, precisely, of its age-old function, a function it continues to fulfill in contemporary ideological struggles: for or against religion and idealism, for or against materialism.

In order to grasp the nature of this epistemological obstacle in the state in which Marx found it before he cleared it from his path, we have to go back to Feuerbach – to his conception of the Human Genus or the generic essence of Man.

The theory of the Human Genus serves, in Feuerbach, to found 'concrete' intersubjectivity (the I–Thou), which stands in for both the Transcendental and the Noumenal Subject in his work; it serves to found the speculary theory of the Absolute Horizon within which man encounters, in his objects, the reflection of his Essence; it serves to 'think' History by distributing the Human Genus among all individual human beings, past, present and future – and is thus the name of the Future whose present stands in perpetual need of a supplement in order to fill its theoretical vacuum; it serves, finally, to represent the 'heart', Man['s] communitarian nature, which images the utopian figure of communism in advance. But – to come to what interests us – the notion of Human Genus also serves to ground the *old spiritualist distinction* that privileges man over the whole natural kingdom.

The human species, says Feuerbach, is not a species like all the others; it must be called a Genus, because it is the 'species of all the species', the *universal* species in the strict sense of the word, the species which, unlike the others (hedgehog, dragonfly, rhododendron), does not take as its object a finite 'world', a minuscule portion of the Universe, but the Universe itself in its totality. This is a disarming way of assigning the Absolute Horizon of the human species the dimensions of the Universe, and the subjectivity of the human species the attributes of objectivity – in a word, a way of repeating the old thesis that the distinguishing feature of the human species is *Reason*.

But, in the good old idealist tradition, to say Reason is, of course, to say *consciousness*. The human species is, for Feuerbach, not just a species, but a Genus, because it is the only species in the world that can take itself as its own object. The hedgehog has many merits, and its 'horizon' (that of its *Umwelt*) has, even when it crosses roads,[65] clear limits – but the poor beast does not possess the privilege of making its species its *object*. It experiences it, but, as we have known since Pascal, *knows nothing about the matter*. Man knows what he is, for he belongs to a Genus that has the immediate privilege of making its species its object:

consciousness is this immediate presence of the Genus [*Genre*] in the individual. Consciousness of all kinds [*en tout genre*], if I may say so, but of course (for this is the crucial point), *moral* consciousness above all (and moral, in Feuerbach, means *religious*).

The notion of the human Genus thus has the function, not of thinking, obviously, but of purely and simply *proclaiming* these Grand Principles of Idealism (they can also be, depending on their mode, the Grand Principles of critical idealism). In Feuerbach, they are the principles of *spiritualist* (religious) idealism: Man is that exceptional being whose attributes are the Universal, Reason, Consciousness (rational, moral, and religious) and Love. As we can readily see, where Grand Principles are involved, there can be no question of going into particulars or offering proof. It is enough to *proclaim* of them; Theoretical Humanism does not suspect the existence of the least little problem here. In its view, these are Established Solutions, established from all eternity.

Under these conditions, one is not surprised to observe the extreme *ideological* importance of the question of the definition of the human species in its distinction from the animal species. In various explicit forms, this question long served and, in transposed forms, still massively serves as a symbolic issue whose stake is (to the extent that it *is* at stake here) the fate of religious and moral ideology – above all, the fate of religion, certain Institutions (the Churches and their powers) and the major political Interests tied to them (in the final analysis, relations of class domination).

It would be a mistake to think that the ideological virulence of this question diminished on the day the Church's prerogatives diminished thanks to progress in the hard sciences, life sciences, and sciences of Man (human palaeontology, etc.). It was merely the ideological exploitation of the question that changed, in both its forms and its point of application: in philosophy on the one hand and science on the other.

1. *In philosophy*, this question is taken directly in hand by spiritualist idealism, in forms that remain crude and obvious even when spiritualist philosophy tries to integrate the results of the life sciences by 'interpreting' them to its advantage. One need only think of Bergsonism, Teilhardism, or – because there

is no avoiding the subject – the echoes that this spiritualist ideology of matter, life and society has found even in certain Marxist circles. But these crude, philosophically discredited forms should not blind us to the more subtle forms in which critical philosophy, too, has simply taken over the great Division that interests so many Interests – that is to say, since to divide is to rule, so many forms of Rule.

Without going back to the Kantian Distinction between Nature and Freedom, which still commands Phenomenology and finally even haunts its own rejection in the Heideggerian problematic of Being and *Dasein*, let us consider the form in which this spiritualist heritage has been taken up by the philosophy of the 'sciences of Man'. It appears in *propria persona* in the great idealist Distinction between the Sciences of Nature and the Sciences of Man. For example, it is manifest in Dilthey's theory[66] of the difference between explanation (the Natural Sciences) and comprehension (the Sciences of Man). It is also manifest in the famous question of the legitimate *object* of the dialectic – to be very precise, in the question of the legitimacy or illegitimacy of a *Dialectic of Nature*.

The thesis of the exclusively human (or historical) privilege of the dialectic (see Sartre, etc.),[67] like the thesis of the irreducible specificity of the form of intelligibility of 'human phenomena' (*comprehension*, phenomenological *description*, and other *hermeneutic* variants), shows that spiritualism's defence of the religious privilege of the Nature and Destiny of Man is an ideological constant. It is against the background of this *ideological struggle* that the Marxist materialist thesis of the epistemological Unity of all the Sciences, the natural sciences as well as the sciences of man, takes on its full significance, as does the thesis of the Dialectic of Nature.

At this level, these theses must be taken for what they are: *the defence of ideological positions* in the field of philosophy, that is, a radical *refusal* to adopt idealist-spiritualist positions (a refusal to privilege the virtues of 'comprehension', 'description', 'hermeneutics', etc. – a rejection of the idea of the non-dialecticity of Nature); and, at the same time, the *affirmation* of counter-theses calling for a fundamental transformation in the way the 'problems' at stake in the debate are defined and posed.

We have seen this in connection with the Dialectic of Nature.

It is no accident that the thesis that there is a Dialectic of Nature[68] has made its way from Hegel into Marxism, and that this question is, even today, one of the absolute touchstones of the materialist party position in philosophy. The thesis that there is a Dialectic of Nature was indispensable to Hegel's theory of History as a *non-anthropological* theory of History: it indicates, in the Hegelian context (which continues to bear the stamp of spiritualism in the teleology of the process of *alienation*), that the dialectic does not begin with Man, and that History is therefore a process without a subject. It is owing to the religious privilege conferred upon the Human Species that all notion of a dialectic of Nature disappears in Feuerbach: for the same fundamental theoretical reason, there can also be no Dialectic of Nature in the *1844 Manuscripts* or *The German Ideology*, in which history is *anthropological*, in whole or in part. It is no accident that, in Marxism, the thesis that there is a Dialectic of Nature comes to the fore during Engels's struggle against Dühring's spiritualism,[69] which was attempting to re-establish the religious privilege of the human species.

But this justified 'revival' of the Dialectic of Nature, which some modern Marxists, and by no means the least of them, condemn with incredible nonchalance, has more than just an ideological function. For epistemological reasons that we can now see, it is closely bound up with the fundamental philosophical category on which *Capital* is based – the category of the *process without a subject*. The thesis that there is a Dialectic of Nature thus plays not only an ideological role (against spiritualism, for materialism), but also a positive epistemological role: against the category of the process of the alienation of a Subject, for the category of the *process without a subject*.

The thesis of the Dialectic of Nature, *in its present form*, has to do less with such dialectics as exist in Nature (an area that is open to scientific and epistemological investigation) than with what is going on in the science of History on the one hand and at the junction of the Natural and Human Sciences on the other. For this threefold reason, ideological, philosophical and scientific, it is today, and will long remain, a key thesis of Marxism on which no theoretical concession can be made if we are not to relapse into idealism and spiritualism.

Such are the ideological and philosophical stakes whose

site is the question of the differential definition of the human species.

2. But the debate has also taken, since the emergence of the life sciences (especially since Darwin), the form of an ideologico-scientific debate pursued on the terrain of the sciences themselves; to be very precise, *at the borderline* between the life sciences and the science of history. Are the sciences that take this *borderline* for their object capable of demonstrating the existence of a *material continuity* in the evolution of species from the animal to the human species? For spiritualism finds, as might be expected, one of its favourite arguments in what it regards as the 'fact' that there is an irreducible discontinuity here, which it loses no time in exploiting to religious ends. Of course, there is something to be gained from denying it the possibility of using this argument. Whence the ideological importance, a function of the ideological struggle defined by the terms of contemporary spiritualism, of scientific discoveries about the nature of the borderline between animal species and the human species.

It would, however, be peculiarly naive to believe that settling this question would leave spiritualism with nowhere to turn. As we know, it is even capable of taking the initiative and 'domesticating' any scientific discovery that might, at the scientific level, radically compromise the 'histories' [*histoires*] in Genesis: think of Teilhard's apologetic operation. Indeed, spiritualism, like any other ideology, not only does not take science seriously; that is what spiritualism is *made for*. Its function is always to 'domesticate' science, whatever its findings. One does not put paid to an ideology by 'countering' it on the terrain of science, for the very good reason that an ideology does not 'spring up' on that terrain, but on the terrain of class relations and their effects. Spiritualism has a bright future ahead of it, even after Darwin, even after the recent discoveries of human palaeontology.[70]

I should like to pause over this point, for when Marxists begin to display this kind of naivety about the basic nature of spiritualism, they not only misjudge the 'conclusive' ideological effects that they expect 'scientific discoveries' to have on the crucial question of the definition of the human species; much more alarmingly, they do not always manage to avoid the ideological contamination that contact with the ideological 'arguments' of the adversary often brings in its wake. When one has to 'follow the adversary' on to his own ground (ideology), one rarely comes away unscathed, unless one is very well armed from a theoretical standpoint.

There is, precisely, no lack of recent examples of 'Marxists' who are only too happy to utilize the Recent Scientific Discoveries of human palaeontology to refute the arguments of traditional spiritualism without pausing to consider that, in hastily bending these Recent Discoveries to the service of a Humanist ideology, even one that is dubbed 'Marxist', they inevitably lapse into modern spiritualism.

I am referring specifically to the following situation. Recent discoveries have cast doubt on the classic Darwinian thesis of man's simian ancestry (a 'scandal' that spiritualism laughed to scorn). It has, it seems, been proven that man's ancestors did not descend from the most 'highly evolved' breeds of the simian species, that the pertinent sign of humanness is not brain size (this is a mechanistic materialist thesis which, moreover, still has an odour of spiritualism about it, since to say 'brain' is to say 'reason' or 'consciousness', etc.). Rather, it would appear that the 'ancestor' of the human line was a creature which had only a modestly developed brain but was distinguished by the fact that it stood upright, so that its hands were free to fashion rudimentary tools under conditions which, it seems reasonable to suppose, were not 'individual' but social. We see straight away the interest that this discovery can hold *for historical materialism*. The object of historical materialism is the nature of the forms of historical existence characteristic of the human species: namely, the structure of social formations, as the condition for the production, and for the reproduction of the conditions of production, of men's material means of existence. The Recent Discoveries supposedly make it possible to 'bridge the gap' between present-day human societies and the animal origins of the human species, since they seem to show that the human species comprised, *from its beginnings*, creatures living 'together' and producing rudimentary tools.

Marxists have not been slow to draw parallels between these discoveries and a famous text by Engels (*Dialectics of Nature*) on the feature that distinguishes the human species from the most advanced animal species – namely, labour – as well as the role that labour played in the 'creation' of the humanness of the human species.[71] Marx had already pointed to this distinguishing feature in *Capital*, citing a phrase of Franklin's that defines man as a 'toolmaking animal'.[72]

The Recent Discoveries are of undeniable ideological, scientific and philosophical interest. We need, however, to spell out the *significance* and *limits* of this interest.

From the ideological standpoint, they render the task of spiritualist apologetics more difficult. Such apologetics can no longer make as demagogic a use of the arguments of derision which decried the Darwinian 'scandal' (the ape!) in an appeal to a crude common sense flattered in its religion by the solacing thought that man could not decently be the son of an ape. But we can count on spiritualist ideology: it will always land on its feet – since, like any good ideology, it does not have any.

From the scientific standpoint, the Recent Discoveries are of undeniable interest. But they add nothing at all to the conceptual content of historical materialism, which did not have to wait for either Darwin or modern palaeontologists in order to emerge and develop, and cannot hope to learn anything about the fundamental problems of the development of its own theory from their revelations. The hypothesis that man is a 'toolmaking animal' living in groups, and that labour transforms 'human nature', has been in general circulation since the eighteenth century,[8] but has remained altogether unproductive. Historical materialism does not spring from it; as we know, it was produced on the basis of very different 'premises'. Indeed, what can we expect the scientific solution of this kind of 'borderline problem' to contribute to the scientific content of a discipline whose object is authentic social formations, not these groups which a profound qualitative difference probably sets apart from the social formations that historical materialism studies? A borderline problem: it must still be demonstrated that the borderline in question *clearly is* the one that runs between ecological and biological laws on the one hand and, on the other, the social laws of history that make human history properly so called what it is – and that it is not a borderline internal to the prehistorical realm, that is, one which is still subject to bio-ecological rather

[8] *Pace* Suret-Canale.

than social laws. On this point, the question is far from being closed.

From the philosophical point of view, these discoveries hold a much broader interest. For they constitute, on one precise point, the edict revoking a *genetic* conception of the evolutionary process, and therefore an *evolutionist* ideology of *genesis*. They offer a totally different image of the dialectic from the teleological dialectic of evolutionism, which is merely the poor man's Hegelianism: a dialectic of *non-genetic mutations*.

What, however, do we see? Certain Marxists rush to embrace these discoveries and put them to the kind of ideological use which, although it is directed against certain spiritualist arguments, throws the door wide open to a new kind of spiritualism: that of Theoretical Humanism. The notion on which this ideological enterprise turns is either that of labour (the essence of Man is labour) or the apparently more 'Marxist', but in fact equivalent, notion of 'social labour'. The ideological operation I wish to denounce is simple. It consists in giving Theoretical Humanism a new 'lease on life' by reactivating the ideological notion of 'labour' against the background provided by the following theoretical complex: Essence of Man = labour (or social labour) = the creation of Man by Man = Man, Subject of History = History as a process whose Subject is Man (or human labour). It looks very much as if the Recent Discoveries of human palaeontology had here given the 'green light' to a 'revival' of Theoretical Humanism.

Since those who profess this spiritualist ideology are not necessarily aware of the implications of their argument, and since their argument gives itself the theoretical benefit of expressions with a Marxist resonance, it is essential that we go into some detail here. I take the liberty of quoting Suret-Canale,[73] whose argument will enlighten us, precisely in so far as it explicitly relates the recent discoveries to the *1844 Manuscripts*:

> Thus what is still mistaken or inadequate in the *1844 Manuscripts* is their philosophical (speculative) approach.
>
> I believe that Althusser, too, thinks this. But his interpretation also seems to reject as 'ideological', that is, speculative or mistaken, the very conception of a universal essence of man, or, if you like – to put the same thing in everyday language – any general definition whatsoever of the human species.

Such a rejection is unjustified, as is any rejection of the general theory to the sole benefit either of a particular science or of certain scientific laws taken separately (an approach typical of positivism).

The core of the general definition of man in the *1844 Manuscripts* is perfectly valid. I would even go so far as to say that this definition of man in terms of social labour is one of Marx's fundamental discoveries, without which everything that follows – the theory of modes of production, the analysis of capitalism – would have been inconceivable. Marx never disowned it; on the contrary, he built on it (for example, in Volume 1 of *Capital*,[74] by showing what basically distinguishes man from animals). Engels, too, developed this definition in *Dialectics of Nature*.

May I be permitted a parenthetical remark? We have all the less reason to call this general conception into question in that it has today been strikingly confirmed by the discoveries of science, of human palaeontology. This is quite recent; it dates from the last ten years. . . . [There follows a résumé of Leroi-Gourhan's theses.] It has been proven that it is social labour, the distinctive sign of which is toolmaking, which originally led to hominization, not the other way round. . . .

But let us turn back to the subject at hand. The definition that Marx gives in the *1844 Manuscripts*, one that has been confirmed and enriched by science, cannot be put on a par with the speculative, erroneous definitions (which are idealist at their root) advanced by Feuerbach or the eighteenth-century philosophers who, for their part, set out to deduce the essence of man from the *appearance* of the bourgeois and petty-bourgeois individual of their day.

To the extent that, in 1845, Marx's break with his earlier conceptions bears essentially on the speculative nature of his approach, not with his general conception of man, the terminology 'theoretical humanism/theoretical anti-humanism' seems to me to be unjustified. It does not get at the essence of the matter.

I shall not reiterate themes that cannot be seriously defended. What is essential about a scientific discovery is not the break with speculation. *Infinitely more* is required than this simple prerequisite; otherwise, Feuerbach, who spent his life breaking with speculation, would have been a great man of science. What is essential about a scientific discovery is that it contribute something new to the *content* of a theory (not its *form*, speculative or not). I agree with the statement – albeit with major reservations which I shall go on to explain – that the novelty of Marx's discovery is not *unrelated to* what an expression like 'social labour' can mean for us, retrospectively, and on condition that it is subjected to a radical critique. But I do not at all agree with (1) the statement that this discovery is contained in the *1844 Manuscripts*; or (2) the idea that it can be designated by the terribly equivocal (I mean *un-Marxist*) expression 'social labour'. Yet one cannot defend the thesis that Marx's discovery is contained in the *1844 Manuscripts* unless one considers this expression Marxist.

The *1844 Manuscripts* defines Man in terms of *labour* (after Hegel and Smith, who are reconciled and given a theoretical blessing whose edifying whys and wherefores I have already discussed). The *Manuscripts* defines this labour in terms of its *originary act*, the (Feuerbachian) externalization of the Essential Forces of the individual producer. Everything takes place between a Subject (labouring Man, the worker) and his products (his Object). On the Feuerbachian definition, the individual's 'absolute essence' is the species; he is therefore Genus in his very essence, and that is why his individual act is, primordially, a *generic act*. Hence the ideological deduction, which the *Manuscripts* develops for us with admirable rigour, of the *social* effects of this originary act of self-externalization/self-manifestation of the Human Essence (for the individual is, as Man, generic in his essence) in the material production of the worker/individual: property, classes, capital, and so on. The adjective 'social' in the expression 'social labour' forged by Suret-Canale designates, in the *Manuscripts*, the effect or phenomenon or manifestation (the Hegelian in-itself–for-itself) of the *generic character* of Man contained in the *originary act* of externalization/alienation of the essence of Man, which is present [in] the worker's labour (the Hegelian in-itself). A close reading of the *Manuscripts* leaves no room for doubt on this score. Everything that is 'social' designates, not the structure of social *conditions* and the *labour-process* or the process of the realization of value, but the externalization/ alienation (via as many mediations as you like) of an originary essence, that of Man.

That, incidentally, explains why Marx can come up with a perfectly idealist formulation about '*the action* [acte] *of world history*' that is man's birth act [acte][75] – which is *originary* in the precise sense of all philosophies of the origin, that is, of the essence as constitutive Subject. Here 'origin' signifies, not *the origins*, that is, *the beginning*, but the present, eternal, constitutive essence that produces, out of its constitutive depths, all the phenomena of history.

Let us extend the scope of the debate. If the expression 'social labour' is ambiguous, it is because 'social' is here simply the *adjective* (in the *Manuscripts*, the Phenomenon, the externalization, the in-itself–for-itself) associated with a *noun* that is its inner essence (its in-itself): *labour*. If we draw the conclusions that follow from this, we have to state plainly, in the face of God-only-knows-how-many appearances and authorities, that the concept of *labour*, in the ambiguity that constantly tempts one to establish it as a basic concept of the theory of historical materialism, *is not a Marxist concept*. Quite the contrary: the concept of labour is itself a major epistemological obstacle blocking the development of Marxist theory.

One can easily convince oneself of this a posteriori by examining all the ideologies of labour, all the idealist interpretations of Marxism as a philosophy of labour – whether they rehearse the themes of the *1844 Manuscripts* or set out to construct a Phenomenology of 'praxis'.[h] But it will be objected that what is involved here is *philosophical* ideology, not historical materialism, which situates itself elsewhere, on the terrain of science.

Very well then; let us talk about historical materialism. If we do, we cannot but admit that Marx's whole critique of classical Political Economy consisted in exploding the concept of *labour* accepted by the Economists, in order to suppress and then replace it with new concepts in which the *word* 'labour' figures, to be sure, but always in conjunction with other words that confer a distinctive meaning upon the new concept, a meaning that can no longer be confused with the ambiguous meaning of the simple *concept* of 'labour'.

The concept of labour, when it 'explodes', breaks down into the following concepts: *labour-process*, the structure of the social conditions of the labour-process, labour-power (not labour), value of labour-power (not of labour), concrete labour, abstract labour, utilization of labour-power, quantity of labour, and so on. All the products of this 'explosion' are merely the precise forms thanks to which the *enormous epistemological obstacle* that

[h] In Italy, the work of Enzo Paci.

the simple, originary notion of *labour* constituted for *historical* materialism is cleared from the path of the science of history. And when Marx talks, in *Capital*, about the 'social' character of labour or the ever more extensive socialization of labour, the word *labour* in these expressions does not refer us to a basic concept that is theoretically prior, and thus scientific in and of itself – the concept of Labour – but, rather, to the *new, complex concepts* of which I have provided a brief list.

That is why Suret-Canale's expression 'social labour' is ambiguous, especially in view of the fact that he explicitly refers to the *1844 Manuscripts* in his comments on it. Of course, this expression has an advantage over others (such as 'the essence of man is labour'): it introduces the adjective 'social' as a 'supplementary', 'remedial' element indispensable to designating Marx's discovery of labour. But Marx's discovery bears, precisely, on the nature of the object designated by the adjective 'social': namely, society. What is involved is not a 'supplement'; it is the *essence of the matter*. Marx's discovery has the effect of *reversing* the order adjective–noun that expresses a phenomenon–essence relationship perfectly adapted to the theses of the *Manuscripts*, and of bringing out the fact that, in order to think the nature of 'labour', *one has to begin by thinking the structure of the social conditions (social relations) in which it is mobilized*. Labour then becomes *labour-power*, mobilized in a *labour-process* subject to, and defined by, the structure of social relations. It follows that the feature distinguishing the forms of existence of the human species from those of animal species is not 'social labour', but the social structure of the production and reproduction of the existence of social formations, that is, the social relations that preside over the mobilization of labour-power in the labour-process, together with all their effects.

This makes it easy to see the *ideological* ambiguity on which the entire 'revival' of Humanism is based, as is any attempt which sets out to ground the 'humanist' character of Marxist theory in the fact that Marx talks about *human* societies, not animal societies. There are two possibilities here: what is in question is a truism that is beneath comment; it would have it that one is quite as much a humanist because one produces a theory of human History as one is a mechanist because one writes a treatise on general mechanics, or a monk because one produces a theory of religion. This alternative is not serious. What is, however, serious – but in this case we are dealing with the seriousness of an imposture – is to produce, as the differential concept distinguishing the forms of existence of human societies from those of animal societies, a concept on whose ambiguity and connotations one then proceeds to play (labour, social labour) in order to base a theoretical-Humanist interpretation of Marxist science or philosophy on that concept's moral overtones.

I do not – I repeat – mean by this that the problem of the origins of the human species is not a scientific problem, or that it is not of some interest to historical materialism. A materialist, scientific theory of human palaeontology certainly does matter to historical materialism, because it does away with a whole set of alibis for the spiritualist ideologies of history that are constantly being opposed to historical materialism. But historical materialism managed to emerge without benefit of the scientific basis provided by the findings of modern human palaeontology (it was barely ten years ago that . . .) and *Capital* was conceived some time before the *Dialectics of Nature*, that is to say, before Engels's celebrated text on the difference between man and the apes.[76] If historical materialism could manage without the palaeontologists, that is because its object is *autonomous* with respect to the findings of human palaeontology, and, as such, can be treated in perfectly independent form.

But we must go even further. Although, as will readily be granted, the 'revival' of Theoretical Humanism is no more based on the Recent Discoveries of palaeontology than the lucubrations of the next Teilhard who happens to come along will be (he will have no trouble at all 'domesticating' the famous Discoveries in an apologetic enterprise of the same stripe), and although this 'revival' of Theoretical Humanism is explained, in the final analysis, by factors that have everything to do with the political conjuncture and precious little to do with scientific rigour, we still have to get to the heart of the matter, and ask for what reasons – not only political, but also *theoretical* reasons – serious Marxists (I am not talking about the jugglers) succumb so easily to this temptation. For I am convinced that, in their case, it is not only a matter of the political conjuncture but, first and foremost, of *theoretical* conviction.

Let us therefore go to the root of this conviction. It is inseparable from what these Marxists conceive to be the requirements of *materialism*.

Let me turn back for just a moment to the ideological advantages of the Recent Discoveries. Their function is to 'fill' a vacuum [*vide*] in the materialist 'conception of the world'. In so doing, they offer 'proof' that the world is 'continuous', and that there is not, between the materiality of life and human existence, the discontinuity of that 'transcendence' in which the master-signifiers of religion find their niche but, rather, the unity of materiality itself. This is important. But we have to recognize that even in our day, another preoccupation can *slip in* under cover of this preoccupation with 'filling a vacuum' (ideology rushes to fill a vacuum), and that it is not unrelated to some of the master-signifiers of religious ideology.

It is, indeed, a remarkable fact that the 'empty spaces' [*vides*] in which religious ideology takes a special interest are the empty spaces of Origins that are merely the small change of the big Empty Space of the Origin. The Origin of Man, the Origin of Life, and so on, are for religious ideology merely exemplars, among hundreds of others, of the Origin of the World, that is, of Creation. It is – let me say in passing – no wonder that some, precisely in connection with the origins of Man, spontaneously speak the language of creation.[77] The example they embody will be rejected as irrelevant, and I am happy to agree that it is. But there is a certain way of rejecting the problematic of Creation and the Origin which, while overtly challenging it, in fact remains subject to it.

That this problem of the Origins (of life, man, etc.) haunts, in particular, many Marxists who are convinced that they are engaged in philosophical (and not merely ideological) work is a fact that can already serve us as a clue. This clue is immediately corroborated by the kind of theoretical principle such Marxists bring to bear in order to 'resolve' these problems of the Origin, problems of which they are especially fond.

Here I would like publicly to denounce the 'spontaneous' persistence (in the Leninist sense of 'spontaneity') of a conception that cannot resist associating *materialism* with *genesis*. In broad circles of Marxist materialism, among not only philosophers, but also Marxist scientists (the latter case is by far the more frequent), materialism is spontaneously thought within and through the category of *genesis*. That is why problems of the Origin hold so important a place in the prevailing conception of dialectical materialism. For the Origins are, *par excellence*, the place where the ideological schema of *genesis* can operate unchecked.

To say genesis is to say, from the depths of an age-old religious ideological tradition, *filiation*; the possibility of *tracking* [*suivre à la trace*] the effects of a filiation; the assurance that one is dealing with the *same* individual, the *same* lineage, whose transformations can be followed step by step. At the heart of every genesis is the need for *assurance*, for a fundamental ideological *guarantee* (every ideology has the function, among others, of producing a *guarantee*-effect): that one will never lose sight, through all its transformations, of the initial Subject; the guarantee that one is always dealing with the *same Subject*. In religious Genesis: that one is always dealing, in everything that happens, with one and the same Subject, *God*. In materialist genesis: that one is always dealing, whatever its transformations, with one and the same Subject, *matter*. The association of materialism and the genetic thus ultimately rests on an ideological schema of *guarantee*.

This ideological schema 'spontaneously' takes the form of *empiricism*. When it comes to *tracking* the transformations of the originary Subject, nothing works better [than] to provide, step by step, an exhaustive tally of what becomes of him amid his very transformations. And when he is transformed, one must be able to reconstruct all the details of the process which, even as it transforms him, maintains the originary Subject's Identity (in every sense of the word). When it comes to not losing sight of the individual whom one has thus *identified*, nothing works better than *never losing sight of him*. Empiricism adopts and spontaneously 'lives' this singular logic of *filiation* in its practice of *tailing* [*filature*].[78]

I maintain that the concept of genesis, constantly 'practised' in the spontaneity of scientific ideology, is currently one of the greatest epistemological obstacles to the development not only of dialectical materialism, but also of historical materialism and the majority of the sciences that depend on it, as well, doubtless, as the life sciences and quite a few other natural sciences. It is wreaking havoc in psychology, history, and so on. This concept is constantly practised; yet its *theoretical* claims to validity have never been tested, so crushing and so slight is the weight of its 'obviousness', that is, its ideological weight.

Consider the tremendous power of this genetic prejudice. At the very moment when the Recent Discoveries compel us to recognize, *in the realm of the facts*, that matters can, between the animal and the human kingdoms, unfold in accordance with a schema that is quite different from that of the dialectic of the genesis of man-from-the-ape (the *guarantee* that, on condition that the ape is properly 'tailed', one will, without losing sight of him for a moment, see him turn into a man); at the very moment when it appears that, on the contrary, it is necessary, in order to understand man, to set out from a *result* without a genesis (i.e. without a filiation in which the identity of one and the same Subject is preserved), to set out from this creature-that-is-not-the-son-of-an-ape, which stands upright, and whose brain (too small) is likewise not a brain of the type son-of-the-brains-of-ape (it is much too big for genetic prejudices to function smoothly amid this scandalous downsizing) – *at this very moment*, there is a rush to embrace genesis in the human realm. For one has at last sighted the guilty party, the Originary Individual; he has been identified, he makes 'tools' of some unspecified sort, he lives in groups: *he's the one, all right. We've got him this time.* It is enough to 'tail' [*filer*] him, to track him, not to lose sight of him, since one is sure that at the end of this manhunt [*filature*], one will rediscover both the *1844 Manuscripts* and *Capital*! No less. At that point, we will finally learn what this thing is made of – this thing that was obviously still quite vague prior to the Recent Discoveries – this thing we call a society and history. We shall, into the bargain, finally learn what *Capital* and Marxism are made of, deep down. Finally, we shall learn, on the same occasion (a rather profitable one), what to think of Humanism and Theoretical Anti-Humanism.

I may perhaps be pardoned for packing a bit of punch into what I say. What is required, what will be required to shake this ineradicable *genetic prejudice*, are storms of a very different order. Of course, I know what I am in for. Well-intentioned folk have wasted no time in telling me:[79] not only philosophers, for whom dealing in (transcendental) genesis is all part of the job, but, alas, historians too, although *they* deal with something quite unlike 'abstractions', for they constantly work on *results* produced by a process [*procès*] without a subject (i.e. the very opposite of a genesis). Yet that concept is overwhelmed by the ideological prejudices of the Subject. The verdict is in: I sacrifice 'genesis' to 'structures'. I am in line for this endlessly repeated trial [*procès*].

I shall not reply, for my accusers must be given their chance: after all, Man can also think. But, precisely because we are dealing with men and monkeys, and in order to remain within range of the sound waves generated whenever the troublesome rock of the man–monkey relation is cast into the ideological pond, I, too, shall take the liberty of utilizing (just this once) a Famous Quotation: the short, very clear sentence in which Marx tells us that it is not the ape who is the key to understanding man, but man who is the key to understanding the ape.[80]

Naturally, our good materialists have, for decades, been putting this quotation to all the geneticist uses they can think of. Marx meant, did he not, just like Hegel, that we see in man the development of what is *in embryo* in the ape – of what was already, even in the ape's day, the Man in the ape. It's a simple matter of making the text easier to read: as in Plato, there are passages in small print, the hard ones, and passages in big print, for the short-sighted. Everybody knows that when you put a short-sighted detective on a suspect's tail, you're better off assigning him a tall one or a fat one. Marx's sentence is, in sum, the proof in reverse of filiation/tailing [*filiation/filature*]: for, in man, there is never anything to be understood except the future of man, even in his ape of a father.

In another text,[81] I put forward the idea that it is difficult to leave this short, very clear sentence standing in the context of the *Contribution* and *Capital* unless one construes it in a completely different, non-historicist and therefore non-geneticist, way. But one always has to say things several times, varying one's discourse, if need be. In the text in question, I discussed, above all, the *epistemological* significance of the short sentence: to wit, that knowledge only ever sets out from a *result*, and that the knowledge of the result (the knowledge of the mechanisms of capitalist society), to the extent that it plainly has to begin as the knowledge of a result, and a highly complex one, provides, for this reason, the keys needed to acquire knowledge of other, earlier, 'simpler' results (pre-capitalist societies). To change tack, let us now discuss this short sentence with respect to the *real result* as such; let us, in other words, talk about the dialectic.

I think Marx's text indicates that capitalism is a result, and that, like any result, it is the result of a *historical process*. In everything that we have written, it has never been a question of anything other than History, which 'They' call, in their language, *genesis*. But capitalism is the result *of a process that does not take the form of a genesis*. The result of what? Marx tells us several times: of the process of an *encounter* of several distinct, definite, indispensable elements, engendered in the previous historical process by different *genealogies* that are independent of each other and can, moreover, be traced back to several possible 'origins': accumulation of money capital, 'free' labour-power, technical inventions, and so forth. To put it plainly, capitalism is not the result of a *genesis* that can be traced back to the feudal mode of production as if to its origin, its 'in-itself', its 'embryonic form', and so on; it is the result of a complex process that produces, at a given moment, the encounter of a number of elements susceptible of [*propre à*] constituting it in their very encounter. Evolutionist, Hegelian or geneticist illusions notwithstanding, a mode of production does not contain, 'potentially', 'in embryo', or 'in itself', the mode of production that is to 'succeed' it. If it did, we would be unable to understand why so many examples of social formations governed by the feudal mode of production failed to 'give birth' to the capitalist mode of production.

Obviously, since things are always 'happening', and, above all, since things have always-already happened, the half-pint historian can, at no great cost, afford himself the 'theoretical' pleasure of tracking them back through time and taking this succession for a *filiation*, in line with the good old religion of genesis. As Voltaire said a long time ago, if all sons have fathers, not all fathers have sons. But Voltaire's critique was still beholden to a dialectic of filiation that is doubtless not unrelated to familial ideology; to be very precise, the *juridical* familial ideology of 'succession' (read: of inheritance rights). We must go much further, and say that the Sons who count in the historical process *have no father*, because they need several, and these fathers are in their turn the sons not *of a single father* (or we would be going round in circles), but of several, and so on.

I do not think that one loses history in this business. One certainly does lose genesis, but that is a good loss. One also loses all the things that are obvious for historical empiricism, but that is an excellent loss. One gains, quite simply, the possibility of understanding History, and that does, after all, present certain advantages. And one also gains a few important perspectives on the dialectic, whose rudiments we shall expound some day.

I come back to our man and ape. If man can provide the key to the ape, the reason is above all that, setting out from man, what we can understand of the ape is how it was possible to make an ape, when one understands that man is not the son of the ape. That is how I would interpret Marx's short sentence. Understanding man provides the key to understanding the ape by showing that neither – the ape no more than the man – is the result of a *genesis*, that is, of a filiation that begins with a Subject who is identified with the origin, and *whose authentic origin is guaranteed* [*garanti d'origine*]. It's a pretty safe bet that those who throw themselves into the ideology of the genesis of the human societies discussed in *Capital*, starting out from the miracle identified by the Recent Discoveries, are in for a disappointment or two if they try to put a tail on this latter-day miracle. No doubt the dialectic of processes (which are not geneses) holds a few surprises in store for them, of the sort that have already devastated – theoretically, of course – all those who have undertaken to put a tail on a mode of production in order to trace its transformation into another mode of production, in a birth without (or with) labour pains.

That, then, is the point I think one has to arrive at in order to track down to its last refuge the ideological argument that sustains, even in the case of serious Marxists, a kind of reasoning which others – who are also Marxists, but not serious ones – hasten to transform into a spiritualist Plea for Marxist Humanism. I apologize for having had to go into such detail. But political experience (for lack of other kinds: but politics is an excellent teacher in this respect) teaches that it is not possible to make the slightest concession to ideology. Marx pointed that out in his *Critique of the Gotha Programme*: one can make concessions in politics – that is known as compromise – one can forge unions in politics, but one can never forge a union with ideology. Marx added that one is especially well advised to respect this absolute rule, *making no concessions whatsoever*, above all when political Union is the order of the day. Duly noted.

German Social Democracy, 'so as not to stand in the way of unity' with the Lasalleans, 'so as not to disappoint them', buried this text of Marx's for fifteen years. For the sake of Unity.[82]

Notes

1. See, for example, Adam Schaff, *Introduction to Semantics*, Oxford, 1962; *Marxism and the Human Individual*, ed. Robert S. Cohen, introduction by Erich Fromm, based on a translation by Olgierd Wojtasiewicz, New York, 1970. When he first met Althusser, Schaff was a member of the Central Committee of the Polish United Workers' Party.
2. This surprising way of referring to the Frankfurt School suggests that Althusser was not well acquainted with it.
3. See, for example, Erich Fromm, *The Sane Society*, New York, 1990 (1955); and, among the works Fromm published after Althusser wrote 'The Humanist Controversy', *The Revolution of Hope*, New York, 1968; *The Crisis of Psychoanalysis*, New York, 1991 (1970).
4. Erich Fromm, ed., *Socialist Humanism*, New York, 1965; London, 1967, which includes contributions by some three dozen hands. Althusser's essay 'Marxism and Humanism' is not among the 'inevitable omissions' that Fromm names and 'regrets' in his Introduction (p. xiii). [*Trans.*]
5. Erich Fromm, letter of 27 September 1963 to Louis Althusser. Althusser kept a file of his correspondence with Erich Fromm; it confirms everything he says here.
6. 'In fact, the objective of the revolutionary struggle has always been the end of exploitation and hence the liberation of man, but, as Marx foresaw, in its first historical phase, this struggle had to take the form of the struggle between *classes*. So revolutionary humanism could only be a "class humanism".' 'Marxism and Humanism', *FM* 221. See also ibid., pp. 121–2n.
7. In a letter dated 18 November 1963, Althusser thanks Jean Laugier for his fine translation, which has not been preserved in Althusser's archives.
8. Erich Fromm, letter of 8 January 1964 to Louis Althusser.
9. *Cahiers de l'ISEA*, June 1964; *Critica Marxista*, no. 2, 1964.
10. Jorge Semprun, 'L'humanisme socialiste en question', *Clarté*, January 1965, reprinted in *La Nouvelle critique*, no. 164, March 1965, pp. 22–31.
11. Jorge Semprun, *The Long Voyage*, trans. Richard Seaver, New York, 1964.
12. In the context of the 'split in the international communist movement', the line followed by the 'Italians' rather closely reflected ideas defended by the Italian Communist Party, in opposition to the leadership of the French Communist Party and also to various 'ultra-left' and pro-Chinese tendencies. The 'Italians' took the helm of the Union des étudiants

communistes (UEC) for a brief period in 1963–64, before the Communist Party leadership reasserted its control over the organization in 1965. Jacques Rancière, *La Leçon d'Althusser*, Paris, 1975 (partially translated as 'On the Theory of Ideology: The Politics of Althusser', in *Radical Philosophy Reader*, ed. Roy Osborn and Roy Edgley, London, 1985, pp. 102–36), offers an interesting analysis of the 'Althusserians'' position and the tactics adopted by the leaders of the Communist Party in response to the conflicts within the UEC.

13. As Althusser learned from Michel Verret's letter of 24 January 1966, the discussions at the 'Journées d'étude des philosophes communistes' (23–24 January 1966), a conference attended by the entire Political Bureau of the Communist Party, focused on the most recent of Roger Garaudy's books, *From Anathema to Dialogue*, trans. Luke O'Neill, London, 1967 (1965), as well as *FM* and *RC*. Unable to attend for health reasons, Althusser asked Verret to read the first part of 'TTPTF' at the conference. Verret's forty-five pages of handwritten notes on the proceedings have been preserved in Althusser's archives, together with a revised written version of Garaudy's presentation, a typed seventy-five-page document that begins with the words 'A fundamental problem has been posed: in the name of science, an attack has been launched against Marxist humanism.' Garaudy's sharp attack on Althusser and his disciples provoked an equally sharp reply from Pierre Macherey, among others.

14. The Central Committee meeting on 'ideological and cultural problems' held in the Paris suburb of Argenteuil on 11–13 March 1966 (for the proceedings, see *Cahiers du communisme*, nos 5–6, May–June 1966 and *Annales, passim*) marked an important stage in the development of the French Communist Party's strategy for the union of the French left and the 'peaceful transition to socialism'. The meeting focused on the theme of the autonomy of 'culture' and cultural production ('to reject or hinder the experimental demands of literature and art is to strike a serious blow to the development of culture and, indeed, the human spirit in general . . . debate and research are vital to the development of science. The Communist Party has not the least intention of thwarting such debate or interfering in it in order to assert predetermined truths, much less of abruptly closing off, in authoritarian fashion, ongoing debate by specialists.') The resolution adopted at the end of the discussion reflected the controversy then raging around the theme of 'Marxist humanism'; virtually every contribution to the discussion made reference to Althusser's essay 'Marxism and Humanism'. The final resolution included the following passage:

> There is a Marxist humanism. Unlike the abstract humanism which the bourgeoisie mobilizes to mystify social relations and justify exploitation and injustice, this humanism derives directly from the historical task of the working class. To uphold such humanism is by no means to reject an objective conception of reality in favour of an impulsive emotionalism. On the contrary, Marxism is the humanism of our times because it is

based on a rigorously scientific conception of the world; but it does not divorce its attempt to understand reality from its resolve to change it for the benefit of all men.

Althusser responded to this text in a typed twenty-seven-page letter addressed to 'the comrades of the Central Committee of the French Communist Party', in which he affirmed, in essence: (1) that the resolution was self-contradictory, because it effectively, albeit tacitly, closed off an ongoing debate; and (2) that it conflated political compromise, which was necessary, with theoretical compromise, which was unacceptable.

15. There follow Althusser's introductory notes to the individual texts he had initially planned to publish in the form of a 'dossier' on the debate about humanism, notably his commentary on Jorge Semprun's contribution to the debate. Since this 'dossier' is not included here, neither are Althusser's introductory notes. (See the Editors' Introduction to 'The Humanist Controversy'.)

16. The phrases Althusser quotes are taken from Semprun, 'L'humanisme socialiste en question'.

17. Althusser expands on this idea in *LP*.

18. Here Althusser intended to insert a note that he seems never to have written. It would probably have been a reference to 'The Historical Task of Marxist Philosophy', pp. 169–80 above.

19. *RC* 119.

20. Althusser incorporated a slightly modified version of the following section of 'The Humanist Controversy' (pp. 233–41) into the paper he presented at Jean Wahl's Hegel seminar in February 1968; the paper was published in 'Sur le rapport de Marx à Hegel', in Jacques d'Hondt, ed., *Hegel et la pensée moderne*, Paris, 1970, and reprinted in *Lénine et la philosophie, suivi de Marx et Lénine devant Hegel*, Paris, 1972 (see the Editors' Introduction to 'The Humanist Controversy'). The translation of the passage given here closely follows Ben Brewster's ('MRM' 176–85), except, of course, where the text of 'Sur le rapport de Marx à Hegel' departs from that of 'The Humanist Controversy'. One or two minor errors in Brewster's translation have been corrected, and a few changes made for the sake of stylistic consistency.

21. See 'On the Young Marx', *FM* 49–86. This essay was dedicated to Auguste Cornu, author of the monumental *Karl Marx et Friedrich Engels*, Paris, 1958–70.

22. In the version of 'Sur le rapport de Marx à Hegel' published in *Lénine et la philosophie* (Paris, 1975, p. 62), Althusser modified this sentence to read: 'Cut the head off a duck and it keeps running all the same.' [*Trans*.]

23. See 'On Feuerbach', pp. 85–154 above.

24. The parenthetical phrase becomes 'Man–Nature–*Sinnlichkeit*' in the version of 'Sur le rapport de Marx à Hegel' in *Lénine et la philosophie*. [*Trans*.]

25. *Gattung*, a word that represents – as Althusser notes in 'On Feuerbach', p. 137 – a 'headache' for translators. The headache is compounded here by the fact that, first, *Gattungswesen* in Marx is usually translated as

'species being', and, second, that the expression Althusser most often uses to translate *die menschliche Gattung, le genre humain* (the human genus), can also mean 'the human race' (*le genre humain* is used in this sense in the chorus of the 'Internationale', for example). [*Trans.*]

26. Althusser is quoting freely from Friedrich Engels's *Ludwig Feuerbach and the End of Classical German Philosophy.*

27. See 'On the Materialist Dialectic', *FM* 200n.:

> One further word on the 'negation of the negation'. Today it is official convention to reproach Stalin with having suppressed the 'laws of the dialectic', and more generally with having turned away from Hegel, the better to establish his dogmatism. At the same time, it is willingly proposed that a certain return to Hegel would be salutary. One day perhaps these declarations will become the object of some proof. In the meantime, it seems to me that it would be simpler to recognize that the expulsion of the 'negation of the negation' from the domain of the Marxist dialectic might be evidence of the real theoretical perspicacity of its author.

28. See 'Letter to Jean Lacroix', *SH* 197–230.

29. See, for example, Jacques Derrida, 'De la Grammatologie', *Critique*, no. 223–4, December 1965–January 1966; the revised and expanded version of this text released in 1967 has been translated as *On Grammatology*, trans. Gayatri Chakaravorty Spivak, Baltimore, MD, 1976. Althusser heavily annotated both the offprint of the first version of this work, given to him by Derrida, and his copy of Derrida's 'Freud et la scène de l'écriture', *Tel Quel*, no. 26, summer 1966 ('Freud and the Scene of Writing', in *Writing and Difference*, trans. Alan Bass, Chicago, 1978, pp. 196–231). Generally speaking, Derrida had a far greater influence on Althusser's thinking than this solitary reference to him in the works Althusser published in his lifetime might lead us to suppose. Althusser's library contained many heavily annotated offprints of texts by Derrida.

30. The section of 'The Humanist Controversy' included in 'MRH' ends here. See Note 20 above.

31. Engels, *Ludwig Feuerbach*, p. 364.

32. Marx, 'Contribution to the Critique of Hegel's Philosophy of Law: Introduction', trans. anon, *CW* 3: 182.

33. Ibid., p. 175.

34. Marx, 'Contribution to the Critique of Hegel's Philosophy of Law', trans. Martin Milligan and Barbara Ruhemann, *CW* 3: 31. See also 'On the Jewish Question', trans. Clemens Dutt, *CW* 3: 154.

35. The *Deutsch–Französische Jahrbücher* (German–French Annals), only one issue of which saw the light, in February 1844.

36. Marx, Letter of September 1843 to Arnold Ruge, trans. Clemens Dutt, *CW* 3: 144–5, translation modified. See also Ludwig Feuerbach, Introduction to *The Essence of Christianity*, in *FB*, 109–10: 'Religion is the solemn unveiling of man's hidden treasures, the avowal of his innermost thoughts, the open confession of the secrets of his love.'

37. *EC*, 112–3:

> The doctrine of the Creation in its characteristic significance arises only

on that standpoint where man in practice makes Nature merely the servant of his will and needs.... When, on the contrary, man places himself only on the practical standpoint and looks at the world from thence, making the practical standpoint the theoretical one also, he is in disunion with Nature; he makes Nature the *abject vassal of his selfish interest*, of his practical egoism.... Utilism is the essential theory of Judaism.

38. Marx, *Economic and Philosophical Manuscripts of 1844*, trans. Martin Milligan and Dirk J. Struik, CW 3: 333.

39. Ibid., p. 290.

40. See, for example, Michel Simon's contribution to the debate on 'Marxism and Humanism', *La Nouvelle critique*, no. 165, April 1965, pp. 96–132; see also Jean Kanapa's intervention at the Central Committee meeting held at Argenteuil, *Cahiers du communisme*, nos 5–6, May–June 1966.

41. Letter of 21–22 September 1890 from Engels to Joseph Bloch, in Marx and Engels, *Selected Correspondence*, ed. S.W. Ryazanskaya, trans. I. Lasker, 3rd edn., Moscow 1975, pp. 394–6. This letter is analysed in 'Appendix to "Contradiction and Over-Determination"', FM 117–28.

42. Antonio Gramsci, 'The Study of Philosophy', in *Selections from the Prison Notebooks*, ed. and trans. Quintin Hoare and Geoffrey Nowell Smith, New York, 1971, p. 353: 'Each individual is the synthesis not only of existing relations, but of the history of these relations. He is a précis of all the past.' Althusser heavily annotated his copy of Gramsci, *Œuvres choisies*, Paris, 1959.

43. The wording of Althusser's translations of the Sixth Thesis varies, as does his use of capital letters. The expression he usually translates as 'the essence of Man' is *das menschliche Wesen*. [*Trans*.]

44. Althusser intended to insert a note here that he seems never to have written. It would probably have been a reference to GI 45: 'As though [nature and history] were two separate "things" and man did not always have before him an historical nature and a natural history.'

45. Althusser intended to insert a note here that he seems never to have written. It would probably have been a reference to ibid., pp. 43, 253:

> Where speculation ends, where real life starts, there consequently begins real, positive science, the expounding of the practical activity, of the practical process of development of men.... When reality is described, a self-sufficient philosophy loses its medium of existence. At best its place can only be taken by a summing-up of the most general results, abstractions which are derived from the observation of the historical development of men.... One has to 'leave philosophy aside' ... one has to leap out of it and devote oneself like an ordinary man to the study of actuality.

46. No doubt an error for 'Feuerbachian'. [*Trans*.]

47. Althusser intended to insert a note here that he seems never to have written. It would probably have been a reference to *The German Ideology*, vol. 2, part 3.

48. Althusser had made plans to write a book 'settling accounts with our former philosophical consciousness' (see Marx, Preface to *A Contribution*

to the Critique of Political Economy, trans. anon, CW 29: 264). Only the first five pages have been preserved in a folder that bears the title '66–67 (unfinished) "*La coupure*" [The break]'. Dated January 1967, Althusser's text begins with the words: 'This book is a settling of accounts: *Abrechnung*.'

49. Althusser's translation is '*rapports de commerce mutuel*'; the English translation of *The German Ideology* usually cited in the present volume has 'forms of intercourse'. [*Trans.*]

50. *GI* 47.

51. Written above the phrase 'doesn't give a damn about' [*se fout*], in a hand that is probably not Althusser's, is the alternative 'couldn't care less about' [*se moque*]. *Se fout* has not been crossed out.

52. *GI* 263; see also 463.

53. Ibid., p. 61:

> This conception of history ... comprehend[s] the form of intercourse connected with and created by this mode of production ... as the basis of all history; and ... describ[es] it in its action as the state, and also explain[s] how all the different theoretical products and forms of consciousness, religion, philosophy, morality, etc., etc., arise from it, and trace[s] the process of their formation from that basis.

Althusser's translation has '*genèse*', genesis, for 'process of their formation'. The German is *Entstehungsprozeß*.

54. Ibid., pp. 89–92.

55. We have emended the text, which reads 'historical materialism', an obvious error.

56. *GI* 61; the German is *idealistische Flausen*. Althusser's translation has *billevesées*, a word which is not found in the translation published by the Party publishing house Éditions sociales, the text Althusser usually cites, but is used in the Pléiade edition.

57. This and the following paragraph also appear in *SISS* 66.

58. See 'The Philosophical Conjuncture and Marxist Theoretical Research' above.

59. Althusser intended to insert a 'note on Lenin' here that he seems never to have written.

60. See Note 48 above.

61. Althusser intended to insert a note here that he seems never to have written.

62. Part II of 'The Humanist Controversy', unlike Part I, is untitled. Moreover, the most recent typed version of the text does not indicate that what follows is the second part; a horizontal line has simply been drawn across the page here. We have introduced this subdivision on the basis of an older version of the text – the only one, in all probability, that Althusser typed himself (see the Editors' Introduction to 'The Humanist Controversy').

63. Althusser intended to insert a note here that he seems never to have written. It would probably have consisted of a few extracts from

the texts he takes issue with. We shall limit ourselves to giving one example:

> Transcendence, if we take the word in the strict etymological sense – to rise above something – has, as applied to man, who rises above nature, and also constantly rises above himself, rises above his proper nature, a perfectly acceptable meaning. I am convinced that the Christians' conception of transcendence is the awareness, in mystified form, of man's vocation to rise above nature.... To the Christians' question (albeit mystified in its very formulation), we can provide a valid response. The theory of transcendence has already been produced: it is everything that has already been acquired by Marxism, even if some things remain to be added. (Jean Suret-Canale, 'Marxism is Both a Science and a Humanism', published version of a presentation at the Central Committee meeting held at Argenteuil, *Cahiers du communisme*, nos. 5–6, May–June 1966, pp. 245–61)

64. Of the six 'problems' listed by Althusser, only the first is discussed here. Althusser nevertheless felt that he had made sufficient progress on the text to have a secretary type it (see the Editors' Introduction to 'The Humanist Controversy').

65. Althusser intended to insert a note here that he seems never to have written.

66. See especially Wilhelm Dilthey, *Introduction to the Human Sciences*, trans. Ramon J. Betanzos, Detroit 1988. Althusser extensively annotated his copy of the first volume of this work.

67. Let us note that Althusser had been attacked on this point by Merleau-Ponty (*The Adventures of the Dialectic*, trans. Joseph Bien, Evanston, Il, 1973 (1955), p. 63n, translation modified):

> Going from Engels to Plekhanov, one easily arrives at the views of contemporary orthodoxy, which are that the dialectic is not a sort of knowledge; it is rather a group of verifications, and it is valid only in its 'general content' (interaction, development, qualitative leaps, contradictions) [*SH* 248]. This mixture of positive spirit and dialectic and positivism transfers into nature man's way of being: it is nothing less than magic.

68. Althusser intended to insert a 'note on Kojève' here that he seems never to have written.

69. Friedrich Engels, *Herr Eugen Dühring's Revolution in Science (Anti-Dühring)*, trans. Emile Burns, *CW* 25: 125 and *passim*.

70. Althusser intended to insert a note here. He probably had the work of André Leroi-Gourhan in mind (for example, *Gesture and Speech*, trans. Anna Bostock Berger, Cambridge, MA, 1993).

71. See, for example, the following passage:

> Labour is the source of all wealth, the political economists assert. And it really is the source – next to nature, which supplies it with the material that it converts into wealth. But it is even infinitely more than this. It is the prime basic condition for all human existence, and this to such an

extent that, in a sense, we have to say that labour created man himself. (Friedrich Engels, *Dialectics of Nature*, trans. Clemens Dutt, CW 25: 452)

72. Marx, *Capital*, trans. Samuel Moore and Edward Aveling, New York, 1967, vol. 1: 179.
73. Suret-Canale, Presentation at the Central Committee meeting at Argenteuil, pp. 246–8.
74. Althusser intended to insert a note here that he seems never to have written.
75. Marx, *Economic and Philosophical Manuscripts*, pp. 297, 336. This phrase comes in for high praise in the article by Suret-Canale that Althusser analyses here. [The word rendered by *acte* in Althusser's translation of the *1844 Manuscripts* and 'action' or 'act' in the *Collected Works* of Marx and Engels is *Akt* in the original German. –*Trans.*]
76. Engels, 'The Part Played by Labour in the Transition from Ape to Man', in *Dialectics of Nature*, pp. 452–64.
77. Althusser intended to insert a note here that he seems never to have written.
78. This passage exploits the verbal links between *filiation; filature* or 'tailing', in the sense in which a detective 'tails' a suspect; and *filer*, 'to tail'. [*Trans.*]
79. Althusser intended to insert a note here that he seems never to have written.
80. Marx, Introduction to the *Critique of Political Economy*, trans. Ernst Wangermann, CW 28: 42: 'The anatomy of man is a key to the anatomy of the ape. On the other hand, indications of higher forms in the lower species of animals can only be understood when the higher forms themselves are known.'
81. Althusser intended to insert a note here that he seems never to have written. In all probability, he would have referred the reader to *RC* 124 ff.
82. The text, which is probably unfinished, ends here.

Index

Printed in the United States
by Baker & Taylor Publisher Services